Studies

on

Anglo-Saxon Institutions

Studies
on
Anglo-Saxon Institutions

by

H. MUNRO CHADWICK

NEW YORK

RUSSELL & RUSSELL · INC

1963

FIRST PUBLISHED IN 1905
REISSUED, 1963, BY RUSSELL & RUSSELL, INC.
BY ARRANGEMENT WITH CAMBRIDGE UNIVERSITY PRESS
L. C. CATALOG CARD NO: 63—15152

PRINTED IN THE UNITED STATES OF AMERICA

PREFACE.

IN recent years the social and economic conditions prevailing in this country in the time of the Anglo-Saxon dynasties have had much light thrown upon them by the researches of various scholars in Domesday Book and other documents of the Norman period. Such investigations afford perhaps the safest means of approaching the difficult problems presented by this subject. Yet those who are interested in the earlier periods of our national life may serve a useful purpose by venturing from time to time on a re-examination of the evidence available for those periods. For some considerable time past comparatively little has been attempted from this side of the subject. Indeed it is often alleged, and unfortunately not without truth, that as a people we show a singular lack of interest in the early ages of our history. This indifference is no doubt partly to be attributed to the reluctance of scholars who are primarily historians to embark on a subject for which a certain amount of linguistic knowledge is essential, but partly also to the fact that linguistic scholars have come to regard the study of philology as an end in itself rather than as a means to the fuller comprehension of the life and thought of past times.

These remarks must serve as an apology for the presumption of one who makes no claim to special historical knowledge in venturing upon ground which may be thought to lie outside his own province. At the present time a re-examination of the early evidence appears to be called for in view of the conclusions reached by those scholars who have been examining the evidence of the Norman period— conclusions which are difficult to reconcile with certain fundamental ideas prevalent among writers on early constitutional history. The researches of Mr F. Seebohm, especially in his latest work, *Tribal Custom in Anglo-Saxon Law*—a book to which I am very much indebted—have likewise contributed to throw doubt upon views which formerly met with general acceptance. Mr Seebohm's statement of the Anglo-Saxon monetary system, however, contains a number of propositions which seem to me to require further consideration. I have therefore deemed it advisable to treat this subject at considerable length.

The present volume makes no claim to offer a comprehensive survey of the problems of ancient English sociology. A few only of such problems are treated, and those mainly of a kind which relate to political institutions rather than to private life. In general my object has been to call attention to those branches of the subject which seemed not to have been sufficiently regarded by previous writers. Thus, for example, in sketching the history of the kingdoms I have given special attention to the evidence relating to Kent, Sussex, Essex and the Hwicce. On the other hand Mercian and Northumbrian history has been treated more briefly because I had little or nothing to add to what had already been said.

Other questions have been omitted for different reasons. Thus I have not discussed the organisation of the village community because, owing to the inadequacy of the information obtainable from early documents, I thought it better to leave such questions in the hands of those who are more qualified to deal with the modern evidence. Again, the conditions of land-tenure during the tenth and eleventh centuries can hardly be discussed with advantage except by those who have made a special study of Domesday Book. In cases where the later evidence could not be neglected I have preferred, as far as possible, to rely on the results obtained by other scholars, realising as I do that the subject is one in which anyone who is not an expert may very easily go astray. To Professor Maitland's *Domesday Book and Beyond* I am under special obligations throughout. In general my own researches are confined to the period anterior to the reign of Aethelred II.

The use which I have made of certain charters is perhaps open to criticism. I am inclined to think that at present there is a tendency to carry scepticism somewhat too far in this respect. When, even in obviously spurious documents, we meet with names and titles otherwise unknown, it is, I think, a mistake to assume that they are necessarily products of the authors' imagination. Again, the persistence of tradition, popular as well as ecclesiastical, is a force which seems to me to have been underrated by writers on ancient English institutions.

In the rendering of ancient terms and the representation of proper names it is impossible to avoid inconsistency. On the whole I have perhaps gone farther than most writers in the use of modern expressions. For example, I do not see that any serious objection can be made to the use of 'earl' for *(e)aldorman*. On the other hand I have retained certain words, such as 'thegn,' on the ground that I know of no satisfactory modern equivalent.

In regard to proper names the plan which I have followed is to use the popular forms when speaking of persons whose names are household words, in other cases to follow the orthography of the best contemporary texts[1]. In order to avoid too great complexity however I have generally used the Mercian forms of names occurring before the time of Alfred.

I am very much indebted to Mr H. M. Macdonald, Professor of Mathematics in the University of Aberdeen and Fellow of Clare College, for the generous way in which he has helped me in the preparation of my work for press; to Mr E. C. Quiggin, Fellow of Gonville and Caius College, for kind assistance in the revision of the proofs of the earlier chapters; to Miss A. C. Paues, Fellow of Newnham College, for reading some of the proofs and for many valuable suggestions and criticisms; to Mr E. Magnússon, the well-known Scandinavian scholar, for several references in Northern literature and for the kindly interest he has throughout shown in my work; and to Professor W. Ridgeway for constant help and encouragement without which I should

---

[1] In the representation of Anglo-Saxon words I have perhaps been biassed somewhat in favour of early forms. I regret now that I have not had the courage to discard the useless and inconvenient symbol *æ*.

hardly have ventured to take up the study of these subjects.

My thanks are further due to Professor T. McKenny Hughes and Mr J. E. Foster for references on several points of antiquarian interest; to Mr C. W. Moule, Fellow and Librarian of Corpus Christi College, for allowing me to consult MSS. in the College Library; and to the Staff of the University Library, especially Mr A. Rogers and Mr O. Johnson, for the unfailing kindness and attention I have received at their hands.

In conclusion I have to express my thanks to the Syndics of the University Press for undertaking the publication of this book, and to the Staff for the careful manner in which they have carried out the printing and the corrections.

H. M. C.

December, 1904.

TABLE OF CONTENTS.

PAGE

CHAPTER IV. THE SOCIAL SYSTEM *continued*.

CHAPTER V. THE EARL.

EXCURSUS II. THE DANELAGH . . . 198

CHAPTER VI. THE ADMINISTRATIVE SYSTEM.

CHAPTER VII. THE ADMINISTRATIVE SYSTEM *continued*.

EXCURSUS III. THE TRIBAL HIDAGE . . 263

CHAPTER VIII. THE HISTORY OF THE OLDER COUNTIES.

Note.   The abbreviations B., Birch refer to documents published in Birch's *Cartularium Saxonicum*.   In Bede's Ecclesiastical
History the references are to Plummer's *Baedae Opera Historica*.

CHAPTER I.

THE MONETARY SYSTEM.

§ 1. *Introduction.*

THE classification of Teutonic society in ancient times may perhaps be most conveniently attempted by observing the gradations in the monetary payments to which persons belonging to different classes were entitled in compensation for various injuries. For this purpose a clear understanding of the monetary system is an indispensable preliminary. The monetary system of early England however in itself presents a number of difficult problems. In the first place the terms in use were more numerous than in most countries. Some of these terms were names of coins, while others denoted units of account and others again units of weight. As examples of the three categories it will be enough here to mention the penny, the (ancient) shilling and the pound. Another serious difficulty arises from the fact that the standards of weight appear to have been continually changing. A further source of trouble is the variation in the relative value of gold and silver. In France the ratio seems to have been 12 : 1 from

the earliest times.   In England however, so far as
I have been able to ascertain, this ratio was not
attained before the end of the tenth century.   In
earlier times the ratio appears to have been considerably lower.

Finally, there is some difficulty in ascertaining
the purchasing power of money.   This is a matter
of considerable importance, as it was customary to
make large payments in livestock.   In the twelfth
century the sheep was valued at six pence and the
horse at a pound.   Somewhat later the ox was valued
at three ores or 48 pence.   But these sums do not
correspond to the prices fixed for such animals in
the laws of the early kings.   For the pre-Norman
period the chief sources of information on this subject are Aethelstan VI. (a code dating from about
930—940), especially cap. 6, § 1 f., and the *Gerædnes
betweox Dunsetan*, which is probably from half a
century to a century later.   It will be convenient
for future reference to tabulate here the more important of the prices given in these two documents:

	Aethelstan	Gerædnes
man (slave)		1 pound
horse	½ pound (or less)	30 sh.
mare		20 sh.
ox	1 mancus	30 pence
cow	20 (pence)	24 pence
pig	10 (pence)	8 pence
sheep	1 sh.	1 sh.
goat		2 pence

The meaning of these monetary terms will be discussed in the following pages.

§ 2.   *The Coins.*

The coins of the Old English period are chiefly of silver or gold.   The only exceptions are the Northumbrian coins which numismatists call *stycas*[1]. These are said to be formed of a composition chiefly of copper, zinc and silver, and are very numerous[2].

The silver coins are of two clearly marked types. The first, called by numismatists the *sceatt*-type, is small and comparatively thick.   The designs are usually copied from Roman gold or copper, less frequently from Frankish, coins[3].   Many of these coins bear traces of inscriptions, but these, when they contain more than two or three letters, appear to be mere corruptions of Roman legends.   Consequently they afford no clue as to the king or moneyer by whom the coins were issued.   The only exceptions are (1) a few coins bearing the inscriptions *pada* and *ædilræd* in Runic letters, which are believed to have been issued by Peada[4], earl (or sub-

---

[1] The word seems to have been created out of O. Engl. *stycce*, 'piece.'   In the Lindisfarne gloss to St Mark xii. 42 *duo minuta* is translated by *twa stycas* (*stycgce*, Rushworth).   But had the translator really such coins in his mind?   These coins must surely have passed out of circulation long before the date of the Lindisfarne gloss.   The only other example of *stycce* in this sense given by Bosworth-Toller occurs in the compound *seolforstycce* for *argentei* (Matth. xxvii. 3).

[2] As the laws and charters which have come down to us apparently contain no reference to these coins, it will not be necessary to discuss their value.

[3] Cf. Keary, *British Museum Catalogue of Coins*, p. xvii. ff.

[4] Is it not more probable that this is really the name of the Mercian king Penda (d. 655)?   At such an early date the umlaut-vowel might quite possibly not be written (cf. *Pantha* in Nennius),

king) of the Middle Angles and South Mercians
(d. 656) and his brother Aethelred (king of the
Mercians, 675—704), and (2) a series of coins bearing
the names of Northumbrian kings who reigned
during the eighth century. In regard to weight
there is great disparity among these coins, the range
being from 9 to 21 grains. In certain types the
average weight is much greater than in others[1].
Hence it is not improbable that the heavier and
lighter types belong to different districts or periods.
The coins with Runic legends mentioned above are
among the heaviest.

The other type of silver coins, called by numismatists the 'penny'-type, is very different, being
both larger and thinner. These coins also invariably
bear legends, including generally the name of a
king. The earliest examples of the new type appear
to be the coins of a certain Beonna, probably a king
of the East Angles[2], and those of the Mercian king
Offa, which are fairly numerous. There are supposed
to be no West Saxon coins bearing the name of any
king earlier than Ecgberht; but the king Beorhtric[3],
whose name occurs on a supposed East Anglian coin

and the omission of the -*n*- is an orthographical peculiarity, which
is found in several Scandinavian inscriptions of the earliest period.

[1] Thus in the *Brit. Mus. Cat.* Type 2 a the variation in
thirteen coins is only from 17 to 21 gr., nine of them weighing
between 19—20 gr. Again in Type 2 c ii. the variation in four
coins is from 9 to 12 gr.

[2] He is in all probability to be identified with the Hunbeanna,
whom Symeon of Durham (*R. S.* II. 39) makes to succeed Aelfwald
in 749, and with the Beorna who appears in the same position in
Florence of Worcester's Appendix.

[3] The form of the name is that of the W. Sax. dialect.

in the British Museum (*Catalogue,* Vol. I. p. 89), can hardly be any other than the West Saxon king of that name (r. 786—802). It is believed that this new type of coin was copied from a similar Frankish type which seems to have first come into existence under Pippin about the middle of the eighth century[1]. In England the type lasted without any very great change until late in the Plantagenet period. In regard to weight there is, as in the earlier type, considerable variation. The majority of Offa's coins weigh less than 19 grains; but under his successors the weight distinctly rises, and again in Alfred's reign there is a very considerable increase[2].

The gold coins of the Old English period are not numerous. A hundred small gold coins, resembling the sceattas both in size and style, were found together with objects of English manufacture at Crondale, Hampshire, in 1828. Some of these were certainly Merovingian coins, but the majority are said to be undoubtedly of English origin, though, with the exception of a few which seem to be derived from Roman prototypes, they were copied from Merovingian coins[3]. Isolated coins of a similar type have also been found elsewhere[4]. Besides these

---

[1] Cf. Keary, *op. cit.* p. xxiii.

[2] Alfred and his successors also issued a similar but much smaller type of coins, which were no doubt intended to be halfpennies.

[3] *Brit. Mus. Cat.* I. xiii. ff.

[4] *Num. Chron.* IV. 31 ff.; *ib.*, New Series, IX. 171 ff. Coins of this type appear to have been found in Kent, Oxfordshire and Gloucestershire. Unfortunately their weight is hardly ever recorded.

a few larger gold coins with legible inscriptions have been found: (i) An imitation of a solidus of Honorius, weighing 67·2 gr. and bearing the inscription *scanomodu* in Runic letters[1]. From the orthographical peculiarities of the inscription it is impossible to date it much after the end of the sixth century. (ii) A copy of an Arabic dinar, bearing the inscription *Offa Rex* in addition to a long Arabic legend[2]. (iii) A gold coin of Wigmund, Archbishop of York 837—853, weighing 68 2 gr.[3] (iv) A gold coin of Aethelred II., weighing 51·5 gr.[4] (v) A gold coin of Edward the Confessor, weighing 54¼ gr.[5] These few examples are obviously insufficient to prove the continuous existence of a gold coinage. Between the coin with the Runic inscription and the coin of Wigmund there is indeed no perceptible difference of weight; but the fact that the gold coins of the eighth and ninth centuries were known by a new and foreign name, viz. *mancus* (p. 10 f.), rather favours the supposition that they were an innovation. On the other hand, between the coin of Wigmund and those of Aethelred and the Confessor there seems to be a distinct change of standard. Unfortunately however there seems to be no means of ascertaining when this change took place, for in documents of the ninth and tenth centuries the

[1] *Brit. Mus. Cat.* i. p. 1.
[2] *Num. Chron.* v. 122 f. The Arabic coin of which this is a copy was minted in the year 157 of the Hedschra, *i.e.* A.D. 773—4. Unfortunately the weight seems nowhere to be given. As a rule however the weight of these Arabic coins is about 65—70 gr.
[3] *Brit. Mus. Cat.* i. p. 193.   [4] *Brit. Mus. Cat.* ii. p. 208.
[5] Ruding, *Annals of the Coinage*, 3 ed. vol. i. p. 108, footnote.

word *mancus* occurs pretty continuously. In King
Eadred's Will (*Liber de Hyda*, p. 153 f.) instructions
are given to coin two thousand mancusas. This
direction may never have been carried out, but at
all events the document, if genuine[1], points to the
existence of a gold coinage about the middle of the
tenth century. Evidence to the same effect is
furnished by a statement at the end of the Will of
Aethelgifu (Birch, *Cart. Sax.* 812)[2] that the sum
paid for a certain estate was *quinquaginta nomis-
mata auri cocti*.

§ 3. *The terms for money.*

The words used in Old English to denote coins
and monetary units are *scilling*, *sceatt*, *penning*, *tryms*,
mancus; to these we may also add *ora*, *marc*, and
pund, though strictly these last three terms denote
units of weight. Of all these words only the first
two can be regarded as old. They occur in poetry[3]
and are found in all the other early Teutonic languages[4]. As a name for English money *sceatt* (*scætt*)

---

[1] The will does not occur, so far as is known, in any early
MS., but there seems to be no reason for doubting its genuineness.
The language appears to be that of the tenth century, though the
text is slightly corrupt in places.

[2] Kemble and Birch date this document 944—6. I am not
quite clear how this date was fixed, but I imagine it is not far
wrong. Like Eadred's Will, this document is preserved only in a
late and somewhat corrupt copy.

[3] *E.g.* Widsith 92, Gen. 2143, Andr. 297.

[4] Goth. *skilliggs*, O. Norse *skillingr*, O. Fris. *skilling*, O. Sax.,
O.H.G. *scilling*; Goth. *skatts*, O. Fris. *sket*, O. Sax. *skat*, O.H.G.
scaz; cf. O. Norse *skattr*, 'tribute.' It is to be observed that

only occurs in Aethelberht's Laws and once in the short document *Be Myrcna Lage*. On the other hand *scilling* occurs everywhere, but, at all events from the eighth century onwards, apparently only as a unit of account, varying in value according to the district. Mr Seebohm[1] has suggested that *sceatt* and *scilling* originally denoted silver and gold coins respectively. In the Gothic Bible *skatts* is used to translate δηνάριον[2], while *skilliggs* occurs in a Gothic charter of the sixth century at Naples as a translation of Lat. *solidus*. There can be little doubt that in Aethelberht's Laws at all events *sceatt* is used to denote a silver coin, in all probability coins of the small and comparatively thick type to which the name has always been applied by numismatists.

The origin of the word *penny* (*pending, penning, pening, penig*, etc.) is altogether obscure. Corresponding forms are found in the Low and High German languages (in the latter case from the eighth century)[3] and in Old Norse, though here of course the word may have been borrowed from English or German. On the other hand no such word occurs

O. Fris. *sket* denotes 'cattle' as well as 'coin.' In view of O. Slav. and Russ. *skotŭ*, 'cattle,' this was probably the original meaning of the word.

[1] *Tribal Custom in Anglo-Saxon Law*, p. 445 f.

[2] Luke vii. 41, xx. 24; Mark xii. 15, xiv. 5. *scotus*, which occurs in a corrupt passage of a Gratz MS. quoted by Soetbeer (*Forsch.* II. 340), seems to be a Latinised form of the same word. It appears to have been the name of some small silver coin.

[3] The earliest occurrence of the word seems to be *phantinc* = *denarius* in the Paris glossary. For the various forms in which it appears see Graff, *Althochd. Sprachschatz*, III. 343.

in Gothic, nor do we find it in the earliest English
poetry. In charters its first occurrence seems to be
in Birch 412 (A.D. 833—9); yet the Laws of Ine
present several examples (cap. 44, 58, 59, 69).
Numismatists think that the word was first introduced into England as a name for the larger and
thinner type of silver coins described above[1], and
there can at all events be no doubt that this was the
name by which such coins were known, probably
from the beginning. Again it may be regarded as
practically certain that the Frankish coins, from
which this English type was originally copied, bore
the same name, although, as the laws are in Latin,
the term by which they are generally described is
denarius. We may further note that in charters
of the ninth century the word occurs in two forms,
pending and *penning*, corresponding to the two forms
which occur in the continental languages. As the
cause of this variation is in both cases unknown, it
is perhaps an additional argument for believing that
the word was introduced from the continent. Yet if
we are to suppose that the word *penny* did not come
into use in England before the middle of the eighth
century we shall have to regard all those passages
in which the word occurs in Ine's Laws as inter-
polations or additions. That is a proposition to which
I am somewhat reluctant to assent. It is of course
true that we have no evidence for any other West
Saxon code until the time of Alfred. Changes therefore may quite possibly have been introduced in the

---

[1] Cf. Keary, *Brit. Mus. Cat.* I. p. xxii. f.

course of the intervening two centuries[1]. Yet the complete substitution of *penny* for *sceatt* is at least curious. It seems to me at least equally possible that the word *penny* came into use both in France and England before the change in the type of the coins.

The word *tryms, þryms*[2], first occurs in a gloss which is common to the Epinal, Erfurt and Corpus glossaries, where it is used in the plural (Ep. *trimsas,* Erf. *trynsas,* Corp. *trymsas*) to translate Lat. *asses.* In the Leiden glossary *trymisas* occurs as a translation of *solidus.* There is therefore reason to believe that the word was current in England before the end of the seventh century. It appears to be derived from Lat. *tremissis* (i.e. *triens*), but in value the English tryms can hardly have been equal to either the Roman or the Frankish coin of that name. No English coins are known which would seem to suit the requirements of the tryms; so it is probably to be regarded, at all events from the eighth century onwards, as no more than a unit of account.

The word *mancus* occurs frequently in charters from the year 799 (Birch 293) onwards. An earlier

[1] Several passages, especially the repetition of cap. 18 in cap. 37 and the apparent discrepancy between cap. 23 § 3 and cap. 32, might seem to suggest not the presence of additions to an original text, but rather a combination of two distinct codes. Perhaps one ought not to leave altogether unmentioned the possibility that part of the code in its present form may be derived from the lost Laws of Offa. But it would hardly be wise to take such a supposition seriously into account until some definite evidence is brought forward in its favour.

[2] The latter is the form used in the document *Northleoda Lagu.* I have not seen any explanation either of the variation in the initial consonant or of the origin of the -*y*-.

though perhaps somewhat less certain example is found in a charter of Offa dating from 785 (Birch 245)[1]. It is the regular word in use for expressing weight of gold[2]—never, apparently, of silver, at all events until very late times. It is derived from Arab. *man-kush*[3], lit. 'stamped,' a word used as equivalent to *dinar*, the name of a gold coin, the traditional weight of which was $71\frac{1}{2}$ barleycorns[4]. Its value was therefore identical with that of the Roman solidus. This etymology is confirmed by the gold coin of Offa described on p. 6, which is clearly copied from an Arabic coin and has the Arabic inscription reproduced upon it. The word, together with the thing which it denoted, probably became known in England during the eighth century, at the time when the Moorish power in Spain and the South of France was at its height[5]. It occurs frequently also in

[1] In a letter of Pope Leo III. to Coenwulf, A.D. 798 (Birch 288), it is stated that Offa paid a yearly tribute of 365 mancusas to the Pope. No importance need be attached to the occurrence of the word in B. 32, a charter which professes to belong to the reign of Wulfhere, though it bears the date 624. The witnesses belong to the time of Aethelbald.

[2] It occurs very frequently in charters (generally with the addition of the word *auri* or *goldes*), *e.g.* Birch 322, 338, 396, 449, 452, 502, 507, 524, 533, 536, 538, 539, 540, 550, 551, etc. That it was used as a unit of weight is shown by such examples as the following: Birch 245 (mentioned above) *C mancusas auri obrizi in una armilla*; 353 (A.D. 815) *uiginti et tres mancusas in uno anulo*; 370 (A.D. 822) *anulus aureus abens LXXV mancusas*; 587 (A.D. 901) *kalicem aureum pensans XXX mancusos*.

[3] *Num. Chron.* v. 122 f.

[4] For this information I have to thank Prof. A. A. Bevan.

[5] Possibly however it may have come direct from the East. Charlemagne had dealings with the Caliph at Baghdad.

Frankish charters, the earliest example apparently
dating from the year 778[1].

The words *ora* and *marc* are of Scandinavian
origin (O. Swed. *öre, mark* ; O. Norse *eyrir,* pl. *aurar,
mörk*) and were introduced in all probability with
the Danish invasions during the ninth century.
They denote not coins but weights of silver and gold,
the amount of which will be discussed later. No
coins at all corresponding to these weights have been
found in England, and the native Scandinavian
coinage belongs to a later date than this. The word
pund (from Lat. *pondo* or *pondus*) must also have
been used originally to denote a weight.

§ 4.   *The value of the shilling.*

It has already been mentioned that, at all events
from the eighth century onwards, the shilling was
not a coin but a unit of account. It was however
not an invariable unit.

i.   After the Norman Conquest the shilling was
reckoned at twelve pence in accordance with Frankish
custom. But there is no satisfactory evidence that
this reckoning was in use before the Conquest. The
only passages, so far as I know, which would favour
such a supposition are (1) a passage in Thorpe's text
of Egbert's *Penitential,* IV. 60 : *se rihtscylling byþ a
be* XII *penegum,* and (2) an addition to Exodus xxi. 10
in the Old English version : *þæt synd twelf scillingas
be twelf penigon.* There is however very considerable
doubt as to the authenticity of the *Penitential,* in

---

[1] Cf. Soetbeer, *Forsch. z. d. Geschichte,* II. 359 ff.

the form presented by Thorpe's text. The first three books are said to be certainly not the work of Egbert, while the history of the fourth book is altogether obscure[1]. Both in this document and in the passage from Exodus continental influence may be strongly suspected.

ii. According to the laws of William I. (I. 11) the English shilling contains four *denarii*, *i.e.* pence[2]. With this statement agree several passages which represent the shilling as $\frac{1}{60}$ of a pound; for at all events during the tenth and following centuries the pound is regarded as containing 240 pence. In the short document *Be Myrcna Lage*, §§ 1, 2, it is stated that a thegn's wergeld is 1200 shillings; a king's wergeld is six times as great, viz. 30,000 sceattas, that is altogether 120 pounds[3]. The document

---

[1] Cf. Haddan and Stubbs, *Councils and Ecclesiastical Documents*, vol. III. p. 413 ff.

[2] *solidum Anglicum quatuor denarii constituunt.*

[3] *ceorles wergild is on Myrcna lage CC scill. þegnes wergild is syx swa micel, þæt bið XII hund scill. þonne bið cynges anfeald wergild VI þegna wer be Myrcna lage, þæt is XXX þusend sceatta, & þæt bið ealles CXX punda.* According to this calculation the shilling seems to be valued at a trifle over four sceattas. Now it would of course be absurd to suppose that there was a contemporary currency of sceattas and pennies differing from one another by only 4 per cent. Either this calculation dates from a time before the term *penny* had come into use or in some (Mercian) district the old word (*sceatt*) survived until late times. In the latter case at all events one would have expected to find 240 sceattas reckoned to the pound, and even in the former case it is difficult to believe that the shilling, being a mere unit of account, was not equated with an even number of sceattas. Clearly the explanation must be that the calculation 60 shill. = 1 pound was only approximate; in practice the weight of 4 sceattas × 60 was found to fall short of one pound by 4 per cent.; cf. p. 28 f.

therefore regards 7200 shillings as equivalent to 120
pounds, *i.e.* 60 shillings = 1 pound. This reckoning
however applies only to Mercia, not to Wessex. We
may compare Will. I. 8, where it is stated that the
thegn's wergeld amounts to 20 pounds in Mercia
and to 25 pounds in Wessex[1]. In both cases, as we
shall see later, the wergeld is reckoned at 1200
shillings. The shilling of four pence occurs again in
a Mercian charter dating from 857 (Birch 492): *hec
libertas huius agri comparata est a rege cum sexa-
ginta solidorum argenti: et ante empta cum tanto
pecunia uno libra et Ceolmunde præfecto.* It is
further to be observed that in other Mercian
charters, when the price of an estate is reckoned
in shillings, the figures are frequently multiples of
60 ; *e.g.* Birch 122 (A.D. 704—9): *DC solidis*; 414
(A.D. 835): *trecentorum solidorum*; 416 (A.D. 836):
sex hund scillinga on golde; 452 (A.D. 848): *nigen
hund scillinga*; 488 (A.D. 855): *CCC^{tos} solidos argenti*;
cf. also 509 (A.D. 864): *XXX solidos.* Again in the
Gerædnes betweox Dunsetan, cap. 7, the value of a
horse is fixed at thirty shillings; in a parallel
passage in Aethelstan's Laws, VI. 6, half a pound is
the sum specified. Again in the *Gerædnes* (*l. c.*) the
pig is valued at eight pence and the sheep at one
shilling[2]; in Aethelstan's Laws (*l. c.*) the corresponding sums are ten pence and one shilling

[1] *La were del thein XX lib. in Merchenelahe, XXV lib. in
Westsexenelahe.*

[2] The traditional price of the pig seems to be twice that of the
sheep; cf. a Kentish charter of 833—9 (Birch 412) where among
the charges laid on an estate are *feower weðras an suin, oððe sex
weðras.*

(*i.e.* five pence, see below). Though these passages
in themselves are hardly conclusive, they certainly
tend to confirm the view that in the districts north
of the West Saxon frontier the shilling was regularly
equivalent to four pence. It will be seen later that
there is some reason for believing the same equation
to have prevailed in the Northumbrian kingdom.
It seems to occur also once in a Kentish charter
(Birch 507) dating from 863. After a statement of
certain charges laid upon an estate there follow the
words: *uel xxx argenteis hoc est semi cum libra
redimatur. argenteus* here can hardly mean anything
else than 'shilling.'

iii. In other documents however the equation
1 shilling = 5 pence is found. Thus according to
Aelfric's Grammar, cap. 50: *fif penegas gemacigaþ
ænne scillingc,* and this statement agrees with several
passages in the "Laws of Henry I.," where one *solidus*
is equated with five *denarii.* So also in Aethelstan's
Laws, vi. 6, where the pig and sheep are valued at
ten pence and one shilling respectively (as against
eight pence and one shilling in the *Gerædnes betweox
Dunsetan,* see above), the Latin version has *v denarii*
for *scilling.* This seems to be the regular West Saxon
reckoning. In Aethelred's Laws, ii. 5, it is ordained
that if a free Englishman slay a free Dane or *vice
versa,* the compensation shall be twenty-five pounds.
If, as there seems little reason to doubt, it is the
1200 shilling wergeld which is meant, this will give
48 shillings to the pound. Indeed the equation
seems to occur as early as the laws of Alfred,
cap. 71, according to which the compensation for

the loss of an eye, hand or foot is *LX scill. and VI scill. and VI pœningas and þriddan dœl pœninges* (*-as* MS.). Clearly the third of the man's wergeld (*i.e.* 200 shillings) is intended[1]. Taken as it stands of course this passage implies a reckoning of $9\frac{1}{2}$ pence to the shilling, which is never found elsewhere. But if we adopt the supposition of an old scribal error of very frequent occurrence, viz. *ui pœn.* for *iii pœn.*, the reckoning 5 pence = 1 shilling will be satisfied.

It does not of course follow that this equation prevailed in Wessex from the beginning. The assumption that the shilling contained five pence in Ine's Laws seems to me somewhat hasty. One passage (cap. 59) points distinctly to a different reckoning: "the tail of an ox is valued at a shilling, a cow's tail at five pence; the eye of an ox is valued at five pence, that of a cow at a shilling." Granting that there may be some scribal error in the passage, it is not easy to see why the expressions 'shilling' and 'five pence' should be used side by side if they were synonymous. As a matter of fact the oldest MS. (B) has *IIII peonega* for *scill.* in the first sentence[2]. Again in cap. 74 a Welsh slave is valued at sixty shillings. In the *Gerœdnes*, cap. 7, and Aethelred's Laws, II. 5, the slave is valued at one pound, *i.e.* 60 Mercian

---

[1] In Aethelberht's Laws the corresponding compensation is half the wergeld; so also in the Lex Saxonum, Lex Frisionum and Lex Angliorum et Werinorum. In the Bavarian Law it is a quarter of the wergeld.

[2] So also in the Pseudoleges Canuti, cap. 64, where this passage is quoted, we find in the last sentence: *oculus bouis quinque et uaccae quatuor denariis.*

or 48 West Saxon shillings. It may of course be conceded that 60 shillings containing five pence of eighth century standard would amount to no more than 48 shillings containing five pence of tenth century standard. But as a matter of fact we do not find that in other cases the increased intrinsic value of the unit of account is matched by a corresponding decrease in the number of units[1]. Thus the amounts regularly payable in fines are 30, 60 and 120 shillings from the time of Ine's Laws until the Norman Conquest; so also the wergelds of the noble and the ceorl remain at the same figures, viz. 1200 and 200 shillings respectively. On the whole therefore it seems probable that the shilling of Ine's Laws contained only four pence. This conclusion is further somewhat supported by a passage in the *Chronicle* (ann. 694), which states that the people of Kent paid Ine 'thirty thousand' as wergeld for the West Saxon aetheling Mul[2], who had been killed by them in 687. It has long been seen that, in spite of the Latin chroniclers, *sceatta* is the word which must here be understood. But 30,000 sceattas is the *anfald wergeld* (*i.e.* the wergeld without the *cynebot*) of the Mercian king (cf. p. 13). Moreover according to the *Northleoda Lagu* the wergeld of the aetheling was equal to that of the king apart from the *cynebot*. Mul's wergeld is therefore in all probability identical with that of a

---

[1] There is indeed a decrease in fines, etc. for offences against a bishop, but for this of course there is a special reason.

[2] *her Cantware geþingodan wiþ Ine & him gesaldon XXX m̄. forþon þe hie ær Mul forbærndon.*

Mercian aetheling. The wergeld of a West Saxon king or aetheling in later times is never specified, but if, like the Mercian, it was equal to that of six thegns, it would amount to considerably more than 30,000 sceattas. The change in the reckoning of the shilling, from four to five pence, is probably to be regarded as the result of a decrease in the purchasing power of money and was perhaps a consequence of the establishment of West Saxon supremacy, especially in Kent[1].

iv. It has already been mentioned that in the text *Be Myrcna Lage* the shilling seems to be reckoned at four sceattas, *i.e.* this sceatt is identical with the penny. In Aethelberht's Laws however, the only other document in which the shilling is reckoned in sceattas, a very different reckoning is found. It has long been seen that several passages in these Laws imply that the shilling contained twenty sceattas[2]. Now it is of course quite possible that the sceattas in the two cases were not of equal value. The only sceattas which are known to be Mercian are among the heaviest coins of this type and practically equal to Offa's pennies in weight. It is possible also that Aethelberht's sceattas were among the lightest. But even supposing that their standard weight did not exceed 10 gr.—an improbable supposition—the weight of twenty such coins

---

[1] It is perhaps worth pointing out that the later wergeld of the West Saxon noble, *i.e.* 5 pence × 1200, is identical, in regard to the number of coins, with the ancient wergeld of the Kentish noble, *i.e.* 20 sceattas × 300.

[2] Cf. Schmid, *Gesetze der Angelsachsen*, p. 594.

would still be more than twice that of four Mercian sceattas. Hence it is clear that the Kentish shilling must have been of much greater value than the Mercian shilling or even than the later West Saxon shilling. This conclusion is corroborated by the fact that the sums of shillings fixed as compensations etc. in Aethelberht's Laws, as well as in the later Kentish codes, usually amount to half or less than half the corresponding sums found in the West Saxon laws.

The later Kentish laws, viz. those of Hlothhere and Eadric and those of Wihtred, make no mention of any monetary unit other than the shilling. They give no indication of any reduction in its value, the figures for compensations etc. being apparently about the same as those in Aethelberht's Laws. After Wihtred we hear nothing of any new laws; but on the other hand Kentish charters become very frequent. Curiously enough, when these charters speak of money, which is frequently the case, they do not make mention of shillings[1] but of pence; *e.g.* Birch 318 (A.D. 805) *tria milia denariorum*; 402 (A.D. 832) *XXVI denarii*; 403 (A.D. 860—870) *C pen.*; 412 (A.D. 833) *D pend', fif hund pend'*, etc.; 497 (A.D. 859 ?) *sexcentis denariis*; 515 (A.D. 860—6) *CCLXX denarios*; 519 (A.D. 868) *CXX denarios argenteis*; 638 (before A.D. 914) *CCCLXXXV denarios*; 637 (A.D. 923) *mille denariis puri argenti*. Large sums are also reckoned by the pound, *e.g.* Birch 328 (A.D. 809) *XXX libras*; 348 (A.D. 814) *VII libras auri et argenti*;

---

[1] Except in the charter already mentioned, dating from 863 (Birch 507), where *argenteus* seems to mean the Mercian shilling.

373 (A.D. 823) *v librum et semis*; 384 (A.D. 825)
pecuniam...cxx librarum; 412 (A.D. 833) *pund
pendinga*; 502 (A.D. 860—2) *pecunio...hoc est xv
pund* etc. The most frequent reckoning of all is in
mancusas (cf. p. 11). In some cases indeed the unit
is not specified, but there is no reason for supposing
that it was the shilling (see below). These facts
would seem to show that some inconvenience had
arisen through the great difference in value between
the Kentish and Mercian shillings when Kent came
into nearer relationship with the latter kingdom,
and that in consequence of this the Kentish shilling
had passed out of use.

§ 5.   *The value of the tryms.*

It has already been mentioned that the tryms
occurs in the earliest texts, though these passages
give no clear indication of its value. It appears
again in the Lindisfarne Gospels as a translation of
stater. Apart from this the only place, so far as
I know, where it is used as a word for money, is the
Northleoda Lagu where it occurs frequently (in the
form *þryms*). In cap. 6 it is stated that 266
þrymsas (the ceorl's wergeld) are equal to 200
(Mercian) shillings. The *þryms* is therefore equal to
three pence. According to the text *Be Myrcna Lage*
the Mercian thegn's wergeld is 1200 shillings. We
should therefore expect the thegn's wergeld here to
be 1600 *þrymsas*, but as a matter of fact we find
(cap. 5) 2000 *þrymsas*. The explanation clearly

is that the thegn has the West Saxon thegn's valuation, viz. 1200 West Saxon shillings, *i.e.* 6000 pence.

The word *tryms* occurs also as the name of a weight. In this sense it is used to translate *drachma*[1] and occurs very frequently in the Old English version of the Herbarium of Apuleius, especially in the first chapter. The drachma was a Roman weight of $52\frac{1}{2}$ gr. and equal to three scripula. May we then infer that the Northumbrian penny (or sceatt) was originally the equivalent of a scripulum ? Such a supposition is distinctly favoured by a statement in the Dialogus of Egbert (Archbishop of York 734—766), cap. 8. The statement is to the effect that the priest was to have a wergeld of 800 sicli. There can be little doubt that this sum is intended to represent the Northumbrian thegn's wergeld; for elsewhere we always find the priest and the thegn put on an equal footing in this respect[2]. Now the siclus was a weight in common use during the eighth and ninth centuries (cf. p. 39 f.). It was a quarter of the Roman ounce and equal therefore to six scripula. Consequently, if the penny was a scripulum, the Northumbrian thegn's wergeld would amount to 4800 pence. That seems to be correct; for in the Leges inter Brettos et Scotos[3], which reckon 16 pence to the ore, the

---

[1] This usage is not peculiar to English; cf. O.H.G. (gloss.) *drimisa, trimisa=dragma.*

[2] Cf. *Northl. Lagu,* cap. 5; Aethelred v. 9, vi. 5, viii. 28; Cnut i. 6; and the fragment on the Mercian Oath.

[3] Cf. Seebohm, *Tribal Custom in Anglo-Saxon Law,* p. 307 ff.

thegn's wergeld is said to be 300 ores. We have seen also that the Mercian thegn's wergeld amounts to 4800 (or 5000) pence. Again the weight of the eighth century Northumbrian coins described in the British Museum Catalogue seems to agree pretty well with the supposition that they were intended to be of the standard of a scripulum. The only coin issued by Egbert himself weighs 16·8 gr. Of those bearing the name of his brother Eadberht (r. 737—758) one weighs between 13—14 gr., three between 14—15 gr., four between 17—18 gr. and one between 19—20 gr. Three coins of Alhred (r. 765—774) weigh 13·5, 17 and 17·2 gr. respectively. One coin of Aelfwald (r. 778—789) weighs 15 gr.

The passages discussed above refer entirely to the Northumbrian kingdom. Yet the occurrence of the word *tryms* in the glossaries renders it probable that the same monetary unit was once known in the South of England. If so it must of course have passed out of use at an early date, as we never find it mentioned in laws or charters[1]. We may note

[1] In a Kentish document (B. 412) dating from 833—9 the wergeld of a reeve, named Abba, is stated to be 'two thousand' (*min wærgeld twa ẟusenda*), the unit not being given. Elsewhere in the same document the monetary statements seem to be in pence. 2000 pence would be the wergeld of a Kentish ceorl, as we shall see later. Yet from the description of the man's property we should certainly have expected a 'thegn's' wergeld. No wergeld of 2000 shillings (whether Mercian, West Saxon or Kentish) is known. Consequently, if the sum mentioned is not 2000 pence, it would seem to be 2000 trymsas, *i.e.* the wergeld of the thegn in the *Northleoda Lagu*. This sum would represent both the wergeld of the West Saxon thegn and that of the Kentish noble (Hloth. and Eadric, cap. 1). There is therefore much to be said in favour

however that a very considerable proportion of the
anonymous silver coins described on p. 3 f. are no
heavier than the Northumbrian coins which we
have just been considering. It is quite possible
therefore that in some part of the South, perhaps
Kent, the sceatt may have been intended to weigh
no more than a scripulum.

§ 6. *The value of the mancus.*

The value of the mancus is given by Aelfric,
Gram. cap. 50: *xxx penega (gemaciga*þ*) œnne
mancus.* This equation goes back at all events to
the reign of Aethelstan, as may be seen from certain
passages in his Laws: thus in VI. 6. 2 the value of
an ox is fixed at one mancus; in VI. 8. 5 the ox is
valued at thirty pence. Earlier than this there is
no definite evidence for the relative value of the
penny and the mancus. But from the very frequent
references to the mancus in charters, from the
beginning of the ninth century onwards, and from
the fact that as early as 836 we find a reckoning of
shillings in gold (cf. p. 49), it is clear that these gold
coins must by this time already have been brought
into some sort of fixed relationship to the English

of this interpretation, if evidence can be produced for the survival
of the tryms in Kent at so late a period. But I have not been
able to find any such evidence, and consequently I am disposed
to believe that Abba really was a ceorl. It will be seen later that
the position of the Kentish ceorl was apparently, in some respects
at least, much superior to that of the ceorl in other parts of
England.

silver currency. Again the absence of all evidence for a different reckoning favours the supposition that the equation 1 mancus = 30 pence had prevailed from the beginning. It may be mentioned that on the Continent the mancus is found equated with thirty denarii as early as the year 816 (cf. p. 66).

§ 7.　*The mark and the ore.*

The word *marc* first occurs in the Treaty of Alfred and Guthrum, cap. 2. In this case however the reference is to a mark of gold; consequently the passage cannot be taken into account until the relative value of gold and silver is discussed. From this time forward the mark and the ore (*ora*) are of fairly frequent occurrence in the laws, and it is clear enough that, as in the North, the mark contained eight ores; but the relationship of these units to the native monetary system is hardly ever explicitly stated. Domesday Book indeed forms a striking exception. In this work it is stated again and again that the ore contains 20 pence. The mark therefore contained 160 pence.

Yet there are some traces of a different reckoning. In Aethelred's Laws, IV. 9, it is stated that the pound contained fifteen ores[1]. As there can be no doubt that the pound at this time contained

---

[1] *et ipsi qui portus custodiunt efficiant per ouerhirnessam meam ut omne pondus sit marcatum ad pondus, quo pecunia mea recipitur, et eorum singulum signetur ita quod XV orae libram faciant. et custodiant omnes monetam sicut uos docere praecipio et omnes eligimus.*

240 pence, this must mean that 16 pence went to the ore. For this statement there are some later parallels. In a document dating from the reign of Henry III. mention is made of a payment of two ores, in value 32 pence[1]. Again, the same reckoning seems to occur in the Leges inter Brettos et Scotos, which are clearly based to a large extent on Old English law. Here the thegn's wergeld (*cro*) is said to be 100 cows or 300 ores; that of a thegn's son 66⅔ cows or 200 ores; that of a thegn's grandson 44 cows and 21⅔ pence[2]. The second of these sums is clearly meant to be two-thirds of the first, and the third sum two-thirds of the second. Strictly of course this calculation gives 16¼ pence to the ore, but the fraction may be attributed to unskilful arithmetic. Whatever may be the age of this document its calculations do not seem to be modern. It has been shown above (p. 21) that there is some reason for believing the Northumbrian thegn's wergeld to have been 1200 (Mercian) shillings or 4800 pence. If the ore contained 16 pence, 300 ores come to the same amount.

There would seem therefore to have been two equations in use, side by side, whether the explanation of the difference is to be sought in the weight of the ore or in that of the coins.

---

[1] Ruding, *Annals of the Coinage*, 3 ed. vol. I. p. 115.

[2] *cro a un fiz a cunt ou a un thayn est C uaches u treis C ores. cro a fiz dun thayn est LXVI uaches & II pars dune uache ou CC ores. cro del neuu a un thain u de un ogettheyrn est XLIIII uacc & XXI đ & deu pars dun deñ.*

§ 8. *The pound.*

The weight of the Old English pound is a question of very considerable difficulty, for two unknown quantities, viz. (1) the number of pence contained in the pound and (2) the exact weight of the penny, are involved. Setting aside for the present the question of weight, it may be observed that payments and valuations by the pound (*i.e.* the pound of silver) are frequently mentioned in laws and other documents from the time of Alfred onwards. In charters they occur still earlier, *e.g.* Birch 328, 338, 436, 450, 502, dating from the years 809, 811, 841, 845 and 860—2 respectively. That the pound was, in theory at least, a pound of money seems to be shown by an original charter of the year 825 (Birch 384) where we find the phrase *pecuniam* ...... *cxx librarum,* for which a later text (Birch 385) has *cxx libras denariorum;* so also by the phrase *pund pendinga* in an original charter of 833—9 (Birch 412). In some instances the pound seems to denote value rather than weight, *e.g.* in an original charter of 823 (Birch 373): *uas electi auri et argenti quod est estimatione v librum et semis.* With this may be compared the phrase *vii libras auri et argenti* in an original charter of 814 (Birch 348); so also *pecunio id est lx punda in puro auro et argento* in a charter of 849 (Birch 455). It is hardly probable that in such cases the figures given represent the total weight of the gold and silver combined, but rather the silver equivalent of the whole. I would therefore compare a passage which occurs in a charter of 864 (Birch 509): *unum chiatum* (*i.e. cyathum*) *pretiosum de auro et argento fabrefactum pulcre in quibus fuit cccc solidos* etc.

The above quotations will be enough to show that the pound of silver was a common unit for payments etc. from the beginning of the ninth century. Unfortunately however, as has already been mentioned, we have no definite information from early times as to the number of pence which the pound contained. It is indeed generally assumed that it contained 240 pence. For Norman times this statement may be accepted without reserve; for then the pound contained 20 shillings (*solidi*), while each shilling contained 12 pence (*denarii*). The same reckoning seems to be implied also in Aethelred's Laws, II. 5, where the wergeld of a Dane slain by an Englishman or *vice versa* is stated to be 25 pounds. Here, in view of cap. 70 and 76 of the "Laws of Henry I.," the twelfhyndeman's wergeld (*i.e.* 1200 shillings) seems to be intended; and, since the West Saxon shilling contains five pence, this will give 240 pence to the pound. Again in Edgar's Laws, II. 8, one of the MSS. has *to healfan punde* in place of *to cxx p̃*, which is the reading of the rest. Beyond this point however we become dependent entirely on inferences. Certain figures indeed which occur in the charters seem to favour the supposition that the pound was already regarded as containing 240 pence. Thus two original charters (Birch 497, 519) dating from 859 and 868 respectively contain the phrases *sexcentis denariis* and *cxx denarios argenteis*. Further it has been shown above that the Mercians apparently reckoned four pence to the shilling and sixty shillings to the pound—which yields the same result. Lastly it may be mentioned that on the Continent 240 pence were reckoned to the pound, at all events from the time of Charlemagne, and in the course of the next sections it will be seen that both the currency and the weight standards of England were from time to time considerably influenced by those in use on the Continent.

The only other reckoning of which I have been able to find any trace is that of 250 coins to the pound. It has already been mentioned (p. 13, footnote) that the passage in the document *Be Myrcna Lage*, referring to the king's wergeld, gives a reckoning of 250 sceattas to the pound. If this passage stood alone we might regard it as an antiquated reckoning surviving from a time when the penny had not yet come into use. But as a matter of fact traces of a similar reckoning seem to be found in some of the later laws. According to both Mercian and West Saxon law the traditional wergeld of the ceorl is 200 shillings, while that of the noble or thegn is 1200 shillings, or six times that of the ceorl. Yet according to the "Laws of Henry I.," cap. 70, the wergeld of the villanus (*i.e.* ceorl) and the thegn in Wessex are said to be four pounds and twenty-five pounds respectively, *i.e.* the ratio is not 1 : 6 but 4 : 25. Again in the Leges inter Brettos et Scotos the thegn's wergeld is said to be 100 cows or 300 ores, which seems to be equivalent to 1200

Mercian shillings. We might therefore expect to find the ceorl's wergeld stated at 16⅔ cows or 50 ores, *i.e.* 200 shillings as in Mercian law. As a matter of fact however the figure given is 16 cows, *i.e.* 48 ores or $\frac{4}{25}$ of the thegn's wergeld. This agreement between the English and Scotch laws is somewhat striking. It seems to suggest that the apparent discrepancy noticed above in the text *Be Myrcna Lage* is due not to any intrinsic difference in the value of the sceatt and the penny, but rather to some peculiarity in the method of calculation, which may be stated somewhat as follows:

ceorl's wergeld	200 shillings	*i.e.* 800 sceattas
thegn's wergeld	200 ,,	$\times 6 = 1200$ shillings
king's wergeld	200 ,,	$\times 6 \times 6 = 7200$ shillings ($= 120$ pounds) $= 30,000$ sceattas.

Strictly, if the thegn's wergeld is reckoned at six times that of the ceorl, it will be 4800 sceattas; if at one sixth of that of the king, it will be 5000 sceattas. In the latter case its ratio to that of the ceorl will be the same as that found in the "Laws of Henry I." and in the Leges inter Brettos et Scotos[1].

---

[1] Another trace of this reckoning may perhaps be found in Alfred's Laws, cap. 3, and indeed in connection with a comparatively small sum of money. It is there stated that the compensation for the king's *borg-bryce* is five pounds, for that of an archbishop three pounds, for that of a bishop or earl two pounds. Again in cap. 15 it is stated that the compensation for fighting in the presence of an archbishop is 150 shillings and for the same offence against a bishop or earl 100 shillings. If the two compensations

As regards the origin of this peculiar method of calculation, the most probable explanation which I can suggest is the following. It has been shown above that it was customary even in the ninth century to pay large sums of money by weight. Now if large numbers of such thin coins as the Old English pennies are weighed, it is clear that some allowance must be made for wear. If 240 pence were coined from the pound of silver, a reckoning of 250 pence to the pound in payments will only mean an allowance of 4 per cent.—which can hardly be regarded as excessive. On the other hand, in the payment of comparatively small sums such as the ceorl's wergeld the old custom of counting in shillings of four or five pence each may have lasted much longer. As a matter of fact the payment by weight of the ceorl's wergeld is not mentioned before the "Laws of Henry I." When it did come into use the disparity which had grown up between the ceorl's and the thegn's wergelds may well have been taken into account.

The only alternative explanation, so far as I can see, would be that at some very early period 250 pence or sceattas were actually coined from the pound; that the thegn's wergeld was at this time weighed but the ceorl's counted; and that subsequently, when the pound of 240 pence had come into use, an extra ten pence in the pound was allowed to the thegn. This explanation seems on the whole less likely,

are intended to be identical, a reckoning of 50 (instead of 48) shillings to the pound will be involved. Possibly cap. 3 is of Kentish origin.

especially as the reckoning of 250 pence to the pound is not found in any of the continental monetary systems[1].

The results of this discussion may be briefly summarised as follows : (1) Payments by the pound were frequent from the beginning of the ninth century. (2) In the time of Aethelred II. the pound contained 240 pence. (3) Previous to this time there is no decisive evidence. (4) The only other reckoning, for which there is any evidence, is one of 250 pence or sceattas to the pound ; this reckoning may however be due to an allowance for wear. On the whole I am disposed to believe that the pound of 240 pence goes back to the beginning of the ninth century, if not earlier. This conclusion is supported especially by the Mercian reckoning, which seems to occur also in the laws of Ine, and by the fact that the Frankish pound likewise contained 240 pence (*denarii*), at all events from the year 779 onwards (cf. p. 65).

---

[1] Except perhaps in the Lex Salica, and here again only in the case of large sums. The amounts usually specified in the larger fines are 15, 30, 35, 45 and 62½ solidi. The fine of 35 solidi is perhaps capable of a special explanation, for it may represent the old price of a slave. The sum of 62½ solidi (for which the later laws have 60 solidi) was equivalent to 2500 denarii. I suspect that this means ten (Roman) pounds of silver. If twenty Merovingian denarii were reckoned to the (Roman) ounce (cf. p. 75 and note), we shall have, as in England, an addition of ten denarii to the pound in large sums. Possibly therefore this practice came to England from the Franks.

CHAPTER II.

§ 1. *The weight of the coins.*

THE question of weight must now be discussed. Was the weight of the pound determined by that of the penny or *vice versâ*? As a matter of fact none of the surviving laws or other documents dating from the period before the Conquest convey any information regarding the standard of either[1]. The only exceptions are certain passages which fix the relationship of the penny or the pound to the ore (cf. p. 24 f.), but as the weight of the ore is itself matter of debate, these passages unfortunately give us very little help. It is indeed often assumed that the old English pound was identical with the later Cologne or Tower pound (5400 gr.). But if, in accordance with the conclusion reached in the last chapter, we are to believe that the pound contained

---

[1] It has often been stated that the weight of the old English penny was regulated according to the weight of 32 wheat grains; but I have not been able to find any authority for this statement earlier than the statute "De ponderibus," which is ascribed to the latter half of the thirteenth century; cf. Ruding, *Annals of the Coinage*, ed. 3, vol. I. p. 7 and footnote.

240 pence, probably from the beginning of the ninth
century, we are confronted with a serious difficulty.
The British Museum Catalogue gives a description
of thirty-eight intact pennies issued by Coenwulf;
of these nineteen weigh between 21—23 gr. Again,
in the same Catalogue, of ninety-one intact pennies
issued by Edward the Elder sixty-six weigh between
24—26 gr., and of about six hundred intact pennies
issued by Cnut over two-thirds weigh between
15—18 gr. From these figures it is evident that the
standard weight of the penny was changed at least
twice. Hence, if the number of pence contained in
the pound was constant, the weight of the pound
itself must have been variable.

In face of this difficulty, the only course open is
to ascertain, so far as possible, the weight of the
coins issued by the various kings. I have therefore
made an analysis of the coins of all the more
important reigns, except those of Alfred and Edward
the Confessor, according to the weights given in the
British Museum Catalogue. All the silver coins
of these reigns given in the Catalogue have been
counted, except 'halfpennies' and damaged coins and
some four or five others, the appropriation of which
seemed uncertain[1].

The coinage of Cnut is evidently based on an
entirely different standard from any of those contained in the following table. Out of five hundred
and ninety-eight intact pennies given in the Catalogue

---

[1] The last fifteen coins of Aethelred II. are also omitted.
Four of these weigh over 30 gr.

Table of Pennies in the British Museum Catalogue, classified according to weight.

No. of grains (Troy)		under 16	16—17	17—18	18—19	19—20	20—21	21—22	22—23	23—24	24—25	25—26	26—27	over ·27
Offa (Merc.)	757—796	5	9	7	12	10	2	3						
Coenwulf (Merc.)	796—821	1	1	1	5	5	6	15	4					
Cuthred (Kent)	798—807			1	1	2	1	6						
Ceolwulf (Merc.)	821—823			1		3	1	6						
Ecgberht (Wessex)	802—839	1		1	2	2	4	7						
Berhtwulf (Merc.)	838—852		2	3	2	7	2		2	1				
Ceolnoth (Archbp. Cant.)	833—870			2	2	8	6	7	1					
Aethelwulf (Wessex)	839—858			5	14	30	25	3	2	1	1			
Burgred (Merc.)	852—874	3	5	13	32	50	82	54	20	2	1			
Aethelberht (Wessex)	860—866	2		2	12	12	9	12	3	2				
Edward the Elder	900 (?)—924	1	1		1	1	1	4	5	8				
Aethelstan	924—940	1	2	2	8	4	5	13	18	38	51	15	2	3
Edmund	940—946	1	1	1	5	7	10	23	18	17	42	17	4	1
Eadred	946—955	1	1	4	4	9	20	19	19	21	20	21	1	
Eadwig	955—959	6				3	7	3	4	4	4	3		
Edgar	959—975	6	8	12	22	28	37	21	25	10	6	2		1
Edward the Martyr	975—979					2	10	6	9	6	3	2		
Aethelred II	979—1016	3	5	11	16	41	41	50	58	33	16	47	32	12
Harold II	1066	2	1	5	11	26	42	31	6	1				

four hundred and ten weigh between 15—18 gr. For the remainder the figures are:

Under 12 grs.	12—13	13—14	14—15	18—19	19—20	20—21	21—22	22—23	Over 23
10	13	36	44	26	9	18	16	11	5

The coins of Harold I. and Harthacnut seem to have the same standard, being all under 19 gr. with the exception of one penny in each reign.

A glance at the table is enough to show (1) that the standard weight of the penny must have varied considerably, and (2) that this variation is between the coins of different periods and not between the contemporary currencies of the different kingdoms. For Offa's reign the maximum number of coins falls between 18—19 gr.; the average weight of his coins is 18·14 gr. In each of the next four currencies, ranging from 796 to 839 and representing the Mercian, Kentish and West Saxon kingdoms, the maximum number falls between 21—22 gr., while the average weight varies from 20 gr. to 20·7 gr. After this there seems to be a slight reduction, the maximum number in the next five (Mercian, Kentish and West Saxon) currencies falling between 19—20 gr.[1], while the average weight varies from 19·2 gr. to 20 gr. In Edward's coinage we find a much higher standard, the maximum number falling between 24—25 gr. and the average weight being 24·3 gr. After this there seems to be a continuous

---

[1] Except for the coins of Burgred, the latest of these kings, where it falls between 20—21 gr. Burgred's coins however are said to be of impure silver (Ruding, *Annals of the Coinage*, ed. 3, Vol. I. p. 120).

reduction till the time of Edgar, at the end of whose reign a new coinage is said to have been issued[1] For the reign of Aethelred II. the maximum number of coins falls between 22—23 gr., though very many attain a much greater weight. In the coinage of the Danish dynasty a standard considerably lower even than that of Offa prevails. Finally, in the reign of Harold II. we find a standard not very different from that of Coenwulf, the maximum number of coins falling between 20—21 gr., and the average weight being 20·24 gr.

The only one of the coinages included in the table which presents any particularly remarkable features in regard to weight is that of Aethelred II. As the question here involved may be of some importance, it is perhaps worth while to give a detailed analysis of Aethelred's coins. Of those contained in the British Museum Catalogue almost all belong to one or other of six varieties. The statistics for these are as follows (the terminology being that of the Catalogue):

	under 16 gr.	16—17	17—18	18—19	19—20	20—21	21—22	22—23	23—24	24—25	25—26	26—27	over 27
Type i	2	3	4	6	12	12	8	3	3	2	4	5	2
„ ii var. a		1		1	5	4	11	3		4	9	5	
„ ii „ d	1			3	1	7	1	6	1	2			
„ (iii), iii „ a				6	4	6	7	12	10	3	21	5	1
„ iv „ a				2	12	9	11	19	10	7	13	17	9
„ viii		2	1	2	4	7	13	10	5				

[1] Cf. Matthew Paris *ad ann.* 975 (*R. S.* i. p. 467): *deinde per totam Angliam nouam fieri praecepit monetam, quia uetus uitio tonsorum adeo erat corrupta ut uix nummus obolum appenderet in statera.* The few heavy coins which appear in the Catalogue may perhaps belong to the new issue.

It will be seen that no variety is represented exclusively by heavy coins, though in types iii. and iv. the light coins are comparatively rare. But on the other hand it can hardly be accidental that type ii. var. d and type viii. contain no heavy coins. The statistics seem to point to a change in the standard after certain types had fallen into disuse. It may be observed that types i. and ii. are found in the coinage of the preceding reign, while types iii. iv. and viii. seem to be entirely new.

The coins of Alfred and of Edward the Confessor vary so greatly among themselves that it would hardly have served any useful purpose to include them in the above table—unless indeed, by combining weight with design, it were possible to distinguish with confidence between the different issues. But this, at all events in the case of Alfred's coins, would require a numismatic expert. It may be observed however that Alfred's coins seem to show a transition between the standard of Aethelberht and that of Edward the Elder. Of the Confessor's coins some are as light as the lightest of Cnut's coins, while others equal the heaviest of Aethelred II. (over 28 gr.). In this case I have noticed a considerable difference in weight between the various types into which the coins in the Catalogue are divided. Thus, the weight of the coins in types i.—iv. and xiii. seems to be about the same as that of Cnut's coins. Almost all the very heavy coins (over 23 gr.), which are pretty numerous, belong to type v.[1]; this type however also contains

---

[1] I have noted only four coins over 23 gr. belonging to the other types.

a number of fairly light coins. In types vii. ix. xi. and xv. which contain almost all the remaining coins given in the Catalogue, the standard seems to be similar to that of the coins of Harold II.

The difficulty of ascertaining the standard weight at which the coins were minted is caused by the uncertainty as to (1) what allowance should be made for wear, and (2) how much variation is likely to have existed among contemporary coins of the same king. In regard to the second point the coins of Edward the Elder clearly show that at that time means were possessed of minting coins of practically equal weight. The variation in the weight of his successors' coins, at all events in those of Aethelstan and Edmund, and probably in those of Eadred also, must therefore be attributed either to carelessness or dishonesty on the part of the moneyers or to subsequent clipping. That such practices were prevalent during Edgar's reign[1] is shown by an entry in Matthew Paris's *Chronicle* (cf. p. 36, footnote) and by Eadmer's *Life of Dunstan*[2].

With respect to the allowance to be made for wear it has been suggested above that the Saxons themselves reckoned this at four per cent. But it is a question whether with the coins which have come down to us we should not reckon it at a higher figure. The coins of Harold II. seem to agree in weight with those of his successors, William I.

---

[1] The figures for Edgar's coins however, as well as for those of Eadwig and (in part) Aethelred II., do really seem to show a recognised reduction in the standard.

[2] Migne, col. 792 f.

and William II.[1] Now it is often stated that from
the time of the Conquest, if not earlier, the pound
in use was the Cologne or Tower pound (5400 gr.),
which gives for the penny a standard of 22½ gr.
But if the coins of these kings are compared with
those of Henry II.[2] it will be seen that there is
a perceptible difference between the two standards.
If, as there seems little reason to doubt, the
standard weight of the coins of Henry II. is
necessarily to be fixed at 22½ gr., that of the earlier
coins will be rather below than above 22 gr.

For these reasons I conclude that the standard of
Harold's coins was intended to be a weight corresponding to about 22 gr. Troy or a trifle less. It
seems therefore that to get the standard weight we
must add about 1½ to the number of grains in that
column of the table which contains the greatest
number of his coins[3]. If we apply the same test to
the coins of Edward the Elder, the result will give
about 26 gr. as their standard weight. This seems to
have been the weight of the *nouus denarius* issued
by Charlemagne (cf. p. 67 f.). It is also a quarter of
the Roman siclus, which was a weight much used in

---

[1] For the coins of these kings, see Ruding, *Annals of the
Coinage*, ed. 3, vol. I. p. 161. The average weight which he gives
for the different types of these coins ranges from 17⅓ gr. to 21½ gr.
The coins found at Beaworth (*ib.* p. 151 ff.), which are supposed
not to have been in circulation, varied apparently between
20¾—21 gr.

[2] The average weight of the coins of Henry II. found at
Tealby was over 21·9 gr.; cf. Ruding, *op. cit.*, p. 172.

[3] This will mean that the average weight of Harold's coins
is reduced from the standard weight by 7—8 per cent. In the

England for silver and gold[1]. This is a strong argument in favour of the calculation being correct; for the advantages to be gained by regulating the standard of the currency by the weight-system actually in use would surely be obvious.

Offa's coinage is clearly based on a lower standard than that of Harold II. If the pound already contained 240 pence at this early period—for which indeed we have no evidence in England—the pound in question can only have been the Roman pound

case of Edward's coins the reduction involved will be under 7 per cent. This method of computation however seems to me less satisfactory than the one followed above, as it allows too much influence to a comparatively small number of coins which may owe the reduction of their weight to clipping or exceptional wear.

It may perhaps be thought that the allowance here claimed for wear is too great. I have therefore tested the weight of a number of threepenny-pieces, the modern coins which most nearly resemble the Old English penny in weight. The standard weight of the threepenny-piece is said to be 21·81818 gr. or 1·41379 grammes. Out of thirty-seven of these coins taken at random and bearing dates from 1866 to 1886 (with the exception of four pieces on which the date was no longer legible) I found that nine weighed over 21 gr., twenty-one between 20—21 gr., five between 19—20 gr., and two between 18—19 gr. The total weight of the thirty-seven coins was 49·004 grammes, giving an average of 1·3163 grammes. The reduction through wear is therefore about 6·9 per cent. As the Old English penny was a much thinner coin than the modern threepenny-piece, it may reasonably be expected to have suffered more through wear. I have to thank Mr H. O. Jones for kindly helping me in ascertaining the above figures.

[1] Cf. the passage from Egbert's Penitential cited above (p. 21). The word also occurs in charters, *e.g.* Birch 271, 321, 509, 513 (dating from 786--796, 805, 864 and 866 respectively). I am not aware that there is any evidence for believing that the siclus varied, like the ounce, according to the variations of the pound.

(5000—5050 gr.), though even this will require the standard weight of the penny to be fixed at about 21 gr.[1], and consequently will involve a somewhat greater allowance for wear. In this case, however, we can hardly get beyond mere conjecture.

Again, the standard weight of Coenwulf's coins and those of his contemporaries and successors, down to about 840[2], will according to the same test be about 23 gr. The origin of this standard is not clear to me. From what has been said (p. 31) it may be concluded with a fair amount of probability that by this time at all events, whatever may have been the case in Offa's reign, the pound was already reckoned at 240 pence. The weight of the pound then would be somewhere about 5520 gr. This certainly very closely resembles the Merovingian pound, the weight of which I have calculated to be about 5550 gr. (p. 74 f.). But there is no satisfactory evidence that the Merovingian pound ever contained 240 denarii.

[1] It may however be observed that three of Offa's coins exceed this weight.

[2] Several other coinages of this period are represented in the Catalogue, but so scantily that it would have been useless to enter them in the table. They may however be mentioned here. Two coins of the Kentish king Eadberht (796—798) weigh respectively 20·4 gr. and 22·3 gr. Three of Baldred (dep. 825) weigh 20·7, 21·2 and 22 gr. Three of Archbishop Aethelheard (792—805) weigh 20·3, 21·3 and 21·9 gr. Three of Archbishop Wulfred (805—832) weigh 20·8, 20·9 and 22 gr. Two of the Mercian king Beornwulf (823—826) weigh 19·2 and 22·2 gr. One of Ludeca (826—828) weighs 22·7 gr., and one of Wiglaf (828—838 ?) 25·7 gr. It will be seen that the average weight of these coins, even without counting the exceptionally heavy coin of Wiglaf, will be over 21 gr., somewhat higher than that of any of the coinages of this period included in the table.

Another possible explanation of this standard is to
connect it with the mancus. If the mancus was at
this time already regarded as the equivalent of
30 pence and if, as is extremely probable, the ratio
of gold to silver at the same time was 10 : 1, there
would be a natural tendency to make the penny
equal to one-third of the mancus in weight. Though
this will require the assumption of a standard as
high as $23\frac{1}{3}$ gr.[1] for the penny and consequently will
involve a somewhat large allowance for wear on the
part of the existing coins, I am inclined to think it
is the true explanation. What especially tells in its
favour is that the same cause seems to have brought
about a similar raising of the Frankish standard a
few years later (cf. p. 68). If the same test be applied
to the coins of the remaining kings the results may
be given briefly as follows: for Aethelwulf and his
successors the standard will be about 21 gr. or
slightly over; for Eadwig and Edgar about 22 gr.; for
Cnut about 18—19 gr. Aethelred's coinage would
seem to have been of two distinct standards, one of
about 24 gr., the other of not less than 27 gr. The
Confessor's coins will require the assumption of three
distinct standards, one similar to that of Cnut,
another equal to the heavier standard of Aethelred II.,
the third apparently identical with that of Harold II.

It will be seen that according to these calculations
the standard weight of the penny must have changed

[1] It is however possible that the English standard of the
mancus may have been slightly lower than its original standard
through the wear which these coins must have undergone before
reaching England.

very frequently. Consequently, if the reckoning of 240 pence to the pound was constant, the weight of the pound must also have varied. It has been mentioned that if this reckoning goes back as far as Offa's time, the pound in use must have been the Roman pound. In Coenwulf's time, assuming that the penny was then minted at 23½ gr., the weight of the pound must have been about 5600 gr. In the time of Aethelwulf, if we are to believe that a recognised reduction took place in the standard of the penny, the pound also will be somewhat lighter. Again, in the time of Edward the Elder, or more probably before the end of Alfred's reign, the rise in the weight of the penny to about 26 gr. points to a pound of about 6240 gr.—more nearly perhaps 6265 gr., the probable weight of the pound of Charlemagne's noua moneta (cf. p. 67 f.). Then, after a temporary reduction about the middle of the tenth century, the standard of Aethelred's penny rises, by one or more steps, to about 27 gr., and the pound consequently to about 6480 gr. Cnut's pound can hardly have exceeded 4500 gr. Lastly, after much variation during the Confessor's reign, the weight of Harold's coins points to a pound of about 5250 gr.

In one case we are fortunately in a position to test the accuracy of the results obtained by the above process. It has already been mentioned (p. 40, footnote) that several charters of the ninth century use the word *siclus* in monetary statements. Now in a charter of Queen Aethelswith[1] dating from 868

---

[1] Though Aethelswith was Queen of the Mercians this charter clearly belongs to Wessex. She was the daughter of the West

(Birch 522) the siclus is clearly identified with the West Saxon shilling[1]: *pecunia......hoc est mille quingentis solidis argenti et auri uel quindecies centum siclis.* As the siclus was about 105 gr. Troy, this statement agrees very well with the conclusion that the standard weight of the penny in the time of Aethelwulf and his successors was about 21 gr.

Apart from this case however there seems to be no way of checking these calculations except by the Scandinavian weight-system, which unfortunately is itself a very complicated problem. It has been mentioned above that the mark contained eight ores. In the North the ore (O. Swed. *öre*) was divided into three *örtogher*, but there seems to be no evidence for the use of such a weight in England. Now in the time of William I. the ore contained 20 pence; consequently, from what has been said above, its weight must have amounted to about 430—440 gr. It has also been seen (p. 24 f.) that a law ascribed to Aethelred II. makes the pound to contain fifteen ores, which gives sixteen pence to the ore, and that the same reckoning is found in later documents, both English and Scotch. If this ore was of the same standard as that of William I. the penny in question must have belonged to the heavier and probably later issue of Aethelred II., for a weight of 27 gr. or slightly more will be required. This

Saxon King Aethelwulf and the grant is made from one of her private estates, apparently in Berkshire. The signatures are chiefly those of West Saxon officials.

[1] We may compare the Introduction to Alfred's Laws, § 21, where *triginta siclos argenti* (Exodus xxi. 32) is rendered by ðrittig scill. seolfres.

perhaps explains how the ore of sixteen pence became traditional in Scotland; for the conquest of the Lothians took place only two years after Aethelred's death.

There can be little doubt that for the eleventh century this calculation of the ore is approximately correct. Unfortunately we find no satisfactory evidence before this time for the existence of such a standard either in England or in the North. In the Cuerdale hoard, which dates probably from the beginning of the tenth century, there were found sixteen ingots of silver, each weighing about 8¼ ounces (3960 gr.)[1]. If·these were really marks, the ore must have amounted to about 495 gr. Such a standard is manifestly incompatible with the reckoning of Domesday; and it is also very much heavier than any of the standards found in the North. The earliest attainable evidence in the North seems to be that of a number of weights found in the island of Gotland, which are said to date from the Viking age[2]. The unit of these weights, presumably an örtogh, is between 8·1 and 8·19 grammes, which will give for the ore a standard of 24·3—24·57 grammes or about 375—379 gr. This again is evidently too low for the ore of Domesday. Coming down to the later Baltic standards we find the Swedish double mark given at 425 grammes and that of Riga at 419 grammes[3].

[1] Hardwick, *History of Preston*, p. 74. There were also a considerable number of smaller ingots; but the weight of these seems unfortunately not to have been recorded.

[2] Cf. Seebohm, *Tribal Custom in Anglo-Saxon Law*, p. 236.

[3] Cf. Seebohm, *op. cit.*, p. 235.

These two standards, which would seem to be derived from a common origin, fix the ore at $26\frac{9}{16}$ grammes (about 410 gr.) and $26\frac{3}{16}$ grammes (about 404 gr.) respectively. These figures also are too low. It may, however, be observed that the double mark of Riga (419 grammes, *i.e.* about 6466 gr.) is practically identical with the (heavier) pound of Aethelred II. Possibly we have here a trace of historical connection[1]. The Baltic standards of the mark and ore may have been reduced, perhaps through German influence, in order to bring them into conformity with the pound[2].

From what has been said it is clear that the standard of the ore was variable. Moreover it appears that three of the standards which we have discussed, namely, the old Gotland standard (375—378 gr.), the Cuerdale standard (slightly under 500 gr.), and the standard of Aethelred II. and William I. (430—440 gr.), go back at least to the beginning of the eleventh century. The explanation which I would suggest is as follows. The ore was originally not a fixed weight but the silver equivalent of a certain weight of gold. As such it would naturally vary with the varying ratio between gold and silver. It will be seen that the three figures

[1] Aethelred's heavier pound was possibly of Scandinavian origin; cf. *Historia Eliensis* II. 19: *appensuram nouem librarum purissimi auri iuxta magnum pondus Normannorum* (in a document professing to date from 1008).

[2] This will mean that the mark was reduced from $\frac{8}{15}$ to $\frac{1}{2}$ of the pound, the ore from $\frac{1}{15}$ to $\frac{1}{16}$. An apparently similar change seems to have taken place in the Frankish weight system soon after the death of Charlemagne (cf. p. 68).

given above stand to one another approximately in
the proportion 6 : 7 : 8. I shall subsequently try to
show that a gold unit of the required weight (about
63 gr.) can be traced, and also that a certain amount
of evidence is to be found even for the ratio 6 : 1 in
the relative value of gold and silver. These suggestions will at all events provide an explanation
for the ore of 430—440 gr. It will hardly be denied
that some explanation of this standard is required ;
for, though it differs comparatively little from the
Roman ounce, the difference is nevertheless appreci-
able. If my explanation is correct the ore in question
must of course be older than that of the Cuerdale
standard.

§ 2.   *The relative value of gold and silver.*

It has been mentioned above (p. 11) that the
weight of the mancus was identical with that of the
Roman solidus, viz. about 70 gr. It has also been
shown (p. 23) that, from the time of Aethelstan at
all events, the mancus was regarded as the equivalent
of thirty pence. Again, if the conclusions reached
in p. 38 ff. are correct, the standard weight of Aethelstan's pennies, like those of Edward the Elder, was
about 26 gr.

The weight of thirty such pennies would therefore be about 780 gr., *i.e.* approximately that of
eleven mancusas. It is true that we have no definite
evidence that the original standard of the mancus
was still preserved in Aethelstan's time and that by
Aethelred's time it was certainly considerably reduced—probably to about 55—56 gr. But if we

are to believe that this reduction had already taken place by the time of Aethelstan, we shall be forced to conclude that the ratio of gold to silver was then not less than 14 : 1, which is scarcely credible. It appears probable therefore that the original standard of the mancus was still preserved at this time, and consequently that the ratio of gold to silver was 11 : 1. There seems to be no reason for supposing that any change took place in the reigns of Edmund and Eadred, whether these kings actually coined mancusas or not. On the other hand in Aethelred's time we have clearly to face a different state of things. Not only the standard of the mancus but also that of the penny was changed. Moreover we have evidence that more than one standard of mancus was known about this time. In a document dating from about 1016—1020, published in the Crawford Charters, p. 9, we find the following statement: *ic Eadnoð bisceop* (of Crediton)...*onborgede xxx mancsa goldes be leadgewihte*[1] etc. If we may believe that the standard here described is that of the original mancus, we obtain some further support for the supposition that the reduction had taken place not very long before this time. As regards the ratio of gold to silver it may be observed that the only extant gold piece issued by Aethelred belongs to type viii. of his coinage (cf. p. 36), a type which contains no pennies weighing as much as 24 gr. Consequently, if this coin was equated in value with thirty such pennies, the ratio of gold to

---

[1] The editors refer to Cockayne's *Leechdoms*, III. 92: *and se sester sceal wegan twa pund be sylfur-gewyht.*

silver can not have been less than 12 : 1, a ratio which is likely enough for the beginning of the eleventh century. Possibly there may be some connection between the two standards of mancus and the two standards of penny in the coinage of Aethelred.

Before the time of Aethelstan there is no direct evidence as to the number of pence with which the mancus was equated. The following points may however be noticed : (1) From the beginning of the ninth century the mancus was the usual standard for payments in gold. (2) Gold must certainly have been brought into some sort of relationship with the English monetary system. This is shown not only by the existence of one or two gold coins of the eighth and ninth centuries, but also by certain expressions which occur in the charters, *e.g. sex hund scillinga on golde* in an original Mercian charter dating from 836 (Birch 416); reference may also be made to certain charters which give values made up in gold and silver conjointly (cf. p. 26). (3) There is no evidence for any tradition that the mancus was ever equated with any other number of pence. (4) On the Continent there is evidence that the mancus was equated with thirty denarii as early as the year 816. These facts taken together favour the supposition that the equivalence of the mancus with thirty pence did not begin in the time of Aethelstan, but was already established far back in the ninth century. If so the thirty pennies with which it was then equated must have been much lighter coins, and consequently the ratio of gold to silver can not have been more than 10 : 1. It has already been suggested (p. 42) that the standard of Coenwulf's penny was fixed on this basis.

The only document, so far as I know, which might throw any light on this question is the Treaty of Alfred and Guthrum. In cap. 2 of this document the wergeld of a Dane slain by an Englishman or of an Englishman slain by a Dane is stated to be eight half-marks of gold, except in the case of a ceorl or (Danish) freedman. The amount specified probably represents a recognised Scandinavian wergeld. But from a comparison of the passage with Aethelred's Laws, II. 5, where the wergeld under the same conditions is said to be twenty-five pounds, it seems likely that the sum mentioned is intended also to correspond, at least approximately, to the wergeld of the West Saxon noble (*i.e.* 1200 shillings[1]). Then if four marks of gold are equivalent to 1200 shillings, one mark will be equivalent to 300 shillings, *i.e.* 1500 pence. But what is to be regarded as the weight of the mark? This question of course can not be answered with certainty; but from what has been said above it seems on the whole most probable that it was identical with the mark of Aethelred II. and William I., *i.e.* about 3440—3520 gr. (430—440 gr. × 8). Then, if the ratio 11 : 1, as in Aethelstan's time, was already established, the weight of the 1500 pence must amount to at least 37840 gr., which will give over 25 gr. for the penny. As the document

[1] It may be noticed that in the *Northleoda Lagu* also the wergeld of the Scandinavian thegn is equated with that of the West Saxon noble (cf. p. 20 f.).

dates apparently from between the years 880 and 890, this weight is hardly probable. On the whole therefore I am disposed to believe that the ratio involved in this statement was 10 : 1, which will give about 23 gr. for the weight of the penny and make the mark of silver equivalent to 150 pence[1]. But of course these conclusions are somewhat uncertain[2].

For the period before Coenwulf evidence on this question is entirely wanting. All that can be said is that if the equation 1 mancus = 30 pence goes back as far as the time of Offa, the ratio then can not have been more than 9 : 1.

§ 3. *The origin of the shilling.*

We have seen (p. 12 ff.) that in early times the term shilling was used to denote two entirely distinct monetary values. The Kentish shilling was the equivalent of twenty sceattas, while on the other hand the Mercian shilling—with which the West Saxon shilling seems to have been originally identical—contained only four pence. As there is no great difference in weight between the pennies of the eighth century and those coins of the sceatt type which bear the names of Mercian kings (cf. p. 3 f.) it may be assumed with some probability that the

[1] This equation is not found elsewhere. If 250 pence be reckoned to the pound (cf. p. 28 ff.) the quarter of the thegn's wergeld will amount to 1562½ pence. Hence it seems possible that, at a ratio 10 : 1, the mark may, as in later times, contain 160 pence. In that case of course the penny of this document will be of the same standard as that of Harold II.

[2] At all events any ratio above 11 : 1 seems to be out of the question.

Mercian shilling contained no more than four sceattas in the seventh century. Again, it has been seen that this difference between the Kentish and Mercian reckonings is not to be explained by any difference in the weight of the coins. Those sceattas which can be identified as Mercian are indeed among the heaviest coins of this class. The Kentish sceattas on the other hand, like those of the Northumbrian kings (cf. p. 22), may have been of a lower standard, though we have practically no evidence to that effect. But even if the Kentish sceatt was of no more than half the value of the Mercian sceatt—which is an extremely improbable supposition—this would be far from accounting for the difference in the two reckonings. Hence it may be concluded that, whatever may have been the case with the sceattas, there was certainly a difference in value between the Mercian and Kentish shillings.

It has already been mentioned that the Kentish shilling disappears from view after the Laws of Wihtred. The Mercian and West Saxon shillings on the other hand, though differentiated already by the ninth century, continued in use until the Norman Conquest. From the eighth century, if not earlier, they were mere units of account, representing a given number of pence. Yet it is à *priori* incredible that such can have been the case from the beginning[1].

---

[1] Of course it might have been borrowed from the Continent as a unit of account. But the Continental evidence is altogether against this supposition. The silver solidus hardly occurs before about the middle of the eighth century and always contained twelve denarii.

The only question can be whether the word *scilling* originally denoted a coin or a weight. The absence of evidence for the use of *scilling* to denote a weight[1], the constant translation of *scilling* by *solidus* in the Latin versions of the Laws, and the analogy of Gothic and early German usage, where *skilliggs, skilling* was the name given to the Roman solidus, all decisively favour the former explanation. Again, from the analogy of Continental usage and from the absence of any silver coins of the required size, we may infer that the coins originally denoted by the word *scilling* were gold coins. If these conclusions are correct the quest becomes greatly simplified, for from the time of Constantine onwards for several centuries there were but two types of gold coins in use in Western Europe, viz. the solidus and the triens. There were indeed differences in these coins, *e.g.* between the Roman and Merovingian standards (cf. p. 71), but that is a matter of comparatively minor importance. The really important question is: Have we reason for believing that the Kentish shilling originated in the solidus and the Mercian (and West Saxon) shilling in the triens?

So far as the Mercian-West Saxon shilling is concerned, a certain amount of evidence somewhat favourable to this supposition is supplied by the gold coins found at Crondale (cf. p. 5). These coins are modelled upon Merovingian trientes and are of the

---

[1] The only example known to me is in the Herbarium of Apuleius, cap. 129. 2 (Cockayne, *Saxon Leechdoms,* I. p. 240): *dust anes scillinges gewihte.* In this case *scilling* is a translation of *drachma.*

same weight. At all events the eight examples given in the British Museum Catalogue all weigh between 19 and 21 gr., which is also the usual weight of Merovingian trientes (cf. p. 71). We may also refer here to the large gold coin with the Runic inscription described above (p. 6), the weight of which is of the Roman standard.

The chief objection to this hypothesis is the ratio which it involves in the relative value of gold and silver. If we take the standard weight of the sceatt to have been the same as that of the Merovingian denarius, *i.e.* about 21 gr., twenty such coins must have made a Roman ounce. Then, if the Kentish shilling was of the standard of the Roman solidus, the ratio of gold to silver would be 6 : 1 ; if it was of Merovingian standard, it would be 20 : 3. The West Saxon and Mercian ratio again, assuming that the silver coins were of the same weight, would be no more than 4 : 1. The possibility, however, is always to be taken into account that in one or other of these currencies the sceatt may have been of lower standard than the Merovingian denarius. It is impossible to believe that all the sceattas given in the British Museum Catalogue were intended to be of a weight of 21 gr. Indeed it has been shown above (p. 21 f.) that there is some evidence for believing that the standard weight of the Northumbrian silver coins was one-third of a tryms or drachma, *i.e.* $17\frac{1}{2}$ gr., and it is hardly likely that the light coins were all of Northumbrian origin. Wherever this lower standard was in use, the ratio of gold to silver would of course be still farther reduced.

But are such ratios impossible? It seems at
first sight very strange that the value of silver
relatively to that of gold should be in Kent twice,
and in the further parts of Britain three times, as
great as it was on the south side of the Channel.
Yet it is to be observed that even in the eastern
part of the Frankish kingdom the ratio was very
different from that which obtained in Gaul. In the
Lex Ripuariorum twelve denarii are reckoned to
the solidus. This denarius—with which the saiga
of the Alamannic laws is probably identical[1]—seems
to have been not a Frankish coin but the old silver
denarius of the Roman emperors. That these coins
long remained in circulation outside the limits of the
Roman empire[2] is shown by the hoard discovered in
Childeric's grave at Tournay[3]. Out of this hoard
ninety gold and forty-two silver pieces were identified.
The gold coins all belonged to emperors of the fifth
century, chiefly Leo I., while on the other hand all the
silver pieces except one dated from before the year 217.
Now the standard weight of these old Roman denarii
is said to have been one drachma, *i.e.* about 52½ gr.
Therefore when twelve such coins were reckoned to
the solidus, the ratio of gold to silver involved was

[1] Cf. Soetbeer, *Forsch.* ii. 329. Into the difficult question
of the monetary values given in the Bavarian laws it is not
necessary to enter. I should however like to suggest that the
Bavarian saiga may in part be the miliarensis of the fourth
century emperors.

[2] Possibly a trace of the same coins is to be found in the heavy
penningar of the Icelandic laws (*Grágás*, vi. 43, viii. 114), ten of
which went to the ore.

[3] Cf. Soetbeer, *Forsch.* i. 547 ff.

9 : 1. Indeed if due allowance is made for wear, considering the fact that they had been in circulation for hundreds of years, it is likely enough that in practice a ratio of 8 : 1 would be more nearly correct[1].

Beyond the old frontier of the Frankish kingdom there seem to be traces of a still lower ratio. At the end of the Lex Saxonum there is a statement that two kinds of solidi were in use among the Old Saxons[2]. One of these contained three tremisses, while the other contained only two. The larger of the two is no doubt the Merovingian gold solidus. The smaller must be a mere unit of account, for there is no evidence that gold pieces of the value of two tremisses or trientes were ever coined. Now what can be the origin of this Saxon monetary unit? So far as I can see, it can only have come into existence as the equivalent of a certain amount of silver. The key to this question seems to me to be given by the monetary system of the Ripuarii, who were the immediate neighbours of the Saxons on the southwest. Among the Ripuarii, as has already been mentioned, the solidus was equated with twelve denarii, apparently silver denarii of the early emperors. Two trientes would therefore be equivalent to eight denarii, *i.e.*, according to the standard weight of the denarius, one Roman ounce. I suspect therefore that the Saxon solidus, or rather *skilling*, was

[1] Cf. Soetbeer, *Forsch.* I. 557.

[2] Lex Sax. cap. 66: *solidus est duplex: unus habet duos tremisses, quod est bos anniculus XII mensium, uel ouis cum agno; alter solidus tres tremisses, id est bos XVI mensium.   maiori solido aliae conpositiones, minori homicidia conponuntur.*   The statement contained in the last sentence seems to be incorrect.

an expression denoting an ounce of silver. But how did the ounce of silver come to be called by such a name? Was the ounce of silver once equated with the Merovingian or Roman solidus? If so, the ratio involved would be in the former case 20 : 3, in the latter case 6 : 1.

This is of course pure hypothesis. In more remote countries, however, there seems to be a considerable amount of evidence tending to confirm the supposition. The Northern monetary and weight system has been discussed above, and it has been mentioned that the mark contained eight örar or ores, while the ore contained three örtogher. It has also been seen that the precise weight of the ore (and consequently also that of the other units) was variable: in Gotland at one time its weight was certainly about 375—379 gr., while in England it must have amounted to about 430—440 gr. Now there are three more important points to be taken into account: (1) The word *öre* (Icel. *eyrir*), is certainly derived from Lat. *aureus*, the vulgar name of the solidus. (2) The difference between the ore of Gotland and the Roman ounce (420 gr.) is the same as that between the Merovingian solidus (cf. p. 73 f.) and the Roman solidus. (3) The division of the ore into three örtogher corresponds to the division of the solidus into three trientes. I do not see how the word *aureus—öre* can have come into use for a weight of 375—440 gr., unless some such weight was at one time the equivalent of the solidus in silver. Further, since the word is Latin, we may infer with some probability that the solidus in question was originally the Roman and not the Frankish solidus, for otherwise we should have expected to find the Frankish word—*skilling*. Indeed, for the same reason it seems probable that the term came into use before Frankish coins were known in the North. This observation distinctly suggests that the ore was originally identical with, or rather borrowed from, the Roman ounce. In that case the ratio of gold to silver would be 6 : 1[1]. The origin of the lighter ore will now become clear. When the Merovingian solidus displaced the Roman one, a change was bound to take place either in the ratio of gold to silver or in the standard weight of the silver ore. Apparently the latter was the course adopted. Hence, as the original ore had been six times the weight of the Roman solidus, so now the new ore was six times that of the Frankish solidus. Then, lastly, the örtogh came into use as the silver equivalent of the triens, the commonest of the Merovingian coins.

If the above conclusions are correct, there seems to be evidence for believing that the equivalence of the solidus with the Roman ounce of silver, involving a ratio of 6 : 1, prevailed at one time over a considerable part of Northern Europe. For the Scandinavians must have acquired their knowledge of Roman coins and weights through the Old Saxons or other neighbouring tribes, and this fact gives some colour to the hypothesis suggested above that

---

[1] It is to be observed that even in the twelfth and thirteenth centuries the ratio was only 8 : 1 in Norway and Iceland; cf. Seebohm, *Tribal Custom*, p. 238 ff., Vigfusson's Dictionary, s.v. *gull*.

the same equation once prevailed among the Saxons. It will also be identical with the Kentish equation if we may believe that twenty Kentish sceattas made an ounce, *i.e.* if the Kentish sceatt was of 21 gr. standard.

Are we to conclude that this equation was prevalent at the time when the 'Saxons invaded Britain, in other words, that the Kentish and Scandinavian monetary systems are historically connected? From what has been said this hypothesis would seem to have certain points in its favour; but the still lower ratio of gold to silver in the West Saxon and Mercian kingdoms is somewhat against it. The Old Saxon and Northern equation is also more likely to have come into existence at the time when communication between the north and south of Europe was at its maximum, *i.e.* during the reigns of Anastasius, Justin I. and Justinian.

If the Kentish shilling was identical with the solidus, the West Saxon and Mercian shilling can hardly be descended from anything but the Merovingian triens. The ratio of gold to silver involved, viz. 4 : 1, is certainly surprising; but it may perhaps be accounted for by the small amount of communication which these kingdoms had with the outer world. It is more of a difficulty that there should be so great a difference in the ratio between these kingdoms and Kent. For this reason I am inclined to believe that the standard weight of the Kentish sceattas really was lower than that of the others. Perhaps it may not be thought unreasonable to suggest that the Northumbrian reckoning by trymsas

was originally derived from Kent. In that case
the standard of the Kentish sceatt would originally
be a scripulum, *i.e.* 17½ gr., and consequently the
ratio of gold to silver would not be more than 5 : 1.
On the other hand the Mercian sceatt was certainly
of Merovingian standard, *i.e.* about 21 gr., as appears
from the evidence of the coins. For Wessex such
evidence is unfortunately wanting; but the fact that
the gold coins found at Crondale were of Merovingian
standard would rather lead one to expect that the
same might be true also of the West Saxon silver
coins, if by any chance they could be identified.

If these conclusions are correct, it will appear
probable that the Mercian and West Saxon coinages
were derived from the Merovingian coinage at some
time subsequent to the reduction of the Merovingian
gold standard, which took place about 575 (cf. p. 71).
On the other hand the existence of an apparently
different standard in Northumbria and perhaps also
in Kent would seem to show that the coinage of
these kingdoms had a different origin. It is commonly assumed that the Kentish coinage was an
outcome of Aethelberht's marriage or Augustine's
mission. If my suggestion is correct, its beginning
will have to be dated somewhat before these events[1].
The evidence of the gold coin already mentioned,
which may now be regarded as a Kentish shilling,
points in the same direction. This coin is not only

----

[1] From Aethelb. 60 it may perhaps be inferred that the
currency was already mainly silver. In any case the extreme
rarity of the gold coins is against the supposition that they were
current for any very long period.

of Roman standard but also of a type long obsolete
in Augustine's time. Moreover it bears a Runic
inscription, while the Roman letters are incorrectly
copied and in part illegible. It is not easy to see
how such a coin as this could come, even indirectly,
from an Italian moneyer living at the end of the
sixth century. I am therefore disposed to believe
that the Kentish monetary system is of native
origin. The reckoning of twenty small silver pieces
as equivalent to one large gold piece may have been
derived from the Continent, though not from the
Franks; but the weight of the coins, like the designs
which they bear, was probably fixed in Britain.

The theory put forward above of course does
nothing to explain the disparity between the Kentish
wergelds, etc. and those of the other English kingdoms. No doubt large sums long continued to be
paid chiefly in live-stock. Unfortunately the price
of animals is never stated in the Kentish laws. But
since in later times the mancus, which was of
identical value with the Roman solidus, was the
price of an ox, and there is no reason for supposing
that the value of gold had increased in the meantime
relatively to that of animals, there seems to be every
probability that the ox was the animal with which
the Kentish shilling was equated. The Kentish
freeman's wergeld will therefore amount to 100
oxen[1]. It will be seen subsequently that this was

---

[1] Mr Seebohm (*Tribal Custom*, p. 493 f.) comes to much the
same conclusion but by a different process of reasoning. He holds
(1) that the wergeld of the Kentish freeman was 200 shillings;
(2) that the value of the cow was two shillings; (3) that the

originally the freeman's wergeld among most of the
Teutonic nations of the Continent. On the other
hand the West Saxon and Mercian shillings were
equated with the sheep, at all events in the tenth
century, as appears from Aethelstan's Laws, VI. 6. 2,
and the *Gerædnes betweox Dunsetan*, cap. 7. From
Kentish shilling was a shilling of two tremisses. In regard to the
first point I do not think the passages he quotes will bear the
interpretation which he puts upon them. This question will be
discussed in the next chapter (§ 4). Setting this aside however
for the present, it will be seen that he gives the gold value of the
cow at four tremisses. Now in the tenth century the ox was
valued at a mancus or 30 pence, the cow at somewhat less (20—
24 pence): cf. Aethelstan, VI. 6; Duns. 7. The weight of four
tremisses would certainly exceed that of a mancus. But it is
contrary to all analogy to suppose that the monetary value of the
ox, even in gold, was actually less in the tenth century than in
the seventh. Again, I cannot assent to the view that the Kentish
shilling was a solidus of two tremisses. It is true that such
solidi are found among the Frisians and Old Saxons at the end
of the eighth century. But by this time these tribes must have
been familiar with Frankish coins, both gold and silver, for two
or three hundred years. Consequently a sufficient length of time
had elapsed for the relative value of the two metals to have
considerably changed. But it is surely incredible that the solidus
of two tremisses should have passed from these tribes into Kent
by the very beginning of the seventh century. The argument
which Mr Seebohm (p. 451 ff.) derives from the amount of the
king's mundbyrd seems to me to be altogether erroneous. The
interpolation in Cnut, I. 3, § 2, contained in MS. G, should have
been quoted in full and in connection with the original text, as
preserved in all the MSS. It will then be seen that the peculiarity
of Kentish custom to which the scribe of MS. G wished to call
attention, both here and in Cnut, II. 62, was that an additional
payment of three pounds had to be made to the archbishop.
The amount due to the king was the same throughout the South
of England. As the kings were primarily kings of Wessex it is
quite unnecessary to suppose that their mundbyrd should be
identical with that of the ancient kings of Kent.

Ine's Laws, cap. 55, we may perhaps infer that this was the case even in the seventh century. The wergeld of the West Saxon freeman would therefore amount to 200 sheep, *i.e.* as we shall see later (p. 156 ff.), probably 33—40 oxen[1].

---

[1] It is however to be noticed that in most nations, after the wergelds had been definitely fixed in terms of money, the number of cattle tended continually to decrease as money became cheaper. In the late Scotch and Welsh laws the cow is valued at three ounces of silver. Hence in the *Leges inter Brettos et Scotos* the 200 shilling wergeld of the Scotch ceorl amounts to no more than sixteen cows.

EXCURSUS I.

THE FRANKISH MONETARY SYSTEM.

As the successive monetary systems of the Franks undoubtedly exercised from time to time considerable influence on the English coinage, it is necessary to refer briefly to this unfortunately somewhat obscure subject.

In the Merovingian period the monetary terms in use were *solidus, triens,* and *denarius.* It is clear from the Salic Law and other documents of this period that the solidus was equivalent to three trientes and to forty denarii. Further, it is certain that the solidus and the triens were gold coins, very many of which, especially of the trientes, are still in existence. There can also be little doubt that the denarius must have been a silver coin. But before the end of the Merovingian period we find that the solidus had passed apparently into a mere unit of account, of the value of twelve denarii[1]. This valuation remained constant during the rest of the period with which we have to deal. Further, at some time during the reign of Pippin (752—768) it was enacted that the pound should not contain more than twenty-two solidi, one of which was to go to the moneyer[2].

---

[1] *solidus id est duodecim denarii* in a document of the year 745; cf. Soetbeer, *Forsch. zur deutschen Geschichte,* IV. 265.

[2] *de moneta constituimus ut amplius non habeat in libra pensante nisi xxii solidos, et de ipsis solidis monetarius accipiat solidum I et illos alios domino cuius sunt reddat* (Pertz, *M. G.,* Leg. I. 31).

This number seems to have been reduced to twenty by the year 779[1]. According to Soetbeer[2] the change took place before the end of Pippin's reign, but others believe it to have come in with the issue of Charlemagne's noua moneta, the precise date of which is uncertain, but at all events not later than 1 Aug. 781[3]. Whatever may be the date the change of course involved a reduction in the number of denarii contained in the pound from 264 to 240— a number which after this seems to have remained constant. From the time of Pippin the currency appears to have been essentially a silver one.

It is in the determination of the weight standards that the chief difficulty lies. Thus (*e.g.*) the denarius of Charlemagne's noua moneta has been variously estimated by Leblanc at 28·8 Paris gr. (*i.e.* 1·528 grammes or about 23½ gr. Troy), by Guérard at 32 Paris gr., and by Fossati at 34 Paris gr.[4] The heaviest of the silver coins appear to be those issued by Ludwig I. (814—840). A large number of these, dating from probably not much later than 822, were found at Belvezet in 1836. Soetbeer (*Forsch.* VI. 38 ff.) has given an analysis, according to weight, of 248 of these, coming from thirty places of mint. The weight of the individual coins varies considerably, the maximum being 34 Paris gr. This weight is however attained by coins of no less than thirteen out of the thirty mints. Moreover the average weight of sixteen coins from Milan is 33½ Paris gr., and that of forty coins from Pavia 33 Paris gr. Several mints are represented only by coins of this weight. From these considerations, in spite of the fact that the average weight of the whole number falls considerably below this

---

[1] Cf. Capitulare episcoporum, A.D. 779: *et unusquisque episcopus aut abbas uel abbatissa, qui hoc facere possunt, libram de argento in elemosinam donet; mediocres uero mediam libram, minores solidos quinque* (Pertz, *M. G., Leg.* I. 39).

[2] *Forsch.* IV. 275 ff.

[3] Cap. Mantuanum, A.D. 781 (Pertz, *M. G., Leg.* I. 41).

[4] Soetbeer, *Forsch.* IV. 295 ff.

figure, I distinctly think that the standard weight of these coins should not be placed below 34 Paris gr., *i.e.* a trifle over 1·8 grammes or nearly 28 gr. Troy. This conclusion is somewhat supported by a calculation which appears in two charters dating from the year 816. In the first, which comes from Freisingen[1], thirty denarii are equated with one gold solidus—presumably a Roman solidus, as the Merovingian solidus had long passed out of circulation[2]; in the second, from Aachen[3], fifty silver solidi (*i.e.* 600 denarii) are equated with twenty mancuses—a reckoning which gives thirty denarii to the mancus. As the mancus was identical in weight with the Roman solidus (*i.e.* 4·54 grammes or about 70 gr. Troy) and there can be no doubt that the ratio of gold to silver at this time was 12 : 1, the silver equivalent required in both cases is about 840 gr. Troy. The calculation will involve for the pound a weight of about

---

[1] Meichelbeck, No. 349; cf. Soetbeer, *Forsch.* II. 335.

[2] There is however in existence a gold coin of Ludwig I. weighing 77 Par. gr. (4·08 grammes) and corresponding therefore to the standard of the Merovingian solidus. At a ratio of 12 : 1 this coin might perhaps represent the value of thirty denarii of Charlemagne's noua moneta, but not that of thirty denarii of Ludwig's issue. Possibly it may have been struck at the very beginning of the reign. The only other gold piece of this king of which I have been able to find mention is a coin weighing 132 Par. gr. (7·01 grammes). At the same ratio this coin would represent very nearly the value of 48 denarii (*i.e.* four silver solidi) of Ludwig's issue. If coins of the former type ever really circulated, the statement in the Freisingen charter cannot be taken as evidence for the weight of Ludwig's denarii. But the fact that there exist also three gold coins of various standards (48, 59 and 69 Par. gr. respectively), which are attributed to Charlemagne, suggests that all these gold coins were experimental issues. For a description of the coins in question see Berry, *Études sur les Monnaies de France*, Tome I. pp. 126 ff., 153 f.—a reference for which I have to thank the Rev. W. G. Searle.

[3] Ughelli, *Italia Sacra*, v. 706; cf. Soetbeer, II. 360, and for its authenticity, *ib.* 363.

433 grammes (6682 gr. Troy), and this is confirmed by the former existence of a copper weight exactly corresponding to what is required[1].

If we turn now to Charlemagne's noua moneta we may probably follow Soetbeer in believing this currency to be represented by the silver coins found at Wyk te Duerstede. But since these coins were probably deposited at the burning of the place in 834 or later, they must have been in circulation for some considerable time. A certain allowance must therefore be made for wear. As a matter of fact the average weight of the coins, thirty in number, was 1·42 grammes. Starting from this fact and taking into account the close agreement between the old French pound (367·1292 grammes), the Dutch Troy pound (369·1258 grammes), the English Troy pound (373·233 grammes), and the Cologne pound (350·7185 grammes), Soetbeer (*Forsch.* IV. 311 ff.) came to the conclusion that Leblanc's figures were the correct ones, viz. 367 grammes for the pound and slightly under 1·53 grammes for the denarius. This conclusion seems to me somewhat hasty. No doubt the close agreement between the various medieval pound weights is an argument for their common origin ; but this common origin is not necessarily to be found in the pound of Charlemagne's noua moneta. As regards the weight of the coins it will be seen that seven out of the thirty have a weight of from 1·6 to 1·65 grammes, and this fact seems to me to be fatal to the hypothesis that the standard weight was intended to be so low as 1·53 grammes. Guérard's calculation, which gives about 1·7 grammes (rather over 26 gr. Troy) for the denarius and about 408 grammes for the pound, seems to me to fit the case much better, though on the whole I should be inclined to prefer a pound of about 406 grammes, *i.e.* one Roman

---

[1] Cf. Soetbeer, *Forsch.* IV. 314, who calculates from it the weight of the pound at 433·24 grammes. It was inscribed *pondus Caroli*, but Soetbeer would ascribe it to Carl the Bald rather than Charlemagne.

ounce less than the (later) pound of 433 grammes[1], and consequently a denarius of about 1·68 grammes. This conclusion rests of course on the assumption of a greater allowance for wear than in the case of the Belvezet coins, but, considering the much greater length of time that the Duerstede coins had been in circulation, this can hardly be considered unreasonable. The point in favour of fixing the pound at about 406 grammes is, that this is the weight of fifteen Roman ounces. Each Roman ounce would then contain sixteen denarii[2], and the transition from a pound of 406 grammes to one of 433 grammes would simply mean the substitution of sixteen (Roman) ounces of fifteen denarii each for fifteen (Roman) ounces of sixteen denarii each. This preservation of the Roman ounce as a unit would not necessarily be incompatible with the preservation of the Roman reckoning of the pound at twelve ounces, though of course these latter ounces had ceased to be of Roman standard.

The increase in the weight of the denarius—and consequently also in that of the pound—during Ludwig's reign may have been partly due to the influence of the mancus. If, as there is every reason to believe, the mancus had come into very frequent use about this time the desirability of equating it with a convenient number of denarii must soon have been felt. This could hardly have been done in a more simple way than by increasing the weight of the denarius by about 7½ per cent., thus making thirty denarii equal in weight to twelve mancuses. The ratio 12 : 1 in

---

[1] The pound of 408 grammes is approximately the weight of 15 Roman ounces according to the old standard when the (Roman) pound stood at 327·47 grammes. The pound of 406 grammes is ⅟₁₈ of that of 433·24 grammes (see above), which seems to reflect the later Roman standard, when the pound stood at about 325 grammes (cf. Soetbeer, *Forsch.* I. p. 264, footnote). It is not necessary however to suppose that the reduced standard had come everywhere into use.

[2] Consequently each siclus—the ordinary unit for small weights at this period, cf. p. 39 f., would contain four denarii.

the relative value of gold to silver seems to have been long established among the Franks, as will be seen below.

As regards the money in use before the issue of the noua moneta, we may no doubt follow Soetbeer in believing this to be represented by the coins found at Imphy. An analysis of sixty-three of these was given by him in the *Forsch. z. d. Gesch.* IV. 276 f., 306. Of fifteen coins issued by Charlemagne the average weight is 1·26 grammes, and of four issued by Carloman 1·33 grammes. Among these were found a larger number of coins issued apparently by Pippin. Soetbeer divides these latter into two classes, the first bearing the legend RXF or PRXF, the latter RP or RPPN. The average weight of the former class, eleven in number, was 1·22 grammes, while that of the latter, thirty-three in number, was 1·26 grammes. From these considerations Soetbeer came to the conclusion that during Pippin's reign two distinct coinages were issued, the coins of the later issue being on the average distinctly heavier than those of the earlier. The coins of the lighter class he believed (*ib.* p. 281 ff.) to have been issued at the rate of 264 to the (Roman) pound (cf. p. 65 above), while the heavier type belonged to a later period of Pippin's reign, when the number of denarii in the (same) pound had already been reduced to 240. These calculations give for the earlier issue a standard weight of 1·23 grammes, and for the later a standard of 1·354 grammes. The coins of Charlemagne in use before the issue of the noua moneta represent, according to Soetbeer, a standard identical with the later standard of Pippin.

Soetbeer's explanation seems to me to be open in three points to serious criticism. In the first place a detailed examination of the coins scarcely bears out the theory of an earlier and later standard. The Imphy coins may be classified as follows:

grammes:	1·0—1·1	1·1—1·2	1·2—1·3	1·3—1·4	1·4—1·5
RXF, PRXF	3	1	5	2	
RP, RPPN	2	5	12	12	2
Carloman			1	3	
Charlemagne	1	2	5	6	1

These figures hardly seem conclusive. Again, if only the earlier coins of Pippin bore the legend RXF, it is curious that some of Charlemagne's coins should bear very similar legends, *e.g.* CA : R.F. and CAROLVS RX.F. Secondly, the evidence for the existence of a reckoning of 240 denarii to the pound before the issue of the noua moneta does not seem to me quite satisfactory. The first example of this reckoning dates from the year 779 (cf. p. 65 above), while the decree of 781[1] is not really a statement that a new coinage was then first being issued, but a prohibition against the circulation of an old issue. Now in the case of a new issue by Ludwig, Charlemagne's successor, several years were apparently allowed to elapse before the circulation of the old money was forbidden[2]. It seems therefore quite possible that the noua moneta was really issued before 779. Thirdly—and this is the most important point—the weight of the coins inscribed RXF and PRXF seems to me quite irreconcilable with the supposition that 264 of them went to a pound of 325 grammes. It is true that this calculation gives 1·23 grammes to the denarius, while the average weight of these coins is only 1·22 grammes ; but it is to be remembered that the deposit at Imphy dates from Charlemagne's reign. Consequently, if these coins represent Pippin's earlier issue, they cannot have been by any means new. Moreover out of the eleven coins no less than six exceed the theoretical standard—five of them attaining a weight of 1·28 grammes or more.

I conclude therefore (1) that no type of Pippin's coins represented in the Imphy hoard agrees with a reckoning of 264 denarii to the Roman pound, and (2) that the evidence for a change of reckoning, from 264 to 240 denarii to the pound, before the issue of the noua moneta is not quite satisfactory[3].

---

[1] *de moneta : ut nullus post Kal. Augustas istos dinarios, quos modo habere uisi sumus, dare audeat aut recipere : si quis hoc fecerit, uannum nostrum componat :* Pertz, *M. G., Leg.* I. 41.

[2] Cf. Soetbeer, *Forsch.* VI. 5 f.

[3] The actual weight of the coins is not incompatible with the supposition that 240 of them went to the Roman pound. It will

The most reasonable explanation seems to be that the reckoning of 264 denarii to the pound was in use up to this time, but that the pound was much heavier than the Roman pound. The money of the Merovingian dynasty has yet to be discussed. It has been mentioned that this was essentially a gold currency, though silver coins were also in use. The first king whose name appears on coins is Theodebert (534—548), but some imitations of Roman coins which appear to have issued from Frankish mints may possibly be still older. Down to the time of Sigebert (561—575) the Frankish solidi and trientes seem to have preserved the Roman standard, *i.e.* about 4·5 grammes (70 gr. Troy) for the solidus, and 1·5 grammes for the triens ; but after this reign there is a distinct and apparently sudden decrease, few of the later coins exceeding 4 grammes for the solidus or 1·4 grammes for the triens[1]. It has been noticed that several of these later solidi have the figures XXI inscribed upon them, while many of the trientes have VII[2], in explanation of which it has been suggested that the standard of weight was now reduced from twenty-four or eight siliquae (the Roman standard) to twenty-one or seven siliquae. Another suggestion, adopted like the last by Soetbeer, is that under the new coinage 84 solidi were made from the pound instead of 72 as formerly. In connection with this, however, it should be pointed out that 21 siliquae × 84 and 24 siliquae × 72 are not exactly identical. If these suggestions are correct, either the reckoning of twenty-one siliquae to the solidus must have been an approximate one, or one of the two units, the siliqua or the pound, must have changed its value.

A considerable number of silver coins are in existence which date apparently from the Merovingian period, though

be seen subsequently that this may have been true even of the Merovingian coins.

[1] Soetbeer (*Forsch.* I. 618) suggests as standard weight 3·96 grammes for the solidus and 1·32 grammes for the triens. But many of the examples which he mentions (especially among the anonymous coins, p. 612 f.) exceed these figures.

[2] Cf. Soetbeer, *Forsch.* I. 619 ff.

few if any bear the names of kings. There is great variation in their weight, some being as low as 0·8 grammes, while others exceed 1·4 grammes. According to Soetbeer's table (*Forsch.* I. 629, ff.) the majority weigh from 1·1 to 1·3 grammes. In face of this discrepancy it might reasonably be questioned whether a standard weight was in existence. Yet there is conclusive evidence that at some time or other such was the case. Among a hundred and seventy coins found at Plassac there were four unstamped pieces of silver. Two of these weighed 1·38 grammes, the third 0·69 grammes, and the fourth 0·37 grammes. The evidence of these pieces is sufficient to show that means were possessed at this time of minting coins of practically equal weight, and that the standard weight of the larger coins was not far from 1·38 grammes. It is of course possible that the Plassac hoard dates from a comparatively late period. Yet it must not be overlooked that the weight of these unstamped pieces agrees in a remarkable way with that of the silver coins of the Vandal and Ostrogothic kings in the sixth century. Thus in a list of nearly fifty Ostrogothic coins given by Soetbeer (*Forsch.* I. 283 f.) all except six fall either between 1·30—1·43 grammes or between 0·61—0·77 grammes. The Vandal coins seem to be somewhat lighter; yet Soetbeer (*ib.* p. 280) calculates their standard weights to have been 1·3 and 0·65 grammes. The same appears to be true also of the Roman silver coins of this period. There is therefore every reason to believe that the silver coin of 1·38 grammes, or thereabouts, was not a late innovation.

It has already been mentioned that in the Lex Salica the solidus is equated with forty denarii and that the word 'denarius' is in all probability used to denote a silver coin. But what silver coin was it? The old Roman denarius (of 3·4 grammes) can hardly be seriously taken into account, for even after making every possible allowance for wear the calculation would involve an inconceivable ratio in the value of gold to that of silver. The choice seems therefore to lie between the two small silver coins which had been in circulation since the fourth century, viz. the siliqua and the half-

siliqua or scripulum[1]. The original and theoretical standard
of these coins was 2·274 and 1·137 grammes respectively.
Now if forty half-siliquae were regarded as equivalent to the
solidus, the ratio of gold to silver involved would be 10 : 1,
which at such a time could hardly be considered unlikely.
But according to Soetbeer's statistics (*Forsch.* I. 273 f.) the
standard was very considerably reduced even by the time of
Honorius, *i.e.* in the first quarter of the fifth century, while
by the beginning of the sixth century the ratio involved by
this equation would be more like 6 : 1. It seems then that
the siliqua must be the denarius of the Lex Salica. According
to Soetbeer (*l.c.*) the average weight of the siliquae of Justin I.
and Justinian is 1·3 grammes, and though the standard
should probably be put somewhat above this figure, it is clear
that this must be the coin which served as a model both for
the heavier silver coins of the Ostrogoths and Vandals and for
the unstamped pieces found at Plassac. If we may take the
standard weight of these (Roman) coins at the beginning of
the sixth century to have been the same as that of the Ostrogothic coins and the Plassac pieces (*i.e.* about 1·35—1·38
grammes) the ratio of gold to silver involved will be 12 : 1.

If the above conclusions are correct a possible explanation
of the reduction in the weight of the Merovingian gold coins
seems to present itself. Since the triens was by far the
commonest of the gold coins, the awkwardness of its relationship to the denarius (1 triens = 13⅓ den.) must have been
a constant source of difficulty in small transactions. If the
ratio of gold to silver was 12 : 1, the advantage to be gained
by reducing the weight of the triens to a level with that
of the denarius, thus making one triens equivalent to twelve
denarii, would surely soon become obvious ; and this is what
I would suggest really took place. There is nothing in the
actual weight of the existing coins which counts against such
a supposition. The only difficulty is in the figures VII and XXI
inscribed on the gold coins. If these figures really do mean
seven and twenty-one (gold) siliquae respectively, I would

[1] Hultsch, *Métrologie*, p. 331 f.

suggest either that the calculation was a very rough one, or that the (gold) siliqua had risen somewhat above its original weight[1].

If my hypothesis is correct, the silver solidus of the eighth century will be the legitimate successor not of the Merovingian solidus but of the triens[2]. It is not necessary to suppose that the triens was ever actually called solidus. The application of the term *solidus* to the silver unit may very well have begun among the Teutonic part of the population, though with them it was no doubt employed only in writing. The word used in actual speech must have been *skilling*, and I can see no reason why this word should not have been applied to the triens as well as the solidus in early times. Possibly the two may have been distinguished as 'large' and 'small' shillings.

Further it will appear from the foregoing discussion that Pippin's enactment quoted above (p. 64) must not be regarded as the establishment of a new monetary system. In appearance Pippin's coins differed considerably from those of his predecessors, but in regard to the standard, if my suggestions are correct, this was not the case. The weight suggested above as the standard weight of Merovingian denarii and trientes, viz. 1·35—1·38 grammes, will suit very well the coins found at Imphy, issued by Pippin, Carloman and Charlemagne. Moreover, a pound containing 264 such denarii, *i.e.* about 356—364 grammes, will very closely approach the figure fixed by Soetbeer for the pound of the noua moneta. And, though his conclusion seems to me to be incorrect on this point, the close agreement between the French, Dutch, and Cologne pounds certainly favours his supposition that they have a common origin, *i.e.* that a pound

[1] Taking 1·365 grammes as the standard weight of the triens, this would give for the (gold) siliqua a weight of 0·195 grammes instead of 0·189 grammes. In any case the standard fixed by Soetbeer for the later gold coins seems to me to be too low (cf. p. 71, footnote).

[2] Cf. p. 59 f., where a similar origin has been suggested for the West Saxon shilling.

of 350—370 grammes must have been in existence at a fairly early date. What I would suggest is that Pippin's enact-ment was in the first place a prohibition against debasement of the currency, which, judging from the weight of existing Merovingian silver coins as compared with the unstamped pieces found at Plassac, would appear to have been by no means unnecessary. It may however also have been intended to limit the profits of the moneyer. By it the moneyer is allowed one (silver) solidus in the pound, *i.e.* one solidus in twenty-two. Now a pound of twenty-two solidi, each of which contains twelve denarii, may of course also be regarded as a pound of twelve ounces, each of which contains twenty-two denarii. Pippin's enactment therefore means an allowance of one denarius in each (Merovingian) ounce. Possibly before this time the moneyer was allowed to appro-priate two denarii in the ounce of silver, and—as there seems to have been no difference in standard between the gold and silver coins—two trientes in the ounce of gold. It is not to be overlooked that if the weight of two denarii or trientes be subtracted, the Merovingian ounce will become the Roman ounce[1]. Indeed the Merovingian ounce may well have had its origin in an increase of 10 per cent. (on the Roman ounce) for some such purposes[2].

[1] If we take the standard weight of the Merovingian denarius to be 1·365 grammes (*i.e.* about 21 gr. Troy), the ounce in question, *i.e.* the weight of twenty such denarii, will be practically the old Roman ounce (27·288 grammes). The old Roman standards may well have survived in Gaul up to this time.

[2] A somewhat parallel phenomenon seems to be presented by the pound of fourteen ounces in use under Constantine the Great (cf. Soetbeer, *Forsch.* I. 292 ff.).

CHAPTER III.

THE SOCIAL SYSTEM.

§ 1. *The Evidence of the Later Laws.*

HAVING discussed the monetary system we are now in a position to deal with the statements contained in the laws regarding the amounts of various compensations and fines. On the subject of wergelds the fullest statement is that contained in the *Northleoda Lagu,* where they are given as follows:

king	30,000	thrymsas
archbishop and aetheling	15,000	„
bishop and earl (*ealdorman*)	8,000	„
hold and king's high-reeve	4,000	„
mass-thegn and secular thegn	2,000	„
ceorl	266	„

This document, which can hardly be earlier than the tenth century, evidently belongs to a Scandinavian district, as appears from the use of the term *hold*; but the monetary system used in the statement of the wergelds seems to be Northumbrian (cf. p. 20 ff.). There is therefore every probability that this table represents the usage of the Scandinavian kingdom in the North of England[1]. The wergeld of the ceorl, which in the text is identified with that of the Mercian ceorl, appears likewise to have been that of the corresponding class in Northumbria[2]. But the wergeld of the thegn seems to be that of the West Saxon and not that of the Northumbrian thegn. As both standards were new to the invaders it is intelligible enough in view of their dominant position, that they should choose the higher one, although it did not belong to that part of the country in which they themselves had settled. No doubt however the choice was partly due to the existence of a Scandinavian wergeld[3], which, at the English value of gold (cf. p. 50), may have corresponded very closely to that of the West Saxon thegn.

All the terms (except *hold*) used in this document are found also in texts referring to the South of England. Setting aside for the present the consideration of the king, the aetheling, the earl, the king's high-reeve, and the ecclesiastics, we find that the distinction between thegn and ceorl is from the time of Aethelstan the broad line of demarcation between the classes of society. The difference may be seen in the amounts of their wergelds and of other pay-

---

[1] The term *NorЗleode* is not used elsewhere in the sense of 'Northumbrians' and is therefore more likely to mean 'Scandinavians.' I suspect that the code originated under the Norwegian kings who reigned in the north of England during the first half of the tenth century ; in which case *NorЗleode* would be equivalent to the more usual *NorЗmen, Northmanni*.

[2] In the *Leges inter Brettos et Scotos* the wergeld of the *carl* is stated to be 16 cows, *i.e.* 48 ores or (strictly) 768 pence.

[3] The origin of this wergeld will be discussed later.

ments due to or from them and in the respective
values of their oaths. Thus in Hen. 64. 2 we find it
stated : *thaini iusiurandum contraualet iusiurandum
sex uillanorum, et si occideretur, plene uindicaretur
in sex uillanis, et si emendaretur, eius weregyldum est
vi uillanorum weregyldum.* This passage is apparently a translation of the fragment *Be Merciscan
Aðe, thaini* being substituted for *twelfhyndes mannes*[1].
The identity of the two expressions may be seen from
Hen. 69. 2 *de twelfhindo, i.e. thaino*; so also ib. 70. 1 :
*in Westsexa...twyhindi, i.e. uillani wera est iv libr.,
twelfhindi, i.e. thaini xxv libr.;* and again ib. 76. 4 :
*twelfhindus est homo plene nobilis, i.e. thainus, cuius
wera est duodecies c sol., qui faciunt libr. xxv*[2]. We
may further compare the short document *Be Myrcna
Lage*, cap. 1, 2, where it is stated that " the ceorl's
wergeld in Mercia is 200 sh.; the thegn's wergeld is
six times as much, *i.e.* 1200 sh." Again, in the
document *Be Wergilde* (Edw. and Guth. 13), cap. 1,
it is stated that the wergeld of the *twelfhynde man* is
1200 sh. and that of the *twyhynde man* 200 sh. As
there can be no doubt that the words *twelfhynde* and
twyhynde are derived from *twelf hund* and *twa hund*
(s.c. *scillinga*)[3], it appears that these terms have their

[1] *uillanus* is the word generally used to translate *ceorl*.
Etymologically of course its equivalent is *tunesman* (cf. *North.
Preosta Lagu* 59).

[2] Cf. Will. i. 8 (quoted above, p. 14 and footnote) ; but the
last sentence (*la were del vilain c sol. en Merchenelahe e ensement
en Westsexene*) must contain some mistake (*c* for *cc.* ?), unless the
ceorl's wergeld had recently been changed in Mercia.

[3] It is very curious that any scepticism should have prevailed
on this point. For the formation we may compare *twiecge* from
twa ecga.

origin in the amount of the wergeld. There seems to be no difference between Mercian and West Saxon custom in this respect, except in regard to the value of the shilling. In the *Northleoda Lagu*, on the other hand, the ratio between the wergeld of the ceorl and that of the thegn is of course different, the former amounting to 200 Mercian shillings, while the latter is equivalent to 1200 West Saxon shillings.

If we turn now to the qualifications of thegnship we find that it was partly inherited, partly acquired. Evidence for the former is given by such phrases as (Duns. 5) *sy he þegenboren, sy he ceorlboren,* ' whether he be of thegnish or of ceorlish birth'; and more explicitly in Hen. 68. 3 : *si tamen (presbyter) occidatur......secundum natale suum reddatur; si de thainis natus est thaini wera reddatur, si de uillanis similiter coniectetur* (cf. 69. 1, 76. 1). We may further compare such passages as Edw. and Guth. 13. 2, where it is stated that if a man be slain, payment is to be made according to his birth (*swa he geboren sy*), and Edm. II. 1 : *sy swa boren swa he sy,* ' whatever his birth may be.' The distinction between the two classes applies also to women, as may be seen from Hen. 70. 13 : *si mulier occidatur sicut weregildum eius est reddatur ex parte patris.* This statement is manifestly to be interpreted by the light of 82. 9, where women are classified as *cyrlisca uel syxhinda uel twelfhinda*; but the latter passage is derived from a much earlier law (Alfr. 18. 1—3). The two points to which we have here called attention, viz. (i) the use of such terms as 'thegnish birth,' and (ii) the application of the distinction to women, are sufficient to show that the thegn was not necessarily a person of official position, but, in some cases at all events, a member of a hereditary class of society.

In other cases, however, the rank of thegn is said to be acquired. Thus according to *Be Leodge-þincðum*, cap. 6, a merchant who had thrice crossed the open sea at his own expense was entitled to the privileges of a thegn. But the most usual condition is the possession of land. Thus in the same document, cap. 2, it is stated that if a ceorl has prospered to such an extent that he possesses five hides of land of his own, a church, a kitchen, a belfry, a castle-gate, a *setl*[1] and special service in the king's hall, he is thenceforth entitled to the privileges of thegnship. According to the *Northleoda Lagu*, cap. 9 f., if anyone kills a ceorlish man who has prospered to such an extent that he possesses five hides of land for military service to the king[2], compensation for his life is to be made with 2000 thrymsas. Nothing is said here of other conditions, but it is added that if he does not possess this amount of land he is still to be accounted a ceorl, even though he has a helmet and coat of mail and a sword overlaid with gold. It is not distinctly

---

[1] For the interpretation of this word see Stevenson, *Eng. Hist. Rev.* xii. 489 ff.

[2] In this expression (*to cynges utware*) the reference is probably to some custom similar to that which according to Domesday Book (p. 56 *b*) prevailed in Berkshire : *si rex mittebat alicubi exercitum de v hidis tantum unus miles ibat*, etc. Military service (*expeditio*) and the repairing of fortifications and bridges were the duties universally required from landholders.

stated in this passage that the ceorl who has acquired five hides becomes thereby a thegn, but only that he is entitled to a wergeld identical with that of the thegn. It would therefore be unwise to conclude that his position was the same as that of the man whose possessions are described in *Be Leodge-þincđum*. In the following passages we find particulars which state how nobility became hereditary : if his son and son's son are so prosperous as to possess as much land as this, the descendants thenceforth will be of *gesiðcund* rank, with a wergeld of 2000 thrymsas ; but if they do not possess this amount and cannot attain to it, compensation is to be made for them as for men of ceorlish rank. It appears from this that permanent nobility of blood was attained after three generations, conditionally however on the possession of land during this period. There is no evidence that any such rule as this prevailed in the South of England, but on the other hand I know of nothing which would be inconsistent with such a supposition.

In Cnut II. 71 a distinction is drawn in regard to heriots[1] between two classes of thegns : the heriot of a king's thegn—'such as stand in immediate relationship to him' (*ðe him nyhste syndon*[2])—consists of four horses, two saddled and two without saddles, two swords, four spears, and the same number of shields, a helmet and coat of mail, and fifty mancusas of

[1] Earlier examples of such payments (dating from the tenth century) are to be found in B. 652, 812, 819, 1008, 1012, 1132, 1174, 1306, 1317.

[2] Cf. Aethelred III. 11, where it is stated that no one is to have jurisdiction over a king's thegn except the king himself.

gold ; the heriot of inferior thegns (*medemra ðegna*[1])
in Wessex consists of a horse and its equipments and
the thegn's arms, or his *healsfang*, while in Mercia
and East Anglia it amounts to two pounds[2]. These
regulations are repeated in Will. I. 20, no distinction
however being made between West Saxon and
Mercian custom[3]. In this case the term *barun* is
applied to the first class of thegns, and the term
vavassur to the second. The use of the latter term
seems to indicate that these persons were regarded
as not being under the immediate lordship of the
king[4]. We may probably identify them with a class
of persons mentioned in the Law of the Northumbrian Priests, cap. 48 ff. Here we find a table of
fines for performing heathen rites and neglecting
church duties. The usual fines are : for a king's
thegn ten half-marks, for any other landowner (*elles
landagende man*) six half-marks, for a ceorl (in place
of which we once find *færbena*) twelve ores. The
position of the landowner who is here placed between
the king's thegn and the ceorl can hardly have
differed much from that of the inferior thegn of
Cnut II. 71[5]. For that the latter was, sometimes at

[1] The Cod. Colb. has *mediocris hominis quem Angli dicunt
lesseþegen* (cf. Cnut III. 2).

[2] According to Hen. 76. 4 the thegn's *healsfang* amounted to
120 sh. (cf. Edw. and Guth. 13. 4). 60 Mercian shillings go to the
pound.

[3] In the latter case, if the man has not a horse and armour,
he is to give 100 sol. (presumably West Saxon shillings).

[4] Indeed the *relief* is said to be due *a sun lige seinur*, while in
the case of the earl we find *relief......ki al rei afert*.

[5] Of course in the North. Pr. Law the division is drawn on

all events, a landowner may be seen from *Be Leodgeþincðum,* cap. 3, where we find a thegn who is
under the lordship of another thegn in possession of
five hides. The fact that the term 'thegn' is not
applied to the landowner in the Northumbrian law
can hardly be considered a serious objection to the
identification. We may note that the *Northleoda
Lagu,* which is also apparently a Northumbrian
document, seems to know of no class intermediate
between the thegn and the ceorl.

It appears then that the thegn-class itself was
divided into a higher and a lower order, the former
being under the immediate lordship of the king, the
latter under that of other persons. The higher order
were subject in certain respects to higher charges
than the lower, and in the North at all events to
heavier fines. We can now understand why the
qualifications for thegnship enumerated in *Be
Leodgeþincðum* are so much greater than those
given in the *Northleoda Lagu.* It is clear from the
mention of the 'special service in the king's hall'
that the person whose qualifications are described in
the former document was a 'king's thegn'; the thegn
of the *Northleoda Lagu* may be only an 'inferior
thegn.' It is quite possible that the term 'thegn'

economic, in Cnut II. 71 on social lines. Presumably, however,
the classes as a rule coincided. The ceorl who acquired five hides
became entitled, as we have seen, to the valuation of a thegn. We
may probably infer that the ceorl who possessed less than five
hides would not be regarded as a *landagende man* (cf. p. 99 ff.).
The case of the landless 'thegn' seems to be omitted in the North.
Pr. Law.

was not universally applied to members of this latter class. No evidence however is to be found for any difference of wergeld between the two classes.

Before the reign of Aethelstan[1] the word þegn occurs in the laws only in the expression *cyninges þegn*, which appears in Wihtr. 20, Ine 45, Alfr. and Guth. 3. In charters also its use is very rare[2] except in this expression or after a possessive or the genitive of a pronoun (*e.g. minum þegne, his þegne*) usually referring to the king. Its Latin equivalents are *minister* (*regis*)[3], which is extremely frequent, and *miles*. In the Old English version of Bede's Ecclesiastical History the expression *cyninges þegn* is used to translate both these Latin terms. In the Chronicle the word þegn occurs fairly often, but until the reign of Aethelstan always under the same conditions as in the charters. From this evidence it is clear that in the earlier texts the word not merely denotes high rank, but also implies a position of subordination to some higher authority. Indeed the notion of rank is not essential, for in a general sense þegn is used for 'servant' both in early and late texts. As this is the prevailing meaning of the corresponding Old High-German word (*degan*), and as the Old Norse þegn denotes 'liegeman' (as well as 'freeman'), the sense of subordination must have

[1] The first examples are in Aethelst. v. 1. 4; 4. 1. The Latin form *thainus* occurs also in Aethelst. III. IV.

[2] An example occurs in B. 384, which will be discussed later.

[3] *e.g.* in a charter of 858 (B. 496): *ego Eðelbearht rex...dabo ...meo fideli ministro Wullafe* etc., and later in the same charter: *Eðelbearht cyning Wullafe sealde his ðegne* etc.

been inherent in the word from early times[1]. The
sense of rank must originally have been due to the
dignity of the person to whom the thegn was
subordinate. In the old poetry we find the personal
retinue of kings and other magnates described as
thegns, and even in charters the traditional phraseology employed (*meo fideli ministro*, etc.) shows that
the grant was originally regarded as a reward for
personal service, though in later times at all events
it often appears to us rather as an act of sale.
According to the *Rectitudines*, cap. 1, the possession of
a charter was the distinctive mark of a thegn; but
it is greatly to be doubted whether even in late
times the term 'thegn' was limited to such persons[2].
Besides the king's thegns we hear also of thegns of
bishops and thegns of thegns, but it was no doubt
through the first of these classes that the term
acquired its sense of rank. How it came to be used
absolutely is not quite clear, though the usage seems
to have been established by the tenth century. It
must not be assumed forthwith that nobility originated in personal service to the king. That is a question
which will require discussion hereafter.

The position of the ceorl class need not be
discussed here. From the tenth century onwards, at

[1] Its original meaning may have been 'boy,' a sense in which
it is found in Old High-German, Old Saxon and Old Norse, and
which points to relationship with τέκνον.

[2] Many persons described as *taini* in Domesday Book seem to
have had very little land, and the little they did have apparently
consisted often of shares in family holdings; cf. Maitland,
Domesday Book and Beyond, pp. 64 f., 165, and the references
there given.

all events in Wessex, it seems to have included all free persons of English blood below the rank of 'thegn.' The class had many subdivisions, some account of which is given in the *Rectitudines*[1]. We find however no evidence for any difference of wergeld within the class. It is indeed stated in Hen. 81. 3 that there was a difference in the amount of the compensations to which the *uillanus* and the *cothsetus* (Old Engl. *cotsetla*) were entitled for *fletgefeoht* and *ouerseunnessa*, the payment to the former being 30 pence and to the latter only 15 pence. But it is doubtful whether this regulation is of great antiquity. In Alfr. 39 we find merely that the ceorl is entitled to 6 shillings (*i.e.* 30 pence) as compensation for *fletgefeoht*. In the corresponding passage of Ine's laws (cap. 6), where the same compensation is awarded, we find in place of *ceorl* the words *gafol-*

---

[1] The various classes of persons mentioned in Domesday Book are obviously described according to their economic rather than their social status. There seems to be little doubt that the *uillanus*, the *bordarius*, the *colibertus* (*bur*) and the *cotarius* all belonged to the ceorl-class. The only difficulty arises in regard to the *liber homo* and the *sochemannus*. The latter is almost confined to those parts of the country which were or had been Danish. Between him and the *uillanus* there seems to be a clear economic distinction. On the other hand apparently no such distinction can be traced between the *sochemannus* and the *liber homo*. It is probable therefore, as suggested by Prof. Maitland (*Domesday Book and Beyond*, p. 106), that the difference in this case really was social, *i.e.* that the *liber homo* belonged to the *twelfhynde* or 'thegn'-class. This explanation is decidedly favoured by Edw. Conf. 12. 4 (as compared with Ine 70, Hen. 69. 2) and by the use of *frigman* apparently in the sense of *twelfhynde man* in Aethelred II. 5.

gelda and *gebur*[1], which may perhaps be regarded as comprehending all persons of ceorlish standing.

§ 2. *The Evidence of the Earlier Laws.*

We have seen that before the time of Aethelstan the word þegn by itself does not occur in the laws. Now it has already been mentioned that in the laws of Henry I. the term *twelfhynde* is occasionally used as a synonym for þegn. These passages are however quoted or derived from passages in the earlier laws. Thus Hen. 69. 2 is derived from Ine 70, Hen. 70. 1

[1] The wording of the passage seems to imply a difference between the two classes, though the gebur alone is mentioned in the next clause and though gafol was paid by the gebur according to *Rect.* 4. From a comparison of Ine 23 with (*ibid.*) 32 and with *Northl. L.* § 7 it appears probable that the Welsh gafolgelda was a man who possessed a hide of land. So far as I am aware, there is nothing to prevent us from believing that the English gafolgelda also was a ceorl who possessed a certain amount of land, though less than five hides. The gebur on the other hand seems to have been a man who received from his lord both land and live-stock, which at his death both returned to the lord (*Rect.* 4; cf. Ine 67). The term *geneat* in Edg. II. 1, IV. 1, and *Rect.* 2 seems to me to refer to persons of the gafolgelda class, in spite of what has been said by Prof. Maitland (*op. cit.* pp. 59, 328 ff.), though persons of superior social position may be included. At all events it is difficult to believe that the ceorlish gafolgelda class is entirely omitted in the *Rectitudines*. In Ine 22 *geneat* may have a wider meaning and refer to dependents generally. When in the Treaty of Alfred and Guthrum, cap. 2, we hear of "the ceorl who resides on gafol-land," this expression must include the gebur as well as the gafolgelda. The ceorl who does not "reside on gafol-land" is presumably the ceorl who has acquired land to the extent of at least five hides, and consequently a wergeld of 1200 sh. (cf. p. 80 f.). In *Cod. Dipl.* 1282 we find a *rusticus* who possessed eight hides.

and 76. 4 from Edw. and Guth. 13, Hen. 82. 9 from
Alfr. 18, and Hen. 87. 4 from Alfr. 29—31. Apart
from the laws of Henry the use of this term is quite
rare in late documents, so far at all events as they
can be dated. The expression *twelfhynde and* (or
oððe) *twihynde*, which occurs in Aethelstan VI. 8. 2,
Edm. III. 2, and occasionally in late charters, may
well have become a traditional formula. The
passage on the Mercian oath (cf. p. 78) may be
derived from a much earlier text.

In Alfred's laws on the other hand the term
twelfhynde is of frequent occurrence. It is found
in all passages of these laws where gradations of
rank are specified. In cap. 29—31 it is contrasted
with *twihynde*, and in cap. 10, 18, 39, 40 with *ceorl*.
In every one of these cases however there stands
between the ceorl (*cierlisc mon, twihynde*) and the
twelfhynde man an intermediate class named *sixhynde*. This term does not occur in the later laws
except in Hen. 82. 9 and 87. 4, which are derived
from passages in Alfred's laws, and in the *Pseudoleges
Canuti*, cap. 6, which is likewise derived from Alfr.
39. The last-mentioned passage gives as a synonym
for *sixhynde man* the word *radcniht*, which occurs
again in the same connection in the Cod. Colb.
version of Alfr. 39. Now in Domesday Book we
find record in the Western Midlands (Worcestershire,
Gloucestershire, Herefordshire, Shropshire, Cheshire,
and the South of Lancashire) of a class of persons
described as *radchenistres* and *radmanni*, who are
mentioned beside and apparently distinguished from
the *milites* (*i.e.* thegns). If these persons are

identical with the *radcnihtas*—of which word indeed
radchenistres looks like a corruption—and if the
identifications of the *Pseudoleges Canuti* and the
Cod. Colbertinus are correct, it would seem that
in this part of the country the *sixhynde* class had
survived till Norman times. Elsewhere, so far as
I am aware, no record of such persons is preserved,
a fact which agrees with the absence of any reference
to the *sixhynde* class in the later laws. The laws of
Alfred themselves give us no clue to the position
of this class. But since, as we have already seen,
the term *twelfhynde* owes its origin to the fact that
members of this class had a wergeld of 1200 sh., it
can hardly be doubted that the term *sixhynde* also is
connected with the amount of the wergeld, whatever
the position of such persons may have been.

It has already been mentioned that in one
passage of Alfred's laws (cap. 31) *twihynde* is
apparently used as a synonym for *ceorl*. These laws
however give us no synonyms for *twelfhynde* or
sixhynde, so that we are left in doubt as to what
constituted the right to a wergeld of 1200 or
(presumably) 600 sh. The only indication that I
have found on this point is in cap. 11, which gives a
statement of compensations for various offences
against unmarried women of the ceorlish class. The
passage ends as follows: "if this happens to a
woman of nobler (or "better") birth" (*æðelborenran*
B., *bettborenran* H.) etc. The right to the higher
wergelds was therefore, in part at least, inherited.
But this seems to be the only information obtainable. Indeed the amount of the wergeld itself would

be a matter of inference if we were dependent solely on the laws of Alfred. The following are the only items of information given by these laws on the relative positions of the classes. In case of adultery with the wife of a *twelfhynde man* the delinquent had to pay 120 sh. compensation, while for the *sixhynde man* and the ceorl the corresponding compensations were 100 sh. and 40 sh. (60 sh. according to the Latin version) respectively (cap. 10). In case of unchastity a betrothed woman of the ceorl class had to pay 60 sh. compensation to her guardian; for women of the *sixhynde* and *twelfhynde* classes the corresponding compensations were 100 sh. and 120 sh. (cap. 18). If a *twihynde man* were killed by brigands, every member of the band had to pay 30 sh. compensation; if the man killed belonged to the *sixhynde* or *twelfhynde* classes, the compensations were 60 sh. and 120 sh. respectively (cap. 29—31). The compensation due to a ceorl for fighting in his house was 6 sh., for a *sixhynde man* 18 sh., for a *twelfhynde man* 36 sh. (cap. 39). The compensations for *burgbryce* were: to a *twelfhynde man* 30 sh., to a *sixhynde man* 15 sh., to a ceorl (in which case the offence is called *edorbryce*) 5 sh. (cap. 40[1]). It will be seen that in the last two cases the compensations vary in the same proportion as the wergelds, the *sixhynde man* being entitled to thrice as much as the ceorl, and the *twelfhynde man* to twice as much as the *sixhynde man*.

In the laws of Ine, cap. 70, the same three

---

[1] The compensation due to a bishop or earl for the same offence was 60 sh., to the archbishop 90 sh., to the king 120 sh.

classes are again brought together. It is stated that the *man-bot* (*i.e.* the compensation payable to a lord for the death of one of his men) is to be 30 sh. in the case of a *twihynde man*, 80 sh. in the case of a *sixhynde man*, and 120 sh. in the case of a *twelfhynde man*. Apart from this passage the terms *twihynde* and *twelfhynde* do not occur in Ine's laws. In cap. 34 however we hear of a man whose wergeld is 200 sh., from which it is clear that the term *twihynde*, as in later times, referred to the amount of the wergeld. The same passage speaks of "persons of a higher birthprice" (*deorborenran*), an expression which shows that the higher wergelds were already, in part at least, inherited. The word *sixhynde* occurs again in cap. 24, where it is stated that a Welshman is *sixhynde* if he possesses five hides. This is the only explicit statement which any of the laws contain as to the origin or position of the *sixhynde man*. It shows that the class consisted in part of Welsh landed proprietors. It would however be somewhat premature to conclude that it consisted solely or mainly of such persons.

At this point it will obviously be convenient to discuss the position of the Welsh peasant. This class is mentioned twice in Ine's laws. According to cap. 23 the Welsh *gafolgelda* (*i.e. tributarius*) is valued at 120 sh. and his son at 100 sh. Again, according to cap. 32 f. if a Welshman possesses a hide of land[1] his wergeld is 120 sh., if he has only

---

[1] It is to be remembered that the expressions *terra v tributariorum* and *terra v familiarum* (*fif hida land*) are synonymous; so also, apparently, the terms *hiwisc* and *hid*.

half a hide it is 80 sh., if he has no land it is 60 sh.; but the Welshman in the king's service who is able to ride on the king's business has a wergeld of 200 sh. With these passages we may compare the *Northleoda Lagu,* cap. 7 f., where it is stated that if a Welshman acquires a hide (*hiwisc*) of land and is able to pay the king's *gafol,* his wergeld is 120 sh.; if he obtains only half a hide it is 80 sh.; if he has no land but yet is free, it is 70 sh. It is plain enough from the general agreement between these passages, in spite of slight differences in points of detail, that the Welshman of the peasant class is valued at about a half (more strictly three-tenths to six-tenths[1]) of the amount at which the English ceorl is valued.

How numerous the class of Welsh peasants was we have no means of ascertaining. But at all events we never find it mentioned beside the *twihynde, sixhynde,* and *twelfhynde* classes in the graduated statements of fines and compensations which occur so frequently in the laws. Hence, as the Welsh landed proprietors within the boundaries of the English kingdoms must have been far less numerous than the peasants, it is extremely improbable that the *sixhynde* class which, in the laws of Alfred, is always included in these statements, consisted solely of such persons. It is manifestly far more probable that the Welsh landed proprietor was equated with some recognised English class, just as the Welsh horseman in the king's service was

---

[1] The gradations in the wergelds may be founded on Welsh custom (cf. Seebohm, *Tribal Custom,* p. 55) ; but I do not know enough about the subject to speak with confidence.

equated with the English ceorl. It may be noted that the amount of land required by the Welshman in order to become *sixhynde* is the same as that required in later times by the Englishman who aspires to the thegn's wergeld of 1200 sh. Now the Welsh peasant has only half the wergeld (more or less) which belongs to the Englishman of the same class. It is likely enough therefore that the same proportion may hold good in the case of the landed proprietor, and consequently that even in the time of Ine's laws the possession of five hides was necessary in order to acquire a wergeld of 1200 sh.

But if the *sixhynde* class did include persons of English blood, what can the position of such persons have been? One indication may perhaps be obtained from some of the passages discussed above. The Welsh population, like the English, seems to have been divided into three classes, with wergelds of 120 sh. (or less), 200 sh., and 600 sh. respectively. The lowest of these classes seems to correspond to the English ceorl or *twihynde* class, and the highest to the English *twelfhynde* class. The Welshman with a wergeld of 200 sh. is one who rides in the king's service. Is it possible that, in spite of the difference in the proportion between the two wergelds, the same qualification held good for the English *sixhynde man*? This idea is certainly favoured by the use of the term *radcniht*, though the word seems not to be known before the eleventh century. The explanation however is not entirely satisfactory, for the English *sixhynde* class included women.

A more satisfactory answer may, I think, be

obtained from a further examination of the laws.
It has been mentioned that in Alfred's laws,
wherever we find a gradation in payments, the terms
used are *twelfhynde, sixhynde* and *ceorl* or *twihynde,*
but that in Ine's laws this series of terms occurs only
once. Now in Ine 51, which deals with the penalties
for neglecting military service, we find a different set
of terms. 120 sh. is the fine for the *gesiðcund* man
who possesses land, 60 sh. for one who does not
possess land, and 30 sh. for the ceorl. These figures
may be compared with those given for *hloðbot* in
Alfr. 29 ff. (cf. p. 90). The first of them is further
identical with the penalty incurred by persons of the
twelfhynde class under various conditions (Ine 70,
Alfr. 10, 18), which have already been mentioned.
The *gesiðcund* man who possesses land is again
brought before our notice in cap. 45, where the compensation due to him for *burgbryce* is stated to be
35 sh. The other figures given in this list are as
follows : for the king or bishop 120 sh., for an earl
80 sh., for a king's thegn 60 sh. No compensation is
stated for any person of lower rank than the *gesiðcund*
landowner. But if we compare the corresponding
passage in Alfred's laws, cap. 40 (cf. p. 90 and note),
we can have little doubt that the lower compensations
were omitted because they were understood to follow
the usual scale. In the same way the classes intermediate between the earl and the ceorl are omitted
in the statement of compensations for *fletgefeoht*
(cap. 6), though they are included in the corresponding statement in Alfred's laws (cap. 39). Now if we
compare the table given in Ine 45 with the parallel

table in Alfr. 40, it will be seen that, in spite of certain differences between the two passages, the *gesiðcund* man who possesses land with his compensation of 35 (probably for 36) sh. appears to correspond to the *twelfhynde* man of Alfred's law with his compensation of 30 sh. Again, we have seen that several passages in the Law of the Northumbrian Priests give a graduated scale of fines for three classes, viz. king's thegns, other landowners and ceorls, and that the landowner of this code seems to be identical with the inferior thegn or *twelfhynde man*[1]. From these considerations it is difficult to avoid the conclusion that the *gesiðcund* landowner of Ine 45 is also identical with the *twelfhynde man*. We are not informed as to the amount of land which he was required to possess, but from cap. 24 one is led to infer that it was, as in later times, five hides.

But if the *twelfhynde man* is a *gesiðcund* man who owns land, the *sixhynde man* can hardly be any other than the person who is mentioned between the *gesiðcund* landowner and the ceorl in Ine 51, viz. the *gesiðcund* man who has no land (or perhaps less than the requisite amount). This conclusion is not necessarily incompatible with the suggestion made above (p. 93) that the *sixhynde man* may have been a man who was able to ride on the king's service. If

---

[1] It may be noted that, if we admit the probable emendation *xxxvi* for *xxxv* in Ine 45, the proportion between the compensations due to the king's thegn and the *gesiðcund* landowner will be the same as the proportion between the fines payable by the king's thegn (10 half-marks) and the landowner (6 half-marks) in the North. Pr. Law.

any hard and fast line of division existed at this time between the upper and lower classes of society, it is quite possible that none but members of the *gesiðcund* class were qualified to perform such a duty. On the other hand this explanation does seem at first sight to conflict with what is stated in the *Northleoda Lagu*, cap. 11. According to this passage when three successive generations had possessed land to the extent of five hides, the descendants were thenceforth *gesiðcund* and entitled to a wergeld of 2000 thrymsas, *i.e.* 1200 West Saxon sh., apparently whether they themselves possessed the requisite amount of land or not. This document however belongs to a period not earlier than the tenth century, and we have seen that the *sixhynde* class is never mentioned in the laws after the time of Alfred, except in one or two passages which are clearly copied from Alfred's laws. Indeed the *sixhynde* class must have died out in the greater part of England during the tenth century, for it is plain enough that in later times there existed no class intermediate between the *twelfhynde man* and the ceorl.

The precise difference however between the *gesiðcund* landowner or *twelfhynde man* and the *gesiðcund* man without land or *sixhynde man* may not be quite so clear as one would at first sight suppose. From the terminology itself and from the analogy of the wergelds assigned to Welsh peasants (cf. p. 91) one might naturally infer that the *twelfhynde man* was the head of a family, and that the junior members of the same family were *sixhynde*. But this explanation can hardly be correct, for the distinction between the two classes applies also to women, as (*e.g.*) in Alfr. 18 (cf. p. 90). Women who are *sixhynde* and *twelfhynde* are presumably the daughters of *sixhynde* men and *twelfhynde* men respectively. It appears then that the distinction between *sixhynde* and *twelfhynde* is a distinction between different families, and not between members of the same family. Again, though, as we have seen, the regulation of the *Northleoda Lagu*, according to which the descendants of a landowner were either ceorlish or *twelfhynde*, may hold good only for the tenth or eleventh century, it is by no means clear that even in early times the descendants of the *twelfhynde man* were ever liable to pass into the *sixhynde* class[1]. If that had been the case the disappearance of this class would be inexplicable : for there must have been many descendants of *twelfhynde* men who did not themselves possess much land[2]. For the same reason it is not likely that the case of a ceorl passing into the *sixhynde* class was at all a frequent one. Indeed the disappearance of this class after the time of Alfred suggests that it had not been recruited either from above or below[3], in

[1] The only evidence known to me for a decline of social status is contained in the *Leges inter Brettos et Scotos* (Seebohm, *Tribal Custom*, p. 308 f.). But even here there is no *sixhynde* wergeld. Indeed the wergelds of the 'thegn's son' and the 'thegn's grandson' do not seem to be English wergelds at all. Probably the Northumbrian social system had been greatly modified by Celtic influence in Scotland.

[2] Cf. p. 85, footnote, and the references there given.

[3] No doubt *sixhynde* men frequently became *twelfhynde*. It was probably through this process that the former class ultimately became extinct.

short that it was an exclusively hereditary class. In this connection we may note a slight difference of terminology between Ine's laws and the Law of the Northumbrian Priests, which may perhaps not be entirely devoid of significance. The latter speaks of the 'landowner' (*landagende man*), the former of the *gesiðcund* landowner (*gesiðcund man landagende*). The case of the landowner who is not *gesiðcund* is not taken into account in Ine's laws. This fact would seem to indicate that the lines which divided the different classes of society were more hard and fast in early times than later.

The word *gesiðcund*, though it occurs frequently in Ine's laws, is very rare elsewhere. One example in the *Northleoda Lagu* has already been quoted. Another which occurs in Wihtred's laws will be noticed later. The second part of the word implies a hereditary qualification as in *þegenboren* (p. 79). We may therefore translate 'descended from a gesith.' The word *gesið* itself occurs occasionally in Ine's laws, but apparently with exactly the same meaning as *gesiðcund man*. Thus in cap. 50 we find the following statement: "If a *gesiðcund man* pleads with the king or the king's earl or with his lord on behalf" (or "account") of members of his household[1], whether bond or free, he, the gesith, shall in such a case receive no payment of *wite*, because he has previously neglected to stop his man from evil-doing at home." In this passage the terms *gesiðcund man* and *gesið*

---

[1] *inhiwan*; Liebermann (*ad loc.*) translates 'Gutsinsassen' and retains the order of words given in the original. The question under discussion however is not affected thereby.

obviously refer to the same person. Again, in cap. 30 we find the word *gesiðman* used in the same sense : "If a ceorlish man is accused of harbouring a fugitive, he is to clear himself by (an oath equal to the amount of) his own wergeld ; if he cannot do so, he is to pay for him according to the amount of his own wergeld ; and the *gesiðman* (under similar conditions is to clear himself or pay) according to his wergeld." It seems clear that what is meant here is that in the circumstances described the ceorl had to swear by or pay 200 sh. and the *gesiðman* 600 or 1200 sh. The only other passage in which the word occurs in this code is cap. 23, where it is stated that if an alien who has no relatives is slain half his wergeld is to be paid to the king and half to the gesith. The following clause adds that "if he (presumably the gesith) be an abbot or abbess, they are to share in the same manner with the king." Here again the word *gesið* may mean the *gesiðcund* man, under whose lordship the alien had been. Elsewhere however, as we shall see later, the term seems to have a technical meaning. The question of its origin must therefore be deferred for the present.

In conclusion it is necessary to notice briefly the meaning of the term *land-* in the expression *land-agende*. I have already suggested that this may mean a certain amount of land (five hides) corresponding to the qualification in later times for thegnship. At all events the appearance of the 'five hides' in Ine 24 suggests that this amount was already a recognised minimum qualification. Of course it does not follow that the usual holding of a

gesiðcund man or family was of this size. Now it is
not to be overlooked that the laws employ the same
terminology to denote the possession of land whether
the amount possessed was one hide or five hides or
more. Yet there clearly was a difference, at least in
later times, in the character of the 'possession.' The
one hide of the gafolgelda may be included in the
five hides of the 'landowner.' Indeed, it may be said
that the lands of all gafolgeldan were included in the
lands of the greater landowners, except of course in
the case of those gafolgeldan who held royal land.
The early laws give us no hint of a different state of
things. The conditions may have been less complicated in Ine's time from the fact that book-lands
were rarely, if at all, held by laymen. But it is clear
from several passages in his laws (cap. 21, 27, 39, 70)
that every man, whatever his position might be, was
supposed to have a lord; and though, as we shall see
later, the payments for *manbot* (cap. 70, 76) may be
regarded partly as compensations for insult, yet it is
hardly likely that the lord got nothing in return for
the protection which he gave his men. Indeed in
the case of the landowner we know pretty well what
his lord did receive. It consisted partly of payments
and partly of services. The former (*feorm, pastus*
etc.) were apparently as a rule rendered in kind.
Regulations for the amount to be paid from an estate
of ten hides are contained in Ine 70 and correspond
pretty closely to the charges due from the owners of
book-lands to their lords in later times[1]. The nature

---

[1] In Ine 70 the expression used is *to fostre*, but there can be
little doubt that this is equivalent to *feorm*. The amount specified

of the services may be inferred from certain statements in charters, especially those of Berhtwulf and other Mercian kings of the ninth century, in which the grantees are said to be freed from the services in question. Besides the duties of military service and the repairing of fortifications and bridges, which were very seldom remitted, the chief items were the maintenance of *faestingmen*, the entertaining of messengers, and the keeping of hunters, horses, dogs etc.[1] Similarly the peasants had in later times to

seems to correspond to the charges due from several Kentish estates to religious houses during the first half of the ninth century (*e.g.* B. 330, 403, 405, 412, 501) ; but since both the size of the estates and the value of several of the items specified are in most cases uncertain, it is impossible to speak with confidence. The *firma unius noctis* etc. of later times probably arose out of such payments as these. We may note that in a document (B. 1010, 1011) dating from 942—958 a set of charges, amounting apparently to about one-quarter or one-fifth of those mentioned above, are said to be 'one day's *feorm*' for the community at Christ Church (Canterbury). It may also be observed that in some grants of *feorm* to religious communities (*e.g.* B. 412, 417), the terms *hlaford* (*hlaforddom*) and *mundbora* (*mundbyrd*) are used to denote the relationship of the head of the community to the testator and his heirs

[1] *e.g.* B. 443, where an estate is said to be freed *a pastu principum et a difficultate illa quot nos Saxonice dicimus festigmen ; nec homines illuc mittant qui osceptros uel falcones portant aut canes aut cabellos ducunt* etc. ; cf. B. 450 : *ab opere regali et pastu regis et principis uel iuniorum eorum, ab hospitorum refectione uel uenatorum etiam equorum regis, falconuum et ancipitruum et puerorum qui ducunt canes* etc.; B. 454 : *ab illis causis quas cum feorme et eafor uocitemus, tam a pastu ancipitrorum meorum omnium quam etiam uenatorum omnium, uel a pastu equorum meorum omnium siue ministrorum eorum, quid plura, ab omni illa incommoditate æfres et cum feorme nisi istis causis quas hic nominamus : praecones si trans mare uenirent ad regem uenturi uel nuntii de gente Occidentalium Saxonum uel de gente Norþanhymbrorum si uenirent ad horam*

render both payments (*gafol*) and services to their lords, and, so far as I am aware, there is no reason for believing that such dues were not in accordance with ancient custom. If the *gafol* which they paid was called 'the king's *gafol*,' it does not follow that it was paid directly to the king or his officials[1]. From Ine 51 it is clear that men of all classes were liable to military service, which was of course service to the king; but it is at least extremely probable that such service was owed primarily to (and enforced by) the man's lord.

If these conclusions are correct we obtain a possible explanation for the origin of the 'five hides.' This amount of land may have been regarded as the least which a man who had any gafolgeldan under his lordship might be expected to possess. A person who possessed less than this amount might in general be expected to have none but geburas and slaves under him. Of course it does not follow that the estate of five hides was the normal holding of the landowner. The fact that in Ine 70 the *feorm* is regulated for ten hides suggests that the latter was the more usual type. Large estates may have been divided for fiscal purposes into units of this size[2].

tertiam diei uel ad medium diem dabatur illis prandium, si uenirent supra nonam horam tunc dabatur eis noctis pastum etc.; B. 488 (489) : *a pastu omnium accipitrum et falconum in Mercensium et omnium uenatorum regis uel principis, similiter et pastu hominum illorum quos Saxonice nominamus Walhfæreld & heora fæsting & ealra Angelcynnes monna & ælþeodigra rædefæstinge, tam nobilium quam ignobilium* etc.

[1] Except of course in the case of gafolgeldan who were under the immediate lordship of the king.

[2] Cf. Seebohm, *Tribal Custom*, p. 419, and the references there given.

§ 3.   *The Mercian and Northumbrian Evidence*[1].

In the preceding sections we have dealt primarily with the social system of Wessex. Incidentally, however, we have already seen that according to the short text *Be Myrcna Lage* the Mercian ceorl's wergeld was 200 (Mercian) shillings, a sum which amounts to 800 pence, while the thegn's wergeld was 1200 sh. In Will. I. 8 the Mercian thegn's wergeld is stated to be 20 pounds, which is the same thing. In the fragment on the Mercian Oath (Schmid, p. 400) we find in place of *þegn* the term *twelfhynde man*[2]. It can hardly be doubted therefore that the persons entitled to the higher wergeld belonged, as in Wessex, to a distinct class of society. We find no reference in the laws to the existence of a *sixhynde* class; but since it is in (Western) Mercia that the *radchenistres* (*radmanni*) appear in Domesday Book (cf. p. 88), the omission would seem to be purely accidental. In regard to wergelds therefore the Mercian and West Saxon systems appear to have been identical before the rise in the value of the West Saxon shilling.

[1] Regarding the social systems of East Anglia, Essex, Sussex, etc. no information seems to be available. The Kentish evidence will be discussed in the next section.

[2] This term occurs also in the Law of the Cambridge Thegns (Thorpe, *Diplomatarium*, p. 611). From the same document we may perhaps infer that the wergeld of the Welshman was, as in Wessex, approximately half that of the ceorl. If one of the thegns killed a ceorl, each of the others had (in certain circumstances) to

In the *Northleoda Lagu* the (Northumbrian) ceorl's wergeld is stated to be 266 thrymsas, *i.e.* 200 Mercian shillings; but the thegn's wergeld is given at 2000 thrymsas, *i.e.* 1200 West Saxon shillings. An attempt to explain the latter sum has already been made (p. 77). In the *Leges inter Brettos et Scotos* the thegn's wergeld (*cro*) is 100 cows or 300 ores. As this document apparently reckons 16 pence to the ore (cf. p. 25), the sum in question will amount to 4800 pence, *i.e.* 1200 Mercian shillings. According to the same authority the ceorl's wergeld is 16 cows, *i.e.* (strictly) 768 pence or 192 Mercian shillings. It is probable therefore that the wergelds were the same in Northumbria as in Mercia. So far as that of the higher class is concerned, some confirmatory evidence is supplied by Egbert's Dialogus, cap. 12, where the priest's wergeld is said to be 800 *sicli*, *i.e.* probably 4800 pence (cf. p. 21); for there can be little doubt that, as in the *Northleoda Lagu*, the priest was put on a level with members of the highest class. The same passage gives ample proof that the Northumbrian wergelds were inherited[1]. There seems to be

contribute two ores; while if the slain man was a Welshman the amount required was one ore. But, since the corresponding payment in the case of the killing of a *twelfhynde man* was only half a mark, the inference must be regarded as somewhat uncertain.

[1] *Quicunque uero ex laicis occiderit episcopum, presbiterum, uel diaconum aut monachum.........reddat precium aecclesiae suae...... pro presbitero octingentos siclos, pro diacono sexingentos, pro monacho uero quadringentos argenteos, nisi aut dignitas natalium uel nobilitas generis maius reposcat precium; non enim iustum est ut seruitium sanctae professionis in meliori gradu perdat quod exterior uita sub laico habitu habuisse iure parentum dinoscitur.*

no evidence for a *sixhynde* class in Northumbria;
but, considering the character and extent of our
authorities, it would be extremely unsafe to argue
from their silence that such a class did not exist.
On the other hand, if cap. 7 f. of the *Northleoda Lagu*
are derived from old Northumbrian law, the treatment of the Welsh population must have been almost
the same as in Wessex (cf. p. 91 f.). On the whole
there seems little reason for supposing that the social
system of Northumbria differed appreciably from
those of Mercia and Wessex.

§ 4. *The Kentish Evidence.*

The terminology of the Kentish laws differs in
many respects from that of the laws which we have
been considering. These differences are no doubt
partly due to the greater antiquity of the Kentish
laws; but it would be rash to assume at the outset
that this explanation would cover every difference.
The terms regularly used in graduated statements of
compensations for persons of different standing are
eorl (*eorlcund*) and *ceorl*. According to Aethelberht
15 ff. the ceorl's *mundbyrd* (a term to which we shall
have to return later, p. 115 ff.) amounts to 6 sh. He
is likewise entitled to a compensation of this amount
from anyone who commits an offence with his serving
maid. The eorl's *mundbyrd* is not stated, but the
compensation to which he is entitled for the same
offence is 12 sh. (cap. 14). The same sum is to be
paid to him if a man commits manslaughter on his

premises (cap. 13). But as the compensation due to
the king under similar circumstances is identical with
the amount of his *mundbyrd*, viz. 50 sh. (cap. 5, 8,
10[1]), and as according to Hloth. and Ead. 13 a man
is entitled to receive his *mundbyrd* if blood is spilt in
his house, there can be little doubt that this sum of
12 sh. was the amount of the eorl's *mundbyrd*. The
mundbyrd of the eorl was therefore twice that of the
ceorl.

The fullest statement in regard to the amount of
the Kentish wergelds is to be found in the laws of
Hlothhere and Eadric. According to cap. 1, "if
a man's servant (*esne*) kills an *eorlcund* man, who is
to be paid for with 300 sh., the homicide must be
given up by his owner and the value of three men
paid in addition." Again, according to cap. 3, "if
a man's servant kills a free man, who is to be paid
for with 100 sh., the homicide must be given up by
his owner and the value of another man paid in
addition." It is unnecessary to discuss at length the
final clauses of these two regulations. In cap. 2, 4 it
is laid down that if the homicide escape, his owner is
to pay the value of an additional man. The *man-
wyrð* in question is therefore, as Mr Seebohm (*Tribal
Custom*, p. 468 ff.) has pointed out, probably the
value of an *esne* and not the standard value of a free
man. The point however which really deserves

---

[1] Here the word used is *mægdenman*, but it is hardly likely
that the distinction is of much importance. It may be noted that
in the case of the eorl only one compensation (12 sh.) is stated,
while in the other two cases (the king and the ceorl) there are
gradations. I have given the highest sum in both cases.

attention is the parenthetic clause in each case. These clauses show that the amount to be paid for the *eorlcund* man is three times as great as that to be paid for the 'free man,' *i.e.* presumably the ceorl. Again, the natural sense of the words *þane þe sio þreom hundum scill. gylde* is "whose value is 300 shillings." This however has been doubted by Schmid, Seebohm, and others, who hold that the sum specified is not the true wergeld but the amount to be paid under the circumstances, *i.e.* the amount to be paid by a man when his *esne* has committed the crime. This interpretation of the passage seems to me extremely forced. The only other statement in the Kentish laws concerning the wergelds either of the *eorlcund man* or of the ceorl occurs in Aethelberht 21: "If a man kill (another) man he is to make compensation with the ordinary wergeld (*medume leodgeld*) 100 sh." This passage seems to agree perfectly well with Hloth. and Ead. 3, the typical 'man' being the ceorl. Mr Seebohm however takes the passage in connection with cap. 18 ff.[1], and understands the payment in question to be due not from the homicide but from the man who has lent him his weapons. He translates *medume* not by 'ordinary' but by 'half,' thus making the wergeld (*i.e.* the wergeld of a ceorl) 200 sh. For this use of *medume* he compares cap. 7: *gif cyninges ambihtsmið*

---

[1] 18: *gif man mannan wæpnum bebyreð þær ceas weorð and man nænig yfel ne gedeð vi scillingum gebete.* 19 : *gif wegreaf si gedon vi scillingum gebete.* 20 : *gif man þone man ofslæhð xx scillingum gebete.* 21 : *gif man mannan ofslæhð medume leodgeld c scillinga gebete.*

oððe laadrinc mannan ofslehð meduman leodgelde forgelde, which he translates (p. 457): "If the king's *ambihtsmith* [official-smith] or *laadrinc* [outrider] slay a man, let him pay a *medume leodgeld*." Then on p. 474 he interprets this expression to mean 'half-wergeld.' The objection to this is that *medume* is not found elsewhere with the meaning 'half'[1]. Dr Liebermann on the other hand translates : "Wenn [einer] des Königs Dienst-Metallarbeiter oder Geleitsführermann erschlägt, entgelte er [ihn] mit mittlerem Wergelde." The word *man* may be carried over from the preceding clause as in cap. 25, 26[2], where it is thus understood by Mr Seebohm himself (*ib.* p. 463). It appears to have been overlooked that the payment in cap. 7 is in reality a *manbot*. The passage must be taken in connection with the preceding one : *gif man frigne mannan ofsleahð cyninge l scill. to drihtinbeage.* The sense will then be as follows : under ordinary circumstances the king is entitled to a sum of 50 sh. as compensation for the death of one of his freemen, but in the case of certain officials this compensation is to be doubled, and consequently amounts to a sum equal to the wergeld of a free man[3]. The wergeld itself was no doubt to be paid (to the relatives) in addition to the sum here mentioned, which was due to the king. Now if we turn

---

[1] Mr Seebohm recognising this difficulty suggests that the expression is due to Latin (clerical) influence and is a translation of *medium werigeldum*. But this is hardly likely.

[2] 25: *gif man ceorlæs hlafætan ofslæhð vi scillingum gebete.* 26 : *gif læt ofslæhð* (*i.e. gif man læt ofslæhð*) etc.

[3] For the expression we may compare cap. 64: *gif man gekyndelice lim awyrdeð þrym leudgeldum hine man forgelde.*

back to cap. 21, it can hardly be denied that Mr Seebohm's interpretation is somewhat unnatural. The form in which the passage opens *gif man mannan ofslæhð* is paralleled by several other passages in these laws where a new subject is introduced, and stands in marked contrast to cap. 20, *gif man þone man ofslæhð*, which doubtless refers back to cap. 19. I am therefore decidedly of opinion that cap. 21 is of general application and that the payment of 100 sh. is the wergeld due from the homicide[1]. I take *medume* in its usual sense of 'ordinary,' *i.e.* 'inferior,' the wergeld of the freeman, as opposed to the higher wergeld of the *eorlcund* man, just as in later times the *medema* thegn is contrasted with the king's thegn. There is another item of evidence which seems to have been overlooked. In cap. 87 it is stated that if the eye and the foot of an *esne* be destroyed his full value is to be paid. Again, in cap. 43, 69 it is stated that the compensation for the loss of an eye or foot is 50 sh. There can be no doubt that this is the payment due to a ceorl, as in all the cases recounted in cap. 32—72. This fact therefore again points to 100 sh. as the wergeld of the ceorl[2]. If this conclusion is correct there can of course be no doubt that the wergeld of the *eorlcund man* was 300 sh. The expressions *þreom hundum scill. gylde* etc.

---

[1] It is perhaps a question whether *gebete* has not crept into the text from the preceding passages. It is true that *gebete* takes the accus. again in cap. 68, 72, but these cases may be due to the expansion of abbreviations.

[2] The compensation for these injuries amounts to one-third of the wergeld in Wessex (Alfr. 71); but in most of the continental laws it is half, though a quarter is also found.

in Hloth. and Ead. 1, 3 seem therefore to point to
the beginning of a system of terminology similar to
that of Alfred's laws, viz. the designation of the
various classes of society according to the amount of
their wergelds.

After the time of Hlothhere and Eadric we find
no reference in the laws to the amount of the
wergelds.   From Hen. 76. 7 however it may perhaps
be inferred that Kentish peculiarities in this respect
were still preserved.   After a statement of the West
Saxon wergelds the passage ends with the following
statement: *differentia tamen weregildi multa est in
Cantia uillanorum et baronum.*   On the other hand
Cnut in a writ dating from the early part of his
reign (Cod. Dipl. 731) addresses the men of Kent
with the words *ealle mine ðegnas twelfhynde and
twihynde*—terms which would of course be quite
inappropriate to the old social classes of Kent.   If
we are to accept the statement in the ' Laws of
Henry I.' as evidence for the survival of the Kentish
wergelds we shall have to suppose that the official
responsible for this writ was ignorant of Kentish
custom.   At all events it seems clear from the will
of the reeve Abba (B. 412) that the Kentish wergelds
were still recognised in the last years of Ecgberht's
reign (833—839).   The testator uses the expression
min wærgeld twa ðusenda, which probably means
2000 pence, *i.e.* the ancient wergeld of the Kentish
ceorl.   But according to the only other possible
explanation, viz. that it means 2000 thrymsas[1], it

---

[1] Cf. p. 22, footnote.

would of course correspond to the wergeld of the *eorlcund man*.

The word *eorlcund*, which occurs again (with reference to women) in Aethelberht 75, shows that the right to the higher wergeld was inherited. Unfortunately the meaning of the term *eorl* in Aethelberht's laws cannot be determined with certainty. It is generally considered to be synonymous with *eorlcund man*; and we may observe that Aethelberht's laws fix compensations only for the king, the eorl and the ceorl, while the only wergelds stated in the laws of Hlothhere and Eadric are those of the *eorlcund man* and the freeman (*i.e.* the ceorl). Again, it may be noted that in two passages in the West Saxon laws (Alfr. 4 and Aethelstan VI. Pref.) the words *eorl* (*eorlisc*) and *ceorl* (*ceorlisc*) are used together apparently as a comprehensive term for all classes of society. Further, we have seen that in Ine's laws the word *gesið* is used synonymously with *gesiðcund man*. On the whole therefore there seems little reason to doubt that the term *eorl* denoted not an official but a person belonging to the (hereditary) nobility. This conclusion is further supported by a passage in the laws of Wihtred. In these laws the words *eorl* and *eorlcund* do not occur. In cap. 4 however we find the *ceorlisc* man contrasted with the *gesiðcund* man, the penalty for illegal marriage[1] being for the former 50 sh. and for the latter 100 sh. Now as the expressions *gesiðcund* and *ceorlisc* are here contrasted clearly in much the

---

[1] This is probably what is intended, though *unriht hæmed* may have a wider meaning.

same way as the terms *eorl* and *ceorl* in Aethelberht's laws, and as the *mundbyrd* of the eorl
appears to have been twice that of the ceorl, we can
hardly avoid concluding that the *gesiðcund* man is
identical both with the *eorl* of Aethelberht's laws and
with the *eorlcund* man of the laws of Hlothhere and
Eadric. The reason for the change of terminology
is not clear; but it is to be observed that Wihtred's
laws are contemporary with those of Ine, in which
the term *gesiðcund* is of frequent occurrence.

In Aethelberht 26 wergelds are stated for a third
class of persons, the *læt*. This word seems not to
occur elsewhere in Old English literature, but it is
almost certainly identical with the Teutonic-Latin
letus, litus, lazzus[1] of the Continental laws. The
persons denoted by these terms on the Continent
were primarily liberated slaves and their descendants,
though it is at least questionable whether all *liti*
were of this origin. Regarding the position of the
Kentish *læt* we have no information. All that can
be gathered from the law above mentioned is that
there were three subdivisions of the class. For the
highest subdivision the wergeld was 80 sh., for the
second 60 sh., and for the lowest 40 sh. It is not
stated who is to receive the wergeld; but according
to Wihtr. 8 if a man gives his slave liberty at the
altar he is entitled to the wergeld of the liberated
man as well as to his inheritance and the *mund*
of his household.

---

[1] The forms in the Salic Law are *letus, leto. lazzus* (*i.e. lāz*)
represents the Old High German and *litus* (*i.e.* *lūts, for earlier
*lēts) probably the Gothic form of the word.

Now if we compare the terms for the different classes of society in the Kentish and West Saxon laws, we see that the same names, viz. *ceorlisc* and *gesiðcund*, are applied to the two main classes in both series, the former being the regular term for the lower of these classes in both cases. But when the monetary values of the wergelds are calculated, it will be seen that the wergeld of the Kentish ceorl, viz. 100 sh. *i.e.* 2000 (silver) coins, is far greater than that of the West Saxon ceorl, viz. 200 sh., *i.e.* 800 or 1000 coins. In the case of *mundbyrd* the difference is still more striking. We have seen that the *mundbyrd* of the Kentish ceorl amounts to 6 shillings, *i.e.* 120 coins. In the next chapter it will be shown that that of the West Saxon ceorl was no more than 5 or 6 (West Saxon) shillings, *i.e.* 20—24 (later 25—30) coins. These facts suggest that the position of the ceorl-class was far better in Kent than in Wessex[1]. Moreover there are certain indications of a different kind which tend to confirm this view. The reeve Abba, whose will is recorded in B. 412, seems to have had only the wergeld of a ceorl. Yet he was able to bequeath his landed property and—if we may judge from the charges laid upon it—this property would seem to have been

---

[1] Mr Seebohm (*Tribal Custom*, p. 494 f.) has suggested that the Kentish ceorl is really to be identified not with the ceorl but with the *twelfhynde man* of Wessex, and that the West Saxon ceorl is to be identified with the Kentish *læt*. To this question we shall have to return later. It may however be pointed out here that the terminology of the laws (especially the distinction drawn in both cases between *gesiðcund* and *ceorlisc*) is a somewhat serious objection to this explanation.

of considerable extent. Occasionally (*e.g.* in B. 1212) we find persons signing Kentish charters with the title *rusticus* (*i.e.* ceorl). Perhaps there may be some connection between these peculiarities of Kentish custom and the conditions of land-tenure, in regard to which Kent is said to differ very much from the rest of England. That however is a question which must be left for others to discuss. In regard to the higher (*eorlcund* or *gesiðcund*) class, we have seen that their wergeld, like that of the West Saxon *sixhynde* class, was three times as great as that of the ceorl; but we have no evidence for any sixfold wergeld in Kent, corresponding to that of the West Saxon *twelfhynde* class. On the other hand, the *læt*-class with its lower wergelds seems to be peculiar to Kent. There can be little doubt therefore that the social systems of the two kingdoms differed very considerably.

CHAPTER IV.

THE SOCIAL SYSTEM, *continued*

§ 1. *The terms 'borg' and 'mund.'*

THE terms *borg* and *mund* seem to have originally meant 'surety' and 'protection' respectively. But they approach one another very closely in meaning[1], and the penalty for infringement is in both cases the same. This may be seen from a comparison of the following passages: Alfr. 3: If anyone violates the king's *borg*, he is to pay five pounds of pure silver as compensation for the offence; the compensation for the violation of the archbishop's *borg* or *mundbyrd* is three pounds; for the violation of the *borg* or *mundbyrd* of any other bishop or of an earl it is two pounds[2]. Aethelred VIII. 5 (cf. Cnut I. 3. 2): The compensation for the *gri*ð[3] of a chief monastery

---

[1] It may be observed that in Aethelberht 75 *mund* is used for the guardianship of widows, while in Ine 31, Alfr. 18, the guardian of a woman (before marriage) is called *byrgea*.

[2] This enactment is repeated in Cnut II. 58, but the word *mundbyrd* is omitted in both cases.

[3] This term is of Scandinavian origin and denotes (1) 'local peace,' *i.e.* the sanctity attached to certain buildings and places, and (2) 'personal peace,' *i.e.* the protection afforded by a person, whether by hand or by decree. In the latter sense *gri*ð is practically synonymous with *mund, mundbyrd*. The word *mundbyrd* occasionally also means 'local peace,' *e.g. Be Gri*ðe, cap. 14.

is to be according to the king's *mund, i.e.* five
pounds in districts subject to English law. *Be Griðe,*
cap. 11: If anyone violates the king's *mund* in any
other way, he is to pay five pounds compensation in
districts subject to English law; the compensation
for violation of *mund* in the case of the archbishop or
an aetheling is three pounds; in the case of any
other bishop or of an earl it is two pounds.

Unfortunately we nowhere find any comprehensive statement of the various offences which
constituted a violation of *mund* or *borg.* It appears
however from *Be Griðe* 9—11 that the act of
fighting in the king's house was regarded as a
violation of the king's *mund*: (9) The law of *grið* in the
South of England (lit. in districts subject to the Law
of the South English) is as follows: if anyone fights
in a church or in the king's house, all his property
is to be confiscated and it shall rest with the king
to decide whether or not he is to have his life.
(10) If anyone fights in a monastery, but outside
the church, full compensation is to be paid according
to the rank of the monastery[1]. (11) If anyone
violates the king's *mund* in any other way etc.
(as above). In Aethelred VIII. 1. 3 we find a similar
statement regarding the penalty for manslaughter
perpetrated within the walls of a church. According
to Alfr. 5 whoever dragged a fugitive away from
a church in which he had sought sanctuary was
liable for violation of the king's *mundbyrd.* Again,
according to Cnut II. 42 anyone who injured or

---

[1] Cap. 10 is evidently to be taken as a parenthesis (cf.
Aethelred VIII. 5).

seriously insulted an ecclesiastic had to render full compensation for violation of *mund* to the man's lord or (*v.l.* 'and') to the king. This passage is probably to be explained by the help of Edw. and Guth. 12, where it is stated that the king or the earl or the bishop is to be regarded as the kinsman and guardian (*mundbora*) of ecclesiastics and aliens who have no kinsmen or guardians of their own. Further in the regulations concerning the payment of wergeld (Edw. and Guth. 13) it is stated that when the homicide has produced twelve of his relatives to act on his behalf the king's *mund* is to be 'set up.' Presumably therefore any further act of violence would constitute a violation of the king's *mund*.

Most of these passages have no bearing on the distinctions between the various classes of society. It may however be noted (i) that in ordinary cases of *mundbryce* (*i.e.* violation of *mund*) the compensations payable were to the king five pounds, to the archbishop three pounds, to a bishop or earl two pounds; and (ii) that for the offence of fighting in the king's house, apparently the worst form of *mundbryce*, the penalty was entire loss of property, while the king could take even the man's life if he wished. Now if we turn to Ine 6, we find there a graduated list of compensations due to various persons for the offence of fighting in their houses. For fighting in the king's house the penalty is the confiscation of the culprit's entire property and the loss of his life too, if the king so wishes. For fighting in a monastery the compensation is 120 sh.

For fighting in the house of an earl or other distinguished councillor it is 60 sh. together with a fine of 60 sh. For fighting in the house of a *gafolgelda* or a *gebur* it is 6 sh. with a fine of 120 sh.[1] Lastly, it is added that a fine of 120 sh. is to be paid even for fighting in the open[2]. Now it will be seen that the penalty for fighting in the king's house is the same here as in the later laws. On the other hand the compensation for fighting in a monastery varies in the later laws (Aethelred VIII. 5 etc.) according to the rank of the monastery, the sums specified being five pounds, 120 sh., and 60 sh. This differentiation may quite well have taken place after the time of Ine's laws[3]. When however we come to the case of fighting in the earl's house, we find that the compensation is 60 sh., whereas in later times the earl's *borg* and *mundbyrd* are valued at two pounds. In order to explain this discrepancy we must take into account the following passages. According to Alfr. 38 if anyone fights at a meeting in the presence of the king's earl, he must pay the proper fine and wergeld, but first he must pay a fine of 120 sh. to the earl; if anyone

[1] It seems strange that it should be a more costly offence to fight in the house of a ceorl than in that of an earl. It is possible however, in view of Alf. 38, that the *fihtwite* (120 sh.) had to be paid to the king in this case also, in addition to the two sums mentioned which were due to the earl.

[2] In the last two cases Lambard's text and the Latin version give the fine at 30 sh. This may possibly rest on old tradition. 30 sh. may have been the amount of the fine when there was no one killed (cf. *Be Griðe*, cap. 13 f.).

[3] Possibly the expression *heafodmynster* applies only to Christ Church, Canterbury; cf. *Be Griðe*, cap. 8.

disturbs a public meeting by drawing his weapons
he must pay a fine of 120 sh. to the earl. According
to Alfr. 15 if anyone fights or draws his weapon in
the presence of the archbishop, he is to pay 150 sh.
compensation; if this takes place in the presence of
any other bishop or of an earl, he is to pay 100 sh.
The last-mentioned sum is clearly identical with the
two pounds due to the earl for violation of his *borg*
or *mundbyrd*[1]. The somewhat larger sum mentioned
in Alfr. 38 is perhaps due to the idea that the
seriousness of the offence was aggravated by the
fact of its having occurred at a public meeting.
Yet the origin of the difference is probably to be
found in the changes which had taken place in the
monetary system (cf. p. 16 ff.). In Ine's time the
pound had apparently contained 60 sh., while in
Alfred's time it contained only 48 (50) sh. I therefore take the sum to have been originally the same
in all these cases. But the compensation specified
in Ine 6 amounts to only half this sum. The only
explanation that I can see for this is that in the
later laws the compensation and the fine have been
added together. This explanation is distinctly
favoured by the fact that in Alfr. 38 the sum
specified is called a 'fine' (*wite*), whereas in Alfr. 15
the verb used is 'compensate' (*gebetan*). In the
first three cases therefore the penalties and compensations may really be identical with those given
in the later laws for violation of *borg* or *mund*. In
the fourth case we find that the *gafolgelda* or *gebur*,

---

[1] Strictly we should of course have expected 96 sh. On this
point cf. p. 29, footnote.

i.e. the ceorl, is entitled under similar circumstances to a compensation of 6 sh. Now no compensations for violation of *borg* or *mund* other than those mentioned above are given in the later laws. Hence Mr Seebohm (*op. cit.* p. 374) has concluded that these terms could only be used in the case of high officials. But from what has been said above it would seem that the act of fighting in a man's house was a form of *mundbryce.* If so the omission must be purely accidental. It is possible however that in certain cases the compensation due to a high official for *mundbryce* included some element which was wanting when the compensation was to be paid to a person of lower rank. Thus in Alfr. 38, after fixing 120 sh. as the sum to be paid for fighting or drawing one's weapon at a meeting in the presence of an earl, the text goes on to say that if anything of this kind takes place in the presence of a subordinate of a king's earl or in the presence of a king's priest a fine of 30 sh. was to be paid[1]. Since this sum is only a quarter of the other, instead of half, as one might have expected, it would seem that the two offences were not regarded as identical. Some element would appear to be included in the offence, when perpetrated before an earl, which would not come into account if the presiding official were of lower rank.

In Ine 6 there is no mention of any class inter-

---

[1] It is not stated that the fine was to go to the subordinate official in question, but probability seems to favour this view. Presumably such a person would be a *gesiðcund man*, and according to Ine 50 members of that class were entitled to fines.

mediate between the earl (and other distinguished councillors) and the *gafolgelda* or *gebur, i.e.* the ceorl. The missing information is, however, supplied by Alfr. 39. According to this passage the compensation due to a ceorlish man for fighting in his house was ·6 sh. If, however, the weapon was drawn without any fight taking place, only half this amount was to be paid. In either of the above cases the compensation due to a *sixhynde man* was three times the amount due to the ceorl under similar circumstances, while for the *twelfhynde man* the amounts were again doubled. We may therefore tabulate the payments due to various persons for the offence of fighting in their houses (*fletgefeoht*) as follows:

earl and other distinguished councillors	60 sh.
twelfhynde man	36 sh.
sixhynde man	18 sh.
ceorl	6 sh.

It remains to be considered, however, whether these sums are to be regarded as the normal payments for *mundbryce*.

Schmid in his glossary (p. 635) seems to have regarded *burgbryce* and *edorbryce* (*i.e.* the offence of damaging or breaking through the wall or fence surrounding a man's dwelling) as a form of *mundbryce*. In Ine 45 the compensations payable for this offence are stated as follows: to the king or bishop 120 sh.; to an earl 80 sh.; to a king's thegn 60 sh.; to a *gesiðcund* landowner 35 sh. (probably for 36 sh.). In Alfr. 40 they are stated somewhat differently: to the king 120 sh.; to the archbishop 90 sh.; to a bishop or earl 60 sh.; to a *twelfhynde man* 30 sh.; to a *sixhynde man* 15 sh.; to a ceorl (in which case the offence is called *edorbryce*) 5 sh. There are two obvious difficulties in the way of regarding this offence as a form of *mundbryce*. In the first place it is frequently stated that the amount payable for violation of the king's *mund* was five pounds, whereas here the compensation is only 120 sh. Secondly, the proportion between the value of the king's *mund* and that of the earl always appears as 5 : 2, whereas here the proportion is 2 : 1. These discrepancies render it clear, I think, that *burgbryce* can not have been regarded as a violation of *mund* in the time of Alfred or at any subsequent period. It is, however, by no means impossible that such may have been the case in earlier times. In the case of *fletgefeoht* discussed above the compensation, strictly speaking, payable to the earl was according to Ine 6 only 60 sh., and it has been suggested that the later amount due to an earl for *mundbryce*, viz. two pounds, was obtained by adding the fine to the compensation. It seems likely enough therefore that the compensations for *mundbryce* may have been doubled in the case of other high dignitaries by the addition of the sums originally payable to them as fines. For *burgbryce* no fine seems to have been required. But if we may assume for the moment that 120 sh. was the original value of the king's *mund*, it is noticeable that when the normal 'king's fine' (120 sh., cf. Aethelred VIII. 5) is added to this the result is 240 sh., *i.e.* five pounds according to the later West Saxon reckoning. The discrepancy in the proportion between the amounts payable to the king and those payable to the earl[1] may have grown up through the changes in the monetary system. I am therefore disposed to believe that *burgbryce* was originally regarded as a violation of *mund*.

Another payment which seems to have been originally regarded in the same light was the *manbot* or compensation payable to a lord for killing one of his men. This may be seen most clearly from Edw. Conf. 12. 5, where the payments for this offence are graduated according to the rank of the lord: *manbote in lege Anglorum regi et archiepiscopo III marc. de hominibus suis; episcopo comitatus, comiti comitatus, et dapifero regis XX sol.; baronibus ceteris X sol.*[2] The authority of this document is not very good, and as a matter of fact the statement is denied in Hen. 87. 4: *manbota secundum legem a persona interfecti secundum weram potius accipiebatur quam per ouerseunessam domini uel personam.* Yet the fact that the *manbot* varied according to the rank of the person slain does not exclude the possibility that it also varied, or had at some previous time varied, according to the rank of the lord. In principle the variation is evidenced by Domesday Book (p. 179) for a Welsh district (Archenfield) in Herefordshire, though the figures only partly agree with those quoted above: *si quis occidit hominem regis et facit*

---

[1] The archbishop of course does not come into account for the earlier period in Wessex.

[2] These amounts are clearly stated according to the Norman monetary system. In terms of the Mercian system the corresponding figures would be 120 sh., 60 sh., and 30 sh.

heinfaram dat regi XX *sol. de solutione hominis et de
forisfactura* C *sol.; si alicuius taini hominem occiderit dat* X *sol. domino hominis mortui.* It is clear
then that the custom was known, at all events in
certain districts. The statement in Hen. 87. 4 must
therefore be understood as meaning that it had
fallen into abeyance or that it was not in general
use. But when it is stated in Edw. and Guth. 12
that the king or bishop or earl is to be regarded as
the kinsman and guardian (*mundbora*) of aliens and
ecclesiastics who have no kinsmen of their own, does
it not follow that the killing of such persons constituted a violation of the guardian's *mund*? If so
it can hardly be doubted that the killing of a king's
thegn or other person in immediate dependence on
the king was regarded at that time in the same
light. It may further be observed that the *manbot*
payable for killing a *ceorl, i.e.* 30 sh. (Ine 70,
Hen. 69), is identical with the compensation due to
a *twelfhynde man* for *burgbryce*. With this we may
compare the fact that in the Kentish laws the sum
due to a ceorl for killing one of his 'breadeaters' is
according to Aethelberht 15, 25 identical with the
amount of the ceorl's *mundbyrd*.

Another offence which may have been regarded
as a violation of *mund* was misconduct with a man's
female slave. At all events the compensations
payable by Kentish law for such an offence were
identical (in the case of a slave of the highest class)
with the compensations payable for violation of
mundbyrd, whether the owner was the king (Aethelberht 10), or an eorl (*ib.* 14) or a ceorl (*ib.* 16). The

only compensation stated in the West Saxon laws is that payable to the ceorl, which according to Alfr. 25[1] was 5 sh., a sum identical with the amount to which the ceorl is entitled as compensation for *edorbryce*.

To sum up briefly the results of this discussion, it seems probable that the *mund* of the earl was originally 60 sh. But since in certain cases a fine also of 60 sh. payable to the same person was involved, the amount of the *mund* was apparently doubled in later times. The original sum remained, however, in cases where no fine was required. The *mund* of the king's thegn and 'distinguished councillor' may originally have been the same as that of the earl; if not the difference was slight. The king's *mund*, except in the case of certain offences for which no compensation was sufficient, seems originally to have been 120 sh. This sum was subsequently doubled in the same way as the *mund* of the earl, but advantage was taken of changes in the monetary system to make the proportion between the king's *mund* and that of the earl 5 : 2 instead of 2 : 1. The *mund* of the ceorl seems to have varied between 5 sh. and 6 sh., a difference to which we shall have to return later (§ 4). The *mund* of the *sixhynde man* was three times that of the ceorl (15—18 sh.), and the *mund* of the *twelfhynde man* twice that of the *sixhynde man* (30—36 sh.).

---

[1] *Gif mon ceorles mennen to nedhæmde geþreahteð mid v scill. gebete þam ceorle and lx scill. to wite.* As the use of violence is involved the case is of course not quite parallel to those quoted above from the Kentish laws. But the difference may be covered by the fine.

Before leaving this subject it may be mentioned that in the laws of Aethelberht the term *mund* is applied to the guardianship of widows. According to cap. 75 the *mund* of the 'best widow,' of *eorlcund* rank, was valued at 50 sh., that of the second at 20 sh., that of the third at 12 sh., and that of the fourth at 6 sh. The distinction between the three last classes is not stated. Possibly the last two belonged to different varieties of the *læt*-class (cf. p. 112). The laws also unfortunately omit to say who the person was to whom the *mund* belonged. That it was regarded as a desirable thing is clear from the following clause: If anyone takes a widow who does not of right belong to him, he is to pay twice the value of the *mund*[1]. The terms *mund* and *borg* were also applied to the guardianship of unmarried women and minors, but the regulations bearing on this subject in the Kentish laws are so obscure and those in the West Saxon laws so fragmentary that the question can hardly be discussed with advantage here.

[1] In Old Norse *mundr* denotes the price paid by the intending bridegroom to the relatives of the bride. The money was given by the relatives to the bride when the marriage took place, and thus practically returned into the possession of the bridegroom, though in case of separation he had to give it up again. But it is very greatly to be doubted whether this was the original custom. From Alf. 18 it may be inferred that the guardian (*byrgea*) had something to gain from the marriage. Are the sums here mentioned (60 sh., 100 sh., 120 sh.) equivalent to the *mund* involved in each case?

§ 2. *The term 'wite.'*

This is the term for fines payable to the king, or other persons endowed with jurisdiction, for infringement of the law. In Ine's laws the figures given in cases where the word *wite* actually occurs are as follows : 30 sh. for not baptising a child within thirty days oɪ birth (cap. 2), and for ordering a slave to work on Sunday (cap. 3). 36 sh. is the fine to be paid by a merchant who has stolen property in his possession for which he is not able to give a satisfactory account (cap. 25). 60 sh. is the fine for theft (cap. 7), for robbery (cap. 10) and for burning trees, which was regarded as a form of theft (cap. 43). 120 sh. is the fine for fighting (cap. 6). 60 sh. is also the fine to be paid to an earl for fighting in his house (*ib.*). The fines for neglecting military service were for a ceorl 30 sh., for a *gesiðcund* man without land 60 sh., for a *gesiðcund* landowner 120 sh. (cap. 51). In Alfr. 9. 1, which refers perhaps only to cases of theft, it is stated that all fines thenceforth were to be 60 sh., except for one who stole men, in which case the fine was to be 120 sh. The fine for the rape of a ceorl's female slave was 60 sh. (*ib.* 25); for harbouring fugitives 120 sh. (*ib.* 37). Fines of 30 sh. and of 120 sh. are also given in cap. 38, which has been discussed above (p. 120). The later laws give no figures other than those mentioned here[1].

[1] Payments of an amount corresponding to the delinquent's wergeld are mentioned in Ine 15, 30, 72, etc. An interesting example dating from the reign of Eadred occurs in B. 1063.

The amounts which appear in fines therefore are 30 sh., 60 sh., and 120 sh. The only exception is the 36 sh. fine of Ine 25, which is probably to be regarded as a variation of the 30 sh. fine and to be explained perhaps in the same way as the variation between 5 sh. and 6 sh. in the value of the ceorl's *mund.* Sometimes it is stated simply that a fine is to be paid without any specification of the amount. Thus in the laws of Edward and Guthrum the expression " he is to pay *wite* among the English and *lahslit* among the Danes " occurs nine times. In one case (cap. 3. 2) the amount of the *lahslit* is specified, viz. 12 ores. Of the sums mentioned above the one which would most nearly correspond to this is the 60 sh. fine[1]. Again, in cap. 7. 1 it is stated that if a freeman works on a festival he is to forfeit his freedom or to pay *wite* or *lahslit.* According to an addition to Ine 3. 2 in the *Textus Roffensis* the payment of 60 sh. was an alternative to the loss of freedom, a statement which, whatever its authority may be, is supported by cap. 7, while in cap. 74 the life of a slave is valued at 60 sh.[2] Further, in Ine 43 the payment of 60 sh. is called *ful wite,* an expression which occurs again in cap. 72, as well as in Cnut II. 48. Lastly, we may refer again to Alfr. 9, where the regular fine, at all events in cases

---

[1] In two passages (cap. 3. 1 and 7 Pref.) it is stated that a man who has committed certain offences is to pay 30 sh. among the English and 12 ores or 3 half-marks among the Danes. I understand these cases to be exceptional. The amounts mentioned must certainly be very different.

[2] Cf. Duns. 7, Aethelred II. 5, Hen. 70. 2, where the value of a slave is stated to be one pound (of silver).

of theft, is said to be 60 sh. From a comparison of all these passages it appears probable that the normal fine was originally a sum of money (viz. a pound of silver) equal to the value of a slave. As *wite* seems to have originally meant punishment[1], and as *witeþeow* is the name for a penal slave, it is quite possible that the fine was originally regarded as a payment in redemption of the man's freedom. The fine of 30 sh. must in that case have been regarded as a half penalty, incurred for comparatively slight offences. On the other hand the fine of 120 sh., the double penalty, is called the 'king's fine' (*cyninges wite*) in Aethelred VIII. 5 and Cnut I. 3. 2. It is partly the fine for exceptionally serious offences such as fighting (Ine 6); partly it is the amount to be paid by a *twelfhynde man* in cases where the ceorl had to pay a fine of 30 sh. (*ib.* 51).

In the Kentish laws the word *wite* only occurs twice. The first case (Aethelberht 9) gives no indication of the amount involved; in the second (Wihtr. 11) it is the amount of the man's *healsfang*. The forfeiture of the *healsfang* is the penalty involved again in Wihtr. 12, 14. Unfortunately the amount of the *healsfang* in Kent is never stated; but from Aethelberht 22, Schmid (p. 608[2]) conjectured with some probability that it was 20 sh. In Hloth. and Ead. 9, 11, 12, 13 we find payments of 12 sh. to the king, which can hardly be regarded except

---

[1] This is the meaning of O. H. Germ. *wizzi*, O. Sax. *witi*. The O. Norse word *víti* has both meanings.

[2] Of course I cannot admit the argument derived from the proportion of the sums.

as fines[1]. Again, in the same code, cap. 14, it is
stated that if bloodshed took place in a man's house
the *mundbyrd* of the householder had to be paid
and a further payment of 50 sh. made to the king.
Here we have clearly a payment corresponding to
the West Saxon *wite* for fighting in a man's
house (Ine, 6). We may compare Aethelberht 6,
where it is stated that if a man slays a free man
50 sh. is to be paid to the king for 'lordship-money'
(*to drihtinbeage*). It seems doubtful at first sight
whether we should identify this payment with the
fyhtwite or with the *manbot* of the West Saxon
laws. But if the passage be compared with Hloth.
and Ead. 14, it will become clear that the sum must
have been paid in every case of manslaughter,
whether the man slain was in the personal service of
the king or not. It seems probable therefore that
in Kent, as in Wessex, there were three grades
of fines, 12 sh., 20 sh., and 50 sh.

It appears that according to Kentish law the
fyhtwite amounted to 50 sh. But this is also
the amount of the Kentish king's *mundbyrd*
(Aethelberht 8). Now if we return to the West
Saxon laws we see that the 120 sh. fine, which was
exacted for fighting, was known as the 'king's fine.'
Moreover reasons have been given above (p. 122 ff.) for
believing that this was also the original value of the
king's *mund*. If so the Kentish and West Saxon
laws must once have been in complete agreement on
this point. It is difficult therefore to avoid con-

---

[1] In Aethelberht 84 we find a payment of 15 sh. to the king,
but the passage is somewhat obscure.

cluding that the 'king's fine,' at all events in so far
as it was a fine for bloodshed, had its origin in a
compensation for violation of the king's *mund*[1].

It may be objected to this explanation that it
involves for early times the application of the king's
grið to all his subjects. But to this I am quite
willing to agree; for, though the word *grið* is
Scandinavian, there is no reason for believing that
the idea which it denotes was new. We must of
course distinguish between persons under the immediate lordship of the king and persons under
the lordship of others. In the former case the king
was entitled to the *manbot* as well as the *fyhtwite*.
In the latter case the immediate lord was entitled
to the *manbot*; but since he was himself, whether
immediately or not, subject to the king, there seems
to be no adequate reason for doubting that the
king was in a wider sense *dryhten*[2] and *mundbora*[3]
to all.

If we are right in believing that the 'king's fine'
originated in a compensation for violation of the
king's *mund*, we must conclude that originally it
was always paid to the king, whatever modifications
may have been introduced in later times. Then

[1] It may be noted that the regular expression used for a corresponding payment in the continental laws is *pro fredo*.

[2] *Dryhten* is the old word (still used in the Kentish laws) which
hlaford has displaced. It is used to denote not only personal
lordship but also (in early poetry) the relationship of a king to his
people (*e.g. Geata dryhten*); *hlaford* seems to have been originally
the antithesis to *hlafæta*.

[3] This term is used to denote the relationship of the East
Anglian king and nation to Ecgberht in *Chron.* 823.

it is at least a curious coincidence that the ordinary
fine (60 sh.) coincides with what seems to have been
the original value of the earl's *mund,* and perhaps
also that of other officials (cf. p. 125). Again, the fine
of 30 sh. coincides with the value of the *mund* of the
twelfhynde man; and it is clear from Ine 50 (cf. p. 98),
that persons of *gesiðcund* rank were entitled to fines.
These facts suggest that the 60 sh. fine was originally
the amount which the royal official[1] was entitled to
claim from persons convicted in his court[2], and similarly that the 30 sh. fine was the amount which the
gesiðcund landowner could exact from his dependants.
No doubt this system had undergone considerable
modification before the time of the earliest laws, for
even there (*e.g.* Ine 51) we find fines graduated
according to the social rank of the delinquent,
apparently without reference to the position of the
person entitled to receive the fine[3]. But from
Will. I. 16 it would seem that in principle some such
system prevailed in Mercia as late as the Norman
Conquest. The passage is as follows : *Li ercevesque*

---

[1] The origin of the earldoms and the relationship between the
terms 'king's reeve, 'king's thegn,' etc. will be discussed in the
following chapters. It may be well however to mention here that
I have not been able to find any evidence for the existence of
'national officers' as distinct from royal officers. This idea, like
that of a 'national peace' as distinct from the 'king's peace,'
seems to be due to the erroneous assumption that royalty was a
comparatively late institution in the English nation.

[2] This explanation is not necessarily incompatible with the
suggestion given on p. 129. The value of the slave may have
determined the amount which the official could claim.

[3] So also in the Kentish laws (see above) we find payments of
12 sh. to the king.

averad de forfeiture xl sol. en Merchenelahe e li eveske xx sol. e li quens xx sol. e li barun x sol. e li socheman[1] *xl den.* It is somewhat surprising to find the *socheman* entitled to a fine; but since in Domesday Book persons of this class are very rare except in districts which had once been Danish, it is likely enough that this peculiarity is of Scandinavian origin.

It may of course be urged that the Normans failed to distinguish between payments of *wite* and payments for violation of *mund*[2]. But if the suggestion given above is correct, the *wite* to which the *twelfhynde man* was entitled was originally a payment for violation of *mund*. In the case of the king and the earl on the other hand the amount payable for violation of *mund* is double that of the *wite*. The reason for this seems to me to be that the amount payable for *mundbryce* consisted originally of two distinct items, one of which was a compensation for personal injury, while the other was the amount to which the king or the earl was entitled as ' guardian' of the nation or province.

---

[1] Some texts have *vilain* (*uillanus*, Lat. version); but this hardly seems likely. The sum mentioned cannot represent the value of the ceorl's *mund*, unless Mercian and West Saxon custom differed greatly in this respect.

[2] This may be seen (*e.g.*) from Hen. 81. 3 : *Quidam uillani qui sunt eiusmodi leierwitam et blodwitam et huiusmodi minora forisfacta emerunt a dominis suis uel quomodo meruerunt de suis et in suos, quorum fletgefoth uel ouerseunessa est xxx den.; cothseti xv den.; serui vi den.*

§ 3.   *The Oath.*

In several passages of Ine's laws and once in those of Alfred the value of the oath required for refuting or substantiating a specified charge is expressed in terms of hides.   Thus in cap. 14 a man accused of brigandage is required to support his plea of innocence by an oath of 120 hides.   So also in cap. 52, a man, apparently possessing magisterial authority, is required to deny a charge of corruption by 120 hides.   Similarly in cap. 46 and 53, charges of theft or possessing stolen property require to be denied by 60 hides.   Again in Alfr. 11 an unmarried woman claiming compensation for rape is required to deny a charge of previous unchastity by 60 hides in order to obtain the full compensation.

It has long been seen that there is a connection between the number of hides required in these oaths and the number of shillings involved in the corresponding fines or compensations.   Thus in cap. 52 the magistrate accused of corruption has to clear himself by 120 hides or pay 120 sh.   Again, in cap. 46, as has been mentioned above, the charge of theft requires a denial by 60 hides.   But from caps. 7 and 43 it is clear that the fine for theft was 60 sh.   Again, according to cap. 54 a Welsh slave can be scourged on an oath of 12 hides; in cap. 23 the Welsh slave's skin is valued at 12 sh., *i.e.* he may escape being scourged by the payment of this sum.   We may also compare the following passages: cap. 14, where the man accused of brigandage is to deny the charge by 120 hides or pay a corresponding compensation; cap. 15, where the man accused of *hereteam* (*i.e.* brigandage on a large scale) is to ransom himself by his wergeld or deny the charge by his wergeld (cf. cap. 30); cap. 45, where the man accused of *burgbryce* against various persons is to pay the compensation involved or deny the charge according to the same calculation; cap. 28, where a charge of theft is to be denied according to the amount of the fine and the value of the property involved (cf. cap. 25, 35).

This expression of the value of an oath in terms of hides is peculiar to the laws of Ine except for the solitary instance in Alfred's laws quoted above. Indeed after this time the value of the oath required is seldom expressed at all. Instances are to be found in Alfr. 4, where the charge of plotting against the king's life is to be denied by the amount of the king's wergeld; so also a man who plots against his lord's life must deny the charge by the lord's wergeld. We may also compare the oath of a pound in value mentioned in Aethelred I. 1. 3 (Cnut II. 30. 2)[1]. As a rule however in the later laws we find in place of these expressions the statement that a certain number of co-swearers is required. This is also the case in the Kentish laws; but in West Saxon documents no example of this kind seems to occur before the Treaty of Alfred and Guthrum (cap. 3).

---

[1] In B. 1064 Eadgifu, who subsequently married King Edward the Elder, is said to have produced an oath of 30 pounds in proof of her statement that her father had repaid the sum (30 pounds) which he had borrowed from a certain Goda.

That the oaths of persons belonging to different classes of society were not of the same value is clear from a fragment of Mercian law (Schmid, p. 400), according to which the oath of a *twelfhynde man* is valid against those of six ceorls. The ratio is therefore the same as in the wergelds. Several passages in Ine's laws seem to point to the existence of similar differences in Wessex. Thus according to cap. 19 a king's *geneat*, if his wergeld be 1200 sh., may swear for 60 hides, if he be a communicant. Again, in cap. 54 it is stated that in denying a charge of homicide the *hynden* must contain one member with a 'king's oath' (*an kyningæðe*) of 30 hides—a passage which unfortunately is somewhat obscure[1].

With the exception of cap. 19, the Laws give us no information regarding the number of hides for which a member of any particular class might swear. The only item of direct evidence available on this question is an explanation given in the Latin version of cap. 19 and 46. Here, after the expressions *pro LX hidis, per LX hidas* (*iurare, abnegare*), we find the words *i.e. pro hominibus VI, i.e. per VI homines* added[2]. But the mistakes of the Latin

---

[1] Liebermann (*ad loc.*) takes *hynden* to mean in the first clause "(every) 100 hides," and in the second clause "100 shillings." This rendering seems to me by far the best. For the word *hynden* cf. Aethelstan VI. 3. 8; for the expression we may perhaps compare a parenthetic clause in the *Lex Saxonum*, cap. 14, *ruoda dicitur apud Saxones cxx sol.*

[2] Mr Seebohm (*Tribal Custom*, p. 411) quotes these passages in support of his contention that the single oath of the *twelfhynde man* was of ten hides value; but it is not stated in the Latin version what the class of the *homo* in question was.

version in the interpretation of Ine's laws are so numerous that it would not be wise to lay much stress on this explanation. If we turn to the English text we find mention in cap. 54 of a person competent to swear for 30 hides, but the passage unfortunately gives us no clue as to the class to which he belonged. Mr Seebohm (*Tribal Custom*, p. 409 ff.) believes him to have been a king's thegn. This explanation is based on the evidently close affinity which the passage in question has with cap. 3 of the Treaty between Alfred and Guthrum. In the latter it is stated that if a king's thegn wishes to clear himself on a charge of homicide, he must have the support of twelve king's thegns; a person of inferior rank under the same circumstances must be supported by eleven of his equals and one king's thegn. The difficulty in the way of Mr Seebohm's explanation is the statement (quoted above) about the king's *geneat* in cap. 19. It is to this passage therefore that we must first turn our attention.

The expression *cyninges geneat* does not occur elsewhere in the Laws. The word *geneat* by itself however occurs in Edg. IV. 1. 1, 2 (cf. II. 1) and *Rect.* 2, in all which passages it seems to denote a *gafolgelda*—presumably therefore, as a rule at all events, a ceorl. In Ine 23, where a lord's responsibility for his *geneat* is stated, the word may have a wider meaning and refer to dependants generally[1].

---

[1] In B. 574, a charter dating from 896, we hear of the *geneat* of a priest, but no clear indication is given as to his social position.

This may also be the case in the expression *cyninges geneat*. In the *Chronicle*, ann. 897, apparently the only other place where the expression occurs, we find record of the death of a king's *geneat*—a fact which would seem to indicate that he was regarded as a person of distinction. The original meaning of the word seems to have been 'companion,' as in Old High Germ. *ginōz*. Quite possibly therefore the position of the king's *geneat* may have differed but little from that of the king's thegn[1]. In poetry indeed *geneat* seems to be used as an equivalent of *þegn, e.g. Jud.* 684: *þa þegnas seo geneatscolu.* So also in *Beowulf* the words *beodgeneatas* and *heorðgeneatas* are used interchangeably with *þegnas*; they are applied (*e.g.*) to the same persons in ll. 194, 261, 343, 400. It would seem therefore that if the two expressions *cyninges geneat* and *cyninges þegn* were not exactly equivalent, the one class must have been a subdivision of the other. But from the qualifying sentence 'if his wergeld be 1200 sh.' it is to be inferred that not all the king's *geneatas* were *twelfhynde men*. Yet it is hardly conceivable that there were any king's thegns who did not possess this wergeld. From this we may probably conclude that *cyninges geneat* was a more comprehensive term than *cyninges þegn*, and that it was applied not only to nobles but also to persons of humbler rank who

[1] It will be seen later that the king's reeve was, sometimes at all events, a king's thegn. In the list of obits in *Chron.* 877 the king's *geneat* is preceded by a king's reeve. It is perhaps worth suggesting therefore that in such cases as this the term *cyninges geneat* denoted a member of the royal household who held no public office.

were under the immediate lordship of the king. In any case however it is hardly possible that the king's *geneat* should have been superior to the king's thegn. If that had been the case we should certainly have heard of such persons more frequently.

If these arguments are correct, the king's thegn ought to be able to swear for at least as many hides as the king's *geneat, i.e.* for 60 hides. The person competent to swear for 30 hides (Ine 54) can therefore hardly have been a king's thegn[1]. It is true that the regulation declared by this passage will then not be identical with that contained in Alfr. and Guthr. 3. But is it necessary that the two regulations should be identical? The earlier enactment declares that the *hynden* must contain a person competent to swear for 30 hides; the later one demands that one of the co-swearers must be a king's thegn. The requirements of the law may have been altered in the course of time.

We must now turn to the later laws. It has

---

[1] It may be suggested that the king's thegn who was not a communicant was entitled to swear only for 30 hides. In Ine 15 it is stated that an oath of only half the ordinary amount is to be required from communicants. But this is not equivalent to saying that the communicant could swear for twice as many hides as the non-communicant. I should prefer to regard the provisional clause 'if he be a communicant' (cap. 19) as meaning that in that case the king's *geneat* would be entitled to the full oath of a king's thegn. In the preceding note it has been suggested that the term *cyninges geneat* was applied especially to the junior members of the royal household. The oaths of such persons would naturally be of less value than those of the king's thegns.

already been mentioned that after Alfred's time in place of the denial by so many hides we frequently find the statement that so many co-swearers are required. Eleven seems to be the usual number, *i.e.* twelve oaths in all. Thus in Aethelstan II. 11 twelve oaths are required to prove the guilt of a thief who has been killed. So in V. 4 a man who has killed a thief in sanctuary requires eleven co-swearers to declare that he was unaware that the immunity existed. Again, according to Cnut II. 48 (repeated in Henr. 66. 5) the man who is charged with preventing *godcund geriht* requires eleven co-swearers to deny the charge. According to II. 65 (Henr. 66. 6) the same number are required in denying a charge of neglecting the national duties generally comprised under the term *trinoda necessitas*. According to Will. I. 3, when a thief has succeeded in escaping, his surety requires eleven co-swearers to affirm that he has not been in collusion with him. A like number of co-swearers are required in I. 14 to deny a charge of theft ; so also in I. 15 to deny a charge of breaking into a house or church. The same number are required also, according to I. 51, by a man accused by four persons at a meeting of the hundred.

In other cases a smaller number of oaths are required. Thus, according to *Duns.* 1, five co-swearers are necessary for the oath that stolen cattle have been rightly traced to another man's land. A similar case occurs in cap. 8. The provisions of this code are however somewhat peculiar, as it was intended primarily to regulate the relations between the

English and Welsh inhabitants of a frontier district. Again, according to Aethelred I. 1. 8, .12 (cf. Cnut II. 30. 7, Will. I. 52, Henr. 41. 6), five co-swearers (thegns) are required by a lord to clear himself of the charge of collusion with a thief or of allowing a thief to escape. Five co-swearers again are required to deny the charge of preventing a condemned man from making his confession (Cnut II. 44, Henr. 11. 9). Again, if a regular deacon or secular priest be accused on a 'simple charge' (*anfeald spræc*), he must clear himself with two co-swearers of the same order; if on a 'triple charge' (*þryfeald spræc*), he must clear himself with six (Aethelred VIII. 20, 21; Cnut I. 5). A regular priest may clear himself on a simple charge by his own oath; on a triple charge he requires two co-swearers of the same order (Aethelred VIII. 19; Cnut I. 5). Four co-swearers are required by the master of a ship in denying a charge of robbery (Aethelred II. 4). The oaths of three persons, kinsmen of the deceased, are required for pleading the innocence of a slain thief (Aethelstan II. 11). Lastly, a lord who is willing to swear to the previous conduct of one of his men in order to get him judged by the simple ordeal requires to be supported by the oaths of two thegns (Aethelred III. 4, cf. Cnut II. 30. 1).

It will be seen from the above list that the usual number of oaths required is twelve, unless the swearers are persons of some official position, such as thegns or priests. In several of the passages quoted above, where a smaller number of co-swearers is required, it is explicitly stated that they must be thegns, while in others (*e.g.* Cnut II. 44) it is extremely probable that such was the case. Other cases again seem to be due to exceptional circumstances. Further, the conclusion that the normal number of oaths was twelve is supported by the evidence of the 'triple denial' (*þrifeald lad*). According to Will. I. 15 this was required by a man charged with breaking into a church or house if he was a previous offender. It is added that 36 oaths (out of 42) were then required. With this passage we may compare Aethelred III. 13, where it is stated that 36 oaths were required by a man who was charged with harbouring one who had broken the king's peace. In Henr. 66. 9 it is stated that in Wessex thirty *consacramentales* were required for the *triplex lada*, out of whom the magistrate is to select fifteen. If this is correct the passage in Will. I. 15 must refer to Mercia, where according to Henr. 66. 10 the number of *consacramentales* required was 35. Considering however the fact that in the cases enumerated above (p. 140 f.) the number of oaths required is usually twelve, six, or three, it may be suggested that the statement in Henr. 66. 9 points to a later modification of West Saxon custom.

At this point it will be well to call attention to a passage quoted above, Aethelred VIII. 19, where it is stated that a regular priest may on a simple charge clear himself by his own oath, while on a triple charge he requires the support of two other regular priests. If, as there seems little reason to doubt, the oaths here refer to the *anfeald lad* and the *þrifeald lad* respectively, it would appear that, at all events under Mercian law, the oaths of three regular priests were equivalent to those of 36 ordinary persons. Consequently the oath of the regular priest will be equal to that of twelve ordinary persons.

We have seen that twelve is the number of oaths, including his own, required by the ordinary person in order to clear himself on most charges[1], such as theft (Will. I. 14), *burgbryce* (*ib.* I. 15), *mundbryce* (Aethelstan V. 4) and neglecting military duties (Cnut II. 65). Now it has been seen above (p. 134) that in Ine's laws the number of hides required in the oath of denial in cases of theft was 60, while in cases of *burgbryce* it varied according to the rank of the person injured. Again, we have seen that the number of hides required in the oath of denial apparently always corresponded to the number of shillings involved in the payment at stake, including both the fine and the *angylde* (*i.e.* the value of the article in dispute). Therefore the number of hides required in the oath of denial in such cases must also have varied. Consequently we are forced to conclude that after Ine's time a certain amount of simplification must have taken place in legal procedure. This process of simplification is clearly to be connected with the regulation contained in Alfr. and Guthr. 3. It is there enacted that not only in cases of manslaughter but also in every case in which a sum exceeding four mancusas

---

[1] It may also be observed that in Aethelstan III. 7, a reeve is instructed to demand from doubtful characters twelve members of their kindred to act as sureties for their behaviour.

is involved, the defendant in order to clear himself
requires to be supported by eleven of his peers and
one king's thegn.   Again, this regulation is surely to
be taken in connection with Alfr. 9, where it is
stated that henceforth all fines are to be 60 sh.
until the *angylde* amounts to 30 sh.[1]; when the
angylde amounts to 30 sh. the fine is increased to
120 sh.   But the fine for manslaughter also was
120 sh.   It seems probable therefore that the cases
in which the defendant required the oath of eleven
of his peers and one king's thegn corresponded to
the cases in which the fine amounted to 120 sh.

Unfortunately we are not informed as to the
number of oaths required when the *angylde* did not
exceed four mancusas, *i.e.* presumably when the fine
involved was one of 60 sh.   We may however compare the following facts :   The fine of 60 sh. was the
usual fine (cf. p. 128 f.); the usual number of oaths
(except where officials are involved) was twelve.
For theft (presumably the most frequent case) the
fine was 60 sh. ; twelve oaths according to Will. I. 14
were required to deny the charge of theft.   Moreover
we never find more than twelve oaths mentioned in
the laws except in connection with the *þrifeald lad*
and in Alfr. and Guthr. 3, where the number is
thirteen.   In the *þrifeald lad* the number of oaths
(at all events in Mercia) was 36.   From these com-
parisons the obvious inference is that when the fine
amounted to 60 sh. twelve oaths were required,

---

[1] It is true that this sum is not identical with four mancusas
(*i.e.* 24 W. Sax. sh.).   The case where the *angylde* amounts to
between 24 sh. and 30 sh. seems not to be taken into account.

i.e. the defendant required eleven co-swearers, but not a king's thegn.

We may now pass on to a further inference. If, when the fine amounts to 60 sh., the defendant requires eleven co-swearers, and if, when it amounts to 120 sh., he requires as co-swearers eleven of his peers and one king's thegn, we are brought to the suggestion that the oath of one king's thegn is equal to that of twelve ordinary persons. But we have seen that in Aethelred VIII. 19 the oath of the regular priest is made equal to that of twelve ordinary persons. Moreover, though it is frequently stated both in Aethelred's laws and elsewhere that the priest possesses the rights of a thegn, we never find a priest ranked above a king's thegn. The equation between the oath of the king's thegn and those of twelve ordinary persons is therefore in all probability correct.

But who were the ordinary persons? The regulation in Alfr. and Guthr. 3 applies to all persons below the rank of king's thegn. The oath required therefore would be of varying value according to the rank of the defendant. How far this was in accordance with ancient custom is not quite clear. In cases where the payment of wergelds was involved one would certainly have expected the value of the oath to be governed by the social position of the person slain rather than by that of the slayer. But we may at all events note that when the king's thegn is contrasted with persons of other ranks (cf. p. 121 ff.), we never find his privileges assessed at more than twice as much as those of the *twelfhynde man* or more than four times as much as those of the *sixhynde man*. The person therefore whose oath is in value only one twelfth of that of the king's thegn must surely be a ceorl.

Now it has been pointed out above (p. 139) that the king's thegn seems to have been entitled to swear for at least 60 hides. If so, the number of hides for which the ceorl was entitled to swear must have been at least five. On the other hand we have now seen that the oaths of twelve ceorls and one king's thegn are apparently required when a ceorl is accused on a charge involving a fine of 120 sh., and further that the cases where twelve oaths are required without the participation of a king's thegn seem to correspond to the cases where a fine of 60 sh. is involved. If these inferences are correct it would seem not only that the value of the ceorl's oath was not less than 5 sh. (or hides), but also that it was no more, or at all events not appreciably more, than this amount. Consequently also the oath of the king's thegn will be worth neither less nor (appreciably) more than 60 sh. or hides.

It is true that according to Ine 35 the oath of denial had to correspond to the total amount at stake, including the value of the stolen article as well as the fine. Now according to the passages discussed above, when the *angylde* amounted to four mancusas, *i.e.* presumably 120 pence, the total amount at stake would come to 84 sh., which, according to the calculation suggested, would give the ceorl an oath of 7 sh. (or hides). But, since all minor variations in the amount of the *angylde* are disregarded in Alfr. and Guth. 3, we are surely forced to conclude that the regulation stated in Ine 35 had by this time fallen into abeyance, and that the value of the oath required was now determined by the amount of the fine alone without reference to the *angylde*. Indeed the old principle that the total value of the oath required should correspond to the total amount at stake seems now to have been superseded to some extent by the principle that the total value of the oath required should vary according to the social position of the defendant[1].

It does not follow however from this that the monetary value of the oath had now been forgotten. We have seen that even as late as Aethelred's laws (I. 1, 3) we find mention of 'an oath of a pound in value' (*pundes wurðne að*). Now according to Will. I. 14 f. an accused man who cannot obtain 12 oaths has to go to the ordeal, while similarly a previous offender who cannot obtain 36 oaths has to go to the triple ordeal. These statements have a distinct bearing on the passage in Aethelred's laws. It is there stated that if the accused man is of good report he may choose either 'an oath of a pound in value' or the 'simple' (*anfeald*) ordeal; if he is not of good report he must go to the triple (*þryfeald*) ordeal. It appears then that the 'oath of a pound

---

[1] According to this hypothesis the total value of the oath required from persons belonging to the higher classes must now of course have been much greater than formerly. In the case of the king's thegn the text (Alfr. and Guth. 3) hardly leaves any room for doubt on this point. It may however perhaps be doubted whether this enactment was of universal and permanent application.

in value' corresponded to the oath of twelve men.
As we can hardly doubt that these regulations were
intended to apply to ceorls, we again come to the
conclusion that the oath of the single ceorl was
valued at 5 sh. or thereabouts[1].

One qualification must however be made. In
Ine 54 we find an oath of 12 hides, *i.e.* a number of
which 5 is not a factor. But we have seen (p. 125)
that in compensations for *mundbryce* and other
similar payments there is an unexplained variation
between 5 sh. and 6 sh. in sums due to the ceorl, as
also between 15—18 sh. and 30—36 sh. in those due
to the higher classes. May we not assume the
possibility of a similar variation in the value of the
ceorl's oath? If so the oath in Ine 54 will be that
of two ceorls. This suggestion may also perhaps
give us an explanation of the statement in Henr.
66. 9 f. that thirty *consacramentales* were required
for the *triplex lada* in Wessex, as against thirty-five
in Mercia.

If the ceorl was entitled to swear for 5—6 hides
and the king's thegn for about 60 hides, there can
be practically no doubt that the *sixhynde man* could
swear for 15—18 hides and the *twelfhynde man* for
30—36 hides. Then the person mentioned in Ine 54
as competent to swear for 30 hides must have been
not a king's thegn but a *twelfhynde man*[2].

[1] The correspondence would of course be exact only for
Mercia; but since the council from which this enactment pro-
ceeded was held at Woodstock, it seems likely enough that it was
intended primarily for Mercia.

[2] The meaning will then be that the oath of one *twelfhynde man*
must be contained in every hundred hides of the total oath

It will be well here to return for a moment to the question of the *triplex lada*, which is the largest oath required in the later laws. In Ine's laws we find no mention of any oath of more than 120 sh. or hides, except in the case of certain very serious offences (cap. 15, 30, 72) where the denial has to be made by the value of the defendant's wergeld. It would seem then that the *triplex lada* corresponded in some way to the wergeld-oath. Now if we are right in believing that the ceorl's oath was of the value of 5—6 sh., it is clear that the value of 36 such oaths would correspond approximately to the amount of his wergeld. The same would of course be true in the case of persons belonging to the higher orders. It seems probable therefore that the *triplex lada* was actually derived from the wergeld-oath.

It may perhaps be thought that a good deal of what has been said above depends too much upon hypothesis. It will be well therefore to see what alternatives are possible. The number of hides represented by the ceorl's oath can hardly be less than five; for, since the number of oaths required in the later laws hardly ever exceeds twelve, it is inconceivable that more should be required in such a case as that stated in Alfr. 11, 4[1]. But can it

(cf. p. 136, footnote). When a ceorl is accused of slaying a ceorl, he will require the oaths of two *twelfhynde men* and (probably) 24 ceorls. The requirements of the law were thus in some cases greater at this time than in the time of Alfred and Guthrum.

[1] This passage seems to me quite irreconcilable with Mr Seebohm's conclusions. If, as he holds (*op. cit.* p. 410 f.), the single oath of the king's thegn was one of 30 hides, and that

represent a larger number? Practically the only possible alternative is ten (with a necessary variation to twelve) hides; for 120 is the only figure above 60 which is of more than sporadic occurrence, whether in hides or shillings, and even for those figures which occur only sporadically no number above 5 (6) except 10 (12) will be a factor[1]. The suggestion that the twelve men's oath of the later laws was originally identical with the oath by 120 hides has certain points in its favour. It is supported by the Latin version of Ine 19 and 46 (cf. p. 136), and at first sight by a passage in Egbert's Dialogus (cap. 1): *ordines supradicti secundum gradus promotionis habeant potestatem protestandi, presbiter secundum numerum cxx tributariorum, diaconus uero iuxta numerum LX manentium, monachus uero secundum numerum XXX tributariorum etc.* The principle involved here is clearly the same as in the laws of Ine, though unfortunately no persons other than ecclesiastics are mentioned. But we can hardly suppose that the oath of the king's thegn, or the Northumbrian official corresponding to him, was of less value than that of the priest. The ceorl's oath may therefore be one of ten hides. But if this was also the case in Wessex, we are surely bound to conclude that the oath by 60 hides was the normal oath of the *twelf-*

of the *twelfhynde man* one of 10 hides, the oath required here, to prove the chastity of a ceorlish woman, would need two king's thegns or six *twelfhynde men* (or 36 ceorls). But this is surely incredible.

[1] The figures (for hides) which actually occur in Ine's laws are 120, 80, 60, 36, 30, 12. In cap. 45 and 54. 2 *xxxv* and *xxxiiii* are probably mistakes for *xxxvi* and *xxiiii* respectively.

hynde man. Then of course the regulation in Ine 19 becomes unintelligible. From all sides therefore it seems most probable that the West Saxon ceorl's oath was an oath by 5—6 hides. The Northumbrian ceorl's oath may have been one of 10 hides, but I do not see that there is any necessity for supposing that the oaths of the various Northumbrian classes were of the same value as those of the corresponding classes in Wessex.

How the ceorl came to possess an oath by 5—6 hides is not clear, for it is incredible that the typical ceorl can ever have possessed this amount of land. The only clue that I have been able to find is the constant identity of the number of hides contained in the oath with the number of shillings involved in the fine or compensation. Indeed the value of the oath itself is sometimes expressed in terms of money. Instances are to be found in Ine 15, 28, 45 and Alfr. 4, all of which have already been quoted, while in later times we find reference to the oath of a pound in value. Now the value of the ceorl's *mund* was 5—6 sh. (p. 125). Again from Ine 6, 45 it appears that the *mund* of the king's thegn was 60 sh., while from considerations which have been discussed above (p. 120 ff.) it has been concluded that the *mund* of the *twelfhynde man* was six times as great as that of the ceorl. It seems therefore that the value of a man's *mund*, whatever his rank, was the amount for which he was entitled to swear.

In conclusion we may turn for a moment to the Kentish laws. In these laws the value of the oath is never stated either in hides or shillings. It is clear however from Wihtr. 18 ff. that the oaths of different persons varied in value. The priest, the deacon, the stranger and the king's thegn were able to clear themselves on their own oath alone, while the monk and the ceorl required the support of three of their peers, *i.e.* four oaths in all. Unfortunately it is not stated how the *eorl, eorlcund man* or *gesið-cund man* is to clear himself. From cap. 23, which is obscure and probably in part corrupt[1], it may be inferred that a man (a ceorl?) who was a communicant had the right of deciding by his own oath whether or not his slave should be scourged. In cap. 10 a payment of six shillings is given as the alternative to a scourging. Since this is also the amount of the ceorl's *mundbyrd* it seems possible that, as in Wessex, the value of the *mundbyrd* was the amount for which a man was entitled to swear. If so we should expect that the *eorlcund man* required only one co-swearer. The absence of evidence for a fine of 24 sh. is however somewhat against these suggestions. Indeed it cannot be regarded as certain that the oath was associated with any monetary value in Kent[2]. At

---

[1] I find some difficulty in accepting the usual interpretation of this passage. Were there ecclesiastical officials who were not communicants?

[2] Yet the transaction described in B. 1064 (cf. p. 135, footnote) belongs entirely to Kentish history. If, as suggested above, the Kentish ceorl was entitled to swear for 120 pence, the oath of thirty pounds mentioned in this document would represent the oaths of sixty ceorls. On the other hand, if West Saxon custom had been adopted by this time, we shall have to suppose that Eadgifu had the support of (probably) 24 or 25 king's thegns or 40—50 *twelfhynde men*.

all events however it is clear that in this respect as in others the custom of Kent differed widely from that which prevailed in the rest of England.

§ 4. *The value of the ceorl's 'Mund.'*

In the course of the preceding discussion we have frequently had occasion to notice a curious variation in the figures for the West Saxon ceorl's *mund* or for compensations which seem to have been originally founded on this *mund.* 5 sh. is the amount to which the ceorl is entitled as compensation for *edorbryce* (Alfr. 40) and for the rape of his female slave (*ib.* 25). A compensation of the same amount is required according to Alfr. 11 for insult to an unmarried woman of the ceorlish class. On the other hand 6 sh. is the amount due to a ceorl as compensation for *fletgefeoht* (Ine 6, Alfr. 39). Again the same variation is found in the number of hides for which the ceorl is entitled to swear; and in this case at all events the variation seems to be evidenced even in the laws of Ine. It cannot be decided with certainty which of the two reckonings is the older. It should however be observed (i) that the number 60 (shillings) appears to be constant for the *mund* of the king's thegn[1], and (ii) that an oath of 60 hides seems to be equivalent to an oath of twelve men. On the whole therefore probability favours the supposition that 5 was the original figure. But how did the variation arise?

[1] Cf. Ine 6, 45, where the lower compensations seem to have followed the scale 6 : 18 : 36.

It seems to me that both the *mund* and the oath of the ceorl must once have been represented by some object of variable value. The clue is perhaps given by Edw. i. 1, 4: if a man could not produce satisfactory evidence for a purchase he had made "six men were to be nominated to him in the same neighbourhood to which he himself belonged; of these six he must obtain (the oath of) one for every ox (*hryðer*) or other amount of stock of the same value"; beyond this amount the number was to increase according to the value of the stock. The ox-unit appears again in Aethelstan vi 3 and vi 8. 5 as the amount of a fine for neglecting public duties[1]. In these cases the alternative payment in money is stated to be 30 pence, *i.e.* 6 West Saxon shillings. The unit may however be traced farther back, even in the laws of Ine. Thus according to cap. 38 "if a ceorl[2] and his wife have a child together and the ceorl dies, the mother is to have her child and bring it up; 6 sh. is to be given her for its support, a cow in summer and an ox in winter." In Ine's laws the sum of 6 sh. is equivalent to 24 pence. Unfortunately an element of doubt is introduced by the cow; for, in later times at all events, the cow is worth less than the ox[3]. Yet there can be no doubt that the purchasing power of silver was much greater at the end of the seventh century than in the time of

[1] So also as a fine for refusing to pay ecclesiastical dues in the North. Priests' Law, cap. 59.

[2] The word *ceorl* should perhaps be translated by 'husband' here, but there can be little doubt that the payment is regulated for people of the ceorlish class.

[3] Cf. Aethelstan vi. 6. 2, *Duns.* 7.

Aethelstan or later[1]. The valuation of the ox at
24 pence therefore can hardly be thought improbable.
But in cap. 70 there seems to be a trace of a still
lower reckoning. Among the charges due from an
estate of ten hides we find as alternative items 'two
full grown oxen (*hriðeru*) or ten wethers.' The
wether can hardly have been worth more than one
shilling (four pence) at this time, for in cap. 55 it is
stated that a ewe with her lamb is to be valued at
one shilling until a fortnight after Easter, and elsewhere we find no trace of any difference in price
between the wether and the ewe[2]. It would seem
then that the ox had been valued at five shillings or
20 pence, though of course this reckoning may have
become antiquated by the time of Ine's laws. We
may note in passing that if the same price prevailed
in Kent the (silver) shilling of that kingdom would
represent an ox[3], and consequently the Kentish
ceorl's wergeld would represent 100 oxen. These
results, it will be seen, agree perfectly with the
conclusions to which we were brought above
(p. 61 f.) when considering the value of the ox in
gold.

I suspect then that the ox was the object by
which the *mund* and the oath of the West Saxon

---

[1] This may be seen (*e.g.*) from Ine 55. The rise in the price of
the sheep may very well have contributed to the change in the
value of the shilling.

[2] Cf. p. 14 and footnote.

[3] I have suggested above (p. 59 f.) that the Kentish coins were
originally of lower standard than those of Wessex and Mercia; but
there is of course no necessity to suppose that this lower standard
was maintained permanently.

ceorl were regulated, and that the calculations which
state the value of these at 5 sh. or 5 hides are
survivals from the time when the price of the ox
was 5 sh.　If so, the difference between the *mund* of
the West Saxon ceorl and that of the Kentish ceorl
(6 Kentish sh., *i.e.* six oxen) is a striking illustration
of the superior economic position of the latter.

§ 5.　*The value of the wergelds in oxen.*

It will be convenient now to consider the value
of the West Saxon and Mercian wergelds when paid
in oxen.　In the time of Aethelstan, when the ox
was valued at one mancus or thirty pence and when
the West Saxon shilling contained five pence, the
figures must have been for the *twelfhynde man*
200 oxen, for the *sixhynde man* (if this class still
survived in Wessex) 100 oxen, and for the ceorl
33 (strictly 33⅓) oxen.　If the ox was valued at the
same amount in Mercia, the corresponding figures
must have been for the *twelfhynde man* 160 oxen, for
the *sixhynde man* 80 oxen, and for the ceorl 26
(strictly 26⅔) oxen.　These figures are hardly open
to question, though it may of course be doubted
whether wergelds were usually paid in oxen at this
time[1].

Now, if we turn back to the time of Ine's laws,
we see that the ox was apparently valued at six
shillings and that the shilling contained four pence

---

[1] In later times (perhaps the twelfth century) according to
Hen. 76. 7 one horse and forty sheep were included in the ceorl's
wergeld ; the rest was paid in money.

in Wessex as well as in Mercia. The wergelds therefore at this time would be the same in both kingdoms, viz. 200 oxen for the *twelfhynde man*, 100 oxen for the *sixhynde man*, and 33 oxen for the ceorl. Further, if we are right in believing that at some previous time the ox had been valued at five shillings, the wergelds would then amount to 240 oxen, 120 oxen and 40 oxen respectively. It is quite possible however that the statements of the wergelds in terms of money do not go back so far as this; for we have seen that the terms *twelfhynde, sixhynde* and *twihynde* are of rare occurrence in Ine's laws.

It may be noticed that these figures differ greatly from those given by Mr Seebohm (*Tribal Custom,* p. 493 ff.). According to him the West Saxon shilling contained five sceattas in the seventh century. The *twelfhynde* wergeld would therefore already amount to 6000 sceattas. At a ratio 10 : 1 this sum would represent 600 gold tremisses, *i.e.* 200 gold solidi, an amount identical with the wergeld of the Frankish freeman. As the ox was valued at two solidi in the laws of the Ripuarii and Burgundians, it may be concluded that the wergeld of the West Saxon *twelfhynde man* amounted to 100 oxen. This explanation, it will be seen, necessitates our believing that the value of the ox in gold was nearly twice as great in the seventh century as it was in the tenth century[1], and, further, that the wergeld of the

---

[1] About 126 gr. or 140 gr. (according to the standard in use) as against 70 gr. It should be added that Mr Seebohm (*op. cit.,* p. 18) seems to have been under a misapprehension about the

twelfhynde man had risen in the intervening period from 100 oxen to 200 oxen. But surely these suppositions are extremely improbable. Mr Seebohm's calculations seem to me to have been made by a wrong method. As the monetary statements of Ine's laws are invariably expressed in terms of silver currency[1], we surely ought, so far as possible, to estimate the value of the ox in silver rather than to translate the statements into terms of gold currency at an (apparently) assumed ratio[2]. Moreover it is clearly inadmissible to reckon by the continental gold value of the ox, for as a rule the price of the ox on the Continent was quite twice as great as it was in England[3].

With the evidence at our disposal the relative value of gold and silver in Ine's time seems to be much more difficult to determine than the silver value of the ox. We have seen that in the tenth century the ox was valued at a mancus. Further, it has been suggested above (p. 53 ff.) that the Kentish

mancus. It is very curious that all recent English writers appear to have gone astray on this question.

[1] Indeed before the end of the tenth century there are only three passages in the laws (Alfr. and Guth. 2, 3 and Aethelstan VI. 6. 2) which contain statements in terms of gold. Only one of these has reference to the payment of wergelds, and the wergeld in question seems to be of foreign origin (cf. p. 50).

[2] I have not been able to find any reason for the choice of the ratio 10 : 1.

[3] The gold values have already been discussed. In regard to silver Mr Seebohm (*op. cit.*, p. 189) gives authorities for 5 sol., 8 sol. and 10 sol. (*i.e.* 60, 96 and 120 denarii) as prices for the ox. In England, as we have seen, it was valued only at 30 pence in the tenth century.

shilling was derived from a gold coin of the same standard as the mancus, and that the same shilling represented the value of the ox. For the latter supposition we have obtained some confirmation in the last section. For the former we can hardly hope to find any direct evidence. Yet, if we may judge by the analogy of the prices which prevailed on the Continent[1], it is unlikely that the value of the ox, even in gold, had decreased between the seventh and the tenth century. Now we have seen that in Ine's time the ox was valued apparently at 24 pence, and somewhat earlier probably at 20 pence. Unfortunately we have no coins which bear Ine's name. But since no silver coins before the time of Offa exceed 21 gr., and since the coins of Aethelred, Ine's contemporary, are known (cf. p. 3 f.), we may conclude with safety that the weight of 24 pence would not appreciably exceed 500 gr. Therefore, if we may assume that the gold value of the ox was constant, the ratio is not likely to have been more than 7 : 1. According to the same mode of reckoning, when the ox was valued at 5 sh., the ratio would not exceed 6 : 1.

If the above conclusions are correct, Mr Seebohm's identification of the wergeld of the *twelfhynde man* with that of the Kentish ceorl cannot be admitted. It is true that the compensations for *mund* seem to have been originally the same (120 pence or sceattas)

---

[1] As the mancus was equated with 30 denarii (cf. p. 66), the ox would be much dearer when it cost eight or ten silver solidi (see the last note) than in former times when it was valued at two gold solidi.

in both cases. In regard to wergelds however the Kentish ceorl clearly corresponds rather to the West Saxon *sixhynde man*. Even this is a curious fact. For an explanation we shall have to consider the meaning of the terms *gesiðcund* and *eorlcund*. But before entering on this question it will be convenient to discuss the position of the various state officials.

CHAPTER V.

THE EARL.

§ 1. *The English and Latin terms for 'Earl.'*

THE most important of the officials was the earl. This title goes back in the form *eorl* to the time of Cnut, in whose Laws it appears twice (II. 15. 2; 71). About the same time it comes into regular use in the Saxon Chronicle. Thus Thurkyll, who according to *ann.* 1017 was entrusted with the government of East Anglia, is described as *eorl* in *ann.* 1021. In *ann.* 1036 (E) we find mention of *Leofric eorl* and *Godwine eorl*, and from this time onwards the term is frequent. Before the reign of Cnut the title *eorl* does indeed occur in the Chronicle, but its use is restricted. In *ann.* 1013 we find *Uhtred eorl*, in 992 *Thorode eorl*, and in 975 *Oslac se mœra eorl.* The last named person is described as *Oslac eorl* in Edg. IV. 15. Both Uhtred and Oslac were certainly Northumbrian earls, and it is probable that Thored also belonged to that part of the country[1]. At all events he bears a Scandinavian name. In the earlier annals of the Chronicle (871, 911, 918, 920, etc.) the word *eorl* is

[1] Cf. Plummer, *Sax. Chr.* II. p. 159 f.

almost entirely restricted to persons of Scandinavian
nationality. The only exceptions occur (i) in a few
charters incorporated in the Laud MS. (*e.g. ann.* 656),
which represent the usage of the eleventh and
twelfth centuries, and (ii) in some poetical passages
(*e.g. ann.* 937) where the word appears to be used in
the old sense of 'noble' (cf. p. 111 f.). In laws anterior
to the time of Cnut the word *eorl* occurs as a title
in Edg. IV. 15, which has already been mentioned,
in Aethelred III. 12, in a code which clearly refers
to a part of England inhabited by the Danes, and
in Edw. and Guthr. 12, in which case also it may
refer to Danish magistrates. In the earlier laws
eorl with its derivatives seems to be used only in
the sense of 'noble.' Outside the Kentish laws it
occurs only twice, viz. Alfr. 4, 2, and Aethelstan VI.
Pref., both times in apparently traditional phrases *ge
ceorle ge eorle, ægðer ge eorlisce ge ceorlisce.* The undated codes in which the word occurs are *Be Griðe and
be Munde, Be Leodgeþincðum and Lage,* and *Be Werum,*
the last of which is a (probably later) variant of the
Northleoda Lagu. All of these may belong to the
eleventh century, but it may be noticed that in the
first two of these texts the word is used in semi-
poetical phraseology. In charters before the reign
of Aethelred II. the title *eorl* seems to be confined
to a small group of documents (B. 815, 883, 890)
dating from the years 946—949[1]. The names to

[1] We find also the signature *Uhtred eorl* in B. 667, a charter
professing to date from 929 or 930. It is clear however from the
list of bishops which it gives that it belongs to the same group
with B. 815, 882, 883, though the names of Aethelstan and
Wulfhelm have been substituted for those of Eadred and Oda.

which it is applied are Morcer (*Imorcer* MS.), Scule, Urm and Uhtred, all of which, except the last, are Scandinavian. Apart from the texts mentioned above the word *eorl* does not occur, so far as I know, before the time of Aethelred II. except in poetry, and there only in the sense of 'noble.' These facts show that, though the word is old and native, its use as a title was due to the influence of the foreign term *iarl* introduced by the Scandinavian invaders.

The term applied to the chief territorial officials of the English state before the time of Cnut was *aldormon* (*ealdorman*). This is a compound word signifying 'chief-man' and occurs also, apart from its technical use, in the sense of 'chief,' 'superior.' It does not appear to have been a very early formation, as it is not found in the old poetry, though its first component (*aldor*) is frequent. We find it however already in the laws of Ine, and in charters it appears frequently from the beginning of the ninth century. It seems to give way to the word *eorl* during the first half of the eleventh century, though it is still used occasionally in the laws of Cnut. No difference in usage seems to be perceptible between the two words at this period[1]. It may be noted that Byrhtnoth, who is called *ealdorman* in the Chronicle (*ann.* 993 A, 991 E), is described as *eorl* in the poem on the battle of Maldon. Again Oslac is called *eorl* in Edg. IV. 15, but his province is described as *ealdordom*.

The most usual Latin term for 'earl' both in

---

[1] Except in the document *Be Werum*; but the *Northl. Lagu* has in the corresponding passage *æðelinges* for *eorles*.

charters and historical works is *dux*. Beside this
we also find *princeps*, which is very common in
early charters. Another term of not infrequent
occurrence in later charters is *comes*. This is the
word used by Asser to translate the *aldormon* of
the Saxon Chronicle. From the time of Alfred it
seems to be applied exclusively to earls[1]. In B. 564
Alfred makes a grant to his *comes Berthulphus*; but
at the end we find the signature *Berthulphus dux* (as
also in B. 539, 558). He is probably the *Beorhtulf
ealdormon* whose death is recorded in the Chronicle
(*ann.* 897). In B. 567 Alfred grants land in Wiltshire to his *comes* Aethelhelm. Two persons of this
name sign the charter with the title *miles,* but the
grantee is more likely to be identical with the
Aethelhelm, earl of Wiltshire, who signs in B. 568
and whose death is recorded in the Chronicle (*ann.*
898). In B. 584, 590 we find mention of a *comes*
Ordlaf. The same name recurs as that of a landowner in B. 591, who may very well be identical
with the *comes*. No *minister* of this name appears
in the charters of Alfred or in those of Edward, but
an *Ordlaf dux* signs very frequently in the latter.
In B. 603 we find mention of the confirmation of
a grant to a *dux* named Aethelfrith. In the signatures the same name appears with the title *comes*
together with three others (Ordlaf, Ordgar, Beorhtulf),
which occur as the names of earls in charters of the
same period. In B. 624 mention is made of a *comes*
Hemele, but the reference is to an event long past

---

[1] The use of *comes* in the early charters will be discussed later.

and the person specified may be one of Beorhtric's
earls, whose signature is to be found in B. 258 etc.
In B. 728 a grant is made to a *comes* named Aethelstan; but this person is the well-known earl of East
Anglia, as may be seen from a note at the end of
the charter, in which he is described as *dux*. Grants
by King Edmund to persons of the same name and
title are recorded in B. 776, 777, 799, but they may
all refer to the same man. As a matter of fact the
name Aethelstan only occurs once with the title
minister in Edmund's reign (B. 753), and this person
also seems to have become an earl shortly after the
beginning of the reign. Grants to a *comes* named
Eadric occur in B. 781, 828, 834 (dating from 943
and 947). There is indeed a minister of this name
in Edmund's earlier charters, but he ceases to sign
with this title in 943 and appears thenceforth as
dux. It is hardly necessary to go further. A few of
the above examples may be somewhat doubtful,
but taking the whole number of instances into
account there can be little doubt that during this
period the title *comes* was confined to earls [1].

---

[1] It is true that no examples occur in original charters, at all
events before the middle of the tenth century; for even in B. 603
the signatures have been added subsequently. But original
charters of the tenth century are somewhat rare.

§ 2.　*The privileges and duties of the earl.*

The privileges enjoyed by the earl have for the most part been discussed in the preceding chapter. It will be sufficient here therefore to recapitulate them briefly. The compensation due to the earl for infraction of his surety (*borg*) or guardianship (*mund*) was two pounds or 96 (100) West 'Saxon shillings (Alfr. 3, cf. 15 ; Cn. II. 58), as against five pounds to be paid to the king and three pounds to the archbishop for the same offence. The corresponding compensation to be paid to an ordinary noble seems to have been 30—36 shillings (cf. p. 125). For fighting in an assembly in an earl's presence the payment due to the earl was 120 shillings (Alfr. 38). It has been suggested above (p. 118 ff.) that this hangs together with the payments for *fletgefeoht* (Ine 6), which amounted to the same sum in the case of an earl, while for the ordinary noble the compensation was 36 shillings. For *burgbryce* the compensation due to an earl was 60 sh., against 120 sh. due to the king, 90 sh. to the archbishop ånd 30 sh. to the ordinary noble for the same offence (Alfr. 40). Lastly, according to Edw. Conf. 12, the amount due to an earl, as also to the king's steward, as *manbot*, was 20 (Norman) shillings in cases where the baron received 10 shillings and the king and archbishop three marks (*i.e.* 40 Norman shillings). In all these cases the bishop is placed on the same footing as the earl.

In the *Northleoda Lagu* it is stated that the earl (*ealdorman*) had a wergeld of 8000 thrymsas, *i.e.* four times the wergeld of an ordinary thegn. Unfortunately none of the other laws give us any information on this subject. It would however hardly be safe to conclude from their silence that the earl in the South of England had no wergeld distinct from that of the ordinary noble. It may be noted that the West Saxon laws never state the king's wergeld, though it is clear from Alfr. 4 and Aethelred v. 30 that the amount was definitely fixed. On the other hand it would be equally rash to assume that the table of wergelds given in the *Northl. Lagu* held good for the South. According to the document *Be Myrcna Lage* the Mercian king's wergeld was six times that of a thegn. If then the earl's wergeld was four times as great as the latter it would be two thirds of the amount of the king's wergeld—which is hardly likely. The earl Aelfred in his will, dating from King Alfred's reign (B. 558), uses the expression *min twa wergeld*. This would seem to imply that his wergeld consisted of two distinct items, presumably to be devoted to different purposes. This was the case with the king's two wergelds, one of which, the wergeld proper, went to his relatives, while the other, the *cynebot*, went to the *leode*[1] (cf. *Northl. L.* 1, *Be Myrcna L.* 4). Now according to the *Northl. Lagu* the wergeld of an aetheling or royal prince was equal to that of the king without the *cynebot*. From this it would seem that half the total wergeld was the king's birthprice, while the other half was

---

[1] This term is never explained. We may conjecture that it means the members of the court, probably both the high officials of the kingdom (earls etc.) and the personal retinue of the king.

a consequence of the kingly office. The earl was by birth apparently an ordinary noble. At all events it is clear that an earl's sons were not necessarily earls themselves[1]. His birthprice was therefore presumably that of an ordinary noble. Then the most probable explanation of the passage in Aelfred's will is that the wergeld was doubled in virtue of the office. There is another piece of evidence which tends to support this conclusion. It has been mentioned that in regard to compensations the bishop is (in the later laws) always put on an equality with the earl. Now according to the Chronicle (*ann.* 918 A, 915 D) King Edward the Elder paid forty pounds as ransom for a bishop named Cameleac. It is of course quite possible that this sum was merely the result of a mutual agreement. But it is certainly somewhat remarkable that it is just twice the amount of the wergeld of a Mercian thegn (1200 Mercian shillings, *i.e.* twenty pounds). Cameleac seems to have been a Welsh bishop ; but if his price was reckoned according to that of an English bishop at all, it is probable that this would be done according to the Mercian reckoning.

The duties of the earl were partly of a military and partly of a civil character. In his capacity of military leader he had to command the forces of his earldom. Examples of this are to be found throughout the Saxon Chronicle, but they are especially frequent in annals of the ninth century. Thus, to

---

[1] To this question we shall have to return later. It will also be seen that most of the earls of the tenth century were thegns (*ministri*) before they became earls.

quote a few examples, we find: 837: Aethelhelm
dux (*ealdorman*) fought against the Danes *mid
Dornsœtum*; 845: *Eanulf aldorman gefeaht mid
Sumursœtum...and Osric aldorman mid Dornsœtum*;
851: *Ceorl aldermon gefeaht...mid Defenascire*; 853:
*Ealhere mid Cantwarum and Huda mid Suþrigium
gefuhton*; in E these two persons are described as
ealdormen. In his civil capacity the earl had according to Edg. III. 5 to attend (doubtless as presi-
dent) the county assembly. An earlier reference to
some such public assembly under the presidency of
an earl is to be found in Alfr. 38. Several examples
of such meetings occur in the *Historia Eliensis*.
Thus in I. 35 we find Byrhtnoth (earl of Essex) calling
an assembly of the county of Huntingdon, and in
I. 45 Aethelwine (earl of East Anglia) holding an
assembly of the county of Cambridge. Again from
Edg. IV. 15 it appears that the earl was responsible
for the carrying out of the laws within his earldom.
He was also responsible for the execution of justice
against those who had set the law at defiance. An
example is to be found in B. 1063, where an earl
named Byrhtferth in the reign of Eadred is represented as confiscating the lands of a certain Aethelstan who had been guilty of theft. In Cod. Dipl.
(Kemble) 1289 we find Leofsige, earl of Essex,
reversing a decision of the reeves at Buckingham
and Oxford. Lastly it appears from Alfr. 42. 3 that
the earl was the authority to whom application was
to be made for the redress of private wrongs when
the complainant himself was not strong enough to
bring his adversary to law.

It can hardly be doubted that some fines or some share of the fines involved in such cases as those cited above went to the earl from the earliest times[1]. In Domesday Book it is stated in connection with several of the counties that the earl received the 'third penny' in fines; but with the exception of Edw. Conf. 27, which refers to the Danelagh, the laws give us practically no information on this subject. Again, it may be inferred from the frequent use of the expression *pastus principum* in charters that the earl, like the king, was entitled to *feorm* from estates lying within his jurisdiction[2]. It is possible also, as Kemble[3] (*Saxons*

[1] The fiscal system of this period is a subject which requires separate investigation. I have only been able to touch upon it incidentally here.

[2] For examples see p. 101, footnote. Another interesting example occurs in B. 416, a Mercian charter dating from the year 836. The freedom of Hanbury monastery was bought from King Wiglaf by a grant to him of 20 hides in one place and 10 in another. One earl (Mucel) received 10 hides in compensation, while, according to the endorsement, another earl (Sigred) received 600 shillings in gold. A somewhat similar case occurs in B. 454. Such payments were intended presumably as compensation for the loss of *feorm*. It will be seen later that in very early times we occasionally find a king and a *comes* making grants together.

[3] It may here be noted that from *Hist. El.* ii. 40, Kemble inferred that a private property qualification of forty hides was required for the earl. The passage is as follows : *sed quoniam ille xl hidarum terrae dominium minime obtineret, licet nobilis esset, inter proceres tunc numerari non potuit.* His inference seems to me somewhat hazardous both on general grounds and in regard to the translation *proceres = ealdormen.* At all events I have not been able to find evidence for the existence of any such qualification in earlier times. The reference here is to the reign of Edward the Confessor.

in England, II. p. 140) pointed out, from such expressions as þæs *aldormannes gemǣre* (*mearc*), which often occur in charters, in the recitation of boundaries, that there were estates permanently and officially connected with the earldoms[1].

§ 3. *The earldoms in later times.*

The jurisdiction of the earl is a subject which requires to be treated more in detail. In Edg. III. 5 and Cnut II. 18, we find it stated that the county assembly was to be held thrice in the year, and that the bishop and the earl (*ealdorman*) were to be present. From this statement it might be inferred that in the reigns of these kings each earl normally had jurisdiction over a county[2]. But the records do not bear this out. According to the Saxon Chronicle (*ann.* 1017) Cnut divided the whole of England into four parts, one of which he kept under his own immediate jurisdiction. It is true that somewhat later we hear of a larger number of earldoms. Thus, in connection with the ravaging of Worcester in

---

[1] Possibly the much disputed *folcland* of B. 558, the disposal of which rested with the king, may have been an estate of this kind. It seems to me quite as likely that Aethelwald had been already provided for as that he was illegitimate. He may very well be identical with the Kentish earl of the same name. Aelfred also had estates in Kent (cf. B. 529).

[2] In regard to the bishops it may be noted that at some periods during the second half of the tenth century there seem to have been as many bishops as counties in the South of England. In the Midlands however, exclusive of the Danelagh and Rutland, we find only six bishops as against seventeen counties.

1041, Florence of Worcester mentions *Thuri Mediter-raneorum, Leofricum Merciorum, Godwinum West-saxonum, Siwardum Northymbrorum, Roni Magese-tensium et caeteros totius Angliae comites.* Either therefore Cnut's arrangement was soon modified, or the great earls had smaller earls under them. But, even granting this, the total number of earls evidenced for any one time during this period never even approximates to the total number of counties in England. Even the less important earldoms seem to have embraced several counties. Thus, according to the Chronicle (1048 E), Odda was made earl of Devon, Somerset, Dorset and Cornwall. We can hardly help concluding therefore that the regulation contained in Cnut II. 18, if it is to be understood as implying that each county had its own earl, was not strictly applicable to the state of things prevalent in Cnut's time. This conclusion agrees well with the fact that the passage in question is copied word for word from Edg. III. 5 and even retains the obsolescent term *ealdorman* in place of *eorl*.

We therefore naturally turn to the reign of Edgar in order to see if the regulation was applicable to the political organisation of the kingdom in his time. As a matter of fact the total number of persons who sign Edgar's charters with the title *dux* is considerable. One charter (B. 1044) contains thirteen such signatures, and there are at least three other persons who sign with the title *dux* both before and after this date. But if we examine the occurrences of these signatures we find that those which occur at all frequently are comparatively few in number. In

charters dating from the beginning of the reign we
regularly find the following names : Aelfhere, Aethelmund, Aethelstan, Aethelwold, and Byrhtnoth. To
these are to be added later the names Aelfheah and
Eadmund (first in B. 1047), Aethelwine (first in
B. 1083), Oslac (first in B. 1113), and Ordgar (first in
B. 1135). All these names occur pretty regularly in
a large number of charters. The remaining names are
of quite rare occurrence and almost entirely confined
to charters dealing with lands north-east of Watling
Street. Uhtred occurs in three charters (B. 1040,
1043, 1044), Urm in two charters (B. 1043, 1044),
Gunner in four charters (B. 1043, 1044, 1112, 1113),
and Eadulf in three charters (B. 1220, 1230, 1266—
none of which refer to the north-eastern counties).
No other name occurs in more than one charter[1]
until the last two years of Edgar's reign. A charter
granting land in Nottinghamshire to Oscytel, archbishop of York (B. 1044), gives the additional names
Leod, Mirdach, Ascured, Halfden and *Ayered.* In
B. 1052 (Yorkshire) we find *Oskytel*, in B. 1112 (ib.)
Durre, in B. 1113 (Durham) *Aelfstan, Aestan, Cytel-
bearn*, in B. 1257 (Gloucestershire) *Osgar*, and in
B. 1266 (Ely) *Malcolm*[2]. It is not to be overlooked

[1] Except in two Westminster charters (B. 1228, 1264), which
are obviously untrustworthy. The historians (Flor. Wig., Malmesbury, and the *Vita Oswaldi* (mention an *Ordmer dux* who was
father-in-law to Edgar, but as his name seems not to occur in any
charter his date is impossible to determine. Is it possible that he
owes his existence to a scribal error (*Ordmer* for *Ordgar*)? The
Aegelfleda of Flor. Wig. and Malmesbury might be due to confusion
with Edmund's second wife.

[2] *Bryctferð dux* in B. 1199 is clearly a mistake for *Bryctferð
minister.*

that many of these names are foreign (Scandinavian and Celtic).

In several cases it is possible to fix more or less definitely the provinces governed by earls whose names are given in the above list. Aelfhere is described in the *Vita Oswaldi* (Raine, *Historians of York*, I. p. 443) as *princeps Merciorum gentis* and in many Worcester charters as *dux Merciorum*. Aethelwold according to the same document (p 428) and Florence (*ann.* 964) was earl of East Anglia. Aethelwine was his brother (ib. p. 429) and appears to have succeeded him in his earldom (cf. Flor. Wig. 975, *Hist. Rames.* c. 38, *Hist. El.* I. 14 etc.)[1]. Oslac according to Symeon of Durham and the tract *De primo Saxonum Aduentu* (Sym. Dur., R. S. II. pp. 197, 382) was earl of York and the districts dependent on it, while according to the latter document Eadulf also had the government of part of Northumbria. Byrhtnoth is described by Florence (991) as *dux Orientalium Saxonum*, and from the poem it is clear that the army which he led at Maldon was that of Essex[2]. Ordgar is called by Florence *dux Domnaniae* and the same description is found in a somewhat doubtful charter (B. 1178)[3]. Aelfheah

[1] It may be noted that Aethelwine begins to sign as *dux* about the time when Aethelwold's signature disappears. In one charter indeed (B. 1135), dated 28 Dec. 964 (probably 963 according to our reckoning), both signatures appear with the title *dux*; but this document has always been regarded with suspicion.

[2] In *Hist. El.* II. 6, he is called *Northanimbrorum dux*, but this statement is not supported by any northern authority and seems to be incompatible with the position held by Byrhtnoth in the *Hist. El.* itself.

[3] These two authorities are hardly independent.

(*Elfegus*) is stated by the same two authorities to have been earl of Hampshire (*Suthamtunensium dux*), and from his will (B. 1174) it is clear that he was connected with that part of the country. Gunner is represented in B. 1113 as receiving a grant of land in the county of Durham, which would favour the supposition that he was a Northumbrian. He is possibly to be identified with Gunner the father of Thored, who is stated to have ravaged Westmoreland in 966 (Chron. E).

There seems to be no means of ascertaining precisely the provinces held by the remaining earls, though several of the names which occur most frequently are included in their number. One circumstance however fortunately enables us to decide roughly which was the part of England to which they belonged. In Edgar's earliest charters (B. 1036, 1037, 1040, 1042, 1043, 1044, 1052) the names Aelfheah and Eadmund do not occur, though they appear regularly in later charters. In five of these charters Edgar is described as king of Mercia, while in B. 1040 he signs as *rex Merciorum et Northanhymbrorum atque Brettonum*. In two charters of Eadwig dating from the same period (B. 1045, 1046) Aelfheah and Eadmund are the only persons who sign with the title *dux*. Now according to the Chronicle (B, C) Edgar became king of Mercia in 957 (cf. B. 1063), two years before Eadwig's death. The kingdom was therefore divided, Eadwig retaining Wessex while the more northern parts went to Edgar. We may conclude then with considerable

probability that the earldoms of Aelfheah and
Eadmund lay in the South, while the earls who sign
in B. 1036, 1037, 1040, 1042, 1043, 1044, must have
belonged to the other parts of England. In the case
of Aelfheah there is some evidence, as we have
already seen, that Hampshire was his earldom.
Eadmund's earldom is never indicated. It may
however be noted that the disappearance of his
signature—the last occurrence is in 963 (B. 1121)—
coincides approximately with the first appearance of
the signature *Ordgar dux*, which begins in 964
(B. 1135). He may therefore have been Ordgar's
predecessor in the earldom of Devon[1]. But are we
justified in concluding that there were only two
earldoms in the South of England at this time ? The
evidence certainly seems to point to this conclusion.
For from the time when Edgar became sole king no
new names of earls appear in his charters till the
year 963 except Aethelwine (whose case has already
been noted), Oskytel (who signs once, in a Yorkshire
charter), Eadmund and Aelfheah, though charters of
the intervening period are pretty numerous. Even
down to the year 974 there are no new names which
occur more than once except (i) in the suspicious
Westminster charters, B. 1228, 1264, and (ii) the
names Oslac, Ordgar and Eadulf, which have already
been located. It would certainly seem therefore
that Aelfheah and Eadmund or Ordgar were the only

---

[1] This cannot be regarded as certain, for not long after this
time we hear in the Chronicle (*ann.* 982 C) of the death of an earl
Eadwine in Sussex.

southern earls during the greater part of Edgar's reign. It will be seen later that in Eadwig's reign there must have been more.

Of the names which appear in charters granted by Edgar before he became sole king three (Aelfhere, Aethelwold, and Byrhtnoth) have already been located. The only other names of frequent occurrence are Aethelmund and Aethelstan. The former seems to disappear in 963, but the latter is found regularly till the last years of Edgar's reign. There seems unfortunately to be no means of locating these names with certainty. It may however be worth while to turn for a moment to the map of England north of the Thames to see what districts are not already assigned. The earldom of East Anglia was at this time of considerable size. It seems to have included not only Cambridgeshire but also apparently Northamptonshire[1]. The earldom of Essex was also very large, at all events in Aethelred's reign; for from Kemble (*Cod. Dipl.*) 1289 it appears that Buckingham and Oxford were under the jurisdiction of Leofsige, who according to (*ibid.*) 698 was earl of Essex. If this was the case also in Edgar's reign[2]

---

[1] Cf. *Hist. El.* i. 11, 34, 45, etc. From *Hist. El.* i. 35, Huntingdonshire seems to have been under the jurisdiction of Byrhtnoth. Yet several passages in the *Hist. Rames.* convey the impression that Aethelwine (of East Anglia) had some authority in this county. On the other hand it may perhaps be inferred from *Hist. El.* i. 38, 44, that Byrhtnoth had some authority in Cambridgeshire. Is it possible that the two earls had concurrent jurisdiction in certain counties? Byrhtnoth's position may have been to some extent subordinate to that of Aethelwine.

[2] It may be noted that in B. 966 (and probably also B. 964) Byrhtnoth is represented as receiving land in Oxfordshire. It is

it is clear that there is no room for the earldoms of
Aethelmund and Aethelstan in the south-eastern
Midlands. Again, the earldom of Mercia can hardly
have been small, as Aelfhere seems to have held the
premier position among the earls[1]. In the eleventh
century we find an earldom of the *Magesœtan* which
apparently corresponded to Herefordshire, though it
may have been of greater extent than the county.
Several of its earls (Ranig, Swegen, Raulf) are well
known. It is not unlikely therefore that this province
may have been an earldom under Edgar. In the
district of the 'five boroughs' also we find earls
during the eleventh century. But if we locate the
fifth of Edgar's earls here, the whole of the country
between the Humber and the Thames will be filled up.
In that case the remaining earls (Uhtred, Urm, etc.)
must be located either in Northumbria or outside
the limits of England altogether—which is hardly
likely. Unless therefore there was really another
earldom in the south-east, in addition to East Anglia
and Essex, the only district left for the fifth earldom
seems to be the north-west (Cheshire, Lancashire, etc.).

If we turn now to Eadwig's charters we find that
the largest number of earls who attest any one
charter is eleven. This number occurs in B. 1029,
a charter granting land in Nottinghamshire to

true that in Aethelred II. Pref., Woodstock is described as being
in Mercia, but in documents of this period (*e.g.* the *Vita Oswaldi*)
the eastern Midlands are also included in Mercia.

[1] It is quite possible that Aelfhere, like Aethelred at an earlier
period, may have had other earls under him. The directions given
in Edg. IV. 15 rather suggest a fourfold division of the whole kingdom, parallel to that found under Cnut (cf. p. 171).

Oscytel, archbishop of York. The charter is to be compared with one of Edgar's (B. 1044) which has been discussed above. It contains five names (*Gunnere, Urm, Leot, Uhred*—for *Uhtred,—Anfred*) which do not occur again in Eadwig's charters, though four of them are to be found in B. 1044. Apart from this case the largest number of earls who sign any of Eadwig's charters is eight, while the total number, omitting those names peculiar to B. 1029, is thirteen. Out of this number seven (Aelfhere, Aethelmund, Aethelstan, Aethelwold, Byrhtnoth, Eadmund and Aelfheah) continue to sign under Edgar and have already been discussed. The new names are Aelfric, Aelfsige, Aelfgar, Byrhtferth, Aethelsige and a second Aethelstan. This last name occurs twice in many charters of the year 956 but only in one (B. 987) of 957, which, as it bears Eadred's name, can hardly be trustworthy. The new Aethelstan is doubtless the person who was surnamed *Halfcyning* or *Semi-rex*, and the father of Aethelwold and Aethelwine. According to the *Hist. Rames.*, cap. 3, he became earl of East Anglia during the reign of King Aethelstan and lived till the reign of Edgar, though he passed his last years as a monk at Glastonbury. His signature occurs beside that of Aethelwold in several charters (B. 925, 934, 945, 946, 974, 982, 983) of the year 956[1], whence it would seem that Aethelwold was associated with his father in the government before the latter's retirement. Byrhtferth's earldom

---

[1] According to Napier and Stevenson (*Crawf. Ch.* p. 82 f.) his signature occurs also in 958, but I have not been able to find it.

is, so far as I know, never directly indicated. From
B. 1063 however it appears that Sunbury (Middlesex)
was in his earldom. As his signatures cease in 956
and Byrhtnoth's begin the same year, though the
two never occur in the same document, we may conclude with considerable probability that he was
Byrhtnoth's predecessor in the earldom of Essex[1].
Aethelsige, who was probably a son of Aethelstan
Half-king, signs charters regularly down to 958
(inclusive). As the signatures of those earls whose
jurisdiction was in the parts north of the Thames
cease in 957, Aethelsige's earldom must be located
in the south. It must however have been distinct
from those held by Eadmund and Aelfheah, as we
find all three signatures together in B. 982, 994,
1027. Moreover Aelfsige and Aelfric, though they
do not appear frequently, both sign charters in 957
and 958, after the division of the kingdom. It would
seem therefore that in these years there were not
less than five earls in the south of England. It is
true that not more than three signatures bear the
title *dux* in any one of these charters; but in B. 1005
Aelfheah is described as *dux*, while Eadmund,
Aelfric and Aelfsige sign with this title. It is clear
that some of these charters have been carelessly
copied or compiled; thus (*e.g.*) the name Eadred has
been substituted for Eadwig in B. 902 and 1022.
Consequently it is quite possible that the succession
has become obscured through corruptions in the dates

---

[1] The first dated signature of Byrhtnoth (as earl) is 29 Nov.
956 (B. 966), though that in B. 930 may be earlier.

contained in the charters[1]. Yet there can be no reasonable doubt that there were more than two earldoms in the south during these years. The signature *Aelfgar dux*[2] occurs only in two charters of 956 (B. 930, 957), in both of which it occupies the first place in the list of earls.

The only charter of Eadwig which dates from 955 (B. 917)[3] bears the signatures of the two Aethelstans, Aethelmund, Eadmund, and Byrhtferth. All these names, together with Aethelsige and Aelfgar, also appear in Eadred's charters. We may further add two names, Urm and Uhtred, which occur again in B. 1029 (cf. p. 178 f.), and a third, Morcer (*Imorcer* MS.), which is identical with a signature found in B. 1044. For the period anterior to this date it will be convenient, in order to save space, to give the names in

---

[1] The facts in regard to the occurrence of these signatures are as follows: Aelfheah signs as *dux* two charters of 956 (B. 979, 982), two charters of 957 (B. 994, 1004), and one charter of 958 (B. 1027); Aelfsige signs as *dux* five charters of 956 (B. 919, 943, 948, 958, 970), one charter of 957 (B. 1005), and one charter of 958 (B. 1032); Aelfric signs as *dux* one charter of 957 (B. 1005), and four charters of 958 (B. 902, 1022, 1033, 1034); Aethelsige signs all the above charters except B. 943, 970, 1005, 1032 ; Eadmund signs all except B. 970.

[2] In a charter of 958 (B. 1027) we find the signatures *Aelfgar dux* and *Byrhtfærh dux*, but from a comparison with other charters of this year it seems clear that *dux* is here a mistake for *minister*.

[3] In this charter we find the signatures *Aelfhere ex parentela regis minister* and *Ælfheah frater eius minister*. Aelfhere must have acquired his earldom at the beginning of 956, as his signature (with the title *dux*) is pretty regular in charters of that year. Aethelwold also must have obtained his promotion early in the year, as his signatures (as *dux*) are frequent. Those of Aelfsige, Aelfheah and Byrhtnoth are only occasional.

tabular form, regulating the order by the date of the last signature[1].

	First signature	Last signature
Aethelstan	940	974
Eadmund	949	963
Aethelmund	940	963
Morcer	946 (B. 815)	958
Uhtred	949 (B. 883)	958
Urm	949 (B. 883)	958
Aethelsige	951	958
Aethelstan	932	956
Byrhtferth	955 ?	956
Aelfgar	946	951[2]
Ealhhelm	940	951
Eadric	942	949
Scule	947 (B. 820, cf. 812)	949 (B. 883)
Osulf	946 (B. 815)	949 (B. 883)

[1] In the case of signatures which only occur rarely, the references are given. I have omitted names which occur in the following charters: two attributed to Eadred (B. 872, 873), one of which is clearly untrustworthy, while the other is really a charter of the West Saxon King Aethelred I. (cf. Napier and Stevenson, *Crawford Ch.*, p. x., note); one of Edmund (B. 779) which, though it is found in the *Textus Roffensis*, contains a very peculiar list of signatures; six of Aethelstan, viz. B. 667, which is based on charters of Eadred like B. 815, 882, 883; B. 670, 671, which are based on charters of Edmund like B. 748; and B. 737, 738 (739) and 785, which are also clearly untrustworthy. Many other charters may be spurious, but I do not think that the earls' names which they give have been invented. I have also omitted certain cases where *dux* is obviously a mistake for *minister*. Odda, who usually signs first among the *ministri* in Aethelstan's and Edmund's charters, appears as *dux* in B. 742, 775, 787, 788; so also Wulfgar in B. 775 and 787, and two other names (*Admund*, *Wllaf*) in B. 775. It is likely also that the *Eadulfus dux* of B. 747 is a mistake for *minister* (cf. B. 741), for no earl of this name is known otherwise.

[2] The question as to the identity of this person with the Aelfgar who signs under Eadwig will be discussed below (p. 187).

	First signature	Last signature
Coll	946 (B. 815)	949 (B. 883)
Grim	946 (B. 815)	949 (B. 883)
Wulfgar	934 ?[1]	946
Aethelwold	940	946
Uhtred	931 [2]	946
Hal(f)dene		946 ? (B. 812)
Aelfwold		944 (B. 796)
Aelfhere	934 ?[1]	941
Wulfstan		939 (B. 742)

Eadmund signs in B. 722, 723, 725 [3]
Aethelsige signs in B. 722, 725 [3]

	First signature	Last signature
Aelfwald	925	938
Osulf	930 ? (B. 700—703)	935 ? (B. 716, 718)
Uhtred	930 [2]	935 ? (B. 716)
Guthrum	928	935 ? (B. 716)
Urm	930	935? (B. 716, 718)

[1] Wulfgar and Aelfhere sign with the title *dux* for the first time in B. 694, a charter professing to date from 933. But this date can hardly be correct. Aelfheah signs here as Bishop of Winchester, whereas his predecessor (Beornstan) signs a charter (B. 702) of 28 May, 934 (cf. Sax. Chron. *ann.* 933, 934 A, 935 F). At all events, whatever may be the true dates, B. 694 is certainly later than B. 701—703.

[2] It is of course impossible to distinguish with certainty between the two Uhtreds. The dates here given are based on the positions in the lists of signatures which the two names occupy (cf. p. 186).

[3] These charters are hardly beyond suspicion. Together with B. 721, 724, 726, which show somewhat different lists of names, they form a group referring to Devonshire and Cornwall. B. 721 bears the date 737, while the other five have the impossible date (A.D.) *DCLXX indictione XI.* If the indiction is correct they must belong to the year 938. The presence of Edmund's signature points to the last years of the reign. It may however be noted that B. 722 seems to be another (and probably spurious) version of the grant recorded in B. 721.

	First signature	Last signature
Scule [1]	931	935 ? (B. 716)
Halfdene [2]	930? (B. 700, 701, 703)	934 (B. 702)
Inhwaer	932	934
Hadder (Hatel, etc.)	931	934
Aelfstan	930	934
Aescberht	931	934
Osferth [1]	926	934
Aldred	930	933
Thurferth	931	932
Regnwald	930	932
Gunner		931 (B. 677)
Hawerd		931 (B. 674)
Aelfred	930 (B. 669)	931 (B. 674)
Styrcaer (Srices ?)		930 (B. 1343, cf. 669)
Grim		930 (B. 669, 1343)
Fraena		930 (B. 1343)
Wulfgar	926 (B. 659)	927 (B. 660)
Ordgar	925 (B. 641)	926 (B. 659)

From this list it will be seen that the 'total number of earls whose signatures appear in Eadred's charters is seventeen, in Edmund's charters eleven, and in those of Aethelstan thirty. But there is of course no need to suppose that so many persons held the title contemporaneously. As a matter of fact the largest number of earls who appear in any one of Eadred's charters is ten (B. 883), in any of Edmund's eight[3], and in any of Aethelstan's fifteen

---

[1] Scule (*Scula*) and Osferth appear again in one of Edmund's charters (B. 779); cf. p. 182, footnote.

[2] This person may be identical with the Halfdene mentioned above.

[3] It is not clear whether B. 812 (which contains ten such signatures) belongs to the reign of Edmund or to that of Eadred. The king's name (*Æduuardus*) is obviously a mistake.

(B. 677, 689). But if we examine Eadred's charters more closely we see that the earls fall clearly into two classes. The first class, consisting of the names Osulf, Morcer, Coll, Grim, Scule, Urm and Uhtred, is practically confined to a small group of charters (B. 815, 882, 883)[1]. Five of these names appear to be Scandinavian and all of them, except Osulf, bear the title *eorl* in one or other of these charters. But it has been pointed out above (p. 161 ff.) that before the time of Aethelred II. this title seems to have been confined to the Danelagh. Osulf signs in B. 880 as *dux*, in B. 815 as *hœhgerefa*, in B. 882 as *bebb.*, and in B. 883 as *ad bebb. hehgr.*—which can hardly mean anything else than 'high reeve at Bamborough.' He is therefore in all probability the Northumbrian earl Osulf mentioned by Symeon of Durham and the *De Primo Sax. Aduentu* (Sym. Dur., R. S., II. pp. 197, 382). There is reason therefore to believe that seven out of Eadred's seventeen earls belonged to the north-east of England. The remaining ten names are all of frequent occurrence except Byrhtferth, who only appears in the latest charters of the reign. Edmund's charters, if we exclude B. 779,812, contain no Scandinavian names. All the ten earls sign frequently except Aelfwold, whose signature occurs only once (B. 796). In Aethelstan's charters we are again confronted with a number of Scandinavian names. These persons do not indeed sign with the title *eorl*, but we can hardly doubt that the bearers of such names at this period were of Scandinavian blood. For it is very improbable that

---

[1] Scule occurs also in B. 812 and Osulf in B. 880.

English noblemen who had been born in the ninth
century, or even in the first years of the tenth
century, would take Scandinavian names. We may
therefore locate thirteen of Aethelstan's earls in the
Danelagh, viz. Guthrum, Urm, Scule[1], Halfdene,
Thurferth, Inhwaer, Hadder, Regnwald, Gunner,
Hawerd, Styrcaer, Grim and Fraena. Again it may
be noted that two of the English names, Aldred and
Uhtred, frequently occur side by side. It is very
likely that they are the two sons of Eadulf of Bamborough mentioned in the *Historia de S. Cuthberto*,
cap. 22 (Sym. Dur., R. S. I. p. 209; cf. Sax. Chron.
ann. 924 A, 926 D). When the name Aldred disappears its place is taken by Osulf. It has been
stated[2] that Osulf of Bamborough (see above) was
the son and successor of Aldred. If this is correct it
appears that we may reduce the number of English
earls, south of the Danelagh, to fourteen.

From what has been said it seems that the total
number of earls, excluding Danes and Northumbrians, whose signatures appear in the charters, was
in Eadred's reign ten, in Edmund's also ten, and in
Aethelstan's fourteen. Of the ten earls in Eadred's
reign not more than seven ever appear together.

[1] Perhaps the person who, according to the *Hist. de S. Cuthberto* 23 (Sym. Dur., R. S. I. p. 209) occupied part of Durham.
Thurferth may be the Danish earl of Northampton, and Regnwald
possibly the (Norwegian) prince in Northumbria mentioned by the
Sax. Chron, *ann.* 942, 944 A (cf. 923 E, 924 A).

[2] Freeman, *Norman Conquest*, I. p. 645; Plummer, Sax. Chron.
II. p. 132. I have not been able to find the authority for this
statement, but it is somewhat confirmed by the fact that in the
lists of signatures Osulf's name usually occupies the position
previously held by that of Aldred.

Byrhtferth's signature begins towards the close of the reign[1], after the disappearance of Aelfgar, while Eadmund and Aethelsige seem to take the place of Eadric and Wulfgar. We may therefore regard the three later earls as the successors of the three earlier ones. Then, as Eadmund and Aethelsige were southern earls (cf. pp. 176, 180), Eadric and Wulfgar will also belong to the south. Aelfgar would seem to have been Byrhtferth's predecessor in Essex. This conclusion is to some extent confirmed by his will (B. 1012), which shows at any rate that his connections lay with the south-eastern Midlands[2]. Of the remaining four earls three, the two Aethelstans and Aethelmund, have already been mentioned (p. 177 ff.), and it has been pointed out that they all belonged to the Midlands[3]. The fourth, Ealhhelm, was according

---

[1] It occurs in B. 887, a charter which bears the date 950. But this must be wrong. The signatures of bishops (Aelfsige, Aelfwold) contained in it show that it cannot be earlier than 953.

[2] Aethelstan 'Half-king' was presumably earl of East Anglia at this time. But the two signatures of *Aelfgar dux* in 956 (p. 181) present a difficulty, if this person is to be identified with the Aelfgar of Eadred's reign. One of these signatures occurs in a charter (B. 930), beside that of Byrhtnoth. Is it possible that there were at this time three earldoms in the South-eastern Midlands? Or was Aelfgar a 'retired' earl? The author of the will was the Aelfgar whose daughter was married to King Edmund.

[3] In charters between 949 and the end of the reign we find only one signature of *Aethelstan dux*. Hence there is a certain amount of doubt as to the identity of these two Aethelstans with the two who sign under Eadwig. On the other hand it must be pointed out that charters dating from these years are few in number, while in the numerous charters of 956 the two Aethelstans sign pretty regularly. No *minister* of this name signs during the period in question, though one is mentioned in B. 885.

to the poem on the battle of Maldon (l. 218) a Mercian earl. It appears then that of the seven earldoms evidenced during Eadred's reign five belonged to the Midlands and two to the south.

Edmund's later charters show nearly the same list of earls as the earlier charters of Eadred. In place of Aelfgar, which does not occur, we find two names, Aethelwold and Uhtred. The former seems from his will (B. 819), which dates from Eadred's reign, to have belonged to the south. It is probable therefore that Uhtred was Aelfgar's predecessor in Essex. Eadric seems to have taken the place of Aelfhere in 941 or 942. If we except the name Aelfwold, which occurs only once, the total number of earls at any one time seems to have been eight, five belonging to the Midlands and three (including Aethelwold) to the south. Four earls (Aethelmund, Aethelwold, Ealhhelm, and one Aethelstan) appear to have been created in 940, as their signatures occur with the title *minister* in certain charters of that year (B. 753, 762).

We have hardly sufficient materials for determining satisfactorily the succession of the earls in Aethelstan's reign. Of those who sign under Edmund four appear as earls in Aethelstan's later charters, viz. Aethelstan, Uhtred, Aelfhere, and Wulfgar. We have seen that the first two of these probably belonged to the Midlands and the last two to the south. Besides these we find the signature *Aelfwold dux* regularly from the beginning of the reign to 938, but at this point it ceases. It is very doubtful therefore whether this can be the Aelfwold who signs once in

944[1]. In a somewhat doubtful group of charters of
uncertain date but belonging to the last years of the
reign (cf. p. 183, note) we find Eadmund and Aethelsige, and in a charter of 939 Wulfstan. In earlier
charters there occur the names Osferth, Aescberht,
Aelfstan, Aelfred, Ordgar, and another Wulfgar. But
it must be noted that of these fourteen names not
more than six occur in any one charter. Nor indeed
does there appear to be any satisfactory evidence
that more than six of these persons were holding
office at the same time. In regard to the last years
of the reign (937—940) there is perhaps a certain
element of doubt, but this is hardly present in
charters dating from before 937. In the earliest
charters of the reign we find only Ordgar, Wulfgar,
Aelfwold, and Osferth. The two first disappear
before the occurrence of any new names. The name
Aelfred ceases before the first appearance of Aethelstan, and the names Osferth, Aelfstan, and Aescberht[2]
all disappear before the first mention of Aelfhere,
Wulfgar, Eadmund or Aethelsige. Charters of the
years 930—934 are so numerous and so fully attested
in other respects, that it can hardly be doubted that
for these years at all events we have a complete list

---

[1] Possibly, as was suggested above in the case of Aelfgar, he
may have retired in 938.

[2] These names occur for the last time in B. 702 (701, 703),
while Aelfhere and Wulfgar appear as earls first in B. 694, which
is certainly later (p. 183, note). They are perhaps to be identified
with *ministri* of these names who sign in B. 701, 703. Osferth
(*Offerdus*) appears again in B. 738 (739), but as this charter likewise
contains the signature of Bishop Beornstan, it must be earlier than
B. 694.

of earls. If that is so, the number, excluding Danes and Northumbrians, cannot have exceeded six.

Before the beginning of Aethelstan's reign it is unfortunately impossible to obtain any satisfactory information regarding the succession of earls, for from the latter part of Edward's reign hardly any charters are preserved[1]. A Mercian charter (B. 632) issued by Aethelfled, probably between 911 and 917, gives the names Aethelferth and Aelfred, the latter of whom may be identical with the Aelfred who signs under Aethelstan. Seven charters (B. 620, 621, 623–5, 627, 628) of the year 909 give altogether seven English names of earls including Ordgar and Osferth, possibly the same persons who sign again during the following reign. But this is not a complete list of earls for the year in question, for it does not include the Mercian earls Aethelred and Aethelferth. The English part of Britain must therefore have contained at least nine earls in the year 909. At an earlier period of the reign there were still more. A charter of 904 (B. 611) gives nine earls, and a charter of 901 (B. 595) eleven, and it is certain that neither of these lists is complete. It is clear then that at the beginning of Edward's reign there must have been an earl for almost every one of the southern counties. For the kingdom was at this time of much smaller extent than it was at the end of the reign. Moreover during Aethelred's lifetime, and indeed probably until the deposition of Aelfwyn, Mercia had a separate council of its own. The list

[1] For a charter (B. 635) which professes to date from 921 cf. Napier and Stevenson, *Crawf. Ch.* p. 74.

in B. 595 probably includes the signatures of one or two Mercian earls (*e.g.* Aethelferth, though not Aethelred), but on the other hand it omits the Kentish earl Sighelm who signs as early as 889 (B. 562), and whose death is recorded in the Saxon Chronicle (A) *ad ann.* 905 (probably for 902).

The evidence of Alfred's charters is too scanty to repay investigation. But it is clear from the Chronicle and other historical works that there were earls in practically all the southern counties during the latter half of the ninth century. Sometimes we find such expressions as *Æðelm Wiltunscire ealdormon* (Chron. 898), *Ceorl Domnaniae comes* (Asser); more frequently the form used is (*e.g.*) *Beorhtulf ealdormon on East Seaxum* (Chron. 897). In other passages we find the statement that a certain earl fought with the militia of a certain county, *e.g. Eanulf aldorman gefeaht mid Sumursætum* (Chron. 845). From a comparison of passages it seems pretty clear that each earl as a rule led the forces of his own county. Thus with the passage last quoted we may compare Asser, cap. 12 : *Eanwulf Summurtunensis pagae comes.* Again in Chron. 853 we find it stated that Ealhhere fought *mid Cantwarum,* and it is abundantly clear from the charters that Ealhhere was a Kentish earl. We may further compare the account of the operations of the Kentish force given in the Chronicle (A) *ad ann.* 905[1]. If we put

---

[1] The only case where the same earl's name appears in connection with the forces of two different counties is that of Osric (845 Dorset, 860 Hampshire). There is no evidence from the charters for two earls of this name. But even if we grant that it is the

together all this evidence we obtain the names of earls for the following list of counties:

Devon : Ceorl (851)[1], Aethelred (901).
Dorset : Aethelhelm (837), Osric (845).
Somerset: Hun (826, *H. Hunt.*), Eanulf (845).
Wiltshire : Aethelhelm (898).
Berkshire : Aethelwulf (871).
Hampshire : Osric (860), Wulfred (897).
Surrey : Huda (853).
Essex : Beorhtulf (897).
Kent : Ealhhere (853), Ceolmund (897), Sigulf and
    Sighelm (905).

The only southern counties which are not represented are Cornwall and Sussex. In the former case there is no evidence for the existence of an earl. Indeed this county was not English in any sense during the period under discussion. It is disregarded in the Burghal Hidage, and even in the time of Aethelstan its people seem to have been treated as a distinct nation[2]. Sussex however certainly had earls during the eighth, and again during part, at least, of the tenth century (cf. p. 176). It is therefore probably a mere accident that the name of no earl of this county has been recorded during the ninth century. Kent seems to have had two earls. Sigulf and Sighelm, who fell at 'the Holme,' are both

same person, is it not possible that he may have been transferred from one earldom to another? It may be noted that in charters of 850—854 we find mention of two earls, named Aethelbald and Aethelberht. Are these not the king's sons?

[1] The references are to the Saxon Chronicle, unless otherwise stated.

[2] Cf. Malmesbury, *Gesta Regum* (R. S.), i. p. 148.

described as earls (Chron. A. 905), and both sign charters with the title *dux*. Again, the former signs with this title as early as 889 (B. 562), while in Chron. 897 we find recorded the death of a Kentish earl named Ceolmund. There must therefore have been two earls in Kent for a number of years. It will be seen later that this was apparently the case also during the first half of the ninth century.

In Mercian charters dating from the time before this kingdom lost its independence we find the signatures of a considerable number of earls. But even under Aethelred and Aethelfled, and probably down to the deposition of Aelfwyn, Mercia still had a separate council of its own. Indeed Aethelred and Aethelfled[1] seem to have issued charters in much the same manner as the Kentish king Cuthred did at the beginning of the ninth century. From the signatures to these charters (*e.g.* B. 552, 557) it appears that about the years 884—888 Aethelred had five other earls under him. Even in a document dating from 896 (B. 574) we find mention of four apparently Mercian earls—Aethelred, Aethelwulf, Aethelferth, and Alhhelm. The first is the well known 'Lord of Mercia.' The second is perhaps to be identified with the brother of Ealhswith, whose death is recorded in Chron. A. 903. His earldom is never stated, but from B. 575 it seems likely that

---

[1] The earliest of these charters (B. 551, 552) do not bear Aethelfled's name and were probably issued by Aethelred before his marriage. Aethelfled appears first in B. 547, which, if the indiction is correct, dates from 887. The year given by the text (880) can hardly be right in any case.

Worcester lay within it. Aethelferth's signatures continue apparently after Aethelred's death (B. 632). From B. 603, 606 it appears that he had inherited estates in Buckinghamshire, which subsequently were in the possession of Aethelstan 'Half-King.' The latter is described in a supplementary note to B. 606 as *filius Etheredi*, and it has been suggested with some probability[1] that -*redi* may be a corruption of -*ferdi*. Of Alhhelm nothing seems to be known, though he may possibly be the person to whom Aethelfled makes a grant in B. 583 under the formula *amico meo*. From this time until the reign of Edmund we find no mention of Mercian earls, and it is consequently impossible to decide with certainty what earls held jurisdiction north of the Thames. From what has been said above (p. 188 ff.) however it seems probable that Aelfred and the later Uhtred, as well as Aethelstan 'Half-King,' were included in their number.

It may now be convenient to summarise briefly the results of this discussion. Under Alfred and his predecessors, probably every one of the southern counties, except Cornwall, had its own earl. Kent seems to have had two, Mercia at least four earls. Under Edward, the number of earls seems to have been greatly reduced, for from the very beginning of Aethelstan's reign we find no evidence for more than six earls at any one time—apart from Danes and Northumbrians. Edmund in his first year seems to have raised the number of earls to eight.

---

[1] Napier and Stevenson, *Crawf. Ch.* p. 83.

If we exclude Northumbrians and refer all persons with Scandinavian names to Northumbria and the district of the Five Boroughs—and, as their signatures are always more or less exceptional, we are probably justified in so doing—we do not find this number exceeded during the rest of the tenth century, except for a short period (about two years) during the reign of Eadwig. Under Aethelstan we have no means of determining the provinces held by most of the earls. It seems probable, however, that at least two of the six earls belonged to the Midlands and at least two to the South. Under Edmund there seem to have been five earls in the Midlands and three in the South. Eadred appears to have reduced the latter number to two. During the first part of Edgar's reign also five earls belonged to the Midlands and two to the South.

Are we to suppose that these six, seven or eight earls held between them the whole of English Britain, or that certain portions of it lay outside their jurisdiction? The question is one which cannot be answered with certainty. But we have seen that under Aethelred II. the earldoms of East Anglia and Essex apparently took up between them the whole of the eastern Midlands exclusive of the Danelagh. Further we have seen that Ordgar is called by Flor. Wig. *dux Domnaniae*; but his successor Aethelweard is described in Kemble (*Cod. Dipl.*) 698 as *Occidentalium Prouinciarum dux*, which implies jurisdiction over more than one county. Again Aelfheah is called by Flor. Wig. *Suthamtunensium dux*; but one of his successors is described in the same charter as *Wentanensium Prouinciarum dux.* It may be noted that we find no mention of any earls in Kent after the battle of the Holme. Is it possible that after this Kent was added to one of the other earldoms[1]? To these questions we shall have to return later. We may, however, at the present moment note the case of Mercia. Edmund in his first year created four new earls, three of whom (Ealhhelm, Aethelmund, Aethelstan) apparently had jurisdiction in the Midlands. The total number of earls in this part of the country was then five. Now the number of bishoprics here was also five at this time, viz. London, Dorchester, Worcester, Hereford, and Lichfield; for the bishopric of Elmham seems not to have been restored before the last years of Eadred's reign. It is hardly likely that the diocese of London coincided with the earldom of Essex, or the diocese of Dorchester with the earldom of East Anglia, but it is very probable that the area of the two dioceses combined[2] coincided with the area of the combined earldoms. It is therefore perhaps worth suggesting that the other three earldoms may have corresponded to the dioceses of Worcester, Hereford, and Lichfield. In later times we hear of a *dux Hwicciorum* and a *dux Magesetensium,* just as we hear of the *episcopus Hwicciorum* and (in Florence) of the *praesules*

---

[1] It does not follow from the importance of Kent that it was valuable as an earldom, for a very large part of it was Church property. See the Addenda.

[2] The diocese of Dorchester also included part of the Danelagh, but this may have been a later addition.

Magesetensium. If the analogy is correct the whole
of Mercia must have been included in the three
earldoms.

It has been remarked that the number of earls
seems not to have been quite constant. In Aethelstan's reign we find apparently six, in Edmund's
eight, in Eadred's seven. If the whole of English
Britain was included in the earldoms, we must of
course conclude that an earldom has been divided,
when we see an increase in the number of earls.
Such may have been the case with Mercia at the
beginning of Edmund's reign. Similarly, when we
find a diminution in the number of earls, we must
suppose that two earldoms have been united or that
one of them has been divided between two (or more)
others. The apparent variation between two and
three earldoms in the South is, however, somewhat
difficult to explain, and it would hardly be wise to
leave out of account the possibility that an earldom
might be temporarily suppressed, the king retaining
the comital rights in his own hand.

EXCURSUS II.

THE DANELAGH.

The term *Dena Lagu* is of frequent occurrence in laws of the eleventh century and is found as far back as the Laws of Edward and Guthrum (cap. 7). It is clear enough that the term has a geographical meaning, but the definition of the territories to which it is applied is attended with some difficulty. Many documents of the twelfth and thirteenth centuries give a list of thirty-two counties classified under the heads *Wessexenelage, Mirchenelage* and *Danelage*. Several of these documents further give the number of hides contained by some of the counties (thirteen in all), a set of statistics which are generally known as the 'County Hidage.' According to Dr Liebermann (*Leges Anglorum*, pp. 7 f.), this list is derived from a text written in English and dating from the eleventh century. The various forms in which it is preserved do not agree absolutely, but there can be little doubt that in the original text the distribution of the counties was as follows: Wessex nine counties, viz. Sussex, Surrey, Kent, Berkshire, Wiltshire, Hampshire, Somersetshire, Dorsetshire, Devonshire ; Danelagh fifteen counties, viz. Yorkshire, Nottinghamshire, Derbyshire, Leicestershire, Lincolnshire, Northamptonshire, Huntingdonshire, Cambridgeshire, Norfolk, Suffolk, Essex, Bedfordshire, Hertfordshire, Middlesex, Buckinghamshire ; Mercia eight counties, viz. Herefordshire, Gloucestershire, Worcestershire, Shropshire, Cheshire, Staffordshire, Warwickshire, Oxfordshire.

In the laws of the tenth century it is frequently stated (Edw. and Guth. *passim* ; Edg. IV. 2, 12, 13 ; Aethelred VI. 37) that the Danes observed laws of their own. But it must not be assumed forthwith that the Danelagh of this period was geographically identical with that of later times. Indeed there can be no doubt that the Danes of the Laws of Edward and Guthrum were the inhabitants of Guthrum's kingdom, *i.e.* the districts east of the Lea and Watling Street. Buckinghamshire and Middlesex were not included in this kingdom ; indeed, so far as we know, these counties were never settled by the Danes. If we turn to the time of Edgar and Aethelred, we find all the counties of the South-eastern Midlands, including Northamptonshire, under English administration (cf. p. 177). In the *Vita Oswaldi* (Raine, I. p. 444) they are described as *orientales Merciorum populi*[1]. About the same time Oxfordshire appears to have been included in the same earldom with Essex, Middlesex and probably Huntingdonshire (cf. p. 177 ff.). It seems unlikely therefore that any of these counties were included in the Danelagh during the period in question[2].

In Edw. Conf. 30 we find the curious statement that the counties of York, Nottingham, Leicester, Lincoln and (according to one text) Northampton were *sub lege Anglorum*. It is added that what elsewhere was called *hundredum* was in these counties called *wapentagium*. This remark is true of the first four counties and also of Derbyshire but not of Northamptonshire[3]. Now it is generally supposed that *Anglorum* in this passage is a mistake for *Danorum*[4]. If so, we have a trace of

[1] The reference is apparently to the districts about Ramsey and Peterborough.

[2] Of course those counties which had formerly been under Danish government may individually have preserved Danish characteristics in their administrative and financial systems. But Danish influence seems to have been felt beyond these counties.

[3] Except in two cases where both terms occur.

[4] Cf. Edw. Conf. 33, where the *Lex Danorum* is said to have prevailed also in Norfolk, Suffolk and Cambridgeshire, except in regard to the *maior emendatio forisfacturae*. But the accuracy of this as a general statement is much to be doubted. In Cnut II. 71 East Anglia is distinguished from the Danish districts. Again, in regard to the treatment of land, if we may judge from Domesday

a smaller and probably older Danelagh than that recorded in the eleventh century text described above. Indeed it seems extremely probable that this was the part of the country governed by Danish law in the time of Edgar and Aethelred II. Aethelred's third code, which is entirely Danish both in its monetary statements and in its official terminology (*eorl*, *on wæpentake*), was clearly intended for the district of the Five Boroughs[1], while Yorkshire had been a Danish stronghold from the year 875, though from the time of Eadred onwards its earls may have been of English blood.

It seems probable then that geographically the meaning of the term *Dena Lagu* changed at least twice. At the beginning of the tenth century it denoted Guthrum's kingdom, together no doubt with the north-eastern districts (Yorkshire, Nottinghamshire, Derbyshire, Leicestershire, and Lincolnshire), which perhaps did not own his supremacy. From the time of Aethelstan onwards it was probably confined to the latter group of counties[2]. Lastly, at some time during the

Book, East Anglian custom differed from that of Cambridgeshire. Danish characteristics were no doubt prominent in both districts, *e.g.* the *forisfactura hundredi* (*i.e.* 120 ores or eight pounds, cf. Edw. Conf. 27, Aethelred III. 1) in Cambridgeshire (cf. Thorpe, *Dipl.* p. 611 f.). But these may be regarded as local survivals from the time of Danish government. They are not sufficient to prove the continuance of Danish autonomy in these districts.

[1] Nottingham, Derby, Leicester, Stamford, and Lincoln ; cf. Sax. Chron. *ad ann.* 942.

[2] Northamptonshire may have remained Danish somewhat longer than the more southern districts. According to the Chronicle its earl, Thurferth, submitted voluntarily to King Edward. If this is the same person whose signatures occur in Aethelstan's charters during 931 and 932 it can hardly have been included in an English earldom before the latter date. In East Anglia proper it is also not quite certain when Danish government came absolutely to an end. The statements of Malmesbury (*Gesta Regum*, R. S., I. p. 98) are hardly of such a character that we can place much reliance on them. In *Hist. El.* I. 49 we hear of a *comes Scule*, presumably a Danish earl, who owned estates in

eleventh century an artificial redistribution of the country was effected, whereby the Danelagh was extended so as to include fifteen counties. This later extension of the term may possibly be connected with the administrative changes introduced by Cnut (cf. p. 171)[1].

Suffolk. Now this name is found among the earls who sign under Aethelstan and again among those who sign under Eadred. It has been suggested above (p. 186, footnote) that the Scule of Aethelstan's time was a Northumbrian. Are we to suppose that the Scule of Eadred's reign was an East Anglian earl? In that case this province must have remained under a Danish governor until after 949, while the original earldom of Aethelstan 'Half-king' must have lain further to the west. But these identifications cannot be regarded as at all certain. There may have been more than two earls of this name.

[1] The distinction drawn between East Anglia and the Danish districts in Cnut II, 71 tells somewhat in favour of a later date. The hidage statistics may of course have been taken over from an earlier survey—a supposition which is perhaps somewhat supported by the fact that they are limited to thirteen counties.

CHAPTER VI.

THE ADMINISTRATIVE SYSTEM.

§ 1. *The Counties of the Midlands.*

IN the last chapter it has been seen that all the southern counties with the exception of Cornwall were already in existence in the ninth century, and that during this period each of them seems to have had an earl of its own. The midland counties on the other hand are rarely mentioned in the Chronicle before the last years of Aethelred II. Later works however offer apparently trustworthy statements as to their existence somewhat before this time. Thus the *Historia Eliensis* speaks of the counties of Cambridge, Huntingdon, and Northampton in connection with events which occurred either before or very shortly after the death of Edgar. Before we proceed to enquire as to the probable date at which these counties were formed we must remember that a considerable part of the Midlands did not come under the West Saxon dynasty before the latter half of Edward's reign. The first serious advancing of the frontier seems to have taken place about 912[1], while by 918 the war was being carried into the Danish strongholds in the north-east. But we have already seen that by the end of this reign the total number of English earls (outside Northumbria) appears to have been reduced to six. We may therefore conclude with certainty that the majority of the midland counties never had earls of their own from the time when they first came under the West Saxon dynasty.

The counties of Northampton, Huntingdon, Cambridge, and Bedford seem to be of Danish origin. In the Chronicle (918—921 A) all these towns are mentioned, apparently as centres to which the inhabitants of the surrounding districts owed allegiance[2]. The district dependent on Northampton may very well have corresponded to the present county, for it extended as far as the Welland, the present northern boundary of Northamptonshire. No other town in these counties is spoken of in the same manner. Moreover Cambridge, Huntingdon, and Northampton each possessed a *here*, which, like the Northumbrian *here* mentioned in Edg. IV. 15, was doubtless not only a military but also a political organisation[3]. Indeed it seems extremely probable that during the period of Danish government each of these districts had an earl of its own. We hear of a *Thurcytel eorl* at Bedford, a *Thurferth eorl*

---

[1] The chronology of this period is unfortunately very obscure. (cf. Plummer, *Sax. Chron.* II. pp. 116 f.).

[2] Cf. *Hist. El.* I. 35: *Toli comes prouinciam de Huntedune... obtinuerat.*

[3] The use of the word in this sense is Scandinavian. We may compare the *allsheriar þing, allsheriar lög*, etc. of Iceland.

belonging to Northampton, and a *Toglos eorl* (*Toli comes*) and a *Mannan eorl* at Huntingdon. It seems very probable therefore that the constitution and demarcation of these counties dates from before the time when they were absorbed into the English realm. On the other hand there seems to be no evidence for the existence of any corresponding territorial divisions before the great invasion. They can hardly be identified with any of the units recorded in the 'Tribal Hidage' (cf. p. 263 ff.)[1].

§ 2.   The 'Burghal Hidage' and the 'County Hidage.'

The earliest evidence for any territorial divisions corresponding to the more western counties of the midlands is to be found in the 'Burghal Hidage' (B. 1335). This text, which occurs only in late and extremely corrupt MSS., gives a survey of a large part of England divided into districts each of which is attached to some place contained in it, for the most part well-known towns. It will be convenient here for future reference to give the substance of the survey[2].

---

[1] Mr Corbett (*Trans. R. Hist. Soc.* XIV. p. 200) has identified with Northamptonshire the five districts of *Arosætna*, *Bilmiga*, *Widerigga*, *East Willa* and *West Willa*, each of which has 600 hides.

[2] For further information see Liebermann, *Leges Anglorum*, pp. 9 f.; Maitland, *Domesday Book and Beyond*, pp. 502 ff. In general the figures of Birch's text seem to be the most probable. I have therefore taken this as the standard throughout. It is to be observed however that in three cases the abbreviation for *hund*

		Hides	
To Heorepeburan (not identified)		324	
Hastings		1500?	(15 B, 500 *al.*)
Lewes		1300	
Burpham		726	
Chichester		1500	
Porchester		650	
Southampton and Winchester	(each?)	2400[1]	
Wilton		1400	
Tisbury		700	
Shaftesbury		700	
Twyneham (Christchurch)		470	
Wareham		1600	
Bridport (or Bredy)		1760	
Exeter		734	
Halwell		300	
Lidford		140	
Pilton near Barnstaple		360	
Watchet		513 (for 516?)	
Axbridge		400	
Lyng		100	
Langport		600	
Bath		3200 (in two items)	
Malmesbury		1500	
Cricklade		1300? (1003 B, 1300 *al.*)	
Oxford and Wallingford	(each?)	2400	

seems to have been omitted, viz. (Hastings) *Quindecim hyd'* for *Quindecim^c hyd'*, (Cricklade) *m and iii hid'* for *m and iii^c hid'*, (Essex), *triginta* for *triginta^c*. There must be a similar omission in the total. When two names occur together with one figure I believe in all cases that repetition is intended. Thus *to Oxeford' and to Wallingeforde xxiiii hund hyd'* I interpret as meaning "Oxford 2400, Wallingford 2400 hides." Similarly by *to Hamtona and to Wincestre hira∂ xxiiii^c hidas* I understand "Southampton 2400, Winchester 2400 hides." It is at all events desirable that uniformity should be observed in this respect.

[1] Other texts give Southampton 50 and 150 hides, perhaps through misreading the symbol for *and*.

Hides

		Hides
Buckingham and *Sceaftesege*[1]	(each?)	1000 (600 *al.*)
Eashing		500 (1800 *al.*)
Southwark		1800

þis ealles XXVII *hid' and hund seofantigi þe hyrde to þan.*

Essex (Wessex *al.*)	3000? (30 B, 1200 *al.*)
Worcester	1200
Warwick	2404 (for 2400?)

It will be seen that the survey begins in the east of Sussex, proceeds along the south coast as far as Devonshire, and returns through Somerset, North Wiltshire, Oxfordshire, Berkshire, and Buckinghamshire to Surrey. At this point a total is given for the districts thus far recorded, though unfortunately the figures given in the text do not correspond to the sum of the figures given for the individual districts. Then at the end we find the statistics for Essex, Worcester, and Warwick added as a sort of appendix. Unfortunately it appears that the document is not only corrupt both in the names and in the figures which it gives but also probably incomplete at both ends. For except on this assumption one can hardly account for the omission of Kent at the beginning, or Gloucester, Hereford, etc. at the end of the list. Consequently it is somewhat hazardous to draw conclusions as to the date of the document from its omissions. There is however one feature in it which certainly deserves attention, namely the inclusion of Oxford and Buckingham in the

---

[1] Not identified. From this point onwards some confusion seems to have been caused (except in Birch's text) by the wrong division of sentences.

same division with the southern districts[1]. So far as I am aware, there was only one period in early English history when these districts were grouped together to the exclusion of Essex, Worcestershire, and Warwickshire, viz. the few years (911—919) immediately following the death of Earl Aethelred. It is stated in the Chronicle (912 A) that on Aethelred's death the king succeeded to London and Oxford with the districts dependent on these towns, and it is likely enough from its geographical position that Buckinghamshire went with them. But from the 'Mercian Register' (cf. Flor. Wig. *ad ann.* 912) it is plain that West Mercia (*i.e.* Worcestershire, Warwickshire, &c.) remained in Aethelfled's hands till her death. Essex, or at all events the greater part of it, was not really in the king's possession at the time of Aethelred's death[2]. Traditionally however it had belonged to the West Saxon dynasty since the year 825 (Chron. 823), and this may be the reason for its inclusion in the survey.

It is to be observed that while the Burghal Hidage is drawn up practically without regard to the shire-system in the south, the divisions which it gives north of the Thames do seem to correspond in some cases to the later counties. Essex, of course,

---

[1] This argument would still hold good even if the insertion of the total for the southern districts were to be attributed to a later scribe; for the survey strikes out in a new direction at the end.

[2] It was not completely reduced till the capture of Colchester in 918 (assuming that the chronology of the Parker Chronicle is here three years wrong). Possibly the prospect of this war may have been the occasion for the survey being made. The absence of Hertford from the list deserves to be noticed.

need not be taken into consideration, for the name at all events is derived from an ancient kingdom. But it is certainly remarkable that the four northern towns which can be identified in the survey, namely, Oxford, Buckingham, Worcester, and Warwick, all appear later as the capitals of counties. Moreover it seems probable that in certain cases the districts attached to these towns actually coincided with the counties. This may be seen by a comparison with the statistics of the 'County Hidage' (cf. p. 198 f.), which it will be convenient to give here in full. They are as follows[1]:

Wiltshire	4800	Herefordshire	1500
Bedfordshire	1200	Warwickshire	1200
Cambridgeshire	2500	Oxfordshire	2400
Huntingdonshire	850	Shropshire	2400
Northamptonshire	3200	Cheshire	1200
Gloucestershire	2400	Staffordshire	500
Worcestershire	1200		

These statistics date no doubt from a time considerably later than the Burghal Hidage, but it will be seen that in two cases (Worcestershire and Oxfordshire) their figures coincide exactly with those given for the corresponding districts in that survey. It is true that in the case of Warwickshire the figures are only half as great as those given for the district attached to Warwick. Consequently we can hardly identify the two. For Buckinghamshire again the statistics unfortunately are not recorded.

---

[1] For more detailed information on these statistics see Maitland, *Domesday Book and Beyond*, pp. 455 ff. The various texts do not entirely agree in the figures, but those given above are almost certainly correct.

But we may note that the figures for Wiltshire, the only southern county which is given, agree very nearly with those of the Burghal Hidage. The total of the figures for the four Wiltshire towns (Wilton, Tisbury, Malmesbury, and Cricklade) in the earlier survey amounts to 4900 hides. Considering the character of the texts it is likely enough that a slight mistake has crept into one of the figures. If so, we need hardly hesitate to believe that the hidages, and consequently also, we may presume, the areas of the more northern ' counties,' underwent no change in the interval between the two surveys.

In connection with the figures of the Burghal Hidage it will be convenient to turn for a moment to the hundred system, in order to see whether this system will throw any light on the distribution of the counties. The evidence for the existence of the hundred goes back as far as the laws of Edmund (III. 5). The question whether the system was in existence before that time must for the present be deferred. Now it has been pointed out by Mr Corbett (*Trans. R. Hist. Soc.*, XIV. 208 ff.), that at the time when Domesday Book was compiled the counties seem to have been grouped together in such a way that each group contained a round number of hundreds. Thus Kent (60) and Sussex (60) together form a group of 120 hundreds. A second group consisting of Surrey (14), Berkshire (22), Hampshire (44) and Wiltshire (40), likewise forms a total of 120 hundreds. A third group, consisting of Somerset (60)[1], Dorset (40)[1], Devonshire (33) and

---

[1] These are corrected figures. The numbers actually traceable seem to be 59 (Somerset) and 39 (Dorset).

Cornwall (7), forms a total of 140 hundreds. In the Western Midlands we again find a group (Gloucestershire 39, Worcestershire 12, Herefordshire 19, Shropshire 15, Warwickshire 10, Staffordshire 5, Cheshire 10, Lancashire 6, and North Wales 4), which amounts altogether to 120 hundreds. Another group in the Eastern Midlands has been calculated by Mr Corbett at the same figure. It is made up as follows: Buckinghamshire 18, Oxfordshire 22, Northamptonshire 30, Rutland 2, Huntingdonshire 4, Cambridgeshire 17, Bedfordshire 12, Hertfordshire $9\frac{1}{2}$, Middlesex $5\frac{1}{2}$. At an earlier date Huntingdonshire may have contained eight hundreds, but at that time Ely (2) and Rutland were possibly not included. Lastly there remains a group (East Anglia 60, Essex 20) containing altogether 80 hundreds[1]. It will be observed that four of the six groups seem to contain 120 hundreds, a fact which can hardly be due to coincidence. The figures raise a suspicion that there may at one time have been a symmetrical distribution of the counties, which later came to be in part disregarded. In particular it may be noted that, if this arrangement took place at all far back, it is likely enough there would be fewer hundreds in Devonshire[2], while Cornwall would probably not be included at all[3].

[1] Mr Corbett groups Essex with Kent and Sussex, making thereby a total of 140 hundreds.

[2] According to Malmesbury (*Gesta Regum*, R.S., I. p. 148) the Tamar was fixed as the boundary of the English and Welsh by Aethelstan. Before that time Devonshire would presumably be of smaller extent.

[3] Cf. p. 192. It may be observed that Cornwall is not included in the eleventh century list of counties described on p. 198. It is

In the Burghal Hidage there is of course no reference to the hundred system. Yet the numbers of hides assigned to the various districts included in the survey are in most cases multiples of 100. Probably the only real exceptions are those assigned to the districts of Sussex and the western part of Wessex. In the former case the figures are as follows : *to Heorepeburan* 324, Hastings (probably) 1500, Lewes 1300, Burpham 726, Chichester 1500. The total number of hides is thus probably 5350. The next name mentioned is Porchester with 650 hides. Now if this figure be added to the sum for the Sussex boroughs it will be seen that the result (6000 hides) corresponds to the 60 hundreds which that county contained. Is it not possible that the boundaries of the counties may have undergone some change between the time of Edward the Elder and that of William I.? If it may be allowed to suggest another slight change in the boundaries of Hampshire, so as to give Christchurch to Dorset, a somewhat remarkable symmetry is obtained in the figures for eastern Wessex. They are as follows :

Southampton	2400	total for Hampshire 4800		
Winchester	2400			
Wilton	1400	total for Wiltshire 4900, probably for 4800 (cf. p. 209)		12,100, probably for 12,000.
Tisbury	700			
Malmesbury	1500			
Cricklade	1300			
Wallingford	2400		Berkshire 2400	

mentioned however together with Cumberland, Scotland, etc. in a statement generally attached to this list and is said to contain seven *paruae scirae* of its own. These are presumably the seven hundreds.

It has been mentioned that the total number of hundreds recorded in these three counties together with Surrey is 120. The distribution found in the Burghal Hidage would seem to be more in accordance with old usage, as Surrey formed no part of the West Saxon kingdom in early times. During the ninth century it belonged to the eastern sub-kingdom, together with Sussex, Kent, and Essex, and even as late as 918 (Chron. A. 921) we find the army of Surrey taking the field together with those of Kent and Essex.

It is to be confessed that no such symmetry is to be found in the remaining portions of the survey. Indeed it is somewhat surprising that we do not get a round number for the total of western Wessex. One cannot help wondering whether an item has been omitted[1] or possibly some serious mistake crept into the figures for one of the boroughs. It is, however, to be noted that the total (incorrect, it is true) given in Birch's text for the whole survey except the last three items is not a round number. Hence perhaps it will be safer to conclude that the hidage of the western districts at this time was due to local calculation rather than to any figure imposed from above. We may note that the total hidage of the three counties (Dorset, Devon, and Somerset) falls far short of the number of hundreds which they contained after the Conquest.

If we turn now to compare the County Hidage with the numbers of the hundreds in the same

---

[1] One would have expected to find Ilchester mentioned. There was a mint there in the time of Edgar.

counties we find here also a certain amount of
agreement. Worcestershire and Bedfordshire each
have 1200 hides and twelve hundreds. Staffordshire has 500 hides and five hundreds. The figures
for Huntingdonshire also perhaps agree in reality.
This county has only four hundreds in Domesday
Book, but they appear to be double hundreds, while
the town of Huntingdon is said to be reckoned at
fifty hides[1]. In the remaining counties the figures
do not agree, though the discrepancy in some cases
is slight. Thus Warwickshire and Cheshire each
have 1200 hides and ten hundreds, Oxfordshire
2400 hides and twenty-two hundreds, Northamptonshire 3200 hides and thirty hundreds[2]. In other cases

[1] These however seem to be included in one of the hundreds.
I suspect that in the survey for the County Hidage the borough
has been counted twice.

[2] It is perhaps worth suggesting that some of these discrepancies
may be due to the fact that in many counties the boroughs do not
appear among the hundreds of Domesday Book. In some cases,
e.g. London, Northampton, and Oxford, they seem not to have
been hidated (cf. Corbett, *l. c.* p. 218). If it may be suggested
that at the time when the hundred system was organised (or
reorganised)—in the reign of Edmund or Edgar (cf. p. 239 ff.)—
many of the boroughs were reckoned as equivalent to two hundreds,
we shall bring the hidage into conformity with the number of
hundreds not only in Warwickshire, Northamptonshire, and
Oxfordshire, but also in Wiltshire. For the Burghal Hidage
has four 'boroughs' in this county, which together with the forty
hundreds will, according to the proposed reckoning, be equivalent
to the 4800 hides of the County Hidage. By the same process the
figures in the Burghal Hidage for Hampshire and Berkshire will
come into conformity with the hundreds. In the former case the
Burghal Hidage has 4800 hides and two boroughs, in the latter
2400 hides and one borough ; while the number of hundreds is 44
in the former and 22 in the latter case. The figures for Dorset

the difference is more serious. Gloucestershire has 2400 hides but thirty-nine hundreds, Herefordshire 1500 hides but nineteen hundreds, Shropshire 2400 hides but fifteen hundreds, Wiltshire 4800 hides but forty hundreds, Cambridgeshire 2500 hides but seventeen hundreds.

It would be of importance to know, if it were possible, whether the distribution of the hundreds, as it appears in Domesday Book, etc., is of earlier or later date than the compilation of the statistics given in the County Hidage. In the western Midlands the figures for the hundreds are greater than the figures given in the County Hidage in the more southern counties and less in those more to the north. The totals are not very different—the

also are not very far out. For this county 39 hundreds are actually recorded. In the Burghal Hidage, if we include Christchurch, it is assigned 4530 hides. Besides Christchurch, which subsequently passed into Hampshire, it included three boroughs, Shaftesbury, Wareham, and Bridport (or Bredy). These three, together with Dorchester, are reckoned as boroughs also in Domesday Book. They are hidated, but only to a very small extent (45 hides in all). A difficulty in the way of this explanation is raised by the cases of Worcestershire and Sussex; for by the process suggested we should destroy the harmony in both cases between the figures for the Burghal Hidage and those for the hundreds. In the first case, where the city of Worcester is hidated only to the extent of fifteen hides, the large amount of Church property may have brought about some peculiarity of treatment. But it is hardly necessary to suppose that such a scheme would have been carried out consistently everywhere. In some cases of course the boroughs are included among the hundreds. If the County Hidage is really later than the distribution of the hundreds found in Domesday Book, some such explanation as this will, I think, necessarily have to be adopted in order to explain the agreements between the Burghal Hidage and the County Hidage.

County Hidage giving altogether 10,400 hides, while the total number of hundreds (exclusive of those in Lancashire and North Wales) is 110. It seems not unlikely therefore that at some time a redistribution of assessment has taken place over the whole area. The number of hides recorded by Domesday Book in Gloucestershire (2388[1]) is so very close to the figures of the County Hidage as to constitute a distinct argument for believing the statistics of this survey to be of later date than the distribution of the hundreds. Unfortunately however the figures for the other counties seem to be quite inconclusive[2]. Outside the western Midlands the most striking difference is in regard to Cambridgeshire. Here the disparity is so great that one cannot help suspecting that the Cambridgeshire of the County Hidage included a larger area than the Cambridgeshire of later days[3]. It may be noted that there is no mention of Hertford in the Burghal Hidage, and again there is no evidence for believing this place to have been the seat of a Danish earl. Is it possible that the county of Hertford was not yet formed when the statistics of the County Hidage were drawn up[4]? A good part

---

[1] Cf. Maitland, *op. cit.*, p. 400.

[2] Prof. Maitland's figures are as follows: Staffordshire 505, Worcestershire 1189, Herefordshire 1324, Shropshire 1245, Cheshire 512, Warwickshire 1338.

[3] In Domesday Book the number of hides is 1233 (Maitland, *op. cit.*, p. 400), which looks like a halving of the assessment in the County Hidage. But this suggestion throws no light on the relation of the latter to the number of the hundreds.

[4] If so the County Hidage must date from before 1011, when we get the first mention of Hertfordshire in the Chronicle. Indeed the *Hist. Rames.* (cap. 55) speaks of it as existing about

of it may have belonged originally to Cambridgeshire. This however need not affect the question of the hundreds, as they might have been fixed before the county was formed.

In spite of the discrepancies noted above it must be agreed that on the whole the numbers of the hundreds correspond fairly well to the figures of the County Hidage and the Burghal Hidage. Is it then permissible to supplement the latter from the evidence of the hundreds? It has been seen that the central counties of the south (including Surrey) form a group of 120 hundreds, and that Kent and Sussex (each with 60 hundreds) together form another such group. But in the Burghal Hidage we find that the central counties (without Surrey) already contain a total of 12,000 hides, and that Sussex seems to contain 6000 hides. Now if we may assume for a moment that Kent likewise contained 6000 hides, corresponding to its 60 hundreds, we shall find that even at this time the south of England was already divided into three approximately equal districts. The western division is indeed smaller than the others, but it is to be remembered that in the eleventh century it had the largest number of hundreds. It has already been mentioned that the counties of the western Midlands together give a total of 120 hundreds; presumably therefore they were once reckoned at 12,000 hides. For the eastern Midlands the figures are not quite so clear. The

the year 990. But it has been pointed out above (p. 201, footnote) that the statistics of the County Hidage may quite possibly be older than the list of counties in which they are preserved.

total number of hundreds, including Ely and Rutland and giving eight hundreds to Huntingdonshire, is 204. To these we have to add for the earlier period 14 hundreds in Surrey, and some account is probably to be taken of the boroughs which are not included in the hundreds, viz. London, Oxford, Buckingham, Southwark, and possibly one or two more. The exact total is not quite clear[1], but it cannot fall far short of 24,000 hides. This part of England may therefore have contained two districts, similar in size to the others, though it is hardly possible now to draw the line of division between them.

We may now summarise briefly the results of this discussion. It seems probable (1) that about 911—919 the South of England (exclusive of Surrey) was already divided into three approximately equal parts ; (2) that the Midlands were divided in the same way at some date subsequent to the conclusion of Edward's Danish war ; (3) that a redistribution was brought about later, whereby Surrey passed

---

[1] It may be noted that the figures of the Burghal Hidage seem to be considerably larger than those of the hundreds in this part of the country :

Burghal Hidage				Hundreds
Oxford	2400	Oxfordshire	2400	22
Buckingham	1000	? Buckinghamshire	2000	18
to *Sceaftesege*	1000			
Eashing	600	Surrey		14
Southwark	1800	? Middlesex	5400	5½ } 39½
Essex	3000	Essex		20

I think we may assume that Middlesex is included in the districts embraced in the last three items, though the absence of any mention of London is very curious. Part of Hertfordshire may also be included, but this will not greatly affect the result.

into the same division with Hampshire, etc. This redistribution apparently destroyed the symmetry of the scheme in regard to the Midlands. It is not necessary to suppose that the hundred system was in existence under Edward or even under Aethelstan. To this question we shall have to return later. For the scheme suggested nothing more would be required than the fact that counties and 'borough-districts' were calculated to contain this and that number of hides.

If these conclusions are correct it is clear that they have an important bearing on what was pointed out in the last chapter (p. 189 f.), namely, that in Aethelstan's reign there seem to have been six English earls. If we may suppose the scheme to have been brought to completion before the death of Aethelstan, it is quite possible that each of the earldoms was reckoned at 12,000 hides. Such a symmetrical division of the nation would have obvious advantages both for military and fiscal purposes, even before the imposition of the Danegeld[1].

---

[1] Cf. p. 100 ff. From the 'Tribal Hidage' it may be seen that in principle such a scheme was no novelty. We may further compare the story told by Florence (*ad ann.* 975) about Edgar's navy. It is said to have been divided into three parts, an eastern fleet, a western fleet, and a northern fleet—each containing 1200 ships. These figures are hardly credible, but the story need not be entirely without foundation.

§ 3. *The Burghal System.*

It is plain that the formation of the great earldoms must have brought about considerable changes in the system of provincial administration. We have seen above that in the Burghal Hidage the shire system is practically ignored in the South. Again, it may be noted that the laws of Edward contain no reference to the shire. In Aethelstan's laws the word *scir* occurs occasionally (II. 8, III. Pref., VI. 8. 4, 10), but there is no reference to any county assembly, except perhaps in the case of Kent (III. Pref.)[1]. On the other hand, the references to 'boroughs' are frequent, and from II. 20 it appears that these are to be regarded as administrative centres. It is there stated that if a man neglects to attend the *gemot* three times the chief men who belong to the borough are to ride to his place and seize his goods. On this passage Prof. Maitland (*op. cit.* p. 185) says : "Already a *burh* will have many men in it. Some of them will be elder-men, aldermen. A moot will be held in it. Very possibly this will be the shire-moot, for, since there is riding to be done, we see that the person who ought to have come to the moot may live at a distance." But if this meeting was a shire-moot, should we not expect some such expression as 'the chief men of the shire'

---

[1] But Kent cannot truly be described as a county. It seems never to have formed one earldom. For the last years of the ninth century this has already been noted (p. 192 f.) ; the evidence for earlier times will be given subsequently. If we are to infer from Aethelstan III. Pref., the holding of an assembly for all Kent, this must be regarded as a survival of the old national assembly.

rather than 'the chief men who belong to the borough'? The first reference to county assemblies after the time of Alfred (cf. p. 169) is in Edg. III. 5, where it is ordained that the *burhgemot* is to be held three times and the *scirgemot* twice in the year. But what was the *burhgemot*? It can hardly have been a meeting for the occupiers of the *hagan* or 'town-houses,' for in that case we should certainly expect it to have met more than three times in the year. As a matter of fact some boroughs, even county towns, were treated as hundreds[1], and consequently, one may presume, held their meetings every four weeks. The *burhgemot* seems rather to have resembled the county assembly. Is it not probable that it was really a meeting of the landowners who possessed *hagan* in the borough and had to provide for its defence[2]? Prof. Maitland (*ib.* pp. 189 ff.) has shown that the boroughs must originally have been supported by the districts surrounding them. In the Midlands, for the most part, each of the counties had but one borough, and we have seen above (p. 208) that some of these counties seem to have grown out of districts

---

[1] One probable case is that of Chester (cf. Maitland, *op. cit.* p. 211). We may note also that according to Domesday Book Cambridge *pro uno hundret se defendebat.* So in *Hist. El.* 34 we hear of a *placitum ciuium et hundretanorum.*

[2] In Aethelstan, VI. Pref., *seo gerædnis þe þa biscopas and þa gerefan þe to Lundenbyrig hyrað gecweden habbað* we seem to have a reference to an assembly of this kind. It is true that London is not mentioned in the Burghal Hidage; but this may be due to the fact that the old kingdom of Essex was in a state of chaos at the time when the Burghal Hidage seems to have been drawn up. We hear of the *burgware* of London in the Chronicle as early as 894.

attached to boroughs. It has been supposed that the burghal districts of the South were of an essentially different character, namely, that they existed for military purposes only. But is such a supposition necessary? We have seen (p. 168 f.) that the earl was the head of the administration within his earldom and also that he was the commander of its forces in time of war. Smaller districts, as we shall see later, were apparently administered by ' king's reeves.' But it is clear from several passages in the Chronicle (*ann.* 897, 1001 A, etc.) that these persons also were fighting men, and indeed that they were the leaders of the local troops. Hence it seems at least doubtful whether we are justified in assuming the existence of a separate system of organisation for civil and military purposes. It has been pointed out above that in Aethelst. II. 20 the boroughs appear to be regarded as administrative centres. They were also mint-places (*ib.* II. 14) and market-places (Edw. I. 1, Aethelst. II. 12, Edg. IV. 3 ff. etc.[1]). These facts ought, I think, to be taken

---

[1] This last feature is of considerable importance. The few references to trade of any kind which we find in the early laws give no indication that it was restricted to certain places, though from Alfr. 34 it is clear that traders at least required authorisation from the king's reeve at a public meeting. Edward's legislation seems to have been directed towards limiting trade to the ' boroughs.' If by this we are to understand the places enumerated in the Burghal Hidage it is clear that such a measure must have had important effects. We shall have to suppose that (*e.g.*) in the counties of Hampshire, Berkshire, Wiltshire, and Dorset buying and selling at ordinary times were limited to some eleven or twelve places. The reason for this limitation is surely to be found, not so much in the fact that the places in question were fortified, but

in connection with the silence of the authorities concerning the administration of the county. What I would suggest is that the formation of the burghal districts, together with the combination of several counties in the hands of a single earl, had deprived the shire system of its importance, if it had not actually caused it to fall into abeyance.

In Edgar's reign the *burhgemot* and the *scirgemot* certainly existed side by side. But by this time considerable changes had taken place. The danger of foreign invasion had passed away for a time before the death of Eadred, and some at least of the boroughs had come to be trading centres of importance[1]. It is likely enough therefore that the thegns of the district were no longer required to

rather in the permanent presence in them of some official (*e.g.* the *portgerefa*) whose duty it was to supervise acts of sale. If so, Edward's legislation would amount to the establishment of standing markets and thus would really conduce to the extension of trade. Before such provision was made any regular dealing must have been practically impossible except on the occasion of assemblies, and we do not know how often assemblies were held before this time. It is not, I think, to be inferred that trading at assemblies (outside the boroughs) was now prohibited (cf. Aethelstan ii. 12). The *Historia Eliensis* records many transactions on such occasions in places which certainly were not boroughs.

[1] According to the *Vita Oswaldi* (Raine, i. p. 454) York (about the year 1000) was *mercatorum gazis locupleta qui undique adueniunt, maxime ex Danorum gente*. In Aethelred iv. 2 we hear that London had trade with Rouen, Flanders, etc. At Cambridge we find mention of Irish merchants before the death of Edgar (*Hist. El.* i. 42). Statistics of population unfortunately are seldom given. According to the *Vita Oswaldi* (*l. c.*) York had a population of 30,000, exclusive of children. That may be an exaggeration, but I suspect that the modern estimates as a rule are too low.

maintain *hagan* in the borough. The revival of the
shire system in the South may indeed have been
due partly to the burdensomeness of the burghal
system. The influence of the Church is also perhaps
to be taken into account. In this part of the country almost every county had its own bishop. The
regulation that the bishop should attend the county
assembly (Edg. III. 5) was probably in accordance
with ancient custom; but he would hardly, in the
capacity of diocesan, be expected to attend the
borough assembly[1]. But whatever were the causes
of this revival, it must have deprived the borough of
its external jurisdiction. Thenceforth the *burhgemot*
was probably a meeting of persons who owned
property in the borough itself, without reference to
the possession of country estates[2].

The counties of the western Midlands present a
somewhat different problem. In one or two cases
they may correspond to old territorial divisions, but
for the most part it is at least doubtful whether they
were in existence before the tenth century. Worcestershire seems to correspond to the district
assigned to the borough of Worcester. Warwick
likewise was a district borough, and from a passage
in the Chronicle (918 A) it is probable that this was
the case also with Gloucester and Hereford. But

---

[1] From Aethelstan, VI. Pref., it may be inferred that any bishop
who owned lands in the burghal district would attend in the same
way as other landowners.

[2] So far as it continued in existence at all. In Henr. 7. 4 it
seems to be confused with the *scirgemot*. Yet Edgar's ordinance is
repeated in Cnut II. 18.

Aethelfled's boroughs were so numerous that, if they were organised on the same principle as those in the South[1], the districts attached to them must have been comparatively small. If the counties were formed out of these districts, several of them must in each case have been combined.

The course of this discussion has led us to infer (1) that in the reign of Edward the Elder the shire system of the south was for a time displaced or at all events deprived of its importance by a new organisation of the country in administrative districts attached to fortified towns, and (2) that this change was connected with the reduction in the number of earldoms. In order to understand the policy involved in these changes it may be well to observe that they synchronised apparently with the disappearance of the Mercian national council[2]. One of the king's main objects probably was to prevent the possibility of Mercia again becoming a separate kingdom—an object which would certainly be furthered both by dividing Mercia, as was done in 911, and by combining the southern counties in such a way as to increase the power of their earls. It is likely enough, however, that the formation of the burghal districts in place of the counties was due primarily to their

---

[1] At all events there were mints in several of these boroughs, viz. Chester, Tamworth, Stafford, Warwick, and 'Weardburg.'

[2] Aethelstan is said to have been elected king by the Mercians (Chron. 924 B, C, D); but the circumstances of course were extraordinary. He and his successors seem to have had the same council for all parts of the kingdom. The division which took place in 957 lasted only two years.

greater convenience for military purposes[1], both for defence and also for bringing together troops at short notice.

The adoption of the burghal system of organisation is probably to be ascribed to Danish influence. Indeed it seems clear that most of the boroughs of the eastern Midlands—Lincoln, Stamford, Nottingham, Derby, Leicester, Northampton, Huntingdon, Bedford, Cambridge, and Colchester, perhaps also Norwich, Thetford, and Ipswich—acquired their burghal character during the period that they were under Danish government. Four or five of these places are mentioned in earlier times, but, with the exception perhaps of Lincoln, there is no evidence that they were administrative centres. The origin of their importance is probably to be found in the fact that Danish officials settled in these places (cf. p. 203 f.) and fortified them for protection against the natives. The ancient English system, at least in Wessex and Sussex[2], seems to have been essentially

---

[1] A permanent garrison seems to have been established in London from the year 886 (cf. Chron. 894, 896). In 895 we hear of *burgware* at Chichester.

[2] In Northumbria a system similar to that of the Danes may have been in use from quite early times (cf. p. 260). Kent had a fortified capital from the time of Aethelberht. In Essex London may originally have had the same character. The case of Tamworth is somewhat more doubtful. It need hardly have been more than a favourite residence of the Mercian kings. From the time of Offa onwards it was by far the most frequent meeting-place of the Mercian council; cf. B. 239, 240 (where it is called *regium palatium*), 259, 293, 326, 350, 351, 430, 432, 433, 434, 435, 436, 450, 455, 488, 489, 492.

different.　Of permanent capitals we have no trace[1].
The kings apparently moved about with their courts
from one royal estate to another, and, in the absence
of all evidence to the contrary, it may probably be
inferred that the earls lived in a similar manner.
We may note that very few of the southern towns
appear to have been places of any importance before the tenth century[2].　Hence we shall hardly go
wrong in tracing their growth to the centralisation in
them of authority over comparatively large districts
through the reforms introduced under Edward the
Elder.

What has been said above applies of course
chiefly to the larger of the districts mentioned in
the Burghal Hidage.　It must not be assumed that
the smaller districts of Sussex and the western part
of Wessex were of precisely the same origin.　The
places mentioned may very well have been genuine
boroughs.　Indeed, though in some cases the
'borough' was moved a few miles[3], the number of
boroughs which disappeared altogether in later

---

[1] Of course individual kings may have had preferences for
particular places.　Thus Aethelwulf seems to have resided chiefly
at Wilton.

[2] Winchester, like Rochester and Worcester, probably owes its
importance to the fact that it had been from early times the seat
of a bishopric.　Malmesbury and Bath also no doubt owe their
development in part to ecclesiastical influences.

[3] Thus Burpham seems to have given place to Arundel, Eashing
to Guildford, Pilton to Barnstaple, Halwell to Totness and perhaps
Tisbury to Warminster.　There were mints at Guildford and Warminster (if this identification of *Worgemynster* is correct) by the
time of Aethelred II. and at Totness by the time of Edgar.

times is remarkably small[1]. But it is at least questionable whether we are justified in speaking of centralisation in regard to districts like those attached to Halwell, Lidford or Lyng. The origin of such districts as these will be discussed in the following chapter.

[1] I have not been able to find any later evidence for boroughs at Porchester or Lyng. On the other hand there seem to be no new places with mints in the South, except Totness and Ilchester, before the time of Aethelred II. The southern mints represented in the British Museum Catalogue during the period in question are those of Bath, Exeter, Winchester, Langport, Wallingford, Wareham, Southampton, Lewes and Wilton. The reign of Aethelred II. adds Chichester, Lidford, Shaftesbury, Southwark and Watchet, and also Warminster, Totness and Ilchester. In other collections Shaftesbury is said to be represented among Aethelstan's coins, and Chichester, Totness and Ilchester among those of Edgar. Coins of Aethelred II. are said to be known also from Axminster, Cadbury, Crewkerne, Salisbury, Cricklade, Malmesbury and Guildford, besides one or two other places the identification of which is uncertain. Kentish mints are of course not taken into account here.

CHAPTER VII.

THE ADMINISTRATIVE SYSTEM, *Continued.*

§ 1. *The King's Reeve.*

THE word *gerefa* (earlier *giroefa*) is of frequent occurrence from the earliest literary times, though it appears to be peculiar to the English language[1]. In the oldest glossaries it is used as a translation of *commentariensis*[2] and (in the plural) *censores, proceres.* In the Old English version of Bede's Ecclesiastical History it is used for *praefectus,* while in other translations of Latin works and in glossaries it appears for *uillicus, procurator, praepositus, comes, consul.* In Latin translations of English works it is generally rendered by *praepositus, praefectus,* or

---

[1] The etymology of the word is not quite certain. The most probable explanation is that it comes from a word *rōf* (O.H.G. *ruoua*), 'number,' preserved in *secgrof,* 'host of men.'

[2] This was the name of a subordinate official under the Roman empire. In Old High German glosses it is rendered by *scultheizzo.* We may compare *actionaris = folcgeroebum* in the Corpus Glossary. The word *actionarius* seems originally to have denoted the official in charge of an *actio,* an administrative subdivision of the Langobardic duchies.

exactor[1], all of which terms occur fairly often in charters.

From the earliest times we find mention both of king's reeves and of the reeves of private persons. A reeve of the latter class seems to have been the bailiff or steward of a wealthy landowner. He had to collect the food rents and other dues from the tenants and to see that they performed their various services to the landowner[2]. From Ine 63 it would appear that a nobleman was usually expected to have a reeve. According to Aethelstan III. 7, a landowner who had more men than he could himself control was required to set a reeve (*praepositus*) over each of his estates (*uilla*), and the latter was to be responsible for the preservation of order among the inhabitants of the estate. In the charters we find mention also of reeves of royal estates, and it is not clear that their position differed essentially from that of the class discussed above. But beside these we find also reeves of counties (*scirgerefan*), reeves of towns (*wicgerefan, portgerefan*) and persons described as high-reeves (*heahgerefan*). It is probably to the higher classes of reeves that the expression 'king's reeve' in the laws usually refers.

The highest type of reeve was the *scirgerefa* or

---

[1] In the earliest glossaries this word is rendered by *scyldhata*, which is clearly identical with the continental *sculdheto, scultheizo*. The latter seems to correspond very closely to *gerefa* in its various usages. Except in glossaries the word *scyldhata* seems not to be known.

[2] A list of the duties of such persons is given in an Old English document published in *Anglia*, Vol. IX. p. 259, ff.

'shire-reeve[1].' Historians seem to have been somewhat at a loss how to distinguish between the
functions of this official and those of the earl. For
it has been assumed that both these officials stood
together at the head of the county, and consequently
various theories have been brought forward to account
for the dual control involved by this hypothesis.
Thus it has been suggested that the earl represented
the nation, while the shire-reeve was a personal
officer of the king. But the difficulty seems to me
to be due to a misapprehension. The word *scirgerefa* itself does not occur until quite late times.
We do indeed find such expressions as *praepositus
comitatus* in Latin works referring to events which
occurred in the tenth century, and in Aethelstan VI.
10 it is stated ðæt ælc gerefa name ðæt wedd on his
agenre scire. But by this time the counties no
longer had earls of their own. There is no evidence
that the king's reeve of the earlier laws was a shire-
reeve. Had such officials been in existence it is
hardly credible that the Chronicle should make no
reference to them in the detailed annals of Alfred's
reign. The only reeves mentioned by name about
this period are Beornulf (897), town-reeve (*wicgerefa*)
of Winchester, Aelfred (906), reeve at Bath, and
Wulfric (897), who is described as *Wealhgerefa*.
These were no doubt persons of importance, but
their position, in the first two cases at all events,
must have been subordinate to that of the shire-
reeve if the latter office already existed. It has

---

[1] Lat. *praepositus comitatus* and (after the Norman Conquest)
uicecomes.

been assumed that the *scirman* mentioned in Ine 6
was a shire-reeve, but this supposition is surely quite
unnecessary. It is true that in the eleventh century
the terms *scirman* and *scirgerefa* are used synonymously. But the word *scirman* can mean no more
than 'a man in charge of a shire.' In the days when
each county had its own earl the term might equally
well be applied to him. I conclude therefore that
the office of a shire-reeve came into existence as
a result of the formation of the great earldoms[1].
Indeed the absence of all evidence for the existence
of such officers in the South during the first half of
the tenth century seems to me to render it doubtful
whether the words of Aethelstan VI. 10 were intended to apply to all the counties[2].

The term *heahgerefa* seems to be older. In the
laws the high-reeve is only once mentioned, namely
in the *Northleoda Lagu*, where he is assigned a
wergeld of 4000 thrymsas, the same as that of a
hold, half that of an earl (*aldorman*) and twice that
of a thegn. In Edm. III. 5 we find the term *summus
praepositus*, but a comparison of the passage with
Aethelstan II. 10 rather suggests that the adjective
may have been added by the translator. In Eadred's

---

[1] It is possible that sometimes the same person was reeve of
more than one county. Thus from *Hist. El.* 27, 45, 59 etc., and
B. 1295, 1296 it would seem that Wulfstan of Dalham was reeve
both of Cambridgeshire and West Kent. But how far this was
customary we have apparently no means of ascertaining.

[2] Is it quite certain that in Aethelstan VI. 8. 4, 10 the word *scir*
is used in its ordinary technical sense? In any case we may
probably compare a passage in the Chronicle (*ann.* 1097) : *manege
sciran þe mid weorce to Lundenne belumpon.*

charters the Northumbrian earl Osulf signs not only
as *dux*, but also as *hœhgerefa* and *ad beƀƀ hehgr̄*,
which apparently means 'high-reeve at Bamborough'
(cf. p. 185). In the Chronicle the term is applied to
several persons in *ann.* 1001 A, 1002 E. In the
earlier annals it occurs only in 778, 779 (E), referring
in both cases to Northumbrian officials. Symeon in
the corresponding passages uses the title *dux*. Unfortunately the date at which these annals were
translated into English is somewhat uncertain. On
the whole the evidence favours the supposition that
the title 'high-reeve' originated in Northumbria.
It has been suggested that the Southern high-reeves
were identical with the shire-reeves, but the fact
that two such persons accompanied the Hampshire
militia in 1001 is somewhat against this explanation.
Another suggestion as to their position will be made
later.

The other specially designated varieties of reeves
need not be discussed at length. The *portgerefa* was
the reeve of a town and is mentioned chiefly in
connection with his duties in supervising trade.
The word *wicgerefa* does not occur in the West
Saxon laws, though we find mention of a person so
described at Winchester in the Chronicle (897).
From the Laws of Hlothhere and Eadric, cap. 16, it
appears that London also had a *wicgerefa* in the
seventh century[1]. Unfortunately the meaning of the

[1] In the glossaries we find *wicgerefa* for *telonarius* and *publi-
canus*. The word *telonarius* occurs frequently in grants of
exemption from a tax on ships at London (*e.g.* B. 149, 150, 152,
177, 188). *actionarius* seems to be used sometimes in the same
sense (*e.g.* B. 173, 177, 189).

word *wic* is not quite clear. It cannot therefore be decided whether this person was really identical with the *portgerefa,* or whether he had jurisdiction over a larger area. The *Wealhgerefa* mentioned in the Chronicle (897)[1] was probably an official entrusted with the duty of collecting tribute from the Welsh. He may also have commanded auxiliary Welsh troops in time of war.

The word *gerefa* by itself or in the expression *cyninges gerefa* is of much more frequent occurrence than any of the compound terms discussed above. Sometimes of course, as in Ine 63, the word refers to the reeves of private persons, but in the majority of cases it is clearly royal officials who are meant. These officials again were in some cases (*e.g.* Alfr. 1) reeves of royal estates. But on the other hand we find from the earliest times (cf. Ine 73, Wihtred 22) king's reeves who seem to have been endowed with some kind of jurisdiction. From Alfr. 22, 34, Edw. II. 8 etc. it is plain that such persons presided over public assemblies. The questions which now require to be discussed are as follows: (1) What was the extent or area of the jurisdiction of the king's reeve? (2) What was the assembly over which he presided? It has already been seen that we have no satisfactory evidence for the existence of shire-reeves before the time of Aethelstan.

In Edw. II. 8 it is ordained that every reeve is to hold a meeting once in four weeks. Now according

---

[1] A has *-gefera* in both the cases cited above from this annal. The confusion of these two words is very common and sometimes causes considerable difficulty.

to Edg. I. 1, the meeting of the hundred was to take
place every four weeks, while according to Edg. III.
5, the borough assembly and county assembly were
held only three times and twice in the year respectively. From a comparison of these passages the
natural inference is that the meeting over which the
king's reeve presided was the meeting of the hundred.
Against this conclusion two objections may be
brought forward. The first is that in Edgar's laws
the head man of the hundred is not described as a
reeve but as *hundredesman* (I. 2, 4, 5) and *hundredes
ealdor* (IV. 8, 10). It has therefore been doubted
whether this person was a reeve. Yet it must be
noticed that the duties assigned to him in Edg. I. 2,
4, 5 are identical with duties elsewhere ascribed to
the reeve. These were (i) to gather together the
men under his jurisdiction for the pursuit of thieves
(cf. Aethelst. VI. 8. 2, 3); (ii) to be witness to the sale
of cattle, the history of which was uncertain
(cf. Edm. III. 5); (iii) to assist in tracing the spoor of
lost cattle (cf. Aethelst. VI. 8. 4). Again in Edw.
Conf. 32, Pref. we find mention of reeves of wapentakes and hundreds[1]. The authority of this document
is of course none of the best, but, so far as the
wapentake is concerned, the statement is confirmed
by Aethelred III. 2. From the evidence at our
disposal therefore it seems probable that the position
of the head man of a hundred was, in some respects

---

[1] The term *praepositus hundredi* occurs in the Latin text of
Will. I. 5, but the French text has nothing corresponding to
this expression.

at least, similar to that of a reeve[1]. The other objection is more serious. We find no reference to the hundred-system either in the laws or elsewhere before the time of Edmund. The discussion of the origin and history of this system may for the present be deferred. It is clear however that for the ordinary administration of justice some subdivision of the nation considerably smaller than the county must have been in use. In Alfred's laws (cap. 38) we find mention of public meetings (presumably county assemblies), at which the earl presided; but we also hear (*ib.* 22, 34) of meetings held in the presence of a king's reeve. These latter are presumably the meetings which in Edw. II. 8 the reeve is directed to hold every four weeks; for it is scarcely credible that such a regulation as this can have been intended to apply to the county assembly. It seems probable therefore that even in the ninth century, beside the county assembly, meetings of much smaller districts were held. These smaller districts, if not identical with the hundreds, must have been at least comparable with them in size.

In Edg. III. 5 we find mention not only of the hundred and the county assembly but also of the *burhgemot*. I have already (p. 220 f.) tried to show that this was originally a meeting of the district attached

---

[1] According to another explanation each hundred had two officials, the reeve representing the king and the *hundredes ealdor* representing the freemen. But no evidence has been produced for the existence of such a dual control before the Norman Conquest. The question whether the king's reeve had jurisdiction over more than one hundred will be discussed later (cf. p. 248, footnote).

to a borough—a system of organisation which we
find in the Burghal Hidage—and that such districts
were used for administrative as well as military
purposes.   Now in the preface to his first code
Aethelstan speaks of 'the reeve at each borough,'
from which it would seem to follow that each of
these districts was under the jurisdiction of a reeve.
It is true that such officials are very seldom
mentioned, but, considering the character of our
authorities before the time of Edgar, that is not
strange.   We have however already heard of a reeve
Aelfred at Bath; and again in B. 591 we find a
reeve Eanulf apparently at Tisbury, another of the
places mentioned in the Burghal Hidage.   Reeves
of this type, at all events those who had jurisdiction
over the larger districts, must have formed a class
distinct from the reeves discussed in the last section.
The districts dependent on Bath, Winchester, and
Southampton were as large as counties; indeed the
district dependent on Wallingford seems to have
been identical with Berkshire.   It is manifestly
improbable that such districts would be called together every four weeks.   We must therefore suppose
that some such rule as that given in Edg. III. 5, viz.
that the *burhgemot* was to be held three times a
year, prevailed already in the time of Aethelstan.

It appears then that there were two classes of
reeves.   One class had jurisdiction in large borough-
districts, the other in smaller districts, whether these
were already organised as hundreds or not.   It
seems likely that the latter class were, in part at
least, subordinate to the former.   But the districts

described in the Burghal Hidage itself, as we have
seen, vary very much in size. In Sussex and western
Wessex we find several quite small districts, one
case containing only a hundred hides. It is hardly
likely that such districts were organised on the same
plan as the larger ones. How then are we to account
for their appearance in the list beside the borough-
districts? The explanation which I would suggest
is that the latter were formed by combining together
a number of the smaller districts, but that this process
was not yet completed when the Burghal Hidage was
drawn up. At the beginning of the century each
county apparently had its own earl, who was responsible for it both in war and peace. So long as the
county system remained intact large administrative
districts like those attached to Bath and Winchester
would not be needed. I conclude therefore that the
higher class of reeves and the districts which they
governed both came into existence with the formation
of the great earldoms.

It would be somewhat strange if the language
possessed no means of distinguishing between these
two classes of reeves. But we have seen that the
position of the Southern high-reeve has not yet been
satisfactorily identified. Hence I am inclined to
think that this official was really the reeve of a
large borough-district. If so we can understand
how two such persons came to accompany the
Hampshire militia in the year 1001. They would
probably be known as 'high-reeve at Winchester,' etc.
or simply 'reeve at Winchester,' etc., just as the
Northumbrian Osulf, who seems really to have had

the rank of earl, describes himself as 'high-reeve at Bamborough.'

Except in the *Northleoda Lagu* (cf. p. 76) we never hear of a special wergeld for any class of reeves; nor do we find any statement of compensations due to them. The penalty to which they were liable for disregard of the king's orders was 120 shillings (the regular payment for *cyninges ofer-hyrnes*). In Aethelstan VI. 11, apparently the only passage which records a gradation in such payments, 120 shillings is to be paid by the reeve, besides the loss of his office[1], and 'half that amount by any of my thegns who holds land' (*ælc minra þegna þe ge-landod sy*). If this phrase means a 'king's thegn' (in the technical sense) it would seem that the position of the king's reeve was superior to that of such persons. Unfortunately there seems to be no means of ascertaining whether the king's reeves themselves were always or usually king's thegns. It is clear that such was the case sometimes. Thus in a Middlesex charter of 845 (B. 448) we find *Werenberhto ministro regis ac praefecto*. The *Aldhun qui in hac regali uilla......praefectus fuit* of B. 319 is identical with the *suo ministro nomine Aldhun* to whom Ecgberht (of Kent) granted land according to B. 293. The reeve Ceolmund to whom Aethelwulf granted land at Rochester in 842 (B. 439) is probably to be identified with one of the persons of this name who sign with the title *minister* or *miles* in B. 447,

---

[1] Cf. II. 26 : *gif minra gerefena hwilc þonne þis don nylle...þonne gilde he mine oferhyrnesse and ic finde oðerne þe wile*, which shows that the appointment of such persons rested with the king.

467, 486. It can hardly be doubted that the shire-reeves in later times[1] were frequently king's thegns. If this was the case generally with the higher class of reeves, it becomes clear why the reeve is never mentioned in graduated statements of fines.

The king's reeve was not the only reeve who had jurisdiction of a more or less public nature. The jurisdiction exercised by (*e.g.*) the reeves of the bishop of Worcester can hardly have differed very much from that of king's reeves. In charters of the eleventh century we find references to reeves of earls, who appear to have been persons of some consideration. An earlier reference to such officials is perhaps to be found in the *cyninges ealdermannes gingra*[2] who is represented as presiding over a public meeting in Alfr. 38.

§ 2. *The Hundred.*

In the last century before the Norman Conquest the counties of the Danelagh (north of the Welland) were as a general rule divided into wapentakes and the English counties into hundreds. The rules for the administration of the hundred are given in Edgar's first code[3]; but the system was not entirely

[1] *e.g.* Wulfstan of Dalham (B. 1295, 1296).

[2] For the expression, cf. B. 450, a charter of 845 : *ab opere regali et pastu regis et principis uel iuniorum eorum* (cf. B. 455).

[3] I have cited this code under Edgar's name throughout, in accordance with general usage. But it is to be remembered that it is really anonymous. There is probably a reference to it in Edg. III. 5 ; and on the other hand it seems from cap. 2 to be later than the time of Edmund. But it may have been issued by Eadred or Eadwig.

new at that time, as we find a reference to it in
Edm. III. 2. Before the reign of Edmund there is
no reference to the hundred in the laws, nor have
I been able to find any such references in charters.
In the *Historia Eliensis* the hundred is frequently
mentioned, in several cases (I. 15, 27, 46, 59) with
reference to events which occurred in Edgar's reign ;
but of course the record does not go back beyond
this point. There seems therefore to be no direct
evidence for the existence of the hundred system
before the reign of Edmund. Consequently it was
suggested by Steenstrup (*Normannerne*, IV. p. 76 ff.)
that the hundred, as well as the wapentake, was a
unit introduced by the Danes. But there is a certain
amount of indirect evidence which tends to show
that, in spite of the silence of the authorities, some
such divisions were known in England before this
time.

We have already seen that in Edw. II. 8 the reeve
is commanded to hold a meeting every four weeks,
and that according to Edg. I. 1 it was at intervals
of four weeks that the hundred was to meet. These
two passages are certainly to be taken together ; but
the parallelism between them is hardly sufficient
to prove that the meeting held by the reeve of
Edward's time was a meeting of the hundred. It is
quite conceivable that between the dates of these
two laws changes may have taken place in the
administrative divisions of the nation, and that the
meeting of Edgar's time was merely the successor of
the earlier one.

But there is some evidence of a different kind to

be taken into account. The hidages of the various counties and districts recorded in the County Hidage and the Burghal Hidage are usually expressed in numbers which are multiples of 100. In the case of the County Hidage this is not surprising as the survey was probably made at a fairly late period. The Burghal Hidage on the other hand dates in all probability from the reign of Edward the Elder. Here indeed we have in certain districts, Sussex and western Wessex, numbers of hides which are not multiples of 100. But in the older parts of Wessex, *i.e.* Hampshire, Wiltshire and Berkshire, as also in the northern part of Somerset and the districts north of the Thames, we find nothing but round figures. In particular we may note the frequent recurrence of the figure 2400 (Warwick, Oxford, Wallingford, Winchester, Southampton), which suggests that the numbers have been fixed according to some artificial scheme.

But this artificial distribution of hides can be traced still further back, namely in the 'Tribal Hidage' (B. 297), a document of doubtful age but at all events anterior to the great invasion. In this document each tribe or administrative unit is allotted a certain number of hides, as in the Burghal Hidage. Unfortunately most of the smaller and some of the larger units cannot now be identified with certainty. But it has been shown by Mr Corbett (*Trans. R. Hist. Soc.* xiv. 187 ff.) that the document is worthy of far more serious attention than has generally been given to it. In one case[1] (Sussex) its evidence is

[1] If the identification of *Suth-Gyrwa* with Bede's *Elge regio* is correct, this is a second case.

corroborated by Bede. Now, though the general scheme of this document is similar to that of the Burghal Hidage, the numbers of hides allotted to the various units are in all cases multiples of 100. As a matter of fact in the whole number of units, thirty-four in all, the figures which occur are only ten or eleven in number, viz. 300, 600, 900 (or 800), 1200, 2000, 3500, 4000 ?, 5000, 7000, 15,000 and 30,000. These figures clearly point to an artificial scheme of distribution. It may be observed (i) that in the last few cases the thousand hides seems to be a unit, and (ii) that the smaller units all apparently belong to a comparatively small area in the Midlands. Hence it is quite likely that the existing form of the scheme has been drawn up with special reference to one part of the country, and that in other forms Kent, East Anglia, etc., may have been subdivided just as minutely. In any case, however, the hundred hides seems to be the lowest unit regarded by the survey.

This observation is of course independent of the identification of the hidages recorded in the document with the hundreds of later times. According to Mr Corbett, however, there is reason for believing that in certain districts there may have been continuity of reckoning. The first case is that of the Hwicce (*Hwinca*, etc.), the territory of which tribe is given at 7000 hides. Mr Corbett identifies this territory with the counties of Worcester, Gloucester and Hereford, which in Domesday Book seem altogether to have contained 70 hundreds. I am inclined to doubt whether this identification is quite correct; for I have not been able to find any evidence

that Herefordshire was included in the kingdom of
the Hwicce. Indeed Bede's language (*H. E.* v. 23)
seems to me rather against such a supposition.
But there is good reason for believing that a small
part of Somersetshire (in the neighbourhood of Bath)
belonged to that kingdom. Quite possibly also it
may have contained a considerable part of Warwickshire. If so, the number of hundreds in later
times would not fall very far short of 70. Secondly,
Mr Corbett identifies a number of units belonging apparently to the southern Midlands, and
containing altogether 12,000 hides, with the counties
of Oxford, Buckingham, Middlesex, Hertford, Bedford,
Cambridge, Huntingdon, Northampton, and the
hidated part of Rutland, which in Domesday Book
contain altogether 120 hundreds. This identification
however involves a considerable element of uncertainty, for there is no continuity either in the
nomenclature or, for the most part at all events, in
the size of the districts identified. On the other
hand it is of course quite impossible to reconcile the
statistics for Kent and East Anglia with the number
of hundreds existing in later times. These discrepancies are probably to be explained by a difference
in the size of the hide[1]. I am inclined to think that

---

[1] Mr Corbett points out that the total number of hundreds in
Kent and Surrey together is 74, or almost half the figure (15,000
hides) given for Kent in the Tribal Hidage. It is quite possible
that Surrey may have been ·included in Kent (cf. p. 279), but
I doubt if the hundreds are trustworthy evidence as to the hidage
of Surrey. There does seem to be some evidence that the Kentish
hide was doubled in later times. In the tenth century it appears
to have been identical with the *sulung* or *aratrum*. Thus in
B. 1295, an original charter of Edgar, we find *decem mansas quod*

a very small hide was in use over the greater part of the Midlands. For Wessex unfortunately the Tribal Hidage gives no detailed information, and the one statement which it contains, viz. that Wessex contains 100,000[1] hides, can hardly be right on any reckoning. I am inclined therefore to think that continuity of hidage is at best limited to a comparatively small number of districts[2].

But, however this may be, it is clear that the distribution of the nation according to hundreds of hides goes back in principle to early times. Moreover we have seen that the king's reeve was from early times endowed with some sort of jurisdiction which, in Edward's time at all events, must have been limited to a comparatively small area. But is this combination of evidence sufficient to make us conclude that the hundred was already an organised unit of administration? There are two objections which may be urged against this conclusion. In the first place the absence of any reference to the

Cantigene dicunt X sulunga. But at the beginning of the ninth century the *sulung* seems to have been equal to two hides; *e.g.* in B. 321, a charter of 805: *aliquam in Cantia partiunculam terrae hoc est duorum manentium, ubi Sueordhlincas uocitantur iuxta distributionem suarum utique terrarum ritu Saxonica án sulung seu in alia loco mediam partem unius mansiunculae id est án geocled,* etc. and in B. 341, a charter of 812: *hoc est terrae particula duarum manentium id est an sulung* etc., and again *demediam partem unius mansiunculae id est an ioclet.* It can hardly be doubted that the *geocled* (*ioclet*) was identical with the *iugum* of Domesday Book which according to Prof. Maitland (*op. cit.* p. 396, footnote) was probably a quarter of a *sulung.*

[1] *hund þusenda* may however mean 'an immense number' of hides. Possibly it is to be taken as meaning that the compiler did not know the hidage of Wessex.

[2] Sussex is perhaps a possible case; cf. p. 265.

hundred in the early laws is very remarkable. We may especially point to Aethelstan II. 20, where a course of procedure is prescribed which certainly was included among the duties of the hundred in later times. Here, however, we hear not of the hundred but of the 'men who belong to the borough.' On the other hand small territorial divisions bore the name *hundare* in Sweden, and perhaps in Denmark also in early times. It is true that in the Danish parts of England the name applied to such districts is generally *wæpentak*[1], but the principle

[1] It is to be remembered that the word *vápnatak* is not found in this sense outside England. Hence the districts designated by this term may at an earlier date have borne the name *hundare*, though *þing* would also be possible. It may be noted that in Edg. IV. 6 the word *wæpengetæc* seems to be used either synonymously with *hundred* or else for the meeting of the hundred. Of course I do not suggest that the unit of 100 hides was known to the Danes. What I mean is that they had territorial divisions corresponding approximately in size to the hundred. As a matter of fact the size of the wapentakes seems to have varied greatly. In Leicestershire they must have been far greater than hundreds, as they contain as much as 600 or 700 carucates. But the wapentakes of Nottinghamshire appear to have been much smaller than this. It seems to me not impossible that some of the hundreds of the Eastern Counties (*e.g.* perhaps those of Huntingdonshire) may once have been wapentakes, whether they ever bore that name or not. The Cambridge Thegns' Law (Thorpe, *Dipl.* p. 610 ff.) presents several points of resemblance to the regulations for the wapentake in Aethelred III., especially in regard to the amount (eight pounds, *i.e.* 120 ores) to which the *gilde*, like the wapentake, was entitled in compensation for violation of its peace. The 'hundreds' of Lindsey were of course of quite a different character (cf. Round, *Feudal England*, p. 73 ff.). Those of Leicestershire (*ib.* p. 196 ff.) more nearly resemble the English hundreds, but I do not know how far they had any organisation of their own. These questions like everything relating to the Danelagh require much further investigation.

on which they were organised seems to have been much the same as in the case of the hundred[1]. Moreover the reign of Edmund is about the time when we should expect Scandinavian influence first to make itself strongly felt in England. Secondly, Edgar's ordinance regarding the organisation of the hundred distinctly conveys the impression that it

---

[1] In Aethelred III. 3 we find mention of 'the twelve senior thegns,' who acted apparently as a kind of judicial council for the wapentake, and who are clearly to be compared with the twelve *lagemanni* of Lincoln and Stamford. But there is a certain amount of evidence that the English hundred had a similar council. The clearest case is that of Chester, which is described as a hundred (cf. p. 220, footnote), and which contained twelve *iudices*. Again it is ordained in Edg. IV. 5 that each hundred is to have at least twelve standing witnesses, and from a comparison with Edg. I. 4 it seems very probable that these were the *hundredes man* and the *teoðingmen*, who were public officials. The arithmetical difficulty involved by this identification occurs again in Aethelstan VI. 8. 1, in connection with an organisation from which that of the hundred seems to have been adapted (see the next note). We may further compare the twelve *lahmen* (a Scandinavian term) of the *Gerædnes betweox Dunsetan*, though this of course is a special case. As there is no evidence for the existence of such councils in the early laws, and as similar bodies of twelve are found in the Danish and Swedish *hæraþ* (*hundare*), it seems probable that they were of Scandinavian origin. It is curious that in Cambridge, which had been a Danish town, we find (*Hist. El.* I. 13, 34) 24 *iudices*. The persons so described must surely be identical with the *lagemanni* of Domesday Book and with the 'thegns' mentioned in Thorpe, *Dipl.* p. 610 ff.; but the number seems to be incompatible with the amount of the payments recorded in the latter document. In Domesday Book the number of *lagemanni* is unfortunately not stated. From the amount of their heriots it may perhaps be inferred that it had been reduced, as at Stamford; but possibly the sheriff was not entitled to the whole sum. I suspect that in the meetings described in the *Hist. Eliensis* two distinct bodies may have been summoned.

was then a new thing¹. It is true that the hundred

¹ The ordinance seems to be modelled on regulations intended
for burghal districts. This may be seen by a comparison with
Aethelstan vi. (*Iud. Ciuitatis Lundoniae*). Thus cap. 1 may be
compared with Aeth. vi. 8. 1, cap. 2 with Aeth. vi. 1. 1; 4; 8. 2, 3,
cap. 3 with Aeth. vi. 8. 5 and cap. 5 with Aeth. vi. 8. 4. It is true
that in Aethelstan's law the *hynden* and the *teoδung* seem to be
associations of 100 and 10 persons respectively, whereas the
hundred and presumably also the *teoδing* of Edgar's law are
territorial units; but that is hardly sufficient to prevent us from
believing that the one system was adapted from the other. Such
an adaptation would be materially facilitated by the existence of
the ten-hide fiscal unit (cf. p. 102). It is quite possible also that
at one time it may have become customary to call upon one man
from each hide for the performance of certain public services—an
arrangement which we find still operative in some districts in the
time of William I. (cf. Domesday Book, p. 262 b: *ad murum
ciuitatis et pontem reaedificandum de unaquaque hida comitatus,*
i.e. Cheshire, *unum hominem uenire praepositus edicebat*). It is
hardly necessary here to discuss the origin of the associations of
100 and 10 men. From the fact that the word *gilde* is Scandinavian (O. Norse *gildi*) it seems probable that they were derived
from the Danes. They may have come into existence for military
purposes, but it is by no means clear that they had not a wider
scope from the beginning. The associations described in Hen. 8. 1,
Edw. Conf. 20, 28 are supposed not to have been in existence before
the Norman Conquest (cf. Waitz, *Deutsche Verfassungsgeschichte,*
i. p. 458 ff.); yet they may have been based on earlier models. At
all events it appears from the Cambridge Thegns' Law that in some
cases artificial associations had come to participate in the privileges and liabilities of the relatives. It is to be remembered
that the invasion of Lothbrok's sons was not a national migration;
moreover many of their troops may subsequently have returned
home. Consequently those who settled in England must have
required some artificial association to take the place of relatives,
while the unreasonably high figure at which the Danish wergelds
had been fixed would tend to render such associations permanent.
The principle of the system seems to have been known in England
from early times, but only in the case of persons who had no

is already mentioned in Edm. III. 2, though unfortunately no information seems to be obtainable about the date and purpose of this code. But is it not possible that in Edmund's time the hundred system was in operation only in certain parts of the country, perhaps those districts which had formerly been under Danish government?

On the whole therefore I am inclined to believe that, though the nation or shire was from early times reckoned in hundreds of hides, these hundreds were not used as units for administrative purposes before the time of Edmund[1], and that the organisation then adopted was borrowed from Danish custom. At the same time it is clear from the references to the duties of the king's reeve that some unit considerably smaller than the county must have been in existence. It must therefore be our endeavour to ascertain what the character of this unit can have been, so far as the very limited evidence at our disposal will permit.

relatives or relatives on one side only (cf. Alfr. 27, 28). In normal circumstances responsibility lies exclusively with the relatives even in the laws of Aethelstan (III. 7, cf. Edw. and Guth. 13). The use of the word *gegildan* in Ine 16, 21 cannot be adduced as evidence to the contrary, for it seems clear from the latter passage that the term refers to the relatives.

[1] It may perhaps be questioned whether every hundred had an independent organisation of its own even in the time of Edgar. In the *Hist. Eliensis* we hear of combined meetings of three hundreds (I. 14, 59), six hundreds (I. 35), and eight hundreds (I. 11, 45), besides the two hundreds of Ely which frequently met together. Such cases at least suggest the possibility of the survival of old administrative divisions, though a different explanation is given in Hen. 7. 5.

§ 3. *The Territorial Divisions of Earlier Times.*

As the laws give practically no information on this subject we are necessarily dependent on the evidence of charters. It will be convenient therefore to begin with Kent, which is the province best represented by charters in early times. Now at the time of the Domesday survey Kent was divided not only into hundreds but also into six districts, to which the term *lest* is applied. Two of these, the *Lest de Sudtone* and the *Lest de Ailesford,* seem to correspond to the present lathes of West Kent. The other four are called *Boruuar Lest, Estre Lest, Linuuart Lest* and *Wiuuart Lest.* All these names can be traced back to early times. In B. 141, a charter of 724, we find the expressions *on Limen-wearawalde, on Weowerawealde.* The former occurs again in B. 248, a charter of 786, while in a charter of 845 (B. 499) we find mention of *Vueowera get* and in one of 858 (B. 499) we find *Wiwara wic.* These forms hang together in all probability with the place-names Lymne (*Liminiae, Liminge*) and Wye (*Wii, Vuiœ, Vueœ*). The latter place is described as a *uilla regalis* in B. 426, a charter of 839, and was the meeting-place of the Kentish council both on this occasion and again in the year 845 (B. 449). The *uillam regalem quae nominatur Wyth* mentioned in a charter of 762 (B. 191) is perhaps a corruption of the same name. That it was an administrative centre may be seen both from this charter and from one of 858 (B. 496): *an Wiwarawic quae ante subiecta erat to Wii.* Lymne was a meeting-place of the Kentish council in 740 or 741 (B. 160)[1] and also apparently an administrative centre, as may be seen from a charter of 689 (B. 73): *unum aratrum......quod pertinebat ad cortem quae appellatur Liminge.* The name *Estre Lest* is doubtless connected with Eastry, which is frequently mentioned in the charters[2]. In a charter of 824 (B. 380) we read of the *terra regis quae pertinet ad Eastræge.* It appears to be used often as the name of a district, as (*e.g.*) in B. 232 *in regione Easterege.* The name *Boruuar Lest* is probably to be connected with the form *Burgwara,* which also appears not unfrequently in charters, *e.g. Burhwaremarce* (B. 5), *Burhwarouualdo* (B. 248), *Burgwaramedum* (B. 497). There can be little doubt that the *Burg* in question was Canterbury. This place is described by Bede (*H. E.* I. 33) as *regia ciuitas* and (*ib.* I. 25) as the *metropolis* of Aethelberht's dominions. Meetings of the Kentish council were frequently held there from the earliest times (cf. B. 4, 5, 35, 36, 42, 148, 159, 190, 191, 195, 227, 303, 328, 419, 445, 516). Lastly it may be mentioned that from B. 1064 Aylesford also would seem to have been a meeting-place on one occasion during the reign of Edward the Elder.

It appears then that the names of the districts into which Kent was divided in Norman times were derived from places which had in early times been royal estates and meeting-places for the Kentish council, and to which the surrounding lands had been in some way attached.

[1] It would seem from this charter that the district attached to Lymne extended as far as Lyminge (*Limining mynster,* B. 98).

[2] It is called *uilla regalis* in Sym. Dur., *Hist. Reg.* § 6.

Now in charters dating from the early part of the ninth century we find mention of a number of reeves, apparently in some cases at all events king's reeves. Thus in a charter of 804 (B. 316) we find the signatures of *Bearnheard præpositus, Wlfheard prepositus* and *Aedred prepositus.* The first mentioned also signs two charters of 805 (B. 319, 321) with the same title. In B. 319 we find the signature of another *præpositus* named Eanred. Again a certain Haehfrith, who signs in B. 321 as *comes*, appears again in a charter of 813 (B. 342) as *præpositus.* Earlier examples are to be found in B. 194 : *Ecgbaldi comitis atque praefecti*, and B. 160 : *Aldberhti prefecti*, who is probably identical with the *Albertus præfectus* of B. 191. In B. 91 we find the signatures of three *præfecti.* The charters give us no information as to the kind of jurisdiction which these reeves held. But in B. 318 we find the will of a certain king's reeve (*prefecto meo*) named Aethelnoth, who describes himself as *se gerefa to Eastorege.* Again in B. 319 (cf. B. 293) we hear of a man named Aldhun, who in the reign of Ecgberht, king of Kent, had been reeve in a certain *uilla regalis*, perhaps at Canterbury[1]. These examples[2], so far as they go, distinctly suggest that the Kentish king's reeve was an official entrusted with the charge of a royal estate (*uilla regalis, cyninges tun*)—in short that he was a *tungerefa* on a large scale.

[1] The text unfortunately is unintelligible : *Aldhun qui in hac regali uilla in huus ciuitatis praefectus fuit.*

[2] The reeve Abba (B. 412) can hardly have been a king's reeve, if we are right in believing him to have been a ceorl (cf. p. 22 f., footnote).

It has been seen above that within the space of
ten years (804—813) we find record of six reeves in
Kent. Though it is not certain that all these persons
were king's reeves, one is rather tempted to connect
them with the six divisions of the county found in
Domesday Book. But on the whole I am inclined
to think that such a conclusion would be rash. The
towns and villages mentioned above are not the only
places at which meetings of the Kentish council were
held. In Wihtred's reign a meeting was held at a
place called *Berghamstyde* (*Berkamystede*, B. 88), at
which the laws which bear his name were drawn up.
This place is probably to be identified with Barham,
which we find later apparently as the name of a district (*e.g. in parte occidente Berham*, B. 294; cf. B. 293,
319). In Domesday Book it is the name of a hundred.
Another meeting during the same reign took place
at Bapchild (B. 91)[1]. In 699 a meeting was held at
a place called *Cilling* (B. 99), which in B. 348 is described as a *portus*. Eanmund held a meeting at a
place called *Godgeocesham* (B. 194). The *ciuitas
supradicta* of B. 228 (A.D. 779) is not made clear, but
perhaps Rochester is meant. If, as there seems little
reason to doubt, this is the place to which the expressions *regio Caestruuara* (B. 199), *Caestruuara-
uualth* (B. 175 etc.) refer, it must certainly have had
a district attached to it[2]. In 843 a meeting of the

---

[1] Another meeting was held there during Coenwulf's reign
(B. 290); but it seems to have been a meeting of ecclesiastics
only.

[2] In B. 439 we find record of a grant of land at Rochester
made by Aethelwulf to one of his reeves (*meo prefecto*) named
Ceolmund.

Kentish council was held at a place called *Meranworð* (B. 442), in 862 a similar meeting at *Willherestrio*, in 863 at *Birenefeld* (B. 507), and in 898 at *Wulfamere* (B. 576). It is true that none of these places are described as royal estates, and it is also true that meetings of royal councils were sometimes held on monastic estates, as may be seen from B. 328 : *actum est......iuxta monasterium quod dicitur Crogedena*; but it is hardly likely that all these places were private property. We may note that in B. 6 Sturry (*Sturigao*) is described as a *uilla*, while in B. 41, 45 (cf. B. 35, 42, 44) it is apparently regarded as a district[1]. It is not unlikely therefore that the royal estates which were used as administrative centres for the surrounding districts were in early times more numerous, and that the organisation of Kent into six administrative districts was the result of gradual centralisation. It may be observed that these districts differed considerably in size. I have not been able to ascertain the exact number of hundreds in each *Lest*; but it appears that the *Lest* of Aylesford contained at least twice as many as the *Lest* of Sutton, judging from the entries in Domesday Book. In East Kent the *Linuuart Lest* seems to contain the

---

[1] It is to be observed that the name *Sturry* (*Sturige, Sturigao*, etc.) has the same ending which is found in *Limin-ge* (*Limin-iae* etc.), *Eastorege* and possibly *Vuiæ*. The same element seems to occur in *Elge, Suðrige*, etc., and is apparently equivalent to *regio*. It is probably to be connected with the *-go* which appears in names of Frisian districts (*Fivelgo, Emsigo*, etc., cf. Germ. *gau*, Goth. *gawi*). *Sturige* seems to be derived from the river-name *Stur*, in the same way as *Liminge* from the river-name *Limen* (*Limin-ea*).

largest and the *Wiuuart Lest* the smallest number of hundreds.

We may next turn to Oxfordshire. In Domesday Book the statistics for the Terra Regis in this county contain unusual statements. The king apparently possessed nine manors varying in size from five to thirty-four and a half hides. In the case of seven of these we find it stated that the jurisdiction (*soca*) over a number of hundreds belonged to the manor. Four and a half hundreds were attached to Bensington, two to Headington, two and a half to Kirtlington, three to Upton, three to Shipton, two to Bampton, and two to Bloxham and Adderbury[1]. Here we have a system similar in principle to that which I have suggested as the origin of the Kentish *Lest*. Is it necessary to suppose that the system came into operation after the organisation of the hundreds? If that was the case one would hardly have expected to find a hundred divided between two royal manors[2]. The remaining three hundreds of the county were in later times called Dorchester, Thame, and Banbury: indeed the first is mentioned by this name in Domesday Book. All these places were manors belonging to the bishop of Lincoln, whose see had formerly been at Dorchester. It is not unlikely therefore, though we find no statement to that effect, that the jurisdiction over the hundreds originally belonged to these manors.

[1] Cf. Maitland, *Domesday Book and Beyond*, p. 92.
[2] It may be noted that in 880 Aethelred transferred to the see of Worcester *sex homines qui prius pertinebant ad uillam regiam in Beonsincgtune* (B. 547).

Now if we compare the organisation of Kent and Oxfordshire with the Burghal Hidage it is clear that we have an analogy in the former to the larger districts, and in the latter to the smaller districts enumerated in that survey. It is true that the Kentish divisions for the most part derive their names not from boroughs but from royal estates. Yet Canterbury was a 'borough' from the earliest times. Lymne was a mint-place in the reigns of Edgar and Edward the Martyr. It may subsequently have been displaced by Hythe, just as Halwell and Eashing seem to have given way to Totness and Guildford (cf. p. 226, note). Similarly Eastry may have been superseded by Sandwich. The coins of Aethelred II. and Cnut which bear the legends ÆGLS, EGELE, etc. may really come from Aylesford and not from Aylesbury. But if we may suppose that the names of the Kentish divisions became fixed before the time of Edward the Elder the difficulty disappears altogether. In earlier times most of the places mentioned in the Burghal Hidage must have been merely royal estates or villages. This may be seen not only from such names as *Hamtun, Wiltun,* etc., but also from the description given to these places in early charters; *e.g. in uilla regali quae nominatur Vuiltun* in several of Aethelwulf's charters[1] (B. 421, 459, 480), *in uilla regali quae appellatur Hamtone* (B. 431). Again, we have seen (p. 236) that the boroughs of Wessex, like the places from which the Kentish divisions

---

[1] In other charters of the same king (B. 468, 469, 471—476) we find *in palatio nostro quod dicitur Wiltun* or *nobili palatio in Wiltune* (cf. p. 226, footnote).

derive their names, were apparently under king's reeves. There seems to be little reason therefore to doubt that the administrative divisions of the two kingdoms were originally of very similar character, though the Kentish divisions have survived while those of Wessex soon disappeared.

On the other hand the divisions of Oxfordshire clearly differed from those of western Wessex in the fact that they did not contain boroughs. At the time when the Burghal Hidage was drawn up they were presumably all subject to one central borough at Oxford. But if Southampton and Wilton were merely royal villages, in the preceding century, it is hardly likely that such places as Halwell and Pilton were anything more[1]. Indeed, so far as I am aware, there is no evidence that they ever were fortified. It seems probable therefore that, at least in early times, such districts as these were organised on precisely the same lines as the divisions of Oxfordshire, except that they were not dependent on a central borough. Now it has been suggested above that the large districts which we find in Hampshire, Dorsetshire, etc. had arisen through a combination of smaller districts. If so they would of course present an exact parallel to the case of Oxfordshire. Possibly some of these smaller districts may be traced. In the year 862 a meeting of the West Saxon council was held at Micheldever (*Mycendefr*), which is called *uilla regalis* (B. 504, 505). Subsequently this estate was granted by Edward the Elder to the New

---

[1] Halwell is mentioned as a royal estate in Domesday Book, but it had been in other hands.

Minster at Winchester, and in the charter which
records the grant (B. 596) it is said to have contained
100 hides[1] (*quendam fundum quem indigene My-
celdefer appellant centum cassatorum quantitatem
continentem*). In the recitation of the boundaries we
find mention of a *gemothus*. Another such case may
perhaps be inferred from the story of the arrival of
the first Scandinavian pirates. According to the
Chronicle (*ann.* 787) a certain reeve ('the reeve')
apparently supposing that they were merchants (cf.
Alfr. 34), wanted to force them to go to the *cyninges
tun*. In Aethelweard's account of the same event
the reeve is described as *exactor regis iam morans in
oppido quod Dorceastre nuncupatur*. Dorchester is
not one of the places mentioned in the Burghal
Hidage, though it was a borough in the eleventh
century. But in a charter dating from 833 (B. 410)
it is called *uilla regalis*, and from this time onwards
it was frequently a meeting-place of the West Saxon
council. The above story leads us to infer that
external jurisdiction, reaching as far as the sea, was
attached to it. According to the Annals of St Neot's
the pirates landed at Portland.

From these considerations it seems very probable
that the type of organisation which we find existing
in Oxfordshire in the time of William I. was only the
survival of a system which had been generally
prevalent in Wessex during the ninth century. It

[1] If districts of this size were at all common they must have
been a contributing factor of some importance towards the
establishment of the hundred system. In the Burghal Hidage
there is one district (Lyng) with 100 hides. We may compare the
early Hwiccian grant recorded in B. 43.

can hardly be doubted, in spite of the absence of any direct evidence to that effect, that the Oxfordshire manors, like the royal estates from which the Kentish divisions derive their names, were under the charge of king's reeves. Again, the boroughs of Wessex, which served as administrative centres for the surrounding districts, were likewise under king's reeves; and further, many of these boroughs had certainly grown out of royal villages. Now it has been pointed out above that the king's reeve mentioned in Alfred's laws, cap. 1, seems to have been the reeve of a royal estate[1], whereas the king's reeve mentioned in cap. 22, 34 is endowed with jurisdiction of a public nature. But after all that has been said we can hardly hesitate any longer to identify the two officials. Consequently we must conclude that in early times jurisdiction in the public courts belonged to the reeve of a royal estate.

It would seem then that originally the position of the king's reeve did not differ in principle from that of the reeve of any other landowner. We have seen that the chief duties of the private reeve were (1) to be responsible for the maintenance of order upon his estate, (2) to collect the food-rents and other dues from his lord's dependents, and (3) to see that they performed their various services. Similarly the king's reeve in his judicial capacity was responsible for the maintenance of order in the district attached to his

---

[1] The passage refers to the case of a man who is imprisoned in a *cyninges tun*: if he cannot obtain food for himself his relatives are to provide for him, but if he has no relatives he is to be provided for by the king's reeve.

estate. That he collected the *feorm* etc. may be inferred from Aethelstan II. Pref.[1] and from the use of the term *exactor*. Further, that he was responsible for seeing to the performance of services, *e.g.* military service, may be seen from the fact that he appears as a commander in time of war (p. 221). In regard to administration therefore we are led to conclude that the territories of the kingdom reflected on a large scale the same system which we find operative in the estates of private landowners.

The Mercian evidence[2] is unfortunately too scanty to give us any satisfactory information on this subject. We do indeed hear of *praefecti* from the earliest times, but many of the persons so described seem really to correspond to the earls of Wessex. In charters of the Hwiccian kingdom however we find occasionally (B. 183, 223, 232) *praefecti* whose position may have been more or less similar to that of the higher Kentish reeves. Somewhat more evidence is to be obtained from documents relating to the early Northumbrian kingdom. It has already been mentioned (p. 185) that in the tenth century we find a high reeve at Bamborough. Long before this we hear of officials who in the Chronicle (778, 779 E) are called *heahgerefan* but by Symeon *duces*. The manner in which they are described in the first of these annals (*Ealdulf Bosing at Ciningesclife...Ecgan æt Helaðyrnum*) suggests that they were attached to

---

[1] *Fram twam minra feorma agyfe mon* etc. The passage is a command from the king to his reeves to feed and clothe the poor.

[2] Oxfordshire may be regarded as West Saxon. It seems not to have been entirely annexed until the time of Offa.

royal estates, however large these may have been, and consequently that they are to be compared rather with the royal reeves than with the earls of the South. In Bede's Ecclesiastical History we find mention of a *praefectus* named Blaecca at Lincoln (II. 16), and again of a *Berctfrid praefectus* who fought against the Picts (v. 24); but the position of the latter seems to have been far above that of the ordinary king's reeve[1]. In Eddius' *Life of Wilfrid*, cap. 35, we hear of a *praefectus* named Osfrith *qui praeerat in Broninis urbe regis*; so also again in cap. 37 : *rex iratus iussit duci (Vilfridum) in urbem suam Dyunbaer ad praefectum nomine Tiidlin*. This evidence is not very extensive, but it tends to show that the Northumbrian *praefectus* or king's reeve was an official charged with the administration of a royal estate or 'borough[2].' From the analogy of the southern evidence we may infer with probability that these places served as administrative centres for the surrounding districts.

It will be convenient now to summarise briefly the conclusions to which we have been led. We have seen:

1. That the office of king's reeve can be traced back to the eighth century or earlier in Kent, Wessex and Northumbria.

---

[1] Cf. Eddius, cap. 58 *Berectfridus secundus a rege princeps*. It is not clear that any other high officials were known in Northumbria. In the Chronicle (*ann.* 779) we hear of an *ealdorman* beside the *heahgerefan*. The Latin text (Symeon *ad ann.* 780) has *patricius* in this case. Again in *ann.* 778 Aethelbald and Heardberht, who are undesignated in the Chronicle, appear as *principes* in the Latin text. But is it not possible that all these persons were members of the royal family?

[2] The word *urbs* seems to be a translation of *burg* (cf. Symeon's *urbs Bebban*).

2. That the evidence for the office of shire-reeve does not go back beyond the reign of Aethelstan.

3. That there is no evidence for the existence of the hundred as a unit of administration before the reign of Edmund, though districts were reckoned according to hundreds of hides at a much earlier period.

4. That in the reign of Edward the Elder the south of England was divided into a number of administrative districts, most of which were attached to fortified towns, and that these administrative centres were apparently under the charge of king's reeves.

5. That Kent was divided from the eighth century onwards, if not earlier, into a number of districts, each of which was apparently attached to a royal estate. In the eleventh century the number of these districts was six, but in earlier times they may have been more numerous.

6. That Oxfordshire in the eleventh century was divided into a number of administrative districts attached to royal manors, each district containing several hundreds; and that apparently similar districts existed in Wessex before the hundred system came into existence. The duties of the officials in charge of such districts seem not to have differed essentially from those of ordinary reeves or bailiffs.

It may very well have been for such divisions as these last that the monthly court was originally ordered to be held. There can be little doubt that some similar system prevailed in Northumbria. There however these estates seem to have been grouped round more important estates or *urbes*, probably under high-reeves, in quite early times. In Wessex the shire-system, so long as it remained intact, prevented this grouping[1]; but with the enlargement of the earldoms at the beginning of the tenth century it was adopted everywhere. A somewhat similar system seems to have prevailed in the eastern Midlands under Danish rule and was continued after the incorporation of these districts with the English kingdom. The place of the Danish *iarl* was taken by the king's reeve, who may at first have been known as 'high-reeve,' though before long the title applied to him seems to have been 'shire-reeve.' The appearance of the shire-reeve in the South hangs together with the restoration of the shire-system, but the change may have been gradual. Lastly, under Edmund and his successors, the small administrative districts attached to royal estates were in most parts of the country displaced by the hundred system, apparently through Danish influence.

[1] Yet the names *Hamtunscir* and *Wiltunscir*, the former of which at least is old, would seem to show that some such grouping had not been altogether unknown in early times. We may also compare the relationship of *Wiltun—Wilsæte* and *Sumurtun—Sumursæte*. Somerton was a royal estate in the eleventh century (Domesday Book, p. 86) and had apparently been a place of some importance in early times (cf. Chron. 733). A meeting of the West Saxon council is recorded to have taken place there in 860 (B. 499).

EXCURSUS III.

THE TRIBAL HIDAGE.

This document is practically our only authority for the ancient territorial divisions of the Midlands, but it is, unfortunately, in so many respects obscure that I have hesitated to use it as evidence in the preceding chapter. In general I am decidedly inclined to follow Mr Corbett's explanation ; in regard to details however some of his conclusions seem to me doubtful. Thus I feel a good deal of hesitation about the proposed identification of *Myrcnaland* with Bernicia, because that name elsewhere is invariably applied to a different district. Again, it is difficult to avoid suspecting that *Wocensætna (Porcensetene)* may be identical with the district which is elsewhere (B. 487, 1119) called *(prouincia) Wreocensetna*, and which seems to have derived its name from the Wrekin. But if Mr Corbett's identifications be rejected in these two points there remains no reason for believing that Northumbria is included in the survey. The hidage of the Midlands will then of course be enormously greater than it was in later times, but that is only what might be expected from the figures for East Anglia. Again, I have some doubt as to the probability of the changes which Mr Corbett has proposed in the order of the items. The order given by the MSS., if we confine our attention to those items which can be identified with reasonable probability, seems to be at least intelligible on the hypothesis that the compiler was dividing the area included in his survey into five approximately equal districts, and following in general a direction from north-west to south-east.

Attention has been called above (p. 242) to the fact that the number of figures which occur in the survey is surprisingly small. The only figures which we find among the smaller units are 300 (five or six times), 600 (eleven times), 800 or 900 (once), and 1200 (three times). There must surely be some reason for the fact that no other figures occur. If we turn to the larger units we find 2000, 3000 or 3500, 4000 (300 *al.*), 5000 and 15,000 once each, while 7000 occurs six times and 30,000 twice. Again, there must be some reason for the frequent occurrence of the figure 7000. Now it is a curious fact that Bede's Ecclesiastical History gives practically the same set of figures, viz. '300 and over' for the Isle of Man (II. 9), 600 for the Isle of Thanet (I. 25), 'about 600' for the Isle of Ely (IV. 19), 1200 for the Isle of Wight (IV. 16), 5000 for South Mercia (III. 24), 7000 for North Mercia (*ib.*) and Sussex (IV. 13). The only new figure is 960 (II. 9), the hidage of Anglesey. Again, we find in the Chronicle (*ann.* 648) a unit of 3000 and in Beowulf (l. 2196) another unit of 7000. Both these cases are grants of land by reigning kings to their nephews; but what the grantee received, at all events in the latter case, was really an earldom or principality.

It is difficult to avoid concluding that the figures 300, 600 and 1200 denote different types of ordinary territorial divisions. But if so the figures for large provinces or small kingdoms ought to be multiples of the smaller figures. Yet this is generally not the case. I suspect that the explanation is to be found in the very rough system of arithmetic employed[1], *e.g.* that a province of 7000 hides was regarded as containing twelve districts of 600 hides each and a province of 5000 hides eight such districts. Similarly I suspect that four provinces or kingdoms of 7000 hides may have been regarded as equivalent to one large kingdom of 30,000 hides. On this principle, if we retain the order given by the MSS., the whole

---

[1] We may compare the figures for the Mercian wergelds (p. 13, footnote).

survey will give five groups of 30,000 hides each. Strictly, of course, the figures will be 30,000, 27,600, 27,500, 30,000 and 29,000 respectively.

A difficulty is caused by the 960 hides which Bede gives for Anglesey. Of course this reckoning dates in all probability from a period long anterior to Beue's time, for we have no evidence that Anglesey remained in English hands after Edwin's death. Hence we may reasonably expect to find an archaic system of reckoning in this case[1]. But the figure in question points not only to the absence of the 300 unit but also to a reckoning in 'long hundreds.' Now have we any other traces of such a reckoning in hidages? Is it possible that when Bede uses the expression *DC familiarum mensura* the unit of which he is speaking really contained 720 hides? This question can hardly be answered with certainty. Yet it may be observed that such a hypothesis would enable us to reconcile the earlier hidage of Sussex with that which is found in later times, viz. 60 hundreds or 6000 hides (cf. p. 211). In that case of course we should have to modify the explanation proposed above of the relationship between the 600 unit and the 7000 unit. The latter would probably contain ten, not twelve, of the former.

It may be suggested that, as no figure between 5000 and 7000 occurs, any province which was too large to be classed in the former category would be set down in the latter. That is quite possible. But if the larger hidages, like the smaller, were chosen from a limited number of types, it does not follow that they were not accurately divided. It is quite conceivable that they were regarded as exact numbers, and that the smaller units were adapted to suit them. Thus in a province or kingdom of 7000 hides the 300 unit would really be one of 350 hides. This suggestion would at all events explain the 87 hides which Aethelwalh gave to Wilfrid. In that case what he granted was a quarter of one of his small territorial divisions[2].

[1] Welsh influence might also be expected; but I am not able to discuss this question.

[2] It may be noted that when Ceadwalla conquered the Isle of

In regard to the character of these small divisions the
Tribal Hidage unfortunately gives us no informatiòn, while
the examples mentioned by Bede are in all cases districts
marked out by natural boundaries. Some of the names in
the Tribal Hidage, *e.g. Pecsætna, Arosætna*, resemble the
names of provinces (*Wilsæte, Magesæte*, etc.)[1]. The choice
seems to be between administrative districts and originally
independent settlements, and in the majority of cases we can
hardly hesitate to decide in favour of the former alternative ;
for it is not only contrary to tradition but also manifestly
improbable in itself that the conquest of Britain was effected
by small bodies of colonists acting independently. Most of
the smaller units in the Tribal Hidage seem to belong to the
ancient kingdom of Middle Anglia, but Bede's examples show
that similar districts were known elsewhere. How far these
districts survived in the wapentakes and hundreds (double
hundreds, etc.) of later times is a question which requires
topographical investigation. The frequent occurrence of the
figure 2400 in the Burghal Hidage suggests combinations of
such districts ; but the smaller figures given in that document
lead one to suppose that a more accurate distribution of
hidage had been attempted in later times.

Several difficulties of course still remain to be explained.
In the first place the hidage of East Anglia and 'the original
Mercia,' together probably with the districts (Middle Anglia)
lying between these two kingdoms, is far greater than we
should expect from their treatment in later times. But is it
not possible that, so far as these districts are hidated at all,
their hidage may have been reassessed[2] on a principle derived

Wight he gave a quarter of it (300 hides) to Wilfrid (*Hist. Eccl.*
IV. 16).

[1] Small districts elsewhere also bear names of this form, *e.g.
Tomsetna* (B. 455), *Lilsætna* (B. 1119). In B. 454 we find the
expression *principibus Tonsetorum*.

[2] The Isle of Wight must have undergone a similar reassess-
ment. Its inhabitants in early times seem to have been a different
people from the West Saxons.

from the South after the establishment of West Saxon supremacy[1]? It has often been remarked that the frequent definition of the hide (especially in the *Hist. Eliensis*) as containing 120 acres points at least to a tradition of a different reckoning. Unfortunately, however, we have practically no means of determining the normal size of the ancient hide in any of these districts, for even in regard to Mercia evidence derived from Oxfordshire or Hwiccia[2] is clearly inadmissible.

Another difficulty is caused by the fact that in one case Bede's evidence is at variance with the Tribal Hidage. The

[1] I do not suggest that the West Saxon and Mercian hides were originally different. Let us take the case of a village which has 200 acres of cultivated land, and let us suppose that at a certain time this village was reckoned at five hides. In course of time the population increases and the amount of land under cultivation is trebled. Two courses are obviously possible. Either the hide may be fixed at 40 acres, and consequently the number of hides may gradually be increased to fifteen; or the assessment may remain fixed, and consequently the hide may gradually grow until on an average it contains 120 acres. It seems to me quite likely that the former of these systems may have prevailed in Mercia and the latter in Wessex. At the same time there is no evidence, so far as I am aware, that even the West Saxon hide contained 120 acres before the tenth century, and it is at least questionable whether hides of this size were normal even then. At all events the figures of the Burghal Hidage in most cases greatly exceed those of Domesday Book. Of course a further element of doubt is introduced by the uncertainty as to the size of the acre, but into that question we need hardly enter. The hypothesis that the normal holding of the *tributarius* (*gafolgelda*) was originally one of 30 or 40 acres agrees well with the evidence obtainable as to the holdings of such persons in the eleventh century and so obviates the necessity for our believing that the economic condition of the peasantry had been seriously depressed during the intervening period.

[2] According to tradition Hwiccia had originally belonged to Wessex; consequently we might reasonably expect an analogy to West Saxon custom in its hidage-system.

former gives only 12,000 hides to Mercia, while in the latter we find 30,000 assigned to 'the original Mercia.' Presumably there is a difference in the size of the hide. But are we to suppose that there has been a change in the reckoning or that the hidage is in one case recorded according to the Northumbrian and in the other according to the Mercian standard? Bede's information may quite possibly date from 655—659, while there is really nothing to prevent us from assigning the Tribal Hidage to the time of Offa or Coenwulf.

It is a more serious difficulty if the hide is a variable unit in the Tribal Hidage itself. One can hardly help doubting whether the 7000 hides of Hwiccia (*Hwinca, Hynica*) are reckoned on the same basis as the 30,000 hides of East Anglia. Yet the former was a frontier province, and in early times its population may have been very sparse. It would hardly be an unparalleled thing for such a district to preserve an antiquated assessment even in official records[1].

In spite of these difficulties enough perhaps has been said to show that the survey presents an intelligible and, with perhaps one or two exceptions, a fairly consistent scheme, the antiquity of which is in principle vouched for by the examples derived from Bede and Beowulf. The essential point to be borne in mind is that, whatever may have been the normal size of the individual hide from time to time, the hide in the aggregate was from the earliest times a unit, presumably for fiscal and military purposes, imposed from above.

---

[1] We may compare the statistics for Devonshire in Domesday Book; cf. Maitland, *op. cit.* pp. 400 ff., 467.

CHAPTER VIII.

THE HISTORY OF THE OLDER COUNTIES.

§ 1. *The South-Eastern Group.*

WE must now turn to the history of the older counties. It will be convenient to begin with those districts which came under the West Saxon crown in 825.

I. Sussex. It has already been mentioned that during the ninth century we find apparently no reference to any earls in this county. In the reign of Offa however we are confronted with a somewhat perplexing number of such persons. In B. 252 we find a grant by an earl named Berhtwald, who at all events owned extensive lands in Sussex. The charter is confirmed by the earl's brother named Eadbald. There can be little doubt that this Berhtwald is identical with the earl of that name who signs Offa's charters from 759 to 790, while Eadbald may likewise be one of Offa's earls who signs from 764 to 790. In other charters of about the same period we find a different group of names. Thus in B. 208, a charter of 772, we find *Osuualdus dux Suðsax'* and three other names, *Osmund, Ælbuuald* and *Oslac*, each of which is followed by the title *dux*. In B. 1334, a charter of 780, the last named person makes a grant under the title *dux Suthsaxorum*. His signature is immediately followed by the names *Ealduulf* and *Ælbuuald*, but they bear no title. Whatever may have been the position of Berhtwald and his brother—they may quite well have been Mercians—it is extremely probable that this latter group of persons belonged to the old royal family of Sussex. For in other charters all these names, except Oswald, appear with the title *rex*. Osmund is described as *rex* in B. 145, 198, and 206, while Aldwulf, Aelfwald, and Oslac (*Osiai* MS.) all sign with this title in B. 197. Here then we seem to have a clear case of the title *rex* passing into the title *dux*. It is somewhat remarkable that Sussex should apparently possess four kings at the same time [1], at least three of whom (Osmund, Aldwulf, and Oslac) were granting land. This however is a feature for which we shall find analogies elsewhere. Indeed in some earlier South Saxon charters (B. 78, 144) we find two signatures (*Nunna, Vuattus*) occurring together with the title *rex*. It may be noted that in the time of Oslac and his colleagues Sussex still had a separate council of its own. Whether this was the case also in the ninth century, or whether the councils of Sussex and Kent were then combined—this is a

---

[1] The expression *regalis omnis dignitas* in B. 145, 1334 is worth noticing. In B. 145, 211, 212 we also find a king named Aethelberht, but he may have been a predecessor (perhaps about 760) of the other four.

question which apparently we have no means of answering.

II. Kent. We have seen that in the latter part of Alfred's reign there were two earls in Kent. This seems to have been the case throughout the ninth century. From the end of Ecgberht's reign the succession was perhaps as follows: for one province, probably that of West Kent, Hereberht (838—841), Alhhere (841—853), Aethelmod (853—859), Dryht-wald (860 —); for the other, Aethelwulf (838 —), Aethelric (855 —), Aethelred (860 —), Eastmund (867 —), Aethelwald (871—888). In the latter part of Ecgberht's reign there seem to have been two earls named Osmod and Dudda. But these lists are probably not complete; and again, if the councils of the South-Eastern kingdoms really were combined, it is quite possible that some of the names given here belonged to Essex, Surrey, or Sussex. It is probable however that there were two earls in Kent at the beginning of the century, for the famous Earl Oswulf, who held office under Cuthred (798[1]—807), is described in B. 445 as *Dei gratia dux atque princeps prouinciae orientalis Cantiae.* Oswulf appears with the title *dux* for the first time in 798 (B. 289). Before this the evidence for earls in Kent is scanty and doubtful[2]. On the other hand we frequently find two kings during the eighth century. When

---

[1] For this date cf. B. 322. A later date is given by B. 1336.

[2] We find *Eathelhun principis* in a charter of 761 (B. 189) and *Baltheardus dux* in a charter of 762 (B. 192). For the application of the term *principes* to the Kentish Council collectively cf. p. 330.

Wihtred died in 725 his kingdom according to Bede
(*H. E.* v. 23) went to his three sons Aethelberht,
Eadberht and Alric. Of these Aethelberht seems to
have reigned till 762, while Alric is otherwise unknown. In regard to Eadberht there is unfortunately
a serious chronological difficulty. According to the
Chronicle he died in 748, but several charters (B. 189,
190, 193) profess to have been granted or attested
by him in 761, 762. These two kings were eventually
succeeded by Eardwulf, son of Eadberht (B. 199),
and Sigered, but the precise nature of the succession
is somewhat doubtful; for Eardwulf signs beside
Aethelberht (B. 175) and Sigered beside Eadberht
(B. 193). All these kings sign with the title *rex
Cantiae* or *rex Cantuariorum*. How the kingdom
was divided is not quite clear, but in one case
(B. 159) it appears that a grant by Eadberht
required confirmation by Aethelberht. That there
was a real division of the kingdom is shown by
B. 194, where Sigered describes himself as *rex
dimidiae partis prouinciae Cantuariorum*. On this
occasion he is accompanied by a king named Eanmund. A little later, in 764 (B. 195), we meet with
a king named Heaberht, and in the following year
(B. 196, cf. 260) we find this king confirming the
grant of another king named Ecgberht. The latter
seems to have been still reigning in 779 (B. 228).
After this the history of the Kentish kingdom becomes altogether obscure. In B. 242, a doubtful
charter dated 781, we find a king *Ethelberhtus,* and
in B. 243, a charter of 784 (cf. Chron. F. *ad ann.*),
a king *Ealmundus.* During the greater part of his

reign Offa seems to have disposed of land in Kent
without reference to the national kings, whereas it
appears from B. 293 that grants made by Kentish
officials without Offa's consent were invalid.

Wihtred appears to have been sole king of Kent
during the greater part of his reign. Before this
there seem to have been divisions again, but the
chronology is unfortunately obscure. According to
Bede Hlothhere succeeded his brother Ecgberht in
673 (July) and reigned till 685 (February), when he
was succeeded by Ecgberht's son Eadric, who reigned
for a year and a half[1]. After this Kent was under
reges dubii uel externi until the time of Wihtred, who
according to *H. E.* v. 23 must have come to the throne
in the autumn of 690. Now during this period we
find charters issued not only by Hlothhere and Eadric
(B. 36, 44, 45, 67), but also by two kings named
Oswine and Swefheard (B. 35, 40, 41, 42, 73), who
clearly were reigning together. Oswine appears to
have belonged to the native dynasty (cf. B. 40, 73),
but Swefheard is stated in B. 42 to have been a son
of Sebbe, presumably the king of Essex. The obvious
inference is that these were the *reges dubii uel externi*
to whom Bede refers; and this conclusion is confirmed by the fact that according to *H. E.* v. 8
Swefheard was still reigning, together with Wihtred,
in 692. The objection is that, though the other
charters are dated only by indictions or regnal years,
one of Swefheard's charters (B. 42) bears the date

---

[1] These dates present a difficult chronological problem, into
which I cannot enter here. On the whole it seems probable that
the true dates are 674, 686, and (for Eadric's death) 687.

676. On the whole I am inclined to think that this charter has been interpolated[1], for Bede's language (*H. E.* IV. 5) distinctly implies that Hlothhere came to the throne immediately on Ecgberht's death, and it is hardly credible that Swefheard can have reigned from 676 to 692. My belief therefore is that Oswine reigned from 688 to 690 (or 691) and Swefheard (whose first year was Oswine's second, cf. B. 35, 42) from 689 to 692 or later. At all events it is clear that these two kings were reigning together for two years or more. It is somewhat surprising to find an East Saxon on the Kentish throne. A satisfactory explanation however is provided by a passage in B. 89, which states that Kent had been conquered by the (East) Saxon king Sigehere. Of course the authority of this charter is very poor, but the statement in question is not one which is likely to have been invented in later times. Swefheard therefore had probably been presented with part of the Kentish kingdom by members of his own family. If we turn now to Hlothhere, it is not clear that even he was sole king throughout his reign. The code which bears his name seems to have been issued by him and Eadric together, and in B. 45 we find the latter consenting to one of Hlothhere's grants. Before the time of Hlothhere however I have not been able to find any satisfactory evidence for a division of the kingdom[2].

---

[1] It may have been the custom about this time for kings to repeat the charters of their predecessors with changes in the names and dates. As a matter of fact we find another edition of this charter issuing from Hlothhere (B. 44), but it is dated 678.

[2] The establishment of a bishopric at Rochester cannot be

III. Essex. Mention has already been made of an earl of Essex whose death is recorded in Chron. 897. From 825, when Essex first came under the West Saxon dynasty, to this time its history seems to be a blank. None of its earls are known, and it is not clear whether it retained a council of its own. Down to 825 it was probably ruled by kings of its own line, subject to Mercian supremacy. The last king of whom we know was Sigered, who signs several Mercian charters, for the last time (as *subregulus*) in 823 (B. 373). For more than a century before this we have no East Saxon charters, though the names of several kings are known. It is to be observed that in early times we find here, as in Sussex, several kings reigning together. Thus in B. 81 and 87, charters dating from 692—695, we find three persons bearing the title *rex*, viz. Sebbe, Sigeheard and Swefred, the two latter being Sebbe's sons. During the greater part of Sebbe's reign the kingdom was divided between him and Sigehere (*H. E.* iii. 30, iv. 6), whose father Sigeberht was Sebbe's cousin. At an earlier period we find Saberht succeeded by his three sons (*ib.* ii. 5). The history of this dynasty is indeed highly instructive and has not received the attention which it deserves. It is therefore worth while to give a list of the kings together with their relationships to one another, so far as these can be ascertained. The chief authority for the genealogy is a ninth

admitted as satisfactory evidence, for Augustine would naturally derive his scheme of ecclesiastical organisation from Continental models.

century text printed in Sweet's *Oldest English Texts,*
p. 179[1].

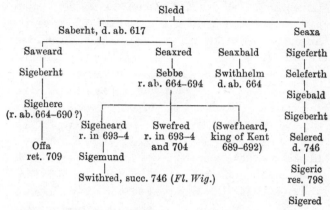

It is very likely that Seaxbald was one of
Saberht's three sons, but this cannot be proved.
Bede mentions two kings named Sigeberht, the
later of whom was reigning in 653 (*H. E.* III. 22).
Since Saberht's sons were young in 617, the son of
Saweard was probably the later Sigeberht. His
predecessor (*Sigberct paruus*) may have been a son
(or brother) of Seaxa. The death of a *Swebriht
Orientalium Saxonum rex* is recorded by Symeon of
Durham (*Gest. Reg.*) *ad ann.* 738, but his position

---

[1] A copy of this text, apparently incomplete, has been used by
William of Malmesbury and Florence of Worcester. The latter
informs us that Swithred was Selered's successor. As Swithred's
genealogy seems to have been unknown to him, this information
is probably correct. With this exception neither of these writers
seems to have had any evidence beyond what we now possess.
The further information which they give us seems to be due to
false readings and (probably incorrect) combinations.

in the genealogy is unknown. He is probably to be identified with the *Swebertus* of the tract *De Primo Saxonum Aduentu.*

IV. Middlesex. This name seems not to be mentioned by Bede. It occurs however in a trustworthy charter of 704 (B. 111), where it is called *provincia*, and again, with the same title, in one of Aethelbald's charters (B. 182). We find it mentioned again in B. 201, a charter of 767, after which it is of fairly frequent occurrence. There seems to be no evidence that Middlesex was originally a separate kingdom, though when Essex was divided (cf. *H. E.* III. 30), it may perhaps represent the territory which fell to one of the kings[1]. It is clear from *H. E.* II. 3 etc. that London was originally included in the East Saxon kingdom, while from II. 5 it appears that at Saberht's death Essex and Wessex were conterminous. From B. 115, which speaks of disputes between these two kingdoms, it may be inferred that this was still the case at the beginning of the eighth century. It is no doubt true that during Wulfhere's reign the whole of the East Saxon kingdom had become subject to Mercian supremacy (*H. E.* III. 30). But his successor Aethelred seems to have lost his hold over the South of England. The course of events is far from clear but, so far as our evidence goes, it seems to indicate a struggle for supremacy between Essex and Wessex. There can be little doubt that the possession of Kent[2] was one of the

[1] The northern frontier of the original Middlesex is of course quite uncertain.

[2] Sussex had become subject to Wessex in the time of Ceadwalla.

chief objects of contention between the two kingdoms. It is perhaps not altogether without significance that the laws of Wihtred were promulgated very shortly after those of Ine, and that one article (Ine 20, Wihtr. 28) is common to both codes. Since Wihtred's accession, or more probably the extension of his power over the whole of Kent, seems to have synchronised with the restoration of peace between that kingdom and Wessex[1], it is not unlikely that he was allied with Ine against the East Saxons. At all events it can hardly be doubted that about 688—693 Essex had succeeded in obtaining some kind of supremacy in Kent. It is further to be noted that Ine in the preface to his laws speaks of Erconwald, who died about 693–4, as 'my bishop,' a fact which seems to indicate that part of the diocese of London had come into his hands. If so the power of Essex must have been broken by this time. In 704 Swefred, king of Essex, granted land at Twickenham (B. 111), but the charter is signed also by the Mercian king Coenred. By this time therefore the supremacy of Mercia had apparently been restored, though Middlesex still belonged to Essex. Eventually the former was annexed by Mercia. The date of this occurrence is unknown, but it would seem to have taken place long before the end of the eighth century. London was a place of meeting for the Mercian council from 748 onwards (B. 177) and Brentford from 780 (B. 235 etc.). There is no

---

[1] Cf. Chron. 694 and B. 86, a charter of 694 : *ego Wythredus rex Cantiae...referens gratias largitori bonorum domino qui dilatauit terminos nostros iuxta paternam antiquitatem* etc.

reason for supposing that Middlesex passed with Essex under the West Saxon dynasty in 825. From B. 400, a charter of 831, it appears that it still remained Mercian. If it had any earls of its own in later times their names have not been preserved.

V. Surrey. Mention has already been made (p. 192) of an earl of Surrey, named Huda, whose death is recorded in the Chronicle, *ann.* 853. In B. 558 we find the will of another earl named Aelfred, who apparently held office in the early part of King Alfred's reign. This province came under the West Saxon dynasty in 825 together with Sussex, Kent and Essex. Before that year it had probably been under Mercia for a considerable time. We have no evidence for the existence of any separate provincial organisation, but in Offa's time it was possibly under the *praefectus* Brorda (cf. B. 275). If the arguments stated in the last section are correct we should expect it to have belonged to Wessex again before the time of Aethelbald; and this suspicion is to a certain extent supported by two unsatisfactory documents (B. 72, 133), which profess to date from the period in question. In Wulfhere's time it was again subject to Mercian supremacy, though it had then a *subregulus* of its own named Frithuwald (B. 33, 34, 39). From B. 34, 39 it would appear that a few years earlier Surrey had been under the Kentish king Ecgberht. This Kentish over-lordship may have been in existence for a considerable time, for in Chron. 568 we find a tradition of hostilities between Kent and Wessex, which implies that the two kingdoms were then conterminous. But it is doubtful whether Surrey belonged originally to Kent. The name occurs in *H. E.* IV. 6, and (in a corrupt form) in B. 34, 39. If, as appears probable, the name means 'southern district' (cf. p. 253, footnote), it would seem to imply that the territory in question had belonged originally to Essex.

§ 2. *The Kingdom of the Hwicce.*

We have already (p. 208) seen that the district assigned to Worcester in the Burghal Hidage seems to correspond to Worcestershire. For Gloucester as an administrative centre we have no early evidence, though from Chron. 918 it appears to have been a place of military importance in Edward's reign. These districts did not come under the West Saxon crown[1] until the time of Earl Aethelred, apparently about 880—883 (cf. B. 551). Together with part of Warwickshire they formed from quite early times the diocese of the Hwicce. From B. 490 it seems probable that an earl named Aethelwulf, whose signatures extend from 836 to 866, had jurisdiction in this diocese[2]. At the beginning of the century it was certainly, at least in part, under an earl named Aethelmund who was killed by the West Saxons in 802. His signatures bear the title *dux* from 792 onwards, but he signs without title considerably

---

[1] According to the Chronicle, however, they had originally (in the sixth century) belonged to Wessex.

[2] It would perhaps hardly be safe to call him earl of the Hwicce; for from B. 416, 454 it appears that several other earls had rights in this district during his lifetime.

earlier. Before this time we find a number of charters, the last of which (B. 232, 233, 238) date from 778—781, issued or attested by two brothers named Uhtred and Aldred, both of whom bear the title *regulus* or *subregulus Hwicciorum*. In earlier charters (B. 183, 187) a third brother named Eanberht appears beside them. Earlier in the century we find (B. 116, 117, 122, cf. 76) grants by three brothers named Aethelheard, Aethelweard and Aethelric, who describe themselves as sons of King Oshere. Grants by Oshere himself occur in B. 51, 85, and by a king named Osric (cf. Bede, *H. E.* IV. 21) in B. 43. Two other persons named Eanhere and Eanfrith, apparently kings of the same nation, are mentioned by Bede in *H. E.* IV. 13. Although the genealogy cannot be traced, there can be little doubt that all these persons belonged to a hereditary line, which ruled, like that of Essex, subject to Mercian supremacy. The extent of their territory cannot be determined with certainty, but since the bishops of Worcester were also known as *episcopi Hwicciorum* it seems probable that the kingdom and the diocese originally coincided. Regarding the administration of the kingdom and its territorial divisions we have no information. Consequently we cannot tell whether anything corresponding to the counties existed in early times[1]. In charters dating from the

---

[1] In B. 309, a document dating from 803 and recording a transfer of lands from the see of Hereford to that of Worcester, we find the heading *into Vuincelcumbe scire*, but the meaning of this expression is not explained. Winchcombe was a borough in the eleventh century.

days of the kingdom we never find Hwiccian signatures with the titles *dux* or *princeps*. On the
other hand the titles *praefectus* and *comes* occur
fairly often. In B. 223 and 232 we find three
praefecti, while in B. 116 (cf. B. 124) four persons
sign with the title *comes* (cf. p. 322).

§ 3. *The Shires of Wessex.*

It has been mentioned (p. 191 f.) that in the
ninth century we find earls in all the West Saxon
counties. Before 825 however there are few references
to such persons which give any clue to the provinces
which they governed. In the Chronicle, *ann.* 800,
we hear of an earl named Weoxtan in Wiltshire,
and in *ann.* 755 of an earl named Cumbra who
clearly had the government of Hampshire. In
charters dating from before 828 the number of signatures is quite small. Indeed I have not noticed
any charter which contains more than seven (excluding the king and ecclesiastics) after the time
of Ine. The title *praefectus* occurs frequently in
signatures, but the persons so described seem to be
really earls[1]. Thus a certain Wulfheard signs in
B. 377, 398 as *praefectus*, but in several other
charters as *dux*. He is probably the person described
as *aldormon* in Chron. 823. Monnede appears as
praefectus in B. 389, 391, 392, 398, as *dux* in B. 395.
Wiohtbrord and Lulla, who sign with the title

[1] Occasionally also we meet with the title *comes* (*regis*) in
signatures (B. 225, 258); but it is not clear that these persons
were earls.

praefectus in B. 300, appear in one of Berhtric's charters (B. 282) with the title *princeps*. Wigferth signs as *praefectus* in B. 258 and as *princeps* in B. 282. Hemele, who appears as *princeps* and *patricius* in B. 258, is probably identical with the *Ham…* who signs as *praefectus* in B. 225[1]. The *praefectus Combra* of B. 169 is in all probability the *aldermon Cumbra* of the Chronicle (*ann.* 755). In Cynewulf's charters, where the same names recur pretty constantly, the abbreviation *p͠r* seems to have been used. This might stand either for *princeps* or for *praefectus*; in one case (B. 186) it has been wrongly expanded into *presbyter*. In some charters, B. 181, 185, 224, 327, no titles are used; but most of these signatures occur elsewhere with the title *praefectus*. Indeed if we omit B. 327, where some of the unspecified signatures are probably those of ecclesiastics, there are only two names in charters dating from 757—827 which do not occur elsewhere with titles (*praefectus, princeps, dux*). On the whole therefore there can be little doubt that almost all the lay signatories to West Saxon charters during this period were earls.

West Saxon charters before the time of Cynewulf are for the most part scantily attested and somewhat unsatisfactory. In two of Ine's charters, B. 101, 108, we find lists of nine unspecified signatures; but in the former several of the names are Mercian and are to be found in charters of Aethelbald. The titles *dux* and *princeps* do not occur, while *praefectus* is quite

[1] Cf. also *Æmele prefectus* in B. 208.

rare[1]; nor do we find any reference to the counties. On the other hand it is clear from several passages in Ine's laws (cap. 8, 36, 39) that 'shires' of some kind were in existence, and that each shire was under an official called *ealdormon*. It cannot of course be proved that these shires correspond to the later counties; but there seems to be no adequate reason for doubting their identity. We hear in the Chronicle (*ann.* 755) of *Hamtunscir* in connection with events which took place in 757; and it is further to be noted that in Cynewulf's and Berhtric's charters the number of *praefecti* is usually six, though seven occur occasionally (B. 200). It is likely enough therefore that the shire-system of Ine's time did not differ greatly from that which we find in existence later. But what was its origin?

Bede (*H. E.* IV. 12) says that after the death of Coenwalh (A.D. 674?) the kingdom was divided among *subreguli* for about ten years, until it was reunited by Ceadwalla. This statement can hardly be strictly correct, for according to the Chronicle the kingdom during this interval was held first by Aescwine and then by Centwine, and in the latter point the evidence of the Chronicle is corroborated by Eddius (cap. 39). But we do find signatures with the title *regulus* or *subregulus* in early West Saxon charters. An example occurs even in one of Berhtric's charters (B. 258), though nothing seems to be known of the

---

[1] Two examples occur in Cuthred's charters, one in B. 169 (see above) and another in B. 179 ; three examples occur in one of Aethelheard's charters (B. 1331). In one of Ine's charters (B. 114) we find the title *patricius*.

person (Lunling by name) so described. In two of
Ine's charters, B. 121 and Kemble's text of B. 142,
we find the signature *Baldredus rex*, which is perhaps to be attributed to the Baldred who grants land
in B. 71. In B. 142 we find reference to *subreguli*
named Baldred and Aethelheard. The latter is probably the person who signs as *frater reginae* in
Kemble's text. Further, if we compare B. 142 with
B. 147, it will be seen that he is in all probability
identical with Ine's successor. Again in B. 107 we
find a grant by a certain *Coinredus,* who uses no title.
It can hardly be doubted however that he is the
Coenredus rex Vuestsaxonum whose signature occurs
in two South Saxon charters (B. 78, 144). In B. 101
we find reference to a grant made by Ine and *Conred.*
Since Coenred, Ine's father, is mentioned in the
Preface to the Laws as being then alive, it is
probable that he is the person to whom all these
notices refer. In B. 101 we also find mention of
a *Cissa rex,* whom Ine describes as one of his *prae-
decessores.* He is perhaps the same person whose
signature occurs in B. 71. At all events he is
without doubt one of the people to whom the
patricius Hea (*Heaha, Haeha,* cf. B. 108) refers in
B. 29, in the expression *parentum meorum qui regni
gubernacula potiri noscuntur*[1].

---

[1] In B. 102 we find the signature *Cuthred rex.* This may be
the later king of Wessex; but in B. 101 we find reference to a
grant of land 'east' (*i.e.* north) of the Thames by a *regulus* of
this name. Since he is associated with Aethelred, it is probable
that he was subject to Mercia. This seems to be the case also with
the *Berhtwald rex,* whose grant is recorded in B. 65 (cf. p. 299).

Bede's evidence as to the existence of *subreguli* in Wessex is therefore fully borne out by the charters. It is true that these charters are not documents of unimpeachable authority. Many of them may have been altered and interpolated, if they are not forgeries altogether. But unless the authors had at least a tradition to go upon, they would hardly have chosen names which are otherwise unknown and given them titles which were not used in Wessex after the eighth century[1]. Moreover the evidence of the charters is confirmed by the Chronicle. In *ann.* 661 we hear of a *Coenbryht cyning*, who was not supreme king of Wessex. Again in 626 E we find a statement, not derived from Bede, that Edwin slew five kings in his campaign against Wessex. What then was the position of these kings? It may be observed that Coenred apparently owned lands in Dorset (cf. B. 107), a fact which agrees with the foundation of Wimborne by his daughter. Baldred and Aethelheard seem to have owned lands in Somerset, while Cissa was perhaps connected with Berkshire. Are we then to conclude that the West Saxon shires were originally separate kingdoms, and that one of them had come to possess supremacy over the rest, just as Essex and the Hwicce eventually became subject to Mercia?

That is not the conclusion to which the evidence seems to me to point. According to the Chronicle, whatever may be the historical value of its early

---

[1] We may compare B. 108. This may be a spurious document, but I can see no reason for refusing to believe that the signatures which it contains are those of Ine's council. If they have been invented the author must have been an expert philologist.

entries, the throne of Wessex was held by one family from the beginning. Both Coenberht and Coenred certainly claimed to be members of this family, as may be seen from the genealogies (Chron. 685, 688), and it is difficult to believe that Aethelheard obtained the throne merely because he was Ine's brother-in-law[1]. Moreover Bede (*H. E.* II. 9) speaks of Cwichelm as *rex Occidentalium Saxonum*, though his father Cynegils was alive and reigning. This fact reminds us of a somewhat parallel case in Essex (p. 275), where we find a father and two sons all signing together with the title *rex*. According to the Chronicle Cwichelm died before Cynegils, the latter being succeeded by another son named Coenwalh. Cwichelm however had left a son named Cuthred[2], and in *ann.* 648 we find it stated that Coenwalh granted Cuthred 3000 (hides) at Ashdown. Now are we to regard this act as the creation of an earldom? Is it possible that the grant in question was the origin of Berkshire[3]? If the event had not been one of permanent importance, such an entry as this would hardly have found its way into the

[1] No great stress need be laid on the statement contained in the Preface to the Parker Chronicle that he traced his descent from Cerdic.

[2] He is called 'king' by three MSS. (B, C, F) in *ann.* 639.

[3] In later times Berkshire was apparently reckoned at 2400 hides (cf. p. 211), but if the 300 hide unit originally amounted to 360 hides (cf. p. 265), continuity of assessment is hardly impossible. I do not understand Mr Stevenson's criticism of Mr Plummer's note on this passage (*Asser's Life of King Alfred*, p. 154, footnote). In view of the Tribal Hidage it is surely incredible that the hidages of early times were determined by any process of counting.

Chronicle. For the division of the kingdom we may compare the case of Sebbe and Sigehere in Essex (p. 275); but a closer parallel is to be found in *Beowulf* (2195 f.), where we find King Hygelac granting 7000 (hides), together with princely authority, to his nephew.

This suggestion of course explains only one of the counties. But it is to be remembered that at the time of Ine's succession the conquest of Somerset was quite recent, if we may trust the Chronicle (*ann*. 652, 658, 682). If Baldred really lived at the time which the charters represent, he may quite well have been the first English ruler of this county. Before the reign of Coenwalh, the kingdom of Wessex—or that part of it which lay south of the Thames—was probably confined to Berkshire, Wiltshire, and part of Hampshire. We cannot trace the origin of the two latter counties; but they may have sprung from a division similar to that between Sebbe and Sigehere[1].

I suspect then that the shires of Wessex owe their origin to divisions of the kingdom between members of the royal family. This explanation enables us to reconcile to some extent the different accounts of the events which took place after the death of Coenwalh. Aescwine and Centwine may have been members of the royal family who held

[1] The early history of Wessex was parallel in many ways to that of Essex. Both kingdoms were subject from time to time to the supremacy of Mercia, and both had been deprived by the latter of large portions of their territories. It was probably not until the time of Ecgberht that the positions of the two kingdoms became essentially different.

sub-kingdoms under Coenwalh, and on the death of the latter they may have succeeded, one after the other, in making themselves supreme over their colleagues. In this connection we may note that according to the genealogies in the Chronicle not one of the four kings who followed Coenwalh was at all closely related to his predecessor. Perhaps it may be objected that the term applied to the head of the shire in Ine's laws is not *cyning* but *ealdormon*. The latter word must therefore be the equivalent of *subregulus*, though elsewhere it is used to translate *princeps*. But is this objection necessarily fatal? The term *princeps* is applied by Bede (*H. E.* III. 21) to Peada[1], though he was a son of King Penda and though the province which he governed is called *regnum*. In Sussex we have seen (p. 270) the same person described first as *rex* and later as *dux*[2]. Moreover the word *aldorman*, as we have seen (p. 163), appears to be of no very great antiquity. The word *aldor*, of which it seems to be merely an extended form, means no more than 'chief,' and is frequently applied in the old poetry even to supreme kings. Indeed *aldorman* itself is sometimes used (with possessive pronouns) to denote any person with authority over others. I can see no reason therefore for disbelieving that in Ine's time the head of the shire may in some cases have been known both as *cyning* and as *aldorman*. Of course it does not

---

[1] So in *H. E.* III. 25 the Northumbrian kings Oswio and Alhfrith are described as *principes*.

[2] In the next chapter it will be seen that the term *comes* is occasionally applied to kings of the Hwicce.

follow that the earls of succeeding ages were necessarily members of the royal family[1]. If a district
originally set apart as a portion for a royal prince
had been retained by him, or possibly by several
members of the family in succession, for a considerable number of years, it may well have been found
convenient to retain such a district as a permanent
administrative unit, even when it had to pass into
the hands of a person of less exalted birth. To this
point however we shall have to return shortly.

§ 4.   *The Divisions of Mercia.*

The history of this kingdom seems to have been
essentially different from that of Wessex. Until the
year 825 the expansion of the latter had, except
perhaps in the southern part of Hampshire, been
gained almost entirely at the expense of the Welsh.
The expansion of Mercia on the other hand seems to
have been due to a gradual course of annexation
among its English neighbours. The last stages of
this process may be seen from the charters. The
kingdom of the Hwicce came to an end about 780
(cf. p. 281), while the South Saxon dynasty seems
to have given up the royal title about the same time
(cf. p. 270). The kingdom of Kent also disappears
after 784, though two abortive attempts were made

---

[1] It is to be noted that on the deposition of Sigeberht (Chron.
755) one 'earl' (Cumbra) seems to have stood out against the
action of the rest. The story is intelligible if the council consisted
of a number of semi-independent princes. But if the person in
question had been an official of lower standing his conduct would
hardly have been tolerated.

later to reconstitute it. But it is clear that the same process had been in operation for more than a century. Large portions of Wessex and Essex had been annexed, and more than one kingdom seems to have come to an end altogether. Thus in *H. E.* III. 21 Bede speaks of the *regnum* of the *Middilangli*; and we know from genealogies that Lindsey had once possessed a dynasty descended from the gods. It is quite possible that other kingdoms also had perished in the same way[1]. Indeed from *H. E.* III. 24 and the Tribal Hidage it would seem that 'the original Mercia' was a comparatively small country, comprising probably the greater part of Staffordshire, Derbyshire and Nottinghamshire together with portions of Warwickshire and Leicestershire. Unfortunately, however, the political geography of the Midlands before the great invasion is a very obscure question, as many of the units mentioned in the Tribal Hidage have not yet been satisfactorily

[1] A not unlikely case is that of the *populi qui ultra amnem Sabrinam ad occidentem habitant* (*H. E.* v. 23), which had a bishopric of their own. This bishopric seems to have been fixed at Hereford by the beginning of the ninth century, but in earlier times it was called *Vestorelih* (MS. C.C.C.C. 183, a text closely related to the one published in Sweet's *Oldest English Texts*, p. 167 ff., but dating from about the time of Aethelstan). I have not been able to identify this place. In Florence's Appendix the name *Hecana* is applied to the see. In the same Appendix mention is made of a certain Merewald, king of the *Westan Hecani*, who is said to have been a son of Penda. Again in Malmesbury's *Gesta Pontificum*, § 163, we find mention of an inscribed monument which claimed to have been set up by Cuthberht (bishop of the same diocese 736—741) to his predecessors and to a certain *regulus Milfrith*. This name recalls those of Merewald's daughters, Milburg, Milthryth and Milgyth.

identified. We have seen that most of the Midland
counties first make their appearance during the tenth
century. It is not clear whether any corresponding
divisions existed before the invasion, but the evidence
of the Tribal Hidage is in most cases decidedly
against such a supposition. In the time of the
Mercian kingdom we find record of a considerable
number of earls (*aldormen*); but the origin of these
officials and the nature of their jurisdiction are alike
unknown. It may be suspected that in some cases
they were resident magistrates set by the Mercian
king over conquered districts[1].

§ 5. *The hereditary principle in succession to earldoms.*

This question has been left until now in order
that the evidence for the earlier period might be
taken into account. In the ninth and tenth centuries
we find a number of cases in which the succession
passed to near relatives. Aelfric, earl of Mercia,
who was exiled in 985, was, according to Florence of
Worcester, the son of Aelfhere (d. 983) who held the
same earldom. The latter had a brother named
Aelfheah, who was an earl in the South (cf. p. 175 f.).
Aethelstan 'Half-king' was succeeded in his earldom
(East Anglia) by his son Aethelwold, and the latter
by Aethelwine, another son (cf. pp. 174, 179). A
third son named Aethelsige held an earldom in the

---

[1] Cf. Bede, *H. E.* III. 24 *eiectis principibus regis non proprii,*
where however the reference is to Northumbrian officials in
Mercia.

South. It has also been suggested (cf. p. 194) that
Aethelstan himself was the son of an earl named
Aethelfrith. The southern earl Aethelwold whose
will is recorded in B. 819 has been connected both
with this family and with other earls of the same
period[1]. Byrhtnoth's predecessor in the earldom
of Essex was named Byrhtferth. As the name of
Byrhtnoth's father was Byrhthelm, it seems not
unlikely that Byrhtferth was a near relative. Ead-
wulf of Bamborough was succeeded by his sons
Aldred and Uhtred; and it has been stated (cf.
p. 186) that the later earl Osulf was a son of Aldred.
Ordlaf, one of Edward's earls, was a grandson of
an earl named Eanulf (B. 590). Aethelred, the
father of Ealhswith, is called *comes* by Asser (cap. 29);
her brother Aethelwulf was also an earl. It seems
not unlikely that the Kentish earl Aethelwald (d.
888) was the son of Aelfred, earl of Surrey (cf. B. 529,
558). In earlier times Aethelmund, earl of the
Hwicce (p. 280), was the son of a certain Ingeld,
who had been one of Aethelbald's earls (cf. B. 202,
203).

Some of the above examples are of course not
free from doubt. A careful examination of the
charters however might bring several more instances
to light. But it would require far more evidence
than this to prove that the succession was hereditary
in any strict sense of the term. Indeed some of the
examples quoted above tell as much against that
view as in favour of it. If Aelfhere, whose ancestry
we do not know, had a hereditary claim to the

---

[1] Cf. Napier and Stevenson, *Crawford Charters*, pp. 74, 86.

earldom of Mercia, his brother Aelfheah can hardly have had any such claim to a southern earldom. Further, what sort of claim can Aethelsige, the son of Aethelstan, have had to a southern earldom? Again, Byrhtferth may have been related to Byrhtnoth; but the predecessor of the former seems to have been Aelfgar, who was Byrhtnoth's father-in-law. Byrhtnoth and Aelfgar can therefore hardly have been near relations. If we turn to an earlier period, we find that Aethelmund left a son named Aethelric, who though a wealthy man (cf. B. 313) seems not to have been an earl. Again, though Aethelmund himself during the earlier part of his career was in the Hwiccian service, his father had been a Mercian official.

The apparent cases of inheritance quoted above are all capable of being explained otherwise[1]. It is not to be overlooked that the earls of the tenth century seem to belong to a comparatively small number of families, and that these families were to a great extent related or connected by marriage both with each other and with the royal family. Aelfhere and Aelfheah may have owed their earldoms to the fact that they were relatives of King Eadwig (cf. B. 917 etc.). Aethelstan 'Half-king' was also of royal descent (*Hist. Rames.*, cap. 3). Aelfgar does not appear as an earl until the reign of Eadred. Therefore his promotion took place in all

[1] An exception is perhaps to be made in the case of the Bamborough earls, who must at first have been practically independent. It is worth observing that the same set of names (Uhtred, Aldred, Osulf) occurs again in the following century.

probability after his daughter's marriage to King
Edmund. Aethelweard the historian was descended
from King Aethelred I. Osferth, one of Edward's
earls, was a relative both of that king and of Alfred
(B. 553, 611, 624). Aethelhelm, earl of Wiltshire
(d. 898), was perhaps a nephew of Alfred (cf. B. 553).
Two of Alfred's brothers, Aethelbald and Aethelberht,
may have been earls before they became kings. At
all events their signatures in charters are frequently
followed by the title *dux*, though these charters are
of doubtful value. This was also the case with the
later Mercian kings; for it is at least extremely
probable that the Beornwulf *dux* of B. 373, the
Ludeca *dux* of B. 378, and the Burgred *dux* of 452,
were identical with the kings who bore those names.
Again, it is to be noticed that almost all the earls of
the tenth century, except the Northumbrians, first
make their appearance in charters with the title
minister[1]. This means presumably that before they
became earls they had held some inferior office,
whether public or private, in the king's service.
Consequently their promotion may have been to
some extent in the nature of a reward. The two
principles however are not mutually exclusive; for
it was no doubt mainly from the leading families,
including those related to the royal family, that the

[1] Among the earls who held office between 940 and 975 the
only ones whose names seem not to occur previously with the
title *minister* are Aethelwold of East Anglia and Byrhtferth.
Some names however, especially Aelfhere, Aelfheah and Byrhtnoth, occur very seldom with this title. On the other hand
Eadmund appears as *minister* from 931 to 949, Eadric from 932
to 943, and Aethelweard from 959 to 975.

king's thegns were drawn. In either case the appointment of a new earl who was related to his predecessor was an event which would be likely to take place without the recognition of any definite hereditary right. The fact that many earls owned large private estates within their earldoms would no doubt be a contributory factor to such appointments.

It may however be urged that in still earlier times, when we get back to the days of *subreguli*, the succession must have been restricted to members of a particular family. In the case of provinces such as Essex (before 825) and the Hwicce, which had once been independent kingdoms, this is no doubt true. In regard to the shires of Wessex however, where the *subreguli*, so far as our evidence goes, appear to have claimed descent from one original stock, it is very much to be doubted. Unfortunately our information for Ine's period is not sufficient to enable us to settle the question. The only fact which stands out clearly is that a great deal of strife took place among members of the royal house. Possibly however an analogous case is to be found in the later history of the kingdom. Ecgberht made his son Aethelwulf king of Kent together with the neighbouring provinces. When Ecgberht died Aethelwulf became king of Wessex and gave Kent to his son (or brother) Aethelstan. It is clear from charters however that in both these cases the senior king reserved in part his sovereign rights. Aethelstan apparently died before 855, as we then find Aethelberht, son of Aethelwulf, reigning in Kent. About the same time Aethelbald, another son, seems to have become king in Wessex. Both these kings also were without doubt expected to be subject to their father during his lifetime[1], but after his death in 858 they seem to have ruled independently of one another (cf. B. 496). The two youngest sons, Aethelred and Alfred, apparently held no public office, probably because they were minors. When Aethelbald died, in 860, Aethelberht succeeded to the whole, Aethelred and Alfred renouncing their claims (cf. B. 553). Again, when Aethelberht died, in 866, Alfred again renounced his claim and Aethelred succeeded to the whole. The latter died in 871, and then Alfred became sole king. His nephews were probably minors at that time. Towards the end of his reign he seems to have associated his son Edward with him in the kingdom, probably in Kent (cf. B. 576). But on Alfred's death Aethelwald, apparently his only surviving nephew[2], at once began hostilities. There can be little doubt that he considered himself entitled to a share in the kingdom.

In this family history it seems clear that the kingdom was treated very much like any other family estate. But is there any reason for believing that a different principle prevailed in early times? If every male member of the royal family, who was

---

[1] There can be little doubt that Aethelberht did reign subject to his father (cf. B. 467, 486). With regard to Aethelbald it will be sufficient here to refer to Stevenson, *Asser's Life of King Alfred*, p. 195 ff.

[2] Osweald seems to have died before the date of Alfred's will. Aethelhelm, if he was identical with the earl of Wiltshire, died in 898. The nature of Osferth's relationship to Alfred is apparently not known.

of age, expected a share in the government, we
obtain an adequate explanation of those family
dissensions which we have noticed. It has been
seen (p. 270) that Sussex at one time possessed at
least four kings, and that the Hwicce (p. 281) had
on two occasions at least three. The latter[1] were in
both cases brothers. But in Essex we find a division
between more distant relatives (p. 275). In this
kingdom it is instructive to notice the fluctuation in
the number of rulers. Saberht, who seems to have
been sole king, was succeeded by his three sons, all
of whom perished together. After them we find
apparently three sole kings in succession. Then we
see two kings reigning together, the survivor of
whom eventually associates his two sons with him
in the government. There can have been nothing
permanent therefore about the divisions of this
kingdom. As for Sussex and the Hwicce, we have
no evidence at all for territorial divisions, though
each king clearly had estates of his own.

In later times provision was made (*e.g.* in Alfred's
Will, B. 553) for princes of the royal house by grants
of bookland. But before the introduction of the
'book' the provision must have taken some other
form. Now we cannot but be struck by the large
number of persons who bear the title 'king' in
early times. We find it applied to sons of the
reigning king, *e.g.* to Cwichelm beside Cynegils in
Wessex, Sigeheard and Swefred beside Sebbe in
Essex, Alhfrith beside Oswio in Northumbria; to

---

[1] Regarding the relationships of the South Saxon kings we
have no information.

brothers, *e.g.* Aelfwine beside Ecgfrith in North-umbria, Eowa (*Hist. Brit.*, Harl. § 65) beside Penda in Mercia; to nephews, *e.g.* Eadric (in the Laws) beside Hlothhere in Kent, and (probably) Berhtwald beside Aethelred in Mercia[1]; and to yet more distant relatives, *e.g.* Coenberht beside Coenwalh in Wessex. We may compare the case of the uncle and nephew, Hrothgar and Hrothwulf, who rule Denmark together in *Beowulf*[2]. In 1. 1181 ff. Hrothgar's wife expresses the hope that, if Hroth-wulf should outlive Hrothgar, he would treat her children, who were apparently minors, with the same generosity which he had received from her and her husband in his childhood. This case has a manifest resemblance to that of Hlothhere and Eadric, though in the latter case Eadric, probably through dissatisfaction with his share in the govern-ment, took up arms against his uncle. It is to be observed that in the South Saxon, East Saxon and Hwiccian cases given earlier in the chapter all the kings seem to be on a footing of equality, whereas in most of those quoted above one king is definitely subordinate to the other. But an examination of the instances will reveal the fact that, so far as our information reaches, the senior king seems always to have come into power before the others. Such was the case at all events with Cynegils, Sebbe, Oswio, Ecgfrith, Hlothhere and Coenwalh. On the other hand, when two or more kings succeed simul-

[1] B. 65; cf. Eddius, cap. 39: *Beorthuald filium fratris Ethel-redi regis Merciorum.*
[2] Cf. *Widsith*, 1. 45 f.

taneously, like Sigehere and Sebbe, their position seems to be equal. The case of Aethelwulf and his sons may therefore have been in accordance with ancient custom.

Again, we have seen that in the smaller kingdoms, Sussex and the Hwicce, we have no evidence for divisions consisting of solid blocks of territory, while the divisions of Essex were continually fluctuating. In Wessex on the other hand we find from the time of Coenwalh one supreme king together with a number of *subreguli*, while, from the eighth century at all events, the 'sub-kingdoms' were permanent territorial units. But is it not possible that this system is a later modification of the other, due in part to the greater size of the area which the West Saxon kingdom covered? It is clear that the chief throne was not confined to any one branch of the family. But is there any reason for believing that the sub-kingdoms were treated on a different principle? All that we know definitely is that Ceadwalla, who had lost his father, 'King' Coenberht, in infancy, was an exile when he grew up. Presumably therefore he had been kept out of his share in the government. It is clear from the constant recurrence of civil strife that the West Saxon system did not work satisfactorily. But there is surely no necessity for believing that this system had been in operation from the beginning. It is at least equally possible that Coenwalh created the 'shires,' as sub-kingdoms for his relatives, in order to avoid the necessity of having to share all his royal rights with them.

In the other kingdoms we find no clear evidence for any divisions exactly corresponding to the shires of Wessex. Northumbria had a sub-kingdom, Deira, which in the time of Oswio was under Oethelwald, the king's nephew; but it had formerly been independent, with a dynasty of its own. It is commonly assumed that Oethelwald was succeeded in the government of this province by Alhfrith and the latter again by Aelfwine; but, so far as I am aware, there is no proof of this in either case[1]. At a later period we find Ecgfrith, the son of Offa, signing charters (B. 253, 257) with the title *rex Merciorum* during the lifetime of his father (cf. Chron. 785). Similarly, as we have seen, Bede speaks of Cwichelm as *rex Occidentalium Saxonum* during the reign of Cynegils. It is not only in the smaller kingdoms therefore that we find a plurality of kings. If we are to give credence to the story of the five kings slain by Edwin, we must conclude that the number of persons who bore the royal title in Wessex was considerable. They can hardly all have had shires or sub-kingdoms of their own. Indeed this story distinctly suggests that the term *cyning* may at one time have been applied to every male member of the royal family.

It may perhaps be objected that Bede does not give the title *rex* to all men of royal birth; that on the contrary he sometimes speaks of such persons as *uir (iuuenis) de regio genere*[2]. The first objection is

---

[1] Cf. Eddius, cap. 7: *Ealfridus qui cum Oswin* (for *Oswiu*) *patre suo regnabat.*

[2] In the Old English version (II. 12 etc.) *regius iuuenis* is

hardly conclusive, as Bede often omits titles. Thus Aelfwine is mentioned three times but only once bears the title *rex*. On the other hand the use of the expression *uir de regio genere* may be evidence for the limitation of the term *rex* to persons actually in authority. Indeed this seems to be the case also with the use of *cyning* itself even in *Beowulf.* Hence it would be rash to assume that it was used otherwise in Bede's time. Yet, in spite of this, we may observe that the word *cyning* is in form a patronymic and would seem originally to have meant 'son of the family[1]' (*i.e.* presumably the royal family or the family of divine origin).

If this suggestion is correct it would appear that *cyning* was originally not a title of authority but rather equivalent to the modern word 'prince.' The title of authority was in all probability *hlaford* or (in earlier times) *dryhten*[2]. The former word is used in the Chronicle, *ann.* 823, to express the

---

translated by *ætheling*. This is the term regularly applied in later times (perhaps even in the eighth century) to princes of the royal family; but it is quite possible that it had originally a wider meaning. It is perhaps worth noting that in Chron. 944 the Scandinavian chiefs Anlaf and Raegenald are called *cyningas* in one text (A) and *cyneborene mœn* in another (E).

[1] Others derive *cyning* from a hypothetical word **kuni-*, 'king.' It is true that *cyne-* has this meaning in many compounds; but this may be a secondary development. In the oldest words of this class, *e.g. cynerice*, the original meaning may have been 'family' ('dynasty'). The O. Norse word *konr* seems properly to have meant 'scion,' 'descendant.'

[2] Cf. p. 131, footnote. It is perhaps worth mentioning that according to *Ynglinga Saga*, cap. 20, the kings of the Swedes had in ancient times borne the title *dróttinn*.

relationship of Ecgberht to the king of East Anglia, and in *ann.* 924 (A) that of Edward the Elder to the Scottish king and others. There can be little doubt moreover that one or other of these terms was used in earlier times to express the relationship of such rulers as Wulfhere or Aethelbald to the kings who were under their suzerainty[1]. Lastly, we need hardly hesitate to believe that the same terms were used of a king in reference to his relatives, even when he had associated them with him in the government[2].

We can now perhaps see why the phenomenon of a number of kings ruling apparently on equal terms occurs so much more frequently in the smaller kingdoms than in the larger. It would not be to the interest of the Mercian or West Saxon overlord that any member of the South Saxon or Hwiccian families should increase his power at the expense of the rest. In independent kingdoms on the other hand it is clear that ambitious princes were always trying to reduce or expel their colleagues. Indeed the history of the Northumbrian kingdom is almost

---

[1] Cf. *H. E.* iii. 30 : *prouinciae Orientalium Saxonum...praefuere reges Sigheri et Sebbi, quamuis ipsi regi Merciorum Vulfheræ subiecti*; v. 23 : *hae omnes prouinciae...cum suis quaeque regibus Merciorum regi Aedilbaldo subiectae sunt.*

[2] According to *Beow.* 2375 Beowulf would have become *hlaford* to his cousin Heardred, the son of Hygelac, if he had consented to accept the (chief) throne on Hygelac's death. So in l. 2604, 2627, 2635, he is called *mondryhten, freodryhten, hlaford,* to Wiglaf, another of his relatives, while in l. 2001 Hygelac is *dryhten* to Beowulf. We may perhaps compare *Byrhtnoth,* l. 224, where Aelfwine says of Earl Byrhtnoth: *he wæs ægðer min mæg and min hlaford.*

as full of family strife as that of Wessex. The fact that the peaceful relations between Hrothgar and Hrothwulf became a theme of poetry in itself goes to show how rarely such a state of things occurred.

Lastly, it may be observed that not only were there kings who apparently had no kingdoms strictly belonging to them; occasionally also we find persons who were not kings ruling over kingdoms. The most striking case is that of Earl Aethelred, Alfred's son-in-law. Aethelweard (*ad ann.* 894) calls him *rex*[1], but I have not been able to find this title in any contemporary writings, while *subregulus* is very rare (B. 561). In the Chronicle and in his signatures to charters he appears with the same titles (*aldormon, dux*) as any other earl. Yet his position seems to have differed but little from that of his royal predecessors, and we find him issuing charters, sometimes (B. 552, 557) even without any mention of Alfred's consent. The explanation of his position is clearly to be found in the expression *Myrcna hlaford* applied to him[2] in B. 582 and in the Chronicle, *ann.* 911

---

[1] So also in Celtic sources; cf. Plummer, *Two Saxon Chronicles*, II. p. 119.

[2] In B. 608 Aethelred and Aethelfled together are described as *Myrcna hlafordas*. Aethelred's power may have been strengthened by his marriage, but there is no reason for supposing that this was the beginning of it. Indeed in his earliest charters (cf. p. 193, footnote) Aethelfled's name does not appear. The continuance of her authority, which was clearly of a personal character (*domina Merciorum*, B. 583; *Myrcna hlæfdige*, Chron. 912 ff., B, C), after Aethelred's death was probably due to the fact that she was the king's sister. It can hardly have been in accordance with ancient custom, in spite of the case of Sexburg. During the earlier period however it is not clear that her position differed essentially from

(B, C). Further, the language used by Bishop Werfrith in B. 608[1] shows that the relationship indicated by this expression was of a personal nature. We must conclude then that, though in respect of rank Aethelred was on a level with the other earls and with the bishops of Mercia, his authority extended over them. His relationship to them seems indeed to have been somewhat analogous to that of the supreme kings to dependent kings in earlier times.

It is true of course that we occasionally hear of kings who were not of royal descent. Besides Harold II. the known cases are Aelle, the last

---

that of Aethelswith, the wife of Burgred (cf. B. 509, 522, 524). The wives of other Mercian kings are not spoken of in the same way, though they use the title *regina*. The position of the king's wife in Wessex is a difficult question which it is hardly necessary to discuss at length here. In the latter part of the tenth century (perhaps earlier) *hlæfdige* was the term regularly applied to her in English, while in Latin *regina* occurs fairly often. In early times we find the word *cwen* applied to Sexburg, Aethelburg and Frithugyth. But between the reigns of Berhtric and Edgar the king's wife had seldom either the title or the status of queen (cf. Asser, cap. 13, with Mr Stevenson's notes, where the references are collected). It is not quite clear whether Alfred was responsible for the explanation given by Asser or merely for the story of Eadburg. One is inclined to suspect that the position of the king's wife may have been determined by her birth. The kings of the seventh century, at all events in Mercia and Northumbria, usually if not always married women of royal birth; but in Wessex after the eighth century this was rarely the case. It is to be observed however that the word *cwen* seems originally to have meant no more than ' wife.'

[1] *þæt is þonne þæt Werfrið bisceop and se hired æt Wigraceastre syllað and gewritað Æþelrede and Æþelflæde heora hlafordum* etc.

English king of Northumbria[1], and probably Ceolwulf II., the last king of Mercia. But the circumstances in all these cases seem to have been
somewhat peculiar. On the Confessor's death the
only male member of the royal house left was a
minor and therefore probably ineligible. Burgred
and Osberht may have been the last of their lines ;
at all events we never hear of their families again.
Moreover, though the circumstances of Ceolwulf's
death or retirement are unknown, he clearly did not
succeed in founding a dynasty, while the reigns of
Aelle and Harold ended in complete disaster. It is
probable therefore that we should regard all these
cases as due to special emergencies or external
pressure and as only partly approved by the national
feeling.

I suspect then that the kingdom was originally
regarded as the property not of the king but of the
royal family, and that every member of the family
who was of age had a right to share in it; and
further, that when a division occurred, it originally
took the form of a division of royal estates and
rights. Such a system as this would, in theory at
least, admit of a redistribution whenever a king
died or whenever a young member of the family
came of age. How far the claim might reach we do
not know. Ecgberht was the great-great-grandson
of Ine's brother. Coenwulf claimed through six
generations from a brother of Penda. If these
persons had been killed before they obtained the

---

[1] The northern part of Northumbria had kings, who were
probably of English blood, for a few years after Aelle's death
(cf. Plummer, *op. cit.*, II. p. 85) ; but their history is obscure.

throne, would their relatives have been entitled to receive royal wergelds[1]? If so one would expect that many earls, West Saxon as well as Mercian[2], must have had royal wergelds. But we have no means of answering the question. Quite possibly some of the ancestors of Ecgberht and Coenwulf bore the title *cyning*, although they did not possess the chief throne[3].

[1] We may note that Oswald, who is mentioned in Chron. 728, 730, belonged to a branch of the royal family which had not held the chief throne for three generations, even if his genealogy is preserved in full. Yet he is called *æþeling*, and therefore presumably he would have an aetheling's wergeld. But this, as we have seen (p. 17 f.), was identical with that part of the king's wergeld which went to the relatives, *i.e.* it was that of a king who had no court of his own (cf. p. 167 and note).

[2] It has been mentioned above (p. 295) that several of the later Mercian kings (Beornwulf, Ludeca, Burgred) first make their appearance as earls.

[3] In this section I have thought it best to discuss the English evidence by itself. It is clear however that similar phenomena are to be found in other Teutonic nations. Thus in its account of the great invasion the Chronicle (*ann.* 871, 875) mentions five Danish kings, and the list is not complete. The ancient kingdom of Sweden had many kings belonging to the same dynasty (cf. *Yngl. Saga* 40); so also Norway after its unification (cf. *Haralds Saga Harf.* 35). The history of the Merovingian dynasty obviously presents several points of striking resemblance to that of the English kingdoms. Even in the earliest times it is by no means clear that the persons described as *principes* (ἡγεμόνες) by the Romans were not as a rule related to one another. At all events the chiefs of the Cherusci, whose names are recorded (Segestes, Segimundus, Segimerus, Segithancus, Inguiomerus, Arminius, Flauus, Italicus), all belonged to one or other of two families, which may quite possibly have been related. Moreover Tacitus (*Ann.* xi. 16) uses the expression *stirps regia* in connection with this tribe. If this explanation is correct the incident related in *Ann.* ii. 88 will be merely one of the familiar attempts to substitute monarchy (not for a 'republic' but) for dynastic government.

CHAPTER IX.

THE CONSTITUTION OF THE NATIONAL COUNCIL.

§ 1. *The King's Thegns.*

OUR information regarding the composition of the national council is derived mainly from charters, though this evidence is supplemented and confirmed by notices in historical works and by the prefaces to some of the laws. Throughout the historical period the council contained two elements, ecclesiastical and lay, both of which are usually represented in the signatures to charters. On the ecclesiastical element little need be said. It consisted of bishops (including archbishops) and frequently also of abbots. In early charters we also find not infrequently the signatures of abbesses[1] and priests; but in the course of the ninth century these become rare. The composition of the lay element in early times is a matter of much greater doubt, owing partly to the uncertainty as to the meaning of the terms used and partly to the fact that many persons attest the

---

[1] It is to be remembered that the abbesses of early times were frequently, if not usually, the widows or daughters of kings.

charters without any title. In the tenth century, however, and indeed from the time of Aethelwulf onwards, it is clear that all the lay members of the council, except members of the royal family[1] and foreign (usually Welsh) under-kings, belonged to one or other of two classes, viz. earls and thegns[2]. The titles of the former class, as well as their numbers from time to time and the character of their office, have already been discussed. We will therefore in the following pages confine our attention to the second class of persons, those who in Latin bear the title *minister* (*regis*) or (less frequently) *miles* and in English the title (*cyninges*) þegn.

The position of the thegn has been discussed to some extent in Chapter III. It was there shown (p. 81 ff.) that the later laws distinguish between the king's thegn and the *medema* þegn, the former being subject in certain cases to higher charges than the latter, and, in the North at all events, to a higher scale of fines. In the earlier laws the word

---

[1] Usually the signatories are sons or brothers of the king, but occasionally we find persons described as *propinquus regis*. In Mercian charters the king's wife (*regina*) generally signs, but in West Saxon charters this is rarely the case, while the use of the title *regina* is still more rare (cf. p. 305, footnote). Aethelfled regularly signs Aethelred's charters from 887 onwards, and after his death seems to have issued charters of her own (cf. B. 632). Aelfwyn's signature occurs occasionally in charters of her father and mother (B. 603, 632). Eadgifu signs frequently in charters of her sons Edmund and Eadred and in those of her grandson Edgar.

[2] We sometimes meet with signatures bearing the titles *discifer*, *dapifer*, *thesaurarius* etc., but from a comparison of the charters it is clear that the same persons elsewhere bear the title *minister*.

occurs only in the expression *cyninges þegn*, the terms applied to the other class being *twelfhynde man* or *gesiðcund man*. But even the king's thegn is only mentioned three times. One case is in Alfr. and Guthr. 3, according to which if a king's thegn were accused of homicide, he required the oaths of twelve king's thegns in order to clear himself; if the same charge were brought against a man of inferior rank, he required the oaths of eleven of his equals and one king's thegn. From this passage it would appear that the oath of the king's thegn was of more value than that of other persons. The same inference may be derived from a passage in the Kentish laws (Wihtr. 20), where it is stated that a king's thegn, like a stranger, is to be allowed to exculpate himself by his own oath at the altar. The third instance occurs in Ine 45, the passage which states the compensations due to various classes of persons for *burgbryce*. The compensation for the king's thegn is 60 shillings, being lower than that of the earl (80 sh.) and higher than that of the land-owning noble (35 sh., cf. p. 121). It seems at first sight somewhat strange that the king's thegn should be omitted in the corresponding table of compensations for *fletgefeoht* (Ine 6). The passage runs as follows: " If any one fight in the house of an earl or other distinguished councillor (*geþungenes witan*), he is to give sixty shillings in compensation and pay a fine of sixty shillings." The same expression occurs again in the Preface to the Laws of Alfred (cap. 49. 7): "Synods have been brought together......throughout England of holy bishops and other distinguished councillors." It seems probable that the reference here is to members of royal councils, though ecclesiastics may also be included in the term. We may compare the last sentence in this Preface: "I Alfred, king of the West Saxons, have shown these things to all my councillors," etc., and the Preface to Ine's laws: "I Ine......by the counsel and instruction of my father Cenred and of my bishops Haedde and Eorcenwald, with all my earls and the chief councillors of my people, have been deliberating," etc. Since there can be no doubt that Alfred's council consisted of ecclesiastics, earls and king's thegns, there is at least a presumption in favour of believing that those members of Ine's council who were not earls or ecclesiastics were likewise king's thegns. If so, the omission of the king's thegn in Ine 6 is only apparent. The 'distinguished councillor' will be identical with the king's thegn, in spite of the fact that he is entitled to the same compensation as the earl[1].

It would be of importance to know, if it were possible, what was approximately the number of king's thegns at any given period. Unfortunately there seems to be no means of answering this question except by counting the signatures of *ministri*

---

[1] It may be observed that even the term 'king's thegn' is sometimes, like the word *witan* in the Preface to Alfred's laws, used in such a way as to include bishops and earls, *e.g.* Sax. Chron. 897: *manige þara selestena cynges þena......forðferdon...... þara wæs sum Swiðulf biscop on Hrofesceastre and Ceolmund ealdormon on Cent* etc.

in the charters. For this purpose I have gone
through those charters of King Edmund which
contain the signatures of such persons. The total
number of times that the words *minister* and *miles*
occur in signatures to these charters is 462, distributed over 34 documents. But the total number
of persons who sign appears to be only 47. Of course
some allowance must be made for the possibility
that signatures of the same name may belong to
different persons, for at this period certain names
were very common. When the same name occurs
twice in one document, I have of course attributed
the signatures to two different persons. So also in
one or two cases where a name occurred only at the
beginning and at the end of the reign, I have assumed that the signatories were different. Possibly
some further allowance should be made, but I should
not be inclined to believe that the total number of
signatories exceeded fifty. On the other hand it
may be pointed out that sixteen (out of the 47)
signatures occur only once, several of them in
charters which are open to suspicion. Again, several
signatures are confined to Edmund's earlier charters,
while others appear only in the later ones. As a
matter of fact the largest number of *ministri* who
sign in any one charter is 23. Taking all these
facts into account I am disposed to think that the
total number of *ministri* at any given time during
this reign was nearer forty than fifty. It may of
course be questioned whether these signatures give
anything like a complete list of king's thegns. Un-

fortunately there seems to be no possibility of answering this question satisfactorily. It may however be observed that 25 grants made to persons bearing the title *minister* are preserved from this reign; that the number of names among the recipients of these grants is 14; and that of these 14 names ten appear among the signatures. The four names which do not occur among the signatures receive only one grant each. On the whole then it seems probable that the list given by the signatures does not fall very far short of the total number of king's thegns.

In other reigns the number may have been larger. In some of Aethelstan's charters a much longer list of such signatures is found, in two cases (B. 677, 702) exceeding fifty. So also in two Abingdon charters (B. 1046, 1047) dating from 959 we find over sixty signatures of *ministri*. Apart from these cases however the number of such signatures in the charters of Eadred, Eadwig and Edgar seldom exceeds 25. The same is true also of Edward's charters, though the total number of signatories in this reign is considerable. In Alfred's charters one is particularly struck with the very large number of names in proportion to the number of signatures. Of course the charters are far more widely separated from one another in point of time than those of Edmund. Again, it appears that at this time there were at least two distinct councils in existence besides that of Mercia, namely one for Wessex and the other (represented by B. 539, 576) for Kent. It is likely enough however that the rate of mortality among king's thegns was pretty high during this reign[1].

If we turn now to the reign of Aethelwulf we find in sixteen charters of this king 121 signatures with the title *minister*. The total number of names is probably 36. They fall clearly into two classes. The first class, which contains 22 names, appears almost only in twelve charters ([B. 451, 457, 468—470, 472—478, 481, 491][2]) belonging to Wessex, while the second class containing the other 14 names appears only in Kentish charters (B. 439, 460, 467, 486). The cases in which a name belonging to one class appears among names of the other class are only four or five in number. Of the 22 names which appear in the West Saxon charters not more than 15 occur in any one document. As the charters cover a period of ten years it is highly probable that some changes took place in the list of *ministri*. If the charters give anything like a complete list, which, considering their character, is somewhat doubtful, it is not likely that there were more than twenty *ministri* at any one time. The largest number of

---

[1] Another explanation might be obtained from Asser's statement (cap. 100) that Alfred's *ministri* resided at court in rotation, one month in every three. Charters of this period are so seldom precisely dated that it is hardly possible to affirm that they were always or even generally issued at special meetings of the council. If this explanation is correct the number of king's thegns may really have been quite considerable. The evidence of Edward's charters is not inconsistent with the continuance of such a custom, but in those of his successors the constant recurrence of the same names clearly indicates a different system.

[2] Several of these charters are said to be spurious; cf. Stevenson, *Asser's Life of King Alfred*, p. 187, note.

persons who sign any of the Kentish charters with the title *minister* is eleven, two of whom are apparently West Saxons. But, considering how few the charters are, it would be somewhat rash to conclude that Kent contained so small a number of *ministri*. A charter (B. 538) bearing the date 874[1], but really belonging to about 840, gives 16 signatures followed by the symbol m̃ (m̃s), six of which are elsewhere accompanied by the title *minister*. Again, in B. 426, 437, 439, 442, 449 there are a number of signatures, giving altogether 31 or 32 names, to which no designation is attached. Seven of these names occur in the later charters among the *ministri*. It is therefore likely enough that some, perhaps most, of the other unspecified names may be those of king's thegns, though some may be the names of ecclesiastics. In B. 426 there are 23 unspecified signatures.

§ 2. *The term 'Minister' in early charters.*

Before the reign of Aethelwulf the term *minister* is rare in signatures to West Saxon charters. The second (Wilton) section of B. 421, if this really dates from Ecgberht's reign, contains eight such signatures, five of which, including apparently two West Saxons, recur in the lists noticed above. In one interpolated document (B. 393) we find sixteen *ministri*, but on this no reliance can be placed. Another isolated case occurs in B. 300, but this charter again is un-

---

[1] This date may be correct for the subsequent confirmation of the charter by Archbishop Aethelred.

trustworthy. King's thegns are however occasionally mentioned in the Saxon Chronicle. In the account of Cynewulf's death (*ann.* 755) the word is several times used in the plural, and in *ann.* 784 it is stated that 84 persons perished with Cynewulf, though probably the great majority of these were attendants.

If we turn to Kent, we find the term *minister* attached to five signatures in an original charter (B. 411) issued by Ecgberht but bearing a wrong date. This is perhaps the earliest genuine occurrence of the word in signatures to any charter. It occurs however in the text of a very much earlier document (B. 192), dating from 762: *ego Dunwald minister dum aduiueret inclitae memoriae regis Ethilberti.* It is also to be noted that grants of land in Kent are conveyed in five Mercian charters (cf. p. 318) under the formula *N. ministro meo.* As a matter of fact the king's thegn is already mentioned in the Laws of Wihtred. Again, in a contemporary postscript to B. 384, a charter of 825, we find the following sentence: (þ)*is earan Cwænðryðe geðincgo and biscopes and þeara þegna on Cantwarabyrg.* The word 'thegns' refers in all probability to the last three men's names in the list of signatures[1]. One of

[1] The last six signatures are those of women. Perhaps five names higher in the list (Nos. 35—37 and 39, 40) may also be included among the thegns. It can not be made out with certainty whether these latter were Mercian or Kentish officials, for, though their signatures are fairly frequent, they occur almost only in documents which concern both the Mercian kings and the archbishop. Their place in the list would lead one to infer that they were Mercians, but two of the same names recur in a charter of the archbishop (B. 406). It is likewise uncertain whether Bola the *pedisecus* belonged to Kent or to Mercia.

these, Alhhere, signs in B. 411 as *minister*, and both
he and Duda (Dudda) appear later as earls. Undescribed signatures are common in Kentish charters
during the whole period from the reign of Hlothhere
to that of Aethelwulf. Before the year 839 the
number of such signatures never exceeds twelve
except in one charter of Wihtred (B. 91). Of course
it is quite possible that such signatures may sometimes belong to ecclesiastics.

In signatures to Mercian charters the word
minister is rare and somewhat doubtful. I have
only been able to find 34 examples, distributed over
13 charters. The largest number (five) occur in a
spurious charter of Wulfhere (B. 22). A charter of
Aethelbald (B. 137) and one of Berhtwulf (B. 433)
each give four. Not a single case occurs in a charter
of which the original has been preserved, though
original Mercian charters are fairly common. Five
examples occur in Coenwulf's charters, but three of
the persons thus specified seem really to have been
earls[1]. Two examples are found in a charter of Offa
(B. 245), which cannot be entirely trusted[2]. On the
examples, sixteen in all, which occur in charters
before the reign of Offa, little stress can be laid, for
the signatures of this period are usually unaccom-
panied by any description. Even in genuine
documents therefore the word *minister* may well
have been added by later copyists. On the other

---

[1] Viz. Ceolmund (B. 295), Eadberht (B. 349), and Sigered
(B. 351).

[2] It may be noted that the names (Cenuulf, Ealhhelm) appear
in West Saxon form.

hand there can be no serious objection to the examples which occur in charters of Berhtwulf and Burgred. From the year 836 onwards there frequently appear at the end of Mercian charters a number of undescribed names, which seem not to be those of earls[1]. The term *minister* (*regis*) was certainly known to the Mercians, as may be seen (*e.g.*) from an original charter of Coenwulf (B. 326) dating from 808 : *meo fideli ministro Eaduulfo.* The same or similar formulae occur in charters from the time of Aethelbald onwards : B. 165, 209 (210), 230, 247, 248, 254, 274, 289, 303[2]. We may further compare the expressions *Eanwulfo regis ministro* (B. 533, 534) and *Cuthulfo ministro regis* (B. 537) in charters issued by Werferth, bishop of Worcester, and Earl Aethelred; so also Sax. Chron. 874 : *anum unwisum cyninges þegne.*

§ 3. *The term 'Comes' in early charters.*

The term *comes* is of fairly frequent occurrence in early charters, both Mercian and Kentish, until about the year 824. After this time it almost disappears until the latter part of Alfred's reign[3]. Its use from this time forward has been already discussed (p. 164 f.) and it has been pointed out that

---

[1] Four or five undescribed signatures occur pretty frequently from 814 onwards, but it is not certain that these persons were Mercians (cf. p. 316, footnote).

[2] We may compare B. 77 (one of Aethelred's charters, dating from 692) : *Oslauuo qui aliquando fuit minister meus.*

[3] In the intervening period I have only noticed one example, viz. in B. 491, a charter of 856.

it appears to be applied only to earls. The last two Mercian signatures with this title occur in a charter of 801 (B. 303). Another is to be found in an undated Surrey charter (B. 275), and a fourth in what is said to be an original charter of 790 (B. 259). One of Aethelbald's charters (B. 157) contains five such signatures. In another (B. 154), an original charter of 736, we find *ego Æthilric subregulus atque comes gloriosissimi regis Æthilbaldi* etc., and *ego Onoc comes*. With this we may compare B. 156: *rex Æthelred cum comite suo subregula Huicciorum Oshere*. Lastly[1] in B. 76, a charter dating from 691 or 692, we find *ego Torchtuuald comes regius* etc. These examples are sufficient to prove that *comes* was a recognised title in signatures during the eighth century. But the word occurs also in the text of charters. Thus in B. 343, an early copy of a charter of 814, Coenwulf is described as granting land in Kent to *Suiðnoðe meo comite*. In B. 201 the purchaser of a grant in Middlesex about the beginning of the ninth century describes himself as *Pilheardus* (for *Wilheardus?*) *misellus comis regis Merciorum Coenuulfi*. In B. 146, 154, 157, 182, 244 (cf. 301) we find grants made by Aethelbald and Offa under the formula *N. comiti meo* etc. Now are we to believe that all these persons were really earls? The evidence is, I think, hardly sufficient to justify this conclusion, though there is no doubt that such was the case sometimes. Thus Byrnwald, who ap-

---

[1] Further examples are to be found in B. 58, 59, 124, 135, 268, but on these little stress can be laid. The same remark applies to the *Cenfrithus comes Mertiorum* of B. 54.

pears as *comes* in B. 303, signs as *dux* in B. 313, 321, 322, 326. The *Eduinus comes* of B. 259 is perhaps to be identified with the *Esuuine dux* of B. 264. The *Esme comiti* of B. 244 is possibly identical with the *Esne dux* who signs in most of Offa's charters. Of the five persons who sign with the title *comes* in B. 157, at least three seem to be earls: Wilfrith signs as *dux* in B. 137, Oba as *patricius* in B. 162 and as *dux* in B. 177, Beorcol as *dux* in B. 162, and as *patricius* in B. 178. The signature *subregulus atque comes* in B. 154 has already been noticed. There still remain however a number of persons described as *comes* in the text of charters, such as Swithnoth and Pilheard, whom we have no reason for believing to be earls.

In Kentish charters the title *comes* occurs frequently from the time of Wihtred to the beginning of the ninth century. In B. 321, an original charter of 805, we find four, and in B. 316, a charter of 804, six persons signing with this title. It is true that both these charters contain Mercian signatures, but we are able to decide that most of the persons described as *comes* belong to Kent. All the *comites* who appear in B. 321 (viz. Haehferth, Aethelgeard, Wihthere and Wynbald) occur again, though without designation, in one or other of the charters B. 303, 318, 319, 328, 1336. Two of these charters, B. 319 and 1336, apparently contain no names other than Kentish, while in B. 318 the only non-Kentish names seem to be those of Coenwulf and the bishops. The other two charters do indeed contain Mercian names, but they are in separate lists. In B. 303 it

is stated that the second list gives the names of the
optimates who confirmed the grant *in urbe Cantuariorum*, though a Mercian abbot named Daeghelm was
present. In B. 328 the second list of signatories
are described as *satrapes Cantuariorum.* It may be
observed that in this list itself one signatory (Esne)
uses the title *comes.* Again, of the six *comites* who
sign in B. 316 four (Oswulf, Swithhun, Sigheard and
Beorhtnoth) appear again in one or more of the
same five charters. One of these signatories, Oswulf,
was apparently an earl (see below). He is again
described as a *comes* in B. 378 (an original charter);
and it is there stated that he had a brother named
Aldberht who is likewise called *comes*, and who is
probably to be identified with one of the persons of
this name who sign in B. 303. The evidence then
leaves no room for doubt that *comes* was a recognised
title in Kent at the beginning of the ninth century,
and that the number of persons who bore this title
was considerable. But there is no reason for believing
that the title was then a new one. In B. 194, a
charter which Birch dates between 759 and 765, we
find, amongst other signatures, *signum manus Ecgbaldi comitis atque praefecti*; in B. 190 (761) *signum
manus Esne comitis*; in B. 189 (about the same date)
signum manus Baltheardi comitis. In a charter of
737 (B. 159) we find the curious formula *ego N.
commites meos confirmari et subscribere feci* repeated
eight times. Lastly, in the second section of B. 91
(dating from 716) we find *signum manus Ædelfridi
comitis.* It is true that the originals of these charters
are not preserved. But they all appear to be fairly

trustworthy documents, and on the whole justify the conclusion that the term *comes* was used in signatures to Kentish charters throughout the eighth century.

Before considering the position of the Kentish *comites* we may turn for a moment to note that the same term occurs occasionally also in charters of the other kingdoms. A Sussex charter (B. 252) dating from the latter part of Offa's reign contains two such signatures, while the formula *N. comite meo* is used in four grants by Osmund, king of Sussex (B. 145, 197, 198, 206). The same formula is used by Oshere and Aldred, kings of the Hwicce, in B. 85, 218. In B. 166 Wilfrith, bishop of Worcester, makes a grant to a *comes* named Leppa; and in B. 116, a charter of Aethelweard, king of the Hwicce, dating from 706, four signatures occur with the title *comes*. In a West Saxon charter of 778 (B. 225) Cynewulf makes a grant to *Bican comiti meo ac ministro*, and at the end of the same charter we find *signum Fadol comitis regis*. In another West Saxon charter, dating from 790 (B. 258), we find *signum manus Wingbaldi comitis*. Lastly in B. 111, a charter (stated by Birch to be an original) of 704, a grant is made by Swefred, king of Essex, and *Pæogthath* (Peohthat) *cum licentia Ædelredi regis comis*[1].

There is no evidence that any of the persons mentioned in the last paragraph were earls. In Kentish charters however there is one clear case. Oswulf, who is described as a *comes* in B. 316, 378, appears as an earl (*dux, aldormonn*) in B. 289, 319, 330.

---

[1] This case ought possibly to be classed among the Mercian examples, for in B. 85 the same person signs in a Mercian list.

Again the *Baltheardus dux* of B. 192 may be identical
with the *Baltheardi comitis* of B. 189; but since this
name never occurs among Offa's earls, it is not
unlikely that the title in B. 192 is a later and
incorrect addition. It is incredible however that
all the Kentish *comites* were earls. We have seen
that six signatures with this title occur in one
charter of 804 and four more in a charter of the
following year. But there can never have been
anything like this number of earls in Kent[1]. Indeed,
so far as Kent is concerned, it is clear that the title
comes is rather to be compared with the later term
minister. It may be noted that in B. 247, 248 Offa,
and in B. 1336 Cuthred, make grants to a certain
Aldberht under the formula *meo ministro*. The
same person is however described as a *comes* in
B. 378, while there is no evidence for any earl of
this name in the reigns of Offa or Coenwulf. Again,
the Swithhun to whom Coenwulf and Cuthred make
a grant in B. 303 is probably to be identified with
the *Swyδun comes* of B. 316. We may compare the
expression *Bican comiti meo ac ministro* in a West
Saxon charter of 778 already quoted. The earl
Oswulf is twice described as a *comes*, but in B. 289
Coenwulf makes a grant to him under the formula
duci et ministro meo. This formula shows that a
person might be described in more than one way.

---

[1] The difference is not, as might perhaps at first sight be
thought, one of terminology merely. In later times we find two
distinct classes of officials in Kent, earls and (king's) thegns; in
earlier times we find only the *comes*. It is far more probable that
the two earls of Kent (cf. p. 271) were appointed after the subjuga-
tion of the country by Mercia in place of the two native kings.

Oswulf was *minister* (*þegn*) primarily in relation to Coenwulf, but *dux* (*aldorman*) primarily in relation to the province (East Kent, cf. B. 445) which he governed—though expressions like *dux Aethelbaldi*, *i.e.* an earl in the service of Aethelbald, do also occur. The formula in B. 289 is closely paralleled by a signature in B. 154, which has already been quoted: *ego Æthilric subregulus atque comes......Æthilbaldi* etc. Aethelric was at the same time king of the Hwicce and a *comes* of King Aethelbald. In B. 157 a grant is made by Aethelbald to the same person with the title *comes* only. Another member of the same family, Osred, perhaps the same who signs together with Aethelric in B. 139, receives a grant in B. 165 under the title *minister*. With the expression *comes Æthilbaldi* we may compare B. 201: *ego Pilheardus misellus comis...Coenuulfi* (cf. p. 319). Further, it deserves to be noticed that out of the nineteen examples of *comes* in the text (apart from the signatures) of the early charters thirteen occur in the phrase *comiti* (*-e*) *meo* or *meo comiti* (*-e*). This predominant use with the genitive and possessive seems to indicate that *comes*, like *minister*[1], implied a sense of personal relationship—generally to a superior, though in B. 159 it would seem to mean no more than 'colleague.' On the other hand the word is sometimes used absolutely. Thus in B. 166 the *comes* Leppa is mentioned without any reference to the existence of an overlord or colleagues ; and in

[1] In the text of the early charters *minister* is always used with a possessive except in one case already quoted (B. 192), where it is used with a genitive.

the same way in B. 378 we find mention of *Oswulf
comes* and *Aldberht comes*. This absolute use of the
word occurs also in Bede's History, as we shall see
later. It should be observed however that we never,
so far as I know, find in early documents such
expressions as *Hamtunensium comes*, where the name
in the genitive denotes the district governed by the
comes[1].

We must now enquire what is the English term
which *comes* is used to translate. The word used to
translate *comes* in the Old English version of Bede's
Ecclesiastical History is *gesið*, and it is to be observed
that in poetry this word, when not used in a technical
sense, seems to correspond exactly to *comes*. Etymologically also the two words appear to be equivalent.
It may further be remarked that in Ine 23 *gesið* is
clearly used in a technical sense to denote a man
with some kind of authority over others. But there
is a serious objection to this answer. The word
gesið does not occur in any charter, nor in the Saxon
Chronicle, nor indeed in any laws later than those of
Ine. In spite therefore of the fact that it is used
in the Old English version of Bede's History, it is
hardly credible that it should have been a term in
general use even as late as the beginning of the
ninth century, when so many *comites* occur in the
charters. But this objection is hardly insurmount-
able. The word *comes* may have been adopted in
England as a translation for *gesið*, and may have been
continued in official use after *gesið* had ceased to be

---

[1] Such expressions as *comes Merciorum* may of course be
parallel to *Merciorum abbas* ('a Mercian abbot') etc.

a current term. This explanation would seem to fit the case satisfactorily; for we have seen that the use of the term *comes* appears to go back to the seventh century, while *gesiδ* is still used in the Laws of Ine.

But what was the term applied in actual speech during the eighth and ninth centuries to the persons described in the charters as *comites*? It can hardly have been anything else than *þegn* or *cyninges þegn*[1]. This word is in later times the regular equivalent of *minister* or *miles*. But we have seen that before the reign of Ecgberht there are no trustworthy occurrences of these titles in signatures, while in the text of the charters, as we get further back, *comes* seems gradually to take the place of *minister*. It is true that in Ine's laws we find both *gesiδ* and *cyninges þegn*. In cap. 23 *gesiδ* is clearly equivalent to *gesiδcund man*, and the same seems to be true of *gesiδman* in cap. 30 (cf. p. 98 f.). On the other hand in cap. 45 the compensation due to the king's thegn is much greater than that due to the landowning *gesiδcund man*, *i.e.* the higher subdivision of the *gesiδcund* class. The position of the king's thegn seems therefore to have been superior to that of the gesith in Ine's laws. This is a difficult question, to which we shall have to return later (p. 346 ff.). But we have seen above that if the table in cap. 6 be compared with that in cap. 45, it can hardly be

---

[1] It is of course impossible to prove this by examples owing to the scarcity of English charters. But the *Esne comes* of B. 328 is in all probability to be identified with the *Esne cyninges ðegne* of B. 318.

doubted that the 'distinguished councillor,' who is classed with the earl in the former, is identical with the king's thegn. Again, we have also seen that we have practically no evidence for the title *minister* being applied to members of the royal councils until towards the close of the eighth century, while *comes* is not unfrequently applied to such persons[1]. Hence we are brought again to the conclusion that during the eighth century *cyninges þegn* and *comes* must have been equivalent terms.

The word *þegn* by itself does not occur in the laws before the time of Aethelstan. It has already been mentioned however that an example occurs in a Kentish charter of 825 (B. 384). It may therefore have come into use in Kent considerably earlier than elsewhere. This is possibly not unconnected with the fact that the evidence for the term *comes* is more frequent and continues later in Kent than elsewhere. For, whereas *minister* is, except in signatures, invariably used with a possessive or genitive in early charters, *comes* is sometimes used absolutely; indeed we find two examples in B. 378, a charter of 824[2].

---

[1] In the text (apart from the signatures) of charters before 765 I have found twelve examples of *comes* against two of *minister*. In (trustworthy) signatures *comes* alone occurs.

[2] It is possible however that there may be a special reason for tne omission of the genitive in B. 384. The government of Kent was clearly in an unstable condition at this time, and the provincial officials may not have been willing to recognise Beornwulf's lordship.

§ 4.　*The constitution of the national council in early times.*

We have seen above that in the ninth and following centuries the royal council consisted of ecclesiastics, earls and thegns. But before the last years of Ecgberht's reign signatures with the title *minister* are rare and doubtful. On the other hand undescribed signatures are numerous, especially in Kentish charters, while *comes* also occurs sporadically in charters of all the kingdoms. In West Saxon charters before the year 825 nearly all the signatories seem to be earls (cf. p. 282 f.), though it is clear from the preface to Ine's laws that these were not the only members of the council. Mercian charters are far more numerous and usually contain a much larger number of signatures[1]. In Coenwulf's reign down to the year 814 (cf. p. 318, note) all the lay signatories seem to be earls[2], except members of the royal family and an official who bears the title *pedes sessor* (*pedisequus*). The only exceptions are some charters which refer to Kent and contain a number of signatures which apparently belong to Kentish officials; but this element is easy to distinguish (cf. p. 320 f.). When we get back to the reign of Offa the evidence is much more complicated owing to the very large number of signatures which appear with-

---

[1] The longest list of signatures that I have noticed occurs in one of Beornwulf's charters (B. 384) dating from 825. The total number of names is 65, but 42 of these seem to be ecclesiastics.

[2] The only doubtful case is that of the *comes* Berhthun in B. 303.

out titles. The total number of (male) lay signatories in charters of this reign, besides Offa himself and Ecgfrith, is probably 58[1]. Included in this number are two *subreguli* and three *praefecti* of the Hwicce (B. 223, 232). Thirty signatories bear the title *princeps* or *dux* in one charter or another; two bear the title *minister* (B. 245, cf. p. 317), and one person is described as *pincerna* (B. 232). The remaining twenty names never appear with any title. Eight[2] of these are probably Kentish, as they occur in charters of the contemporary Kentish kings. Of the remaining twelve signatures three occur twice and the other nine only once. I doubt if any of them are the names of Mercian officials[3]. It is at least questionable therefore, whether any lay officials other than earls are to be found among the Mercian signatories to Offa's charters, though in view of the West Saxon evidence it would be unwise to conclude that no persons of lower rank attended his council. Further back than this it would be useless to pursue the investigation, for even in Aethelbald's charters, though *princeps* is frequent, the proportion of undescribed signatures is very large.

---

[1] I have omitted one charter (B. 208) which contains a number of West Saxon names.

[2] Viz. Baduheard, Ecgbald, Swithhun, Eangisl, Wigheard, Heared, Boba and Heaberht.

[3] Of the three names which occur twice two, Bobba and Caec, are probably Hwiccian (cf. B. 183); the third, Cian, from its position in the lists of signatures (B. 213, 214), would seem to be Kentish. Of the other nine names I suspect that two, Lulling and Bryne, belong to Sussex (cf. B. 80?, 197, 208). The rest occur only in Worcestershire and Gloucestershire charters.

In Kentish charters of the eighth century the terms *dux* and *princeps* rarely occur in signatures. I have only been able to find one example of each (B. 189, 192). But as a title for the Kentish council collectively the word *principes* is of fairly frequent occurrence. An early example is to be found in B. 45, an original charter of 679: *ego Hlotharius rex Cantuariorum...cum consensu archiepiscopi Theodori et Edrico filium fratris mei necnon et omnium principum* etc. We may compare B. 99, a charter of 699: *ego Wihtredus rex Cantiae...cum consensu principum meorum quorum nomina subterscribenda sunt* etc. The list of signatures which follows contains, besides that of the king, eighteen names, of which seven bear ecclesiastical titles while the rest are undesignated. Further examples of the same expression are to be found in B. 86, 189, 190, 194, charters ranging in date from 694 to 761 or later. In the same way we find *patricii* in B. 67 and *duces* in B. 91. As there is no reason for supposing that the persons so described were earls we are forced to conclude that the application of these terms was less restricted than in later times. It may be observed that in other respects no difference of terminology is to be detected in the description of the Mercian and Kentish councils. Thus we find the word *optimates* applied to the former in B. 157, 162, 178 and to the latter in B. 175, 194.

Besides these terms however we also find the word *comites* used in charters of the same period, apparently without any difference of meaning. In

B. 89 the term is applied to the Mercian council, though in the signatures given below five out of the seven lay councillors bear the title *princeps.* In a Sussex charter of 714 (B. 132) we find *ego Nunna rex...coram episcopo...necnon et abbatibus comitibusque meis congregatis,* with which we may compare a Hwiccian charter of 680 (B. 51): *ego Oshere rex... confirmantibus episcopis ac principibus et abbatibus.* In another charter (B 145) issued by Nunna we find *consentientibus omnibus comitibus una mecum.* In B. 155 the same term seems to be applied to members of the West Saxon council: *ego Æthelhardus...una cum comitibus supter nominatim descriptis,* though the signatures are lost. These instances are not numerous, but at all events they give further confirmation to the view put forward above (p. 327) that *comes* was a recognised term for describing the members of the royal council. We may further note an expression which occurs in B. 195, a Kentish charter of 764. Offa grants twenty ploughlands to Eardwulf, bishop of Rochester, together with the meadows, woods etc. belonging thereto, *sicut olim habuerunt comites et principes regum Cantiae et cum omni tributo quod regibus iure competit.* The persons so described were clearly royal officials with territorial jurisdiction; but is it necessary to suppose that any distinction is intended between the two classes?

From what has been said above it is clear that the same set of terms (*principes, optimates, comites,* etc.) were applied to the councils of Mercia, Wessex, Kent, Sussex and the Hwicce, when these bodies are described collectively. When the reference is to individual councillors *comes* and *praefectus* seem to occur everywhere, but there appears to have been a reluctance to use *princeps* in the smaller kingdoms. There can be little doubt that the latter is a translation of *aldorman,* and we may note that this word also does not occur in the smaller kingdoms before the end of the eighth century. The obvious inference is that the councils of the various kingdoms were all constituted alike, but that the dignity of the individual councillor varied according to the size of the kingdom. This fact would only make itself felt when the kingdoms came into close contact with one another. When (*e.g.*) the Mercian and Kentish councils began to meet together it would be found difficult to place the Kentish officials on a level with the earls of Mercia, some of whom probably were in charge of provinces almost as large as Kent. Yet, if the Mercian or West Saxon kings wished to retain their hold on Kent by any other means than mere force, they would clearly find it convenient not only to admit those Kentish officials who had submitted to them to their councils, but also to get the signatures of such persons to grants of land in Kent. The solution seems to have been found in raising two of the Kentish officials to a level with the earls (cf. p. 323, footnote), while the rest were equated with the minor royal officials of the larger kingdoms. The disappearance of the term *comes* from charters may have been partly due to these arrangements. Another probable consequence, at least in Wessex, was that the minor officials of that kingdom begin to sign charters very shortly after the acquisition of Kent.

When we turn to Bede's works we find that in the Northumbrian kingdom also in his time it was customary for royal grants to be signed by both ecclesiastical and lay dignitaries[1], presumably the members of the royal council. But unfortunately he gives us no precise information as to the constitution of these councils. The terms which he uses when speaking of the councillors are *primates* (II. 9), *principes et consiliarii (regis), optimates, sapientes, maiores natu ac regis consiliarii* (II. 13). Apparently, however, he speaks neither of *ministri* nor of *comites* (except perhaps in I. 25) in this sense, though both these terms are common in other connections.

§ 5. *The terms 'Minister' and 'Comes' in Bede's works.*

It has been pointed out above that *minister* is decidedly less common than *comes* in charters of the first half of the eighth century. In the second half of this century however it becomes the more frequent term, while after 824 *comes* practically disappears. It seems then that *minister* gradually takes the place of *comes*. In Bede's Ecclesiastical History however we find both terms, as well as *miles*, in use, just as in Ine's laws we find both

---

[1] Cf. *Ep. ad Ecgb.* 12: *litteras...pontificum, abbatum et potestatum seculi obtinent subscriptione confirmari etc.; ib.* 17 : *cartas... nobilium personarum subscriptione confirmatas.*

gesið and *cyninges þegn*. It will be advisable therefore at this point to ascertain what distinction is made by Bede in his use of these terms.

As a matter of fact Bede's terminology is unfortunately somewhat vague. The reader can not help suspecting that in his day the Latin terms for the various dignitaries of the English state were not yet definitely fixed. Thus, like the early charters, he seems to use the words *patricius, princeps* and *dux* to a great extent indifferently. Again, as we have seen above, in his account of the meeting of the Northumbrian council (II. 13) he gives six terms, all apparently for the same body of men. Turning to the word *comites*, we find this term in II. 9 applied to the retinue of Aethelberge on her journey to the north—in which case it probably means no more than 'companions.' When therefore in I. 25 he speaks of King Aethelberht *cum omnibus qui aderant eius comitibus*, we may doubt whether he intends the word to bear any technical meaning. In III. 21 he states that Peada was baptized *cum omnibus qui secum uenerant comitibus ac militibus*; but does he mean to draw a distinction between the two classes? There are however cases which are not open to the same doubt. In the account of Sigeberht's death in III. 22 we find the expression *unus ex his qui eum occiderunt comitibus*, where it is clear from the context that these persons were not mere chance companions of the king. Again, in III. 14 we hear of a *comes* Hunwald, in v. 4 of a *comes* Puh and in v. 5 of a *comes* Aedde. In none of these cases is the word *comes* used with any genitive or possessive.

In the last two passages there is no mention of any over-lord. The same is the case in IV. 10, where a *comes* is mentioned, whose name is not given. Indeed I have not noticed any example of *comes* in the singular, where the word is used with a possessive, and only one, viz. IV. 20 (22), where it is used with a genitive.

Both *minister* and *miles* are words of frequent occurrence in the Ecclesiastical History. They are translated by the same expression (*cyninges þegn*) in the Old English version, and there are indications that Bede himself regarded the two terms as synonymous. Thus in his account of the attempted murder of Edwin (II. 9) we find the following passage : *Quod cum uideret Lilla minister regi amicissimus, non habens scutum ad manum, quo regem a nece defenderet, mox interposuit corpus suum ante ictum pungentis ; sed tanta ui hostis ferrum infixit ut per corpus militis occisi etiam regem uulneraret.* Before the murderer was killed he slew *alium de militibus.* Again, in IV. 20 (22) a certain Imma is described both as *miles* and *minister regis.* So in Bede's *Hist. Abbatum*, cap. 1, Benedict Biscop is said to have been a *minister Osuiu regis*, but it is stated that he renounced *militia, i.e.* the life of a *miles,* in order to become a monk. Speaking generally we may believe the word *miles* to have been chosen to describe these persons primarily with reference to their duties in war, while *minister* was used to denote their position in time of peace. But it may be observed that in III. 1 Bede speaks of Oswald's companions during his exile in Scotland as *milites*, though we have no hint of warlike operations in this connection. So in II. 20 the man who convoyed Edwin's family and Paulinus to Kent after Edwin's death is described as *Basso milite regis Æduini fortissimo*. In all these cases there can be no doubt that *miles* is distinctly a technical term[1].

It has been remarked that in III. 21 the words *comites* and *milites* occur together. So in III. 14 and again in IV. 20 (22) we find mention of a *comes* and a *miles* side by side. But there is nothing in either of these passages to suggest that the two terms are synonymous. I have not been able to find a single case in which they are applied to the same person. Moreover, the Old English version, though it has the same expression (*cyninges þegn*) for *minister* and *miles*, uses a different word (*gesið*) for *comes*. We seem to be justified therefore in concluding that some difference existed between the *miles* (*minister*) and the *comes*. This difference can hardly have been one of social rank. The *comites* who figure in the Ecclesiastical History seem to have been men of high position. Those mentioned in III. 22 appear to have been relatives of the king of Essex. The *comites* Puh and Aedde (v. 4, 5) had built churches of their own. So in the anonymous History of the Abbots, cap. 2, Ceolfrith is said to have been *nobilibus...editus parentibus*, while in cap. 34 we find *siquidem pater ipsius cum nobilis-*

---

[1] It may be noted that in IV. 20 (22) where 'soldiers' (in the modern sense of the word) are mentioned, they are described as *uiri (hostilis) exercitus*.

simum comitatus ageret officium etc. In Eddius 35
the word *comes* is applied to the *praefectus* of a
' city.' But the *milites* also, so far as we have any
means of ascertaining, seem to have belonged to the
nobility. Such was the case with Tilmon in v. 10 :
*ad saeculum quoque nobili, qui de milite factus fuerat
monachus.* So, in *Hist. Abb.* cap. 1, Bede says that
Benedict Biscop, who had been a *minister* of Oswio,
was *nobili...stirpe gentis Anglorum progenitus*; and
again Eastorwine (Biscop's cousin) is in cap. 8
described as *uir ad saeculum nobilis.* In III. 14 it
is stated of Oswine, king of the Deiri : *unde contigit
ut...undique ad eius ministerium de cunctis prope
prouinciis uiri etiam nobilissimi concurrerent.* Moreover, it is distinctly implied in IV. 20 (22) that the
miles Imma belonged to the nobility. We may also
compare a passage in III. 3 with another in III. 1.
In the former it is stated that Oswald, while in exile
among the Scots, was baptized *cum his qui secum
erant militibus*; in the latter that Aethelfrith's sons,
including Oswald, were in exile among the Scots
and Picts, *cum magna nobilium iuuentute.*

The nature of the distinction between the two
classes must therefore have been something different
from this. Now if the various occurrences of the
words *comes* and *miles* (*minister*) be examined, it will
be seen that the former appears to have been a man
with an establishment of his own, and, in certain
cases at all events, some kind of jurisdiction over
others. The *miles* on the other hand seems to have
been a young man, apparently unmarried, and
employed in the personal service of the king or some

other member of the royal family[1]. I have noticed altogether six passages in the Ecclesiastical History, in which the term *comes* is certainly applied in its technical sense to English officials. In four of these (III. 14, 20, v. 4, 5) he is represented as having a house of his own. In two cases (IV. 10, v. 4) the wife of the *comes* is mentioned. In the latter passage he is also in possession of a *uilla*. In the sixth case (IV. 20) the *comes* is described as the *dominus* of certain soldiers. We may compare a passage (IV. 4) where mention is made of an Irish *comes* who owned or had rights over land: *emitque (Colmanus) partem eius (s.c. loci) non grandem......a comite ad cuius possessionem pertinebat.* The term *comes* would hardly have been chosen to describe this person, if his position had not been somewhat similar to that of an English *comes*. It has already been remarked that in Eddius 35 the term is applied to the *praefectus* of an *urbs*. On the other hand I have not been able to find any example of a *minister* or *miles* who possessed an establishment of his own. Nor is there, apparently, any mention of married *milites*, though in the *Epistola ad Ecgberctum*, cap. 11, we hear of the sons of *emeriti milites*. So far as we can trace them, the *milites* seem to be young men. Biscop was twenty-five, Eastorwine twenty-four years old, when they ceased to be

---

[1] The *miles* Imma in IV. 20 (22) is said to have been formerly the *minister* of Queen Aethelthryth. So also the monk Owine (IV. 3) had been the chief of her *ministri* and had accompanied her from East Anglia. We may compare the *fæmnan þegn* of *Beow.* 2060.

ministri. The *milites* of III. 3 correspond to the
nobilium iuuentus of III. 1 (see above). In IV. 20
the *miles* Imma is described as a *iuuenis.* He does
indeed state that he was married, but this seems to
be part of his plan for escaping detection[1] and goes
to show that the *miles* was expected to be unmarried.
Nor does there appear to be any satisfactory reason
for supposing that the *miles* possessed any jurisdiction over land. At all events the *milites* who
come most before our notice were young nobles who
shared the king's hearth in time of peace, as in the
case of Oswine (*H.E.* III. 14), and accompanied him
not only in war but even in exile (*ib.* III. 3). The
last point shows clearly that the bond between
the king and the *miles* was essentially of a personal
nature. We may note that in the *Ep. ad Ecgb.* 13
the king's *ministri* are classed together with his
famuli.

Briefly then the difference between the two
classes seems to have been the following. The *miles*
or *minister regis* was a young nobleman employed in
the personal service of the king and apparently, as
a rule at least, unmarried; the *comes* on the other
hand was often a married man, possessing an establishment of his own, and, sometimes at all events,
endowed with territorial jurisdiction of a public
nature. The distinction between the two classes
may be clearly seen from the story of Ceolfrith's
father given in the anonymous *Hist. Abb.,* cap. 34.
Here we find the married *comes* preparing, evidently

[1] *Timuit se militem fuisse confiteri; rusticum se potius et
pauperem, atque uxoreo uinculo conligatum fuisse respondit* etc.

at his own home, a great banquet for the king and
his *ministri*. It was the custom, as may be seen
from (Bede's) *Hist. Abb.* I.[1], for the king to reward
his *milites* with grants of land, which enabled them
to marry[2]. It must not be assumed however that
the *miles* thereupon passed into the *comes*. That is
a question which unfortunately we cannot answer
with certainty[3]. But it seems extremely probable
that the *comites*, at all events the king's *comites*,
were drawn from the *milites*.

It has been mentioned above that in the Old
English version of the Ecclesiastical History the
word *comes* is translated by *gesið*, and the terms
minister regis and *miles* by *cyninges þegn*. But
were these really the current terms in use during
Bede's lifetime? Reasons have been given above
(p. 326 f.) for believing that the *comes* of the Southern
charters was in Bede's time known in English as
cyninges þegn. This expression is already in Ine's
laws applied to persons of apparently the same class.
They had fortified houses of their own, and the compensation for breaking into these was much greater

---

[1] The reference is to Benedict Biscop: *denique cum esset
minister Osuiu regis et possessionem terrae suo gradui competentem
illo donante perciperet annos natus circiter xxti. et v. fastidiuit
possessionem caducam* etc.

[2] Hence Bede's complaint in the *Ep. ad Ecgb.* 11 that so much
land had been given away to spurious monasteries *ut omnino desit
locus ubi filii nobilum aut emeritorum militum possessionem accipere
possint; ideoque uacantes ac sine coniugio...perdurent* etc.

[3] To this we shall have to return later (p. 370 ff.). If *comes* and
praefectus are always synonymous we may of course give a negative
answer at once.

than the sum to be paid under similar circumstances
to a gesith or noble. The relative position of the
two classes is therefore clearly not what Bede's
terminology would lead us to expect.

Again it is not to be overlooked that the Old
English language possessed a word, the meaning of
which seems in early times to have corresponded
closely to that of Bede's *minister* and *miles*. This
word was *hagustald* or *hægsteald*. In later literature
it is used only in the sense of ' young, unmarried man
or woman' (*caelebs, ephebus, iuuenis, uirgo*). In the
older poetry however we find it apparently in the
sense of ' young warrior.' It may specially be noted
that in *Beow.* 1890 it is applied to the warriors who
accompanied Beowulf and in *Finn.* 40 to the retinue
of Hnaef. The corresponding Old Norse form *hök-
staldr* seems to be used in much the same sense.
Etymologically it is said to mean ' occupant of a *haga*.'
The word *haga* is frequently used in Domesday Book
and in charters of the eleventh century to denote a
town dwelling attached to some (rural) manor. For
the history of such dwellings it will be sufficient
here to refer to Maitland, *Domesday Book and
Beyond*, p. 196 ff., who shows that originally they
were occupied by soldiers, though in course of time
these gave way to merchants. The use of *haga* to
denote town property goes back indeed to the early
part of the ninth century, as may be seen from
B. 335 (336), a charter of 811. Now since most of
the boroughs of the tenth and eleventh centuries
were at some time the dwelling-places of kings or

other important personages, including ecclesiastics[1], it is likely enough that *haga* was originally the term applied to the dwelling-places set apart for the members of their retinues. Such may have been the *domus* occupied by Coenred's officer whose fate is described in *H. E.* v. 13.

On the other hand we must not leave out of account the probability of a continuity in the translation of English and Latin terms. The word *þegn* (*cyninges þegn* etc.) is used not unfrequently in the old poetry in a sense corresponding to that of Bede's *minister regis* and *miles*, though it is a term of wider application. As a matter of fact we find it applied to the followers of both Beowulf and Hnaef. It is therefore quite possible that this was the word which Bede meant to translate. If so however we can hardly avoid concluding that the Northumbrian terminology of his day differed from that which obtained in the South. It is indeed not unlikely that even in the South the king's *hagustaldas* were sometimes included under the term 'king's thegns.' Many of those who are mentioned in the story of Cynewulf's death may have belonged to this class, though there was an earl amongst them. But the king's thegn whose *burgbryce* was valued at 60 shillings can hardly have been a *hagustald*. It is probable therefore that the *hagustald* of the South

---

[1] Cf. p. 226, notes, and the places described as *uillae regales* in Chapter VII. § 3. A similar development may have taken place in Northumbria at an earlier period, for Eddius' *urbs* seems to be a translation of *burg* (cf. p. 260, footnote, and the Addenda).

was designated by some distinct term. This may quite possibly have been *cyninges geneat* (cf. p. 138, footnote), though in the absence of precise information as to the persons so described it is impossible to speak with certainty.

But if *cyninges þegn* was the English term which Bede renders by *minister regis*, it is clear that he must have had some other term in mind when he uses *comes*. Is there anything to prevent us from believing that this term was *gesiδ*? We have seen that both etymologically and in its general sense this word is an exact equivalent of *comes*. Again it has been shown (p. 330 f.) that the term *comes* was applied in the South to members of the royal councils, both individually and collectively, though in the latter case *optimates* and *principes* are more usual. But in the Corpus Glossary, which in its present form dates probably from the eighth century, we find *gesiδas* given as a translation of *optimates*. There is therefore much to be said in favour of the identification.

But we must first ask whether the position of the Northumbrian *comes* was exactly similar to that of the persons who bore this title in the South. Unfortunately the information which Bede gives regarding the *comites* whom he mentions is somewhat meagre. But in *H. E.* IV. 4 he speaks of an Irish *comes* who sold land for a monastery in Mayo. It has already been pointed out that the term would not have been used here, unless the position of the person in question had been to some extent comparable with that of the English *comes*. The *comes* then had, sometimes at all events, rights of some kind over land. Again it has been noted that Eddius speaks of a *praefectus Osfrid qui praeerat in Broninis urbe regis.* This person is shortly afterwards described as *comes supradictus,* as if the two terms were synonymous. The *comes* was therefore sometimes a king's reeve. For this parallels are to be found in the charters. Thus in a Kentish charter of 759–765 (B. 194) we find *signum manus Ecgbaldi comitis atque praefecti*; in a Mercian charter (B. 535) *Nodehardus praefectus et comes regis in Magansetum*; in another Mercian charter dating from 784 (B. 244) *Esme comite praefectoque meo*—though the last named person may really have been an earl. Again the *Haehferð comis* who signs in a Kentish charter of 805 (B. 321) is probably identical with the *Hœhferth praepositus* of another Kentish charter (B. 342), dating from 813. So in a Hwiccian charter of 757 (B. 183) we find *Beornhardus praefectus,* who is probably to be identified with the *Beornheardo comite meo* of B. 218 (dating from 757–775). It was clearly then no very rare thing for the *comes* to be a king's reeve. Moreover it has been seen above (p. 319 f.) that even in early times the earl is not unfrequently described as a *comes,* and after all the difference between the earl and the king's reeve in the eighth century was not a very definite one[1].

---

[1] It would perhaps be more true to say that the earls of Wessex at this period corresponded to the shire-reeves of later times and the high-reeves of Northumbria. The king's reeve of Wessex in early times seems to have been a less important official (cf. p. 233 ff.), but the difference was probably one of degree only.

Again it has been mentioned (p. 170) that the earl
was certainly entitled to profits of some kind or other
from the lands under his jurisdiction, as may be seen
(*e.g.*) from B. 416, a charter of 836. The same seems
to be true also of the *comes* in early times. A charter
(B. 195) has already been quoted, wherein Offa grants
land in Kent *sicut olim habuerunt comites et principes
regum Cantiae et cum omni tributo quod regibus iure
competit.* The reference clearly is to what is called
in the charters *pastus regum et principum.* This
explains why in the early charters we occasionally
find the consent of a particular *comes* stated. Thus
in B. 85, a charter of 693, Oshere, king of the Hwicce,
grants land *consentiente comite meo Cutberhto.* In
B. 111, a charter of 704, the grant is made jointly by
Swefred, king of Essex, and *Pæogthath cum licentia
Ædelredi regis comis.* It can hardly be doubted that
in such cases the *comes* is a royal official who has
jurisdiction over the lands in question and consequently is entitled to some share in the profits
derived from them. As territorial officials then the
comites of the Southern charters seem not to differ
from those mentioned by Bede. It is true that there
is no certain case of the application of the term by
Bede to members of the royal councils. Yet, after
what has been said, we need hardly hesitate to
interpret in this sense the passage in *H. E.* i. 25:
(*Aedilbercto*) *una cum omnibus qui aderant eius
comitibus.*

Of course it cannot be proved that all the *comites*
mentioned by Bede were royal officials.. That their
position was in some sense an official one seems

indeed to be shown by the expression used of Ceolfrith's father in the anonymous *Hist. Abb.*, cap. 2 (*cum comitatus ageret officium*, cf. p. 336 f.). But did they always hold their office directly from the king ? In cases such as those quoted above from Eddius, where the *comes* is also the *praefectus* of a royal *urbs*, and again in cases where we find expressions like *comes Aedilredi, comites eius* (referring to a king) etc., this may no doubt be taken for granted. There remain however a number of *comites*, such as Puh and Aedde, regarding whose position in this respect no information is obtainable.

Concerning the gesith of Ine's laws we hear little except that he was a nobleman, and that he had apparently some kind of jurisdiction over other men. But it is clear from cap. 50 (cf. p. 98) that he was not necessarily under the immediate lordship of the king. The king's thegn was a person of higher rank than the gesith. Now this fact might be explained in two ways. He may have been endowed with a larger sphere of jurisdiction; or again he may owe his superior position to his personal relationship to the king. As the word *gesið* in itself can not be taken as implying a lower position than that denoted by the word *þegn*, and as the gesith (the *gesiðcund man landagende*) in other respects seems to correspond to the *medema þegn* of the later laws (cf. p. 95), the second explanation seems to be the more probable. In that case we must conclude that the West Saxon gesith was never under the immediate lordship of the king[1].

[1] An exception is to be made in the case of the king's *geneat*

It is curious that the word *gesiƌ* should be used
in Wessex in a different sense from that which it
bore apparently in the other kingdoms. We shall
have to suppose that originally it was applied both
to the 'king's gesith' (*comes regis*) and to the gesith
who was under the lordship of another person[1], but
that in Wessex it had become obsolete in the former
sense. The expression which took its place (*cyninges
þegn*) was not however entirely new. Indeed we find
it in this sense even in the old poetry. Thus in
Beow. 1672 f. the hero says to Hrothgar: "I promise
thee that thou shalt be able to sleep in Heorot without anxiety...(thou) and every thegn of thy people"
(*þegna gehwylc þinra leoda*[2]). Here the word is
clearly applied to all the members of the court, old
and young[3]. Again in l. 1309 Aeschere, a distinguished member of Hrothgar's court, is described
as *aldorþegn,* which seems to mean 'chief thegn[4].'
But in l. 1298 it is stated of the same person: *se
wæs Hroðgare hæleða leofost on gesiðes had, i.e.* "there
was no warrior of gesith status for whom Hrothgar

(cf. p. 137 f.); but it is not quite clear that such a person, though
a *gesiðcund man,* would bear the title *gesið.*

[1] We may compare the 'thegn's thegn' of *Be Leodgeþincðum,*
cap. 3.

[2] The word *leode* here, as in Aethelberht 2, seems to refer
specially to the king's *leode* (cf. p. 167).

[3] The expression *duguðe and iogoðe* in l. 1675 (cf. ll. 160, 622)
seems to correspond to Bede's *comites et milites.*

[4] Cf. the expression *ealdorapostol,* which is used for *princeps
apostolorum* (St Peter) in the Old English version of the Ecclesiastical History. We may also compare the case of Owine who
was *princeps ministrorum* to Aethelthryth (*H.E.* IV. 3).

entertained greater affection." It may perhaps be suggested that in this case *gesið* ought to be translated 'companion' and not taken in a technical sense. But the distinction between the ordinary and technical meanings of the word is in reality very slight. Thus in *Widsith*, l. 125, we find it applied to the great Gothic chiefs Wudga and Hama, and again (l. 110) to a number of famous Gothic nobles. In both these cases the word is used without a genitive or possessive; yet the persons so described in the latter case are called "Eormenric's household troop" (*innweorod Earmanrices*). Again we find the expression *self mid gesiðum* applied both to Beowulf with the young warriors who accompany him (l. 1314) and to King Hygelac with his court (l. 1925). But Beowulf's followers are elsewhere (l. 400, 1628) described as *þegnas,* and we have seen that the same word is used also of the members of Hrothgar's court. It is clear then that in early times the terms *þegn* and *gesið* could be applied to the same person, both to the official noble and to the young *hagustald,* and in both cases with reference to their relationship to their lord. The difference seems to be that the former apparently always implies subjection to a higher authority, whereas the latter can in the case of officials be used absolutely. What we have to conclude then is that the meaning of both words has become specialised in Northumbria and Wessex in different senses.

We may now give a brief summary of the conclusions to which we have been brought in the course of this discussion. The West Saxon gesith was a

nobleman, sometimes at all events endowed with
some kind of jurisdiction over other men, but apparently not under the immediate lordship of the
king. The West Saxon king's thegn was a royal
official and a member of the royal council; his
position consequently was superior to that of the
gesith. The Northumbrian gesith, if we may judge
from the *comes* of Eddius and Bede, seems to have
corresponded to the king's thegn of Wessex, but it is
possible that the term was also applied to persons
similar to the West Saxon gesiths. The Northumbrian king's thegn on the other hand was a *hagustald*,
i.e. a young man in the personal service of the king.
It is clear then that the systems of terminology
employed in the two kingdoms were different. But
the difference seems to have been one of terminology
only. If we examine the descriptions of the two
councils, or if we compare the position of the West
Saxon king's thegn with that of the *comites* in the
North, we fail to distinguish any real difference in
this respect between the kingdoms[1]. Again the
description given in the prologue to Ine's laws would,
so far as the lay element is concerned, apply equally
well to the councils of Edmund or Edgar. In both
cases we find the members described as earls and
other chief councillors, who are elsewhere spoken of
as king's thegns; nor is there any reason for believing
that the position of the persons so designated had
undergone any essential change. We must conclude

[1] This remark of course does not apply to the territorial
divisions of the two kingdoms. We have no evidence that the
Northumbrian divisions were permanent like those of Wessex.

therefore that though the council, like the kingdom, had increased in size, no substantial changes had taken place in its composition.

I am aware that this conclusion is directly opposed to views which have frequently been put forward on the history of the Anglo-Saxon state. It has been supposed that owing to the growth of the royal power the 'noble by service' gradually took the place of the 'noble by birth'; and again that in provincial government the king's officers invaded the positions formerly held by the elected heads of the local community. The former statement seems to me to be a mistaken inference from changes in Latin terminology. It is true that about Coenwulf's time we find the term *minister* (*regis*) displacing the term *comes*. But the two terms are applied to the same persons, and it is clear from the evidence adduced above (p. 323 f., cf. p. 347 f.) that even in the earliest times the *comes* derived his title from his relationship to the king. Moreover *minister regis* is merely a translation of *cyninges þegn*, which we find in use a hundred years before Coenwulf's time. Indeed it occurs in the same sense even in the old poetry. We cannot, it is true, except in the poems actually prove that these high dignitaries were chosen from the king's personal retinue, but at all events there is every probability that such was the case.

As for election by the local community I think we may wait until evidence has been produced for the existence of such a custom in England. The evidence hitherto brought forward, viz. the " Laws of Edward the Confessor" and the remarks of Tacitus and other Roman writers on the institutions of the ancient Germans, is manifestly inadequate. The former document is admittedly a poor authority. Amongst other things it seems to confuse the institutions of Saxon England with those of the Danelagh, where the principle of election may really have been known. As for Tacitus, there is no evidence that he was acquainted, even at second hand, with the political institutions of the Angli[1]. We have seen

---

[1] Unfortunately it has been customary to assume that Tacitus' account of the ancient Germans gives a true picture of the institutions of every Teutonic nation—an assumption which has brought endless confusion into the study of English sociology. Two distinct questions are of course involved in this matter, (1) whether Tacitus' account applies truly to any tribe, and (2) how far the institutions of the various tribes were identical. Into the first question we hardly need enter. If the account holds good anywhere we should expect it to apply primarily to those tribes with which the Romans had themselves come into contact. I have already, in regard to the Cherusci (p. 307, footnote 3), expressed a suspicion that what Tacitus regarded as 'republicanism' was really a form of dynastic government. We may further note that the institutions of the Frankish kingdom, when it first comes prominently under our notice, are difficult to reconcile with the description given by Tacitus. The really important question for us however is the second. Now Tacitus himself gives clear indications that he was aware of differences in the political organisation of the various tribes. Thus when he speaks of the Goths (*Gothones*), a tribe somewhat remote from the Roman frontiers, he says: *regnantur paulo iam adductius quam ceterae Germanorum gentes, nondum tamen supra libertatem* (*Germ.* 43). To the Swedes (*Suiones*), the most distant tribe of all, he attributes absolutism of a pronounced type: *est apud illos et opibus honos eoque unus imperitat nullis iam exceptionibus non precario iure parendi* etc. (*ib.* 44). In the eleventh century we find Adam of Bremen (iv. 22) describing the government of the Swedes as follows: *reges habent ex genere antiquo, quorum tamen*

that in early times the reeve was either the king's reeve (*i.e.* the reeve of a royal estate, cf. p. 257 ff.) or the reeve of some other person. Presumably therefore he was appointed and subject to removal by his lord just as much as in the time of Aethelstan. Similarly the earl was in Alfred's time the 'king's earl' (*cyninges ealdormon*). In Ine's time he could be deprived of his jurisdiction 'unless the king had mercy on him.' For the other kingdoms evidence to the same effect is given by such expressions as *dux et praefectus Aeðelbaldi, comes Aedilredi, principes non proprii regis* etc. Again we have seen that many of the earls of the tenth century were related by blood or marriage to the kings. But the same is true also of early times. Peada had been appointed *princeps* of the *Angli Mediterranei* by his father.

uis pendet in populi sentencia. Quod in commune omnes lauda-uerint illum confirmare oportet nisi eius decretum pocius uideatur quod aliquando secuntur inuiti. itaque domi pares esse gaudent. Evidence to the same effect is given by St Ölaf's Saga (Heimskr.) cap. 81. Rembertus' statements, though not so clear, perhaps justify us in supposing that a similar form of government prevailed two centuries earlier. Hence we may conclude that in the ninth, or at all events in the eleventh century, the position of the Swedish kings was not unlike that of some German kings in the time of Tacitus. But it is certainly not justifiable to ignore Tacitus' account of the Swedes and to state that Sweden 'retained' the original type of Teutonic government. Surely the obvious inference from the evidence at our disposal is that the popular control which we find prevailing among the southern tribes in Tacitus' time did not make itself felt in the North until a later period. Now Angel lies geographically about half-way between Sweden and the Roman frontiers; but its affinities in tradition and religion were with the former. What right then have we to assume that in early times it must have had the same form of government as the frontier tribes?

Cuthred received a grant which clearly amounted to an earldom from his uncle Coenwalh. Berhtwald was a *praefectus* under his uncle Aethelred. Aethelheard seems to have been a *subregulus* under his brother-in-law Ine.

It will be convenient, in conclusion, to turn once more to the poems; for surely, if traces of that organisation which prevailed before the government fell into the hands of the king's nominees are to be found anywhere, it should be in these traditions of prehistoric times. Yet even here we find no hint of popular election. Beowulf's cowardly retinue had looked forward to grants of land in precisely the same way as the *ministri regis* of Bede's time, viz. as a reward for their personal service to the king. Similar grants are made to the court poets Widsith and Deor; and in the latter case, when the poet has lost the royal favour, the grant is taken away and given to his successor. Aeschere, Hrothgar's senior councillor, had fought beside him in former days, presumably as a member of his retinue. Hygelac grants his sister's son a great earldom, and the grant, it is to be observed, is accompanied by the presentation of a sword. We have an allusion to the same custom in the account of Beowulf's cowardly thegns. So also in later times (*e.g.* B. 553, 1012) we find kings presenting swords to their earls. It is a fact which shows clearly the personal nature of the relationship between the king and even the highest officials of the state. Again Hygelac rewards another of his warriors with an immense grant of land and treasure together with his daughter's hand. There seems to be no office indeed, small or great, which it is not in the king's power to bestow. It may of course be urged that the king's power was limited by the existence of the council even in the earliest times[1]. But from the evidence brought forward above it seems probable that such councils were composed exclusively of the relatives and nominees of the kings.

---

[1] Several probable references to royal councils occur in *Beowulf* (*e.g.* ll. 157, 779, 937, 1099), though no clear distinction seems to be drawn between the council and the court. This remark however may hold good also for later times.

EXCURSUS IV.

THE FUNCTIONS OF THE COUNCIL, ESPECIALLY WITH REFERENCE TO THE ELECTION OF KINGS.

I have not thought it necessary to discuss at length the nature of the powers possessed by the council, for in spite of all that has been said there can be little hope of arriving at any definite conclusions on this subject. Indeed it seems at least doubtful whether the functions of the council were ever properly defined. In the latter part of the tenth century we frequently find the leading men of the kingdom acting with a good deal of freedom, and Aethelred II. towards the close of his reign seems to have definitely admitted his dependence on popular support. But it is very difficult to point to cases of concerted action on the part of the council[1]. Again it must not be assumed that such powers as we find the leading officials exercising during this period had belonged to them from time immemorial. The course of events during the tenth century was such as would naturally lead to a diminution of the royal power. A long period of peace—longer perhaps than any before—under a succession of youthful

---

[1] It would be of great importance to know, if it were possible, when and how often the councils of the various kings were accustomed to meet. But so far I have not been able to ascertain anything worth recording on this question (cf. p. 314, footnote).

kings[1] gave place to a time of most unfortunate and apparently incapable government. It is possible also that the autonomy conceded to the Danelagh may not have been without effect on the rest of England. But in early times such conditions as these did not exist[2]. The kings seem almost invariably to have been fighting men. When the councils are brought before our notice their functions appear to have been of a deliberative character. Edwin calls together his council to discuss the adoption of Christianity, but he does so in order to ascertain their views. There is nothing to show that he could not act without their consent or that, if they disagreed, he would have to follow the opinion of the majority. When Oswald and Cynegils give Dorchester to Birinus, when Aethelberht gives Augustine land in Canterbury, when Coenwalh gives an earldom to Cuthred or Hygelac to Beowulf, we hear nothing of the consent of the council. All we know is that the grants roused no effective opposition. The presence of the leading officials of the kingdom was no doubt a source of moral support to the king and to a certain extent guaranteed the permanence of his acts[3], though there can be little doubt that the king's probable successor was the person whose acquiescence it was most desirable to obtain. But of combined action on the part of the council as against the king we have, so far as I am aware, no example. Indeed

[1] It is to be remembered that for nearly a third of the period between 940 and 1000 the kings were under twenty years of age. No king during this period seems to have attained the age of thirty-three.

[2] The influence of the Church, as an organisation both wealthy and permanent and extending beyond the jurisdiction of any single king, may have tended from the beginning to limit the royal authority.

[3] I doubt whether it is wise to lay much stress on the use of the ' consent-clause ' in charters of certain periods—at all events so far as the lay members of the council are concerned. Is there any reason for believing that the scribes were required to give a verbal translation of what they had written before the councillors' names were affixed?

the frequence with which kings were murdered or expelled in itself suggests that the council knew no means of enforcing their wishes in a 'constitutional' manner.

There is one point however which requires to be discussed more in detail. It is generally stated that the council both possessed and exercised the right of electing the king ; and it is true that authorities of the tenth and following centuries use an expression, *ceosan (geceosan) to cyninge*, which may be interpreted to mean some form of election. But it deserves to be pointed out that, except possibly in the case of Edward the Martyr[1], we never get so much as a hint that a vote was taken on any of these occasions. If we examine the royal succession from the time of Alfred to the reign of Cnut[2] we

---

[1] Cf. Flor. Wig. *ad ann.* 975, a passage perhaps derived from the *Vita Oswaldi* (Raine, I. p. 449), though the latter does not actually state that a vote was taken. It is difficult to believe that a child seven years old can have been seriously considered as a candidate. So far as I know, English history before the Conquest provides no parallel for such a proceeding. In any case it seems at least as likely that Aethelred's 'candidature' arose out of an intrigue, possibly on the part of Aelfthryth, as that it was due to any feeling on the part of the electors that they had a constitutional right to choose anyone they wished. It is true that this right is stated by Aelfric (*Hom.* I. 212) : *ne mæg man hine sylfne to cynge gedon, ac þæt folc hæfð cyre to ceosenne þone to cyninge þe him sylfum licað; ac siððan he to cyninge gehalgod bið þonne hæfð he anweald ofer þæt folc and hi ne magon his geoc of heora swuran asceacan.* But is there any reason for believing that the former statement is any more true than the latter? Ecclesiastical writers are always liable to the suspicion that they have foreign institutions in their mind. In this case the remark may have been suggested by the election of Hugh Capet.

[2] There may have been a genuine election in the case of Harold I., though the circumstances are far from clear. But this case obviously cannot prove anything. It is expressly stated in the Swedish laws that the throne of that kingdom was elective. The election had to take place at the Morathing and the rules for the procedure to be followed are carefully laid down. From Saxo I. p. 10 f. (Holder) it appears that a similar custom prevailed at

see that it followed the ordinary system of primogeniture[1], with the qualification of course that minors were ineligible[2]. This observation leads us to suspect that the 'election' was a more or less formal act, and the use of such phrases as *a primatis electus* (Aethelweard, IV. 4), *electione optimatum subrogatus* (B. 815), can hardly be regarded as evidence to the contrary.

If we examine the cases individually we find in the course of the tenth century only two occasions on which the 'election' of a king seems to have amounted to anything more than the recognition of the deceased king's natural successor. The first is the election of Aethelstan in 924. Edward and his son

one time in Denmark. It is clear then that the principle might have been introduced into England in the time of Cnut.

[1] It has been suggested (Freeman, *Norman Conquest*, I. p. 675 ff.) that Edmund Ironside was elected over the head of his brother Aethelstan. The evidence that Aethelstan was still alive at this time is derived from Thietmar, VII. 28, but it is admitted that Thietmar has to a certain extent confused the two brothers. I think it is a probable inference from the evidence of other documents dealing with the same events that Thietmar's informant was mistaken as to the identity of the prince who was in London with Edmund.

[2] It is hardly necessary to mention that in historical times succession through the female line was not recognised. At all events no instance is known before the Norman Conquest. This is an important point of difference between English and Scandinavian custom, for in the latter such succession seems to have been known at all times. How far this difference goes back is of course uncertain. Succession through the male line seems to date from the time of the kings of Angel, but we do not know that succession through females was then excluded. There is no reason for supposing that the claim of William I. was in accordance with English law. The principle that a parent could derive a title from his or her child, and the throne thus pass to an alien line (as in the succession of Halfdan the Black to Sogn), is, so far as I am aware, known only in Norway. It is probably connected with the rules for succession to private property (*e.g. Gulathingslög*, 103 f., *Grágás*, IV. 1.

Aelfweard had died within sixteen days of one another and, so far as we know, no other member of the royal family was of age. Aethelstan, whose legitimacy is doubtful, is said by Malmesbury to have been brought up in Mercia. According to the Chronicle (B, C, D) he was now *gecoren to cynge of Myrcum*. But does it necessarily follow that this was a regular and formal act of the council? As a matter of fact we have no evidence that the Mercian council continued to meet as a separate body. Is it not at least equally possible that Aethelstan, taking advantage of the very exceptional circumstances of the case, called together the leading nobles of Mercia and obtained recognition from them? It is to be observed that we hear nothing of a subsequent election in Wessex. The second case is the election of Edgar, also by the Mercians, in 957. But it is generally agreed that this was the result of a conspiracy on the part of the Mercian nobility. They transferred their allegiance from the reigning king to another member of the royal family, thus restoring for a time the form of government which had prevailed in the preceding century. There is no evidence however that this was done by a formal vote.

The last case of 'election' before the full recognition of Cnut's sovereignty was that of Edmund Ironside in 1016. It is stated in the Chronicle that he was 'elected king' by the members of the council who were in London and by the *burhwaru*[1]. From this passage it has been inferred that 'the people' had a right to take part in the election of kings. But surely the text may equally well mean that Edmund obtained recognition as king only from the members of the council who were with him and from the troops who belonged to London.

These examples are hardly sufficient, I think, to show that the election of kings was regarded as lying within the province of the national council during the period in question. There seem to be traces, especially towards the end of the period

---

[1] It is hardly correct to translate this word by 'citizens'; 'garrison' would be a more appropriate term.

(cf. p. 357, footnote), of a feeling that election of some sort was required. But it is at least doubtful whether in practice this proceeding usually amounted to anything more than recognition on the part of the chief men of the kingdom individually.

We must now turn to the period before the tenth century. It is somewhat curious that the terms used for succession in early times are seldom or never given, for it is not generally contended that election was an innovation of the tenth century. As a matter of fact references to 'election' seem to be very rare though they are not absolutely unknown[1]. The phrase for succession used by the Chronicle, except when the throne was gained by violence, as in the cases of Ceadwalla and Cynewulf, is almost invariably *feng to rice* (*onfeng rices*). When (*ann.* 836) it speaks of succession in a dependent kingdom, it uses the expression: "he (Aethelwulf) gave (*salde*) Kent etc. to his son Aethelstan." Both these forms of expression are used by Bede. With the latter we may compare the phrase *donauit regnum* (Oswio to Peada) in *H.E.* III. 24. For succession in the independent kingdom we find the phrase *succedere in regnum* (*imperium*) etc. used of Hlothhere (Kent), Swithhelm (Essex), Ceolred (Mercia), Coenwalh and Ine (Wessex), Aldfrith and Osred (North.), while *succedere* alone is used of Osric (North.) and *successor* of Eorpwald and Anna (East Anglia). The phrase *regnum suscipere* (*regni gubernacula suscipere* etc.) is used of Eadbald, Erconberht and Ecgberht (Kent), Osric (Deira), Eanfrith (Bern.), Oswio and Coenred (North.), *regnum accipere* and *regno potiri* of Sigeberht (E. Anglia). All these phrases are somewhat ambiguous. Sometimes however the expression used refers to the dying or resigning king. Thus we find *regnum* (*imperium*) *relinquere* etc. used of Eadbald and Erconberht (Kent) and Wulfhere (Mercia); *regni heredes* (*heredem*) *relinquere* of Saberht (Essex), Wihtred (Kent) and

[1] An example occurs in the *Baedae Continuatio* (Plummer, I. p. 363) *ann.* 758, where it is stated that Aethelwald (Moll) *a sua plebe electus intrauit in regnum*. But it is to be observed that his predecessor had been murdered.

Oswio (North.).   In the case of Ine's resignation the phrase used (v. 7) is *relicto regno ac iuuenioribus commendato.*   But in some cases we find still more definite statements.   Thus in v. 19 it is stated of Aethelred (Mercia) : *Coinredum quem pro se regem fecerat,* and again (v. 24) *Coenredo regnum dedit.* In v. 23 the Northumbrian king Osric is said to have died *cum ipse regni......successorem fore Ceoluulfum decreuisset.* The only expression which can be understood as pointing to election is *leuato in regem Vulfhere* (III. 24).   But this was a case of revolution.

These examples suggest that in Bede's time the succession was not left to election but settled beforehand by the reigning king.   Aethelwulf's action in bequeathing his kingdom by will can therefore hardly be regarded as a startling innovation. The practice of associating the king's son in the government, which we find as late as the time of Offa and perhaps even in that of Alfred (cf. B. 576), points in the same direction.   It may be urged however that the expression *geceosan to cyninge* implies at least some form of election, and that even if it generally amounted to nothing more than formal recognition in later times, it must originally have had greater significance. It will be well therefore to consider briefly the meaning of this expression.

In the first place it should be noted that 'elect' is not an entirely satisfactory translation of *(ge)ceosan,* for the latter very frequently has an individual subject.   Apart from this expression the usual meanings of the word are 'select,' 'acquire,' 'approve.'   Again, it has been suggested above (p. 301 f.) that the title *cyning* was originally obtained by birth and not by office, and that the title of authority in early times was *hlaford* or *dryhten.*   If so the use of such an expression as *geceosan to cyninge* would of course at one time be impossible[1]. Moreover we have already had instances of a parallel expression, *geceosan to hlaforde* ; indeed both this and the similar phrase *secan (niman) to hlaforde* occur frequently in

---

[1] The expression *cyning geceosan* occurs in *Beow.* 1852, but *cyning* appears to be an official title in this poem (cf. p. 302).

the Chronicle, especially in the annals of Edward's reign. It is not unlikely therefore that *geceosan to cyninge* may have come into use on the analogy of *geceosan to hlaforde* when *cyning* had come to be a title of authority.

Whatever may have been the nature of the ceremony denoted by the phrase *geceosan to cyninge* there can be no doubt that *geceosan to hlaforde* meant the giving of allegiance to a higher authority. It was the act of an individual[1] and involved the relationship of 'lord' and 'man,' though when the 'man' had dependents (or lands) of his own these passed with him to the superior lord[2]. Now it is clear that all king's thegns were under the immediate lordship of the king. Therefore when the king died they became *hlafordleas* and had to 'select' or 'accept' a new lord. The need for doing so was no mere convention, since the possession of, office and all the profits arising therefrom were at stake. In later times it was doubtless necessary that all the king's thegns should 'select' the same lord. But the reason for this may have been that Edward the Elder had been strong enough to break with the old régime and to deprive his cousin Aethelwald of his rightful share in the government. But in earlier times, as we shall see presently, it is not clear that unanimity was always required. In the days of divided kingdoms we may suspect that the arrangements of a deceased king were sometimes set aside in favour of the more popular and liberal members of the family.

In addition to the power of election it has been supposed that the council also had the right of deposing kings. Instances of kings who lost their kingdoms are not rare

[1] It is perhaps worth noticing that the Latin *eligere* is often used in the same sense, e.g. in Florence's account of the 'election' of Edward the Martyr : *quidam......Edwardum quidam uero fratrem illius elegerunt Aegelredum.*

[2] Even when both 'lord' and 'man' were kings the superior seems to have had some right over the lands of the inferior ; cf. *H.E.* iii. 7 : *donauerunt...ambo reges eidem episcopo ciuitatem quae uocatur Dorcic.* Cynegils had no doubt 'accepted' Oswald *to hlaforde.*

during the seventh and eighth centuries, but as a rule they give little colour to the idea that the 'deposition' was due to a formal act of the council. There are however two cases which have been ascribed to 'constitutional' action on the part of the council. For the first we are dependent wholly on Symeon of Durham (*ann.* 774) : *Alcredus rex consilio et consensu suorum omnium regiae familiae ac principum destitutus societate exilio imperii mutauit maiestatem. primo in urbem Bebban, postea ad regem Pictorum nomine Cynoht cum paucis fugae comitibus secessit.* But do the words *consilio et consensu suorum omnium* necessarily imply a formal act of deposition ? If that had been the case it is hardly likely that the deposed king would have been allowed to make his way to what was probably the most important fortress in the kingdom. The expression *suorum omnium* is clearly to be interpreted by the following words. But these distinctly suggest that the king was deserted by all his *ministri* and *comites,* to use Bede's terms, acting as individuals, and that he fled (from York) for his life before any further action could be taken. It is to be remembered that Alhred had himself obtained the throne by revolution and that the king who now succeeded him was the son of his predecessor. Indeed the history of the Northumbrian kingdom during this period gives little countenance to the idea that its councillors were scrupulous about the observation of constitutional forms.

The other case, that of Sigeberht in Wessex, is more important. The words of the Chronicle (*ann.* 755) are as follows : " Cynewulf and the West Saxon council deprived Sigeberht of his kingdom, except Hampshire, because of his evil deeds[1]." It is generally assumed that this also was a formal act of deposition on the part of the council. But surely the fact that Cynewulf is especially mentioned suggests conspiracy. The words which immediately follow in the

---

[1] *Her Cynewulf benam Sigebryht his rices and West Seaxna wiotan for unryhtum dædum buton Hamtunscire; and he hæfde þa oþ he ofslog þone aldormon þe him lengest wunode* etc. For the account of this transaction given by Henry of Huntingdon see Plummer, *Two Saxon Chronicles,* II. pp. 44 f.

Chronicle are very seldom quoted, and it is assumed that Hampshire was left for the deposed king's maintenance. But the omitted words are not without significance : "but this (Hampshire) he kept until he killed the earl þe him lengest wunode." The last sentence can hardly mean anything else than "who remained (faithful) to him longer than the rest." The reason why Hampshire was left in Sigeberht's possession is therefore in all probability to be found in the fact that its earl, Cumbra, did not transfer his allegiance. There is no necessity then to believe that a formal vote took place at all. Most of the king's thegns individually 'selected' for themselves a new lord and carried with them the provinces which they governed.

Another passage in the same annal deserves notice. Cynewulf was eventually attacked and killed by Cyneheard, Sigeberht's brother. His thegns, who had come on the scene after the murder, were offered life and money by Cyneheard. But they refused his offers and fought until they were all killed except a Welsh hostage who was badly wounded. The following day an earl named Osric arrived with a larger number of king's thegns. Cyneheard offered them their own terms in money and land if they would grant him the kingdom, and added that their relatives were with him and would not leave him. But the thegns replied that no kinsman was dearer to them than their lord, and that they would never serve a man who had killed him, though they were willing to grant a safe pass to their relatives. In the fight which followed Cyneheard and all his party were slain with the exception of one wounded man, who was the earl's godson.

In this story—which incidentally gives a good illustration of the personal relationship between the king and his thegns —we have the record of an unsuccessful attempt to seize the throne. It is not fair, with the evidence at our disposal, to draw a distinction between this proceeding and the deposition of Sigeberht, and to call the one 'revolutionary' and the other 'constitutional.' There can be little doubt that if Osric and his companions had accepted Cyneheard's offers their action would have been regarded as a case of *geceosan to cyninge* just as much as the other. No doubt Cyneheard was in a desperate position when he made such lavish promises; but we may suspect that the offer of land and money was no very rare inducement to enter the service of an ambitious prince.

An interesting parallel, or rather contrast, to the above story is provided by the episode of Finn and Hnaef in *Beowulf* (ll. 1069 ff.). Hnaef was killed and his followers after a long resistance were won over by the promise of reward to enter the service of his adversary, though vengeance was effected later. There is another passage (ll. 2370 ff.) in the same poem which deserves to be cited in this connection. King Hygelac had lost his life on a foreign expedition, leaving only a son who was very young, perhaps actually a minor. Beowulf, who seems to have been the next nearest relative to the deceased king, was invited to accept 'the treasury and the kingdom' (*hord and rice*). But the invitation, it should be observed, is represented as coming not from the royal council but from Hygelac's widow, *i.e.* the person actually in possession of the treasury. Perhaps doubt may be thrown on the historical truth of this story. But is the incident in itself any more incredible than the fact that Coenwalh's widow kept the throne for herself[1]?

I suspect then that the 'election' of a king was originally the selection or acceptance of an overlord, and that the 'electors' acted not as the representatives of the nation but as individuals, though they naturally carried their own dependents with them. Such an act would not differ essentially from the submission which we find recorded to persons who were already kings by those who had not previously been under their jurisdiction, *e.g.* by Hengest to Finn, by the East Anglian king to Ecgberht, and by the Danish earls Thurcytel and Thurferth to Edward the Elder. It was probably customary to reward the electors with treasure and in particular perhaps to give them swords, as if

---

[1] It is possible that both these cases may be explained by a marriage custom, but the authorities themselves do not suggest this.

they were taking up their office anew (cf. p. 353). This feature appears very clearly in Saxo's account (II. p. 67) of Wiggo and possibly also in the story of Finn and Hengest[1]. A Norwegian instance, referring to the ninth century, is to be found in *Haralds S. Hárf.* (Heimskr.), cap. 8[2].

From the story of Sigeberht's deposition it would seem that in early times unanimity on the part of the electors was not essential. In the smaller kingdoms we find a system which admitted of a number of kings, apparently on a footing of equality ; and I have suggested (p. 298 ff.) that this is to be regarded as the original type of kingdom in England. No doubt however it was a familiar occurrence at all times for an ambitious prince to deprive his relatives of their rights, and consequently the kingdom was from time to time brought together under one head. In Mercia and Northumbria the sole kingdom seems to have been established in quite early times. But, so far as our evidence goes, the succession appears to have been settled beforehand by the reigning king, though of course such arrangements were largely dependent on the goodwill of the chief territorial officials. In Wessex we have to take into account (i) the existence of a number of *subreguli*, (ii) the constant recurrence of dynastic strife, (iii) the fact that the king was seldom succeeded by a near relative. The last point might at first sight seem to point to freedom of election, but, if I am right, this election was really a recognition of lordship—generally perhaps to that *subregulus* who had the greatest influence among the deceased king's followers. From the evidence of the Chronicle (*e.g. ann.* 685, 729, 755) it seems probable that the throne was not generally acquired without bloodshed.

---

[1] *Beow.* 1143 ff. The passage unfortunately is obscure. Possibly some lines are lost.

[2] Cf. also the famous story of Harold and Aethelstan (*ib.,* cap. 41).

EXCURSUS V.

THE TENURE OF LAND IN PRE-HISTORIC TIMES.

The character of the grants to *milites* mentioned in Bede's *Epistola ad Ecgberctum*, cap. 11, and *Historia Abbatum*, cap. 1, is a subject on which a good deal of obscurity prevails. In the first place we have to ask whether the land thus granted was *bocland*. There are, I think, three distinct reasons for giving a negative answer to this question (i) We have elsewhere little or no evidence for grants of *bocland* made to laymen, except for religious purposes, unti after the time of Bede. (ii) There are two at least probable cases of the possession of *cyninges folcland* by king's thegns in later times. The first instance occurs in a charter (B. 496) dating from 858, which records an exchange of lands between Aethelberht, king of Kent, and his thegn Wullaf (Wulflaf). The persons who hold the *cyninges folcland* are called Wighelm and Wulflaf. Both these names occur among the signatories to the charter, and the latter may also be identical with the person who makes the exchange. The other example is in the will of Earl Aelfred (B. 558). The testator, after bequeathing certain lands to his son Aethelwald, makes provision that he is to have an additional estate if the king will not grant him 'the *folcland*,' presumably the *folcland* which the testator himself holds. As the disposal of the land in question was in the king's hand it is natural t infer that it was royal land[1]. Otherwise we should expect any dispute as to its ownership to come into the reeve's court (cf. Edw. I. 2). As to the position of the testator there is of course no doubt, and it is at least extremely likely that his son also would be a king's thegn, even if he was not an earl himself (cf. p. 171, footnote). (iii) In the old poetry we find references to grants of land to persons of similar position. Thus in *Beow.* 2885 ff., Wiglaf addresses Beowulf's cowardly thegns in the following words : " Your relatives (or perhaps ' offspring') shall be deprived of the receiving of treasure and the presentation of swords, of all the pleasure of landed estates, of (all such) sustenance (?); every member of the kindred will have to go destitute of property in land, when princes (even) far from here learn the story of your flight[2]." The custom therefore seems to go back far beyond the days of charters.

The next question which we have to consider is whether these grants were heritable. It must be confessed that the evidence at our disposal on this question is scanty. Yet I think we have enough to decide again in favour of a negative answer. Bede complains that the amount of land available for the support of king's thegns was rapidly decreasing. If the grants to king's thegns themselves had been heritable

---

[1] According to Prof. Vinogradoff (*Eng. Hist. Rev.*, VIII. p. 10) we should in that case have not *folcland* but *lænland*. But does not the same objection apply to the case of Wighelm and Wulflaf? May not the term *lænland* have been limited, originally at least, to *bocland* which was let on lease by its owner to others? It is worth noticing that the word *lænland* seems not to occur before the latter part of the tenth century. *Læn* itself is found somewhat earlier, but apparently not before the time of Alfred. In general of course I follow Prof. Vinogradoff's interpretation of the term *folcland*.

[2]   *nu sceal sincþego and swyrdgifu,*
        eall eðelwyn eowrum cynne,
        lufen alicgean : londrihtes mot
        þære mægburge monna æghwylc
        idel hweorfan syððan æðelingas
        feorran gefricgean fleam eowerne etc.

this process would have taken place just the same, though perhaps not so rapidly. Again, it was clearly in the king's power to decide whether the *folcland* held by Earl Aelfred should or should not be continued to his son; and I have already remarked (p. 171, footnote) that the supposition that the latter was illegitimate seems to me to be not sufficiently grounded. Clearer evidence on this point may be obtained from the poems. In *Widsith*, 90 ff., the poet states that he had been presented by Eormenric with a valuable bracelet. On his return home he gave it to his lord, Eadgils, king of the Myrgingas, "in requital of his kindness, because he had given me land, (even) my father's estate[1]." From *Deor*, 38 ff., it would seem that such grants were revocable at the king's pleasure. Deor was another court poet and had likewise received a grant of land. "I have had a good office and a gracious lord for many years, until now Heorrenda, a man skilled in poetry, has received the domain (property in land) which the king formerly gave to me[2]." It appears then that

[1]   *leofum to leane þæs þe he me lond forgeaf,*
         mines fæder eþel etc.

This passage shows clearly that the word *eðel* does not necessarily mean an inherited estate, as has often been stated. We may compare *Genesis* 962, 1052, 1485, 1896, 1927, where the words *eðel, eðelstow, eðelstol, eðelsetl* are applied to the dwelling-places of Adam and Eve after the Fall, of Cain after the murder of Abel, of Noah after the Flood, and of Abraham and Lot. The mistake seems to have arisen from the fact that *eðel* is also used in the sense of 'native country' (*patria*) and from foreign usage.

[2]   *ahte ic fela wintra folgað tilne*
         holdne hlaford oþ þæt Heorrenda nu
         leoðcræftig monn londryht geþah
         þæt me eorla hleo ær gesealde.

In Bosworth and Toller's Dictionary the word *londriht*, both here and in *Beow.* 2887 (see above), is taken to mean 'rights of a native,' 'rights of those who live in the land.' This seems to me scarcely probable, for in that case we should surely require *folcriht*. Again, one would hardly expect a man bearing the name *Heorrenda* to be a 'foreigner' to the Heodeningas. For the translation above we may compare *Gen.* 1910 f.

these grants, so far from being heritable, were tenable only at the king's pleasure. We may suspect, however, that as a rule they were held for life, and it is clear that they were sometimes, as a mark of favour, continued to the grantee's son. In principle therefore the conditions of tenure seem not to differ from those of earldoms. We have seen (p. 292 f.) that in the latter cases of a father being succeeded by his son are by no means rare ; and similar instances are recorded by tradition from the earliest times. Thus according to Saxo IV. p. 107[1], when Frowinus (Freawine), the *praefectus* of Slesvig, had been killed in battle, King Wermund appointed his sons, Keto and Wigo, to the same office[2].

We must next enquire what lands were and were not liable to be granted in this way. Now in the last chapter the question whether the *miles* (*minister*) necessarily became a *comes* on receiving a grant of land was left open. There can be little doubt however that such *milites* were distinguished from *praefecti*. This may, I think, fairly be inferred from the following passage (cap. 13): *sic per annos circiter triginta... prouincia nostra uesano illo errore dementata est ut nullus pene exinde praefectorum extiterit qui non huiusmodi sibi monasterium in diebus suae praefecturae comparauerit...ac praeualente pessima consuetudine ministri quoque regis ac famuli idem facere sategerint.* Again, it is important to notice the exact point of Bede's complaint. He does not say that the royal exchequer had been depleted, but that the lands applicable to the maintenance of *milites* were becoming exhausted. Now it would of course be absurd to suppose that such persons were tillers of the land. What they received therefore must have been the revenue of the lands in question. But we have seen (p. 259 f.) that the Northumbrian *praefectus* appears to have corresponded to the

---

[1] The references are to the pages of Holder's edition throughout.

[2] *Frowini filios Wermundus paterne dignitatis honoribus euehit, extincti pro patria amici liberos iusto ad modum beneficio prosecutus.*

king's reeve of Wessex. We must suppose then that the
normal size of the district under his jurisdiction was at least
100 hides, more probably 300 or 600 hides. It is true that in
later times we find churches with estates of this size. The
church of Hereford had 300 hides in Herefordshire, the church
of Worcester 300 hides in Worcestershire, and the church of
Lincoln (Dorchester) 300 hides in Oxfordshire. But such
cases were quite exceptional. If the multitudinous grants of
Bede's day had been of this character we should have heard
that the kings were being threatened with financial ruin.
Further, they would hardly be open to the objection which
Bede actually points out; for churches with estates of this
size must surely have had lay tenants who were capable of
fighting. On the other hand we saw (p. 254) that the royal
uillae of Oxfordshire had not only jurisdiction over several
hundreds attached to them, but also lands of much smaller
extent, varying from 5 to 34½ hides, which actually constituted the royal estate. It must surely be such lands as
these which the Northumbrian *praefecti* alienated from *militia*
by turning their establishments into monasteries.

It is perhaps possible to press too far the fact that Bede
makes no allusion to the depletion of the royal exchequer.
But the readiness of the kings in making these grants in
itself suggests that they had been no great losers by the
establishment of such monasteries. Now if we turn to
H.E. III. 24 we find that Oswio after his victory over Penda
devoted twelve estates of 10 hides each *ad construenda
monasteria*. We have seen (p. 100) that in Ine 70 ten hides
is the unit for which a payment apparently identical with
the king's *feorm*[1] is regulated. But it must not be supposed
that these grants were grants of the king's *feorm* merely, for in
that case they would of course have been inadequate for the
support of even a humble monastery. They were clearly
grants of ownership over the estates in question. There can

---

[1] Cf. B. 551 where the community of Berkeley are exempted
by Earl Aethelred from *þære cyningfeorme ge on hlutrum alað ge on
beore ge on hunige ge on hryþrum ge on swynum ge on sceapum.*

be little doubt that one of their privileges was that, like most
Church estates in the south, they were exempt from payment
of the king's *feorm*. It has also been supposed that they
were freed from the obligation of military service. This
supposition is based on the words *in quibus ablato studio
militiae terrestris ad exercendam militiam caelestem suppli-
candumque pro pace gentis eius aeterna deuotioni sedulae
monachorum locus facultasque suppeteret*. But I am not sure
that this interpretation is necessary. Is it not possible that
the word *militia* here may mean the support of a king's
thegn? If so we can see at once what the character of the
grants to *milites* really was. It was a grant not of the king's
feorm but of (temporary) ownership over a certain amount of
royal land, perhaps normally ten hides. So far as I am
aware, there is no reason for believing that the king's *feorm*
was paid from royal land. As such land belonged to the
king, he or the person placed in possession by him would be
entitled to all that could be obtained from it. I suspect then
that the lands belonging to *praefecti* and *milites*, to which we
have allusion in the *Epistola ad Ecgberctum*, were of this
character, *i.e.* that they were royal estates held on lease. The
transformation of such lands into monasteries would thus
make no immediate difference to the king, though of course
in time the royal estates would become exhausted by this
process.

It would, however, be somewhat premature to assume
that the king's *folcland* always consisted of scattered estates
of 10 hides or thereabouts. In *H.E.* IV. 13 Aethelwalh, king
of Sussex, is said to have granted to Wilfrid an estate of
87 hides (*terram* LXXXVII. *familiarum...uocabulo Selæseu*),
together with all its inhabitants. Now it has been suggested
that this grant was a transference of royal rights, including
the king's *feorm*, over the district in question. This explanation seems to me extremely improbable. It is true that in
later times we find grants of this kind. In the laws of
Alfred, cap. 2, we hear of churches which were entitled to the
king's *feorm*, and still earlier examples are to be found in
some Kentish charters (cf. p. 101, footnote). But among the

inhabitants of this Selsey estate there were 250 slaves whom Wilfrid liberated. Whose slaves were they? Is it likely that Wilfrid would inaugurate his rule with an act of wholesale robbery? He can hardly have been in a position to give the requisite amount of compensation. The answer surely is that the slaves, or at least the majority of them, had belonged to the king and had been transferred by him to Wilfrid. If so we must conclude that a considerable part of the estate had been *inland* and cultivated by slave-labour. Bede's language seems distinctly to imply that the whole of the 87 hides lay in the peninsula of Selsey. But even if this was not the case (cf. B. 64), the South Saxon hide at this time cannot have been large. If we make allowance for a certain number of *geburas* and for work done by the *gafolgeldan*, we can hardly reckon the *inland* at less than 30 or 40 hides[1]. It is clear then that the grant was not that of a small estate together with jurisdiction over a number of neighbouring landowners, but that it was a grant of ownership over the whole 87 hides.

If this explanation is correct we shall have to suppose that in early times there were districts of quite considerable extent which had no other landowner than the king. Now it is of course a very difficult matter to determine how many of the grants to churches and thegns recorded in the charters were made from royal land. There has been a tendency of late to suppose that the charter frequently amounted only to a remission of national (primarily fiscal) obligations to estates

---

[1] It is more likely to have amounted to 50 or 60 hides or even more. Let us suppose for a moment that all the slaves of the *gafolgeldan* are included, and that the proportion 250 slaves to 87 hides was normal. This will give 20,000 slaves for the kingdom of Sussex. Then according to the statistics of the Tribal Hidage we must conclude that the whole of England contained not less than half a million slaves, even making allowance for a smaller hide in the Midlands. But this is surely incredible unless the proportion of *inland* was vastly greater than in later times. I suspect however that the number of slaves in this case was above the average.

which were already in private hands; and there is no doubt
that such was the case sometimes. Yet I cannot persuade
myself that this is the natural interpretation to be put on
the language generally used in the charters. On the other
hand, if we conclude that the majority of grants were made
from royal lands, we shall of course be forced to believe that
these were constantly diminishing, and that in early times
they were of much greater extent than later. But is there
any cogent reason for denying that this may have been the
case?

We must now consider briefly the tenure of *folcland*
which was not royal. This is a question on which very little
evidence is available. As a matter of fact the word *folcland*
occurs only three times, and in two of these cases we have
seen reason for believing that the land in question belonged
to the king. The third example occurs in Edw. I. 2, and
from it we learn only that disputes as to ownership were to
be settled in the reeve's court. There can be little doubt
that land of this character was held by some sort of hereditary
tenure, probably by a system similar to what we find in other
Teutonic nations. It was also subject, as we have seen, to
certain payments (*feorm*) and services. But why was the
term *gesið* applied to landowners?

There is another question which is closely bound up with
that of prehistoric landownership in England, namely the
question how this country was settled after the Saxon
invasion. Those who hold that Britain, like Iceland, was
occupied by small bodies of settlers acting• independently
may regard the landowning nobility of the seventh and
eighth centuries as the descendants of local chieftains who
were at first independent but subsequently recognised the
supremacy of kings. For others who like myself regard this
view of the invasion as entirely incredible some different
explanation must be found. Now if we turn to the history
of the great Danish invasion, which may reasonably be
expected to present certain analogies to that of the Saxons,
we find it stated in the Chronicle that in 876 King Healfdene
'distributed' the territories of Northumbria. What form the

distribution took we are not told. But on the occasion of a subsequent invasion we find (*Hist. de S. Cuthberto*, cap. 23) a Scandinavian king named Regenwald dividing the lands of St Cuthbert between two of his followers, named Scula and Onalafball. These examples suggest that the settlement of the land was determined from above: that the kings divided their territories among their chief men, and that the latter again distributed their possessions among their own followers. Is there any valid reason for denying that a similar plan may have been followed in the case of the Saxon invasion[1]? By this explanation we shall at all events obtain a satisfactory explanation of the use of the word *gesið* in its two senses, (i) the *comes regis* or royal official who held directly of the king, and (ii) the *gesið* or *gesiðcund man landagende* of Ine's laws who held, whether immediately or not, of the royal official.

It may perhaps be thought that this explanation lays too much stress on the etymology of the word *gesið*. No doubt this term was originally used of a man who was connected with another man by a personal bond. But when we find it applied to ordinary landowners is it necessary to suppose that this original force was still inherent in the word? Yet, as a matter of fact, there are other traces of this personal bond. There is the *manbot* (cf. p. 123 f.) and more especially the heriot (cf. p. 81 f.). Even in the eleventh century we find the reeve (sheriff) receiving heriots from the *lagemanni* of Cambridge (cf. p. 246, footnote). By this time it had for the most part been commuted into a monetary payment which we should perhaps call a death duty. But surely its origin is

---

[1] It is perhaps worth noting that in Chron. 534 the first Kings of Wessex are said to have given the Isle of Wight to their nephews, Stuf and Wihtgar, though the statement may be a fabrication. No stress can be laid on the use of the word *aldormen* (i.e. *principes*) in *ann.* 495. With the traditions of early Wessex I hope to deal elsewhere. The dynasty claimed descent from Freawine and Wig, who are said to have been *praefecti* of Slesvig (cf. p. 370). But the term *praefectus* could, as we have seen, be applied to persons of royal birth.

to be found in the outfit of weapons and armour which the
lord supplied to a man who entered his service, instances of
which are to be found in *Beow.* 2637, 2867, and which
returned to the lord at his man's death. In the Continental
laws we sometimes find it stated that at a landowner's death
his armour was to go to the man (kinsman) who succeeded
him in the possession of his land, *e.g. Lex Angl. et Wer.*,
cap. 31: *ad quemcumque hereditas terrae peruenerit ad illum
uestis bellica, id est lorica...debet pertinere.* The fact that in
England the heriot went to the man's lord is an argument
for believing that originally the land also reverted to the
same quarter. It must certainly not be assumed from the
absence of any reference to heriots in the earliest wills that
this custom was an innovation of later times. Its appearance
is that of an institution coming down from remote antiquity,
though it was regulated by later legislation. We may note a
passage in *Beowulf*, l. 452 ff. The hero gives directions to
King Hrothgar, before entering on a conflict which was likely
to prove fatal to him, that in the event of death the latter
should send his coat of mail to his lord, King Hygelac. That
the coat of mail had been given to Beowulf by Hygelac may
be inferred from the fact that it had formerly belonged to
Hrethel, Hygelac's father.

It is true that from what has been said above we should
not expect the tenure of land held on such a system as this
to be hereditary. But the two centuries which elapsed
between the invasion and the laws of Ine may have brought
about considerable changes in this respect. Very possibly,
as Mr Seebohm has suggested[1], the lease for three lives may

---

[1] *Tribal Custom in Anglo-Saxon Law*, p. 525. In another
passage (p. 417 ff.) in the same work Mr Seebohm has arrived at
conclusions similar on the whole to those stated above by a
different and very forcible line of argument. He is clearly right
in laying stress on the 'official' position of the gesith, but I do
not think he is right in calling the (West Saxon) gesith ('gesith-
cundman') a 'gesith of the King' or his lands 'Royal domains'
(cf. p. 346 ff. above).

in principle not have been entirely foreign to ancient English custom. The regulation quoted above (p. 81) from the *Northleoda Lagu* points in this direction, and analogies are to be found in other Teutonic nations[1]. Land held, whether of the king or of his subordinates, by members of the same family for three generations may have become permanently alienated, though it was still liable to payments and services, and though traces of the personal bond formerly subsisting between the landowner and his superior were still preserved in the *manbot* and the heriot. We have seen that, in some districts at least, slaves appear to have been far more numerous in early times than in the eleventh century. Presumably they passed as a rule into *geburas*; but this class also is a small one in Domesday Book. Hence we are forced to conclude that the *uillani*, who in a sense had land of their own and thus corresponded to some extent to the earlier *gafolgeldan*[2], had largely been recruited from the classes beneath them. But the change of status involved in the transition from *gebur* to *gafolgelda* (cf. p. 87, footnote) seems to be precisely analogous to that suggested above in the status of the landowner.

[1] Cf. (for Norway) Seebohm, *op. cit.*, p. 271 ff.

[2] The holding of the *gafolgelda* seems originally to have been at least one hide (see the Addenda, p. 412 f.), whereas the normal holding of the *uillanus* was very much less; but this may be due to an increase in the size of the hide (cf. p. 267, note). The term *gafolgelda* seems not to be used in official documents after the time of Ine.

CHAPTER X.

THE ORIGIN OF THE NOBILITY

§ 1. *The terms ' gesiðcund' and ' eorlcund.'*

IN Chapter III. we saw that the English
population of Wessex in the time of the early laws
was divided into three classes, distinguished by the
amount of their wergelds, as also by the compensations to which they were due for breach of their
mund, by the fines to which they were liable, and
by the value attached to their oaths. The wergeld
of the highest class was 1200 sh., that of the second
600 sh., and that of the third 200 sh. The same
three classes, with corresponding wergelds, existed
in Mercia and probably also in Northumbria, though
in the latter case we cannot produce definite evidence
for the intermediate class. In Wessex and Mercia
the highest class was called *twelfhynde*, from the
amount of its wergeld. Similarly the second class,
at least in Wessex, was called *sixhynde*; while the
lowest class was everywhere known as *ceorlisc*.
From the laws of Ine we learn further that the
twelfhynde man was a *gesiðcund* man who owned

land, and that the *sixhynde* man was a *gesiðcund* man without land. Lastly, the distinction between the three classes seems everywhere to be, at least in part, hereditary.

It appears then that the two higher classes were 'gesith-born[1].' Now in the last chapter we have seen that *comes*, which seems originally to have been a translation of *gesið*, was a term applied to royal officials in all the ancient English kingdoms, though it is not clear that it was limited to such persons. Again, the word *gesiðas* (plural) itself occurs as a translation of *optimates, i.e.* probably the members of the royal council (cf. p. 343). In Ine's laws however *gesið* denotes a nobleman, possibly only a landed nobleman, who was not under the immediate lordship of the king. We know that the word originally meant 'companion,' a sense in which it is used in the old poetry. We should therefore expect the dignity

---

[1] It may perhaps be thought that this translation lays too much stress on the etymology of -*cund* (*i.e. genitus*). In many compounds of this class, *e.g.* *eorðcund, engelcund, weoroldcund,* the original meaning of the second element has no doubt been forgotten (as in Goth. *airþakunds* etc.). But these theological terms, which must be of fairly late formation, are clearly of a different order from ancient words like *gesiðcund* and *eorlcund*; for the latter are always applied to persons, whereas the former are comparatively seldom so used. Quite possibly -*cund* no longer retained its original force even in Ine's time. But it is surely improbable that *gesiðcund* and *eorlcund* had been synonymous with *gesið* and *eorl* from the beginning. When we find *eorlcund* applied to women what other meaning can it have except 'eorl-born'? It is true that no example of *gesiðcund* happens to occur in reference to women, but since we do find *gesiþwif*, this must be a mere accident. Cf. the O. Norse (poet.) *kundr*, 'descendant.'

of the gesith to be dependent to some extent on the
rank of his lord; and it is true that in compensations
for *mund* and in regard to the value of his oath the
cyninges þegn or *comes regis* is put on a higher level
than the gesith. But we have no reason for believing
that the two orders had different wergelds.

In the Kentish laws we again meet with the
terms *ceorl* and *gesiðcund*. The former is frequent,
but the latter occurs only once, in the latest of the
codes, while *gesið* does not occur at all. In the
earlier codes we find the term *eorlcund*, which seems
to be used in the same sense as *gesiðcund*. The
wergeld of the higher class, like that of the *sixhynde*
class in Wessex, is three times as great as that of
the ceorl, but we find no trace of anything corresponding to the *twelfhynde* class. On the other hand
we do meet with a lower class, the *læt*, apparently
peculiar to Kent and possessing wergelds which vary
from 2 : 5 to 4 : 5 relatively to that of the ceorl.
Lastly, it is to be noted that the wergeld of the
Kentish ceorl is considerably greater than that of
the West Saxon, Mercian, or Northumbrian ceorl.
In the time of Ine and Wihtred the former would
amount to (100 sh., *i.e.*) 2000 coins, *i.e.* probably
100 oxen, while the latter would be (200 sh., *i.e.*)
800 coins or (probably) 33 oxen (cf. p. 156 f.). The
mund of the Kentish ceorl was apparently six times
as great as that of the West Saxon ceorl.

The questions which we have now to set before
us are two: (1) What is the relationship of the
Kentish social system to that of the other kingdoms?
Are we to suppose that two different social systems

were in existence before the invasion of Britain, or
that the differences between them are due to
subsequent development ?   (2) What was the origin
of the higher class or classes ?

To the second question an answer seems to
present itself at once.   If *gesiðcund* means " gesith-
born," and if the gesith was a man of official position,
are we not justified in concluding that the *gesiðcund*
class were the descendants of such persons ? Nobility
then would be a result of official position.   But there
are difficulties in the way of this explanation.   In
a sense we may regard all landowners as officials.
But how can we regard the landless *gesiðcund man*
or *sixhynde man* in this light ? It can hardly be the
mere fact of service in itself which ennobled a man ;
for in that case we should surely not find the king's
men placed on the same level as those who were in
the service of other persons.   Again, we have seen
(p. 96 f.) that our authorities give no support to the
idea that *sixhynde men* were the descendants of
twelfhynde men.   Moreover there is another consideration which may make us pause.   In the
Kentish laws we find the term *gesiðcund* displacing
an earlier term *eorlcund,* and it is by no means clear
what the word *eorl* originally meant.   Nor can we be
certain that this objection applies only in the case of
the Kentish system.   The laws of Aethelberht and
those of Hlothhere and Eadric, in which the term
eorlcund occurs, are older than any West Saxon or
Mercian code which we possess.   It is quite possible
therefore that the term *eorlcund* was once in use
elsewhere.   As a matter of fact we do find the word

eorl in the West Saxon laws, *e.g.* Alfr. 4: *be eallum
hadum ge ceorle ge eorle*; Aethelstan VI. Pref.:
ægðer ge eorlisce ge ceorlisce[1]. These are clearly
traditional formulae like *twihynde and twelfhynde* in
later times. If we note further that the word *eorl* is
of very frequent occurrence in the old poetry, we
shall be forced to admit that it is not likely to have
been a specifically Kentish term.

This consideration obviously complicates the
question at issue. In place of one term (*gesið*) of
known etymology but somewhat ambiguous application, we now come to another (*eorl*) which is obscure
in every respect. We have seen no reason for
believing that the word *eorl* in Aethelberht's laws
denotes a royal official. In Wihtred's time at all
events the term used for this purpose was *cyninges
þegn*. On the other hand in the Scandinavian
languages the word *iarl* does bear this meaning.
The person so denoted was a kind of lieutenant
governor, like the English earl. Moreover even in the
earliest English poems we find such expressions as
eorl Beowulfes, which imply subordination to a higher
authority. But in other passages we find the term
eorl applied to kings, even to supreme kings, *e.g.
eorl Ongenþio* (*Beow.* 2952), where any such idea is
of course excluded. Again, it can hardly be doubted
that the expression *ge ceorle ge eorle* (Alfr. 4) is used
in the sense of 'simple and noble,' without reference
to the possession of office in the latter case. Lastly

[1] Further examples probably occurred in Aethelstan IV. 3
(cf. III. Pref.) and Edm. III. 7, of which the English originals have
been lost.

it is to be observed that in Old Saxon poetry the word *erlos* means no more than ' men.' So far therefore as our evidence goes we seem to get nothing more definite than 'noble' or 'distinguished man' as the original meaning of the word[1].

There is no difficulty in understanding how *gesiðcund* came to displace *eorlcund*. From what has been said it is likely enough that the terms *eorl* and *gesið* were applied to the same persons—the latter primarily with reference to their relationship to a higher authority. But, if so, it is clearly not safe to explain the origin of the nobility from the etymology of the word *gesiðcund*.

§ 2.   *The social systems of the Continent*[2].

As the English evidence in itself is inconclusive, we must now turn our attention to the laws of other Teutonic nations. It will be convenient to begin with the Frankish laws. Here the wergeld of the Frankish freeman was 200 solidi, while that of the Roman was 100 sol. or less[3]. Officials and persons in the service of the king had in either case a triple wergeld, *i.e.* 600 sol. for the Frank and 300 sol. for

[1] In the earliest Scandinavian inscriptions the word *erilaz* occurs several times, but only once with a genitive, in an inscription (Kragehul) which has hardly been satisfactorily made out.

[2] In this and the following sections I am under special obligations to Mr Seebohm's *Tribal Custom in Anglo-Saxon Law*. As the subject is discussed at considerable length in that work (chapters v.—viii.) I have thought it sufficient here in most cases to indicate briefly the main features.

[3] Cf. Seebohm, *op. cit.* pp. 147 ff., 167 f.

the Roman. As there seems to be no evidence that these triple wergelds were inherited, the system obviously has little resemblance to either of those which prevailed in England. On the other hand we clearly find gradations of rank in the laws of the Burgundians and the Alamanni. In the former case[1] the wergelds are as follows: *optimatus nobilis* 300 sol., *mediocris* 200 sol., *minor persona* 150 sol.; while those of the Alamanni[2] are: *primus* 240 sol., *medianus* 200 sol., *baro de minoflidis* 170 (probably for 160) sol. Unfortunately the nature of the distinctions is in neither case explained. It appears, however, that among the Alamanni officials of the duke had triple wergelds. In the Bavarian laws[3] we find definite evidence for the existence of a hereditary nobility, though it was limited to six families. The wergelds were: for the ducal family 640 sol., for the other five noble families 320 sol., for the freeman 160 sol., for the stranger 100 sol., for the freedman 40 sol.

In the Frisian laws we should certainly expect to find greater affinity to the English systems, since of all the continental languages Frisian is the most nearly related to English. But this expectation is hardly borne out by the evidence. We do indeed find three social classes, the noble (*nobilis*), the freeman, and the *litus*, which may quite well correspond to the three classes of Kentish society. The nobility also appears to have been hereditary; at all events it included women as well as men. But the

---

[1] Seebohm, *Tribal Custom*, p. 124.
[2] *Ibid.* pp. 172 ff.
[3] *Ibid.* pp. 174 ff.

proportions which the wergelds bear to one another are different. Into the actual amounts we need not enter; for owing to changes in the monetary system the evidence is conflicting. The wergeld of the noble is however double that of the freeman, and the latter again is double that of the *litus*—except in the central district, where the proportion is in both cases 3 : 2[1]. Of royal and official wergelds we know nothing, as the laws date from a period later than the Frankish conquest. An interesting analogy to English custom is to be found in the fact that the oaths of different classes are of different value, the proportion being in general, though not universally, the same as in the amounts of the wergelds.

In the *Lex Chamavorum* and the *Lex Angliorum et Werinorum hoc est Thuringorum*, two codes dating from not earlier than the ninth century[2], the freeman (*liber, ingenuus*) possesses, as in the Frankish laws, a wergeld of 200 sol. In the former code the *litus* (*lidus*) has a wergeld of 100 sol. In the latter this class is not mentioned; but the manumitted slave has a wergeld of 80 sol. (§ 45), though the value of the slave is only 30 sol. In both codes however we find a higher class with a wergeld of 600 sol. In the *Lex Chamavorum* the persons entitled to this triple wergeld are the *comes*, the royal *missus* and the *homo Francus*. The two former are of course officials, and their treatment is in accordance with the Frankish laws. But the position of the *homo Francus* is unfortunately not made clear. If, in spite of the

---

[1] *Ib.* pp. 197 ff.

Cf. von Amira in Paul's *Grundriss d. germ. Phil.* III.[2] p. 66 f.

preface, we might believe that the population of the district in question was really not Frankish, we might regard the triple wergeld of the *homo Francus* as the result of conquest—in which case it would probably be hereditary. In the other code there can be little doubt on this point. The person entitled to the triple wergeld is called *adalingus*, a word which in itself implies a hereditary qualification. Moreover it holds good for women as well as for men (§ 48 f.). Apart from the wergelds and compensations for injuries this code has far more affinity with the Frankish than with the English laws. That may be due to the fact that the nation to which it belonged, whatever its geographical position[1], had doubtless long been subject to Frankish supremacy. We may however in passing note two striking points of resemblance to the Kentish social system. In both systems the triple wergeld belongs to a hereditary nobility, and in both cases there is a lower wergeld which bears the proportion 2 : 5 to that of the freeman. In the continental code this lower wergeld belongs to the manumitted slave; in the Kentish laws it belongs to the lowest class of *læt*.

We now come to the laws of the Old Saxons. Bede (*H. E.* I. 15) distinctly states that the Saxons of Britain were sprung from this nation. We may therefore reasonably expect to find resemblances

---

[1] According to the generally accepted view these Anglii and Werini were descendants of the Suabi whom Chlothar and Sigibert introduced into North Thuringia. A different view has been put forward by Bremer (*Grundriss* III.[2] pp. 851 ff.), but his arguments are not convincing.

between English and Old Saxon custom. It is true
that in respect of language there is far less affinity
than in the case of English and Frisian. But this
fact is not incapable of explanation. When first we
hear of the Saxons, in the second century (Ptolemy),
they were settled in what is now the province of
Slesvig[1]—presumably the western part of that
province—and in certain islands (apparently Sylt,
Amrum, Föhr etc.) off the west coast of the peninsula.
But in the fourth century, perhaps to some extent
even in the third century, they had formed permanent
settlements in Western Germany, and eventually
they conquered the greater part of the country
between the lower Rhine and the mouth of the Elbe.
It is of course to this district that the laws refer.
Now the earliest texts in the 'Old Saxon' language
belong to the ninth century. It is likely enough
therefore that in the interval between the fourth and
the ninth centuries the invading people had lost their
own language and adopted that of the population
which they had conquered[2].

Here again, as among the Frisians, society was
divided into three classes, the noble (*nobilis*), the
freeman and the *litus*. The oaths belonging to these

[1] Not in Holstein, as is frequently stated. The orientation of
the coast-line as given in Ptolemy's map is of course incorrect; but
all the indications which he gives are against that view. It would
moreover involve the separation of the Saxons on the mainland
from those in the islands. Of course the territory of the Saxons
may have extended somewhat to the south of the Eider.

[2] As a matter of fact forms of an entirely different type and
closely resembling English are by no means wanting; cf. Bremer,
Grundriss III.[2] p. 861 f.

classes seem to have been of different value. At all events, according to *Lex Sax.* 17, the oath of the noble was worth more than that of the freeman. A further analogy to English custom is to be found in the different scales of fines to which the three classes were liable[1]. In many cases however, where we might have expected to find resemblances to the English laws, capital punishment has been introduced—no doubt as a result of the Frankish conquest.

There is not the slightest doubt that the nobility of the Old Saxons was hereditary. The term used in the laws is *nobilis*, but historians, such as Nithard and Hucbald, constantly speak of the nobles as *edilingi*. The difference in the amount of the wergelds again seems to apply also in the case of women. But beyond all this we have a definite statement in the *Translatio S. Alexandri*, cap. 1, not only that the nobility formed a distinct class, but also that intermarriage between the different classes was prohibited. The passage is as follows: *id legibus firmatum ut nulla pars in copulandis coniugiis propriae sortis terminos transferat, sed nobilis nobilem ducat uxorem et liber liberam, libertus coniungatur libertae et seruus ancillae. si uero quispiam horum sibi non congruentem et genere prestantiorem duxerit uxorem, cum uitae suae damno conponat.* If we may admit this statement—and it is difficult to see how it can have been invented—we are driven to conclude that the class-system of the Old Saxons amounted really to a system of caste.

[1] C⨍. *Lex Sax.* 36; *Cap. de part. Sax.* 19 ff.

Our information regarding the wergelds of the Old Saxons is derived from the *Lex Saxonum*. For some unexplained reason however the wergeld of the freeman is omitted. Those of the noble and the *litus* are 1440 sol. and 120 sol. respectively (*ib.* §§ 14, 16). It is stated however that the solidus contained in the former case two tremisses and in the latter three[1]. The proportion therefore between the two wergelds was really 8 : 1 (cf. *ib.* § 18). In the *Lex Ripuariorum*, § 36, the wergeld to be paid when a Saxon is killed by a Frank is said to be 160 sol. (*i.e.* of course solidi of three tremisses). If we may accept this as the true wergeld of the Old Saxon freeman— and it is by no means certain that we are justified in so doing—the proportion between the wergeld of the noble and that of the freeman would be, as in the English laws, 6 : 1. It is true that we do not find any class corresponding to the English *sixhynde* men, but in course of time such a class might have died out, as it did ultimately in Wessex.

It is not to be overlooked however that, though the proportion between the wergeld of the noble and that of the freeman may be identical in the English and Old Saxon systems, the amounts themselves are very different. Indeed objection has been taken to the statements of the *Lex Saxonum* on the ground that the amounts of the noble's wergeld and of the payments to which he was entitled for various injuries are incredible. This may freely be granted

---

[1] The statement in § 66 that wergelds were paid in the smaller solidus and other compensations in the larger is clearly due to a misunderstanding.

if we are bound to suppose that such payments were usually made in gold or silver. But it is obviously much more probable that they were for the most part paid in livestock. As the ox is valued at two solidi (§ 34)—presumably solidi of three tremisses (cf. § 66) —the three wergelds would apparently amount to 480, 80 and 60 oxen respectively. Even these figures are of course very large. In the first two cases they are twice as great as those for the corresponding classes in England. But there is another consideration to be taken into account. We do not know how numerous the Old Saxon nobility were. It is quite possible that by the end of the eighth century they had become reduced to a comparatively small number of princely families[1]. In that case there would be nothing extraordinary about the wergelds.

It will be convenient at this point to summarise briefly the evidence of the continental laws. A hereditary nobility is to be found among the Bavarians, the Frisians, the 'Anglii and Werini' and the Old Saxons. In the first two cases the wergeld of the noble is double that of the freeman, while among the 'Anglii and Werini' the noble has a three-fold, among the Old Saxons perhaps a six-fold wergeld. In all these nations again we find a class of *liti* or freedmen with a wergeld less than that of the ordinary freeman. In regard to the actual amount of the wergelds we find that that of the freeman is 200 sol.—originally gold solidi—among

---

[1] Cf. Bede, *H. E.* v. 10. From Nithard iv. 2 it may at least be inferred that the nobility were far inferior in numbers to the other two orders.

the Franks, the 'Anglii and Werini' and the 'Chamavi.' As the value of the ox is usually two gold solidi, there can be little doubt that this wergeld originally amounted to about 100 oxen. The wergelds of the other nations are not quite so clear. In the *Lex Ripuariorum*, § 36, it is stated that the amount to be paid by a Frank for slaying a Burgundian, Alaman, Bavarian, Frisian or Saxon was 160 sol. If we are to accept this as a true statement of the freeman's wergeld in those nations we must conclude that the wergeld in question amounted to only about 80 oxen. But, since the Franks were in a dominant position, it is at least questionable whether the sum specified is not a reduced wergeld. In the case of the Burgundians and Alamanni at all events it would appear that the amount payable was less than the wergeld of the average freeman according to the laws of those nations (cf. p. 384)[1]. Hence it seems not unlikely that the Bavarians, Frisians and Saxons also, before they were conquered by the Franks, had a wergeld of 100 oxen (or even more). It is for this reason that I admit a certain hesitation in using the evidence of the *Lex Ripuariorum* for filling up the lacuna in the wergelds of the *Lex Saxonum*. It seems to me quite possible that the proportion between the wergelds of the Saxon noble and freeman may really have been 4 : 1 instead of 6 : 1.

In any case however it is clear that the wergeld of the freeman in all these continental nations greatly

[1] In the case of the Alamanni the question is complicated by the extraordinarily low price of the ox; cf. Seebohm, *op. cit.* p. 178.

exceeded that of the English ceorl. We have seen that the latter appears to have originally amounted to 33 (or 40) oxen. That is a figure which corresponds rather to the wergeld of the continental freedman or *litus*. It is apparently identical or almost identical with that of the freedman in the *Lex Angliorum et Werinorum*, while that of the Frisian *litus* was at least as large. In the *Lex Chamavorum* and the *Lex Saxonum* the value of the *litus* seems to be 50 oxen and 60 oxen respectively.

§ 3.   *The social systems of the North.*

In conclusion it is necessary to review briefly the evidence of the Scandinavian laws. The Danish laws unfortunately give us extremely little information on the structure of the social system. The only wergelds which they mention are those of the freeman and the freedman. According to the old Law of Skåne[1] the former was 15 marks and the latter half as much as that of the freeman. But that further social distinctions existed, or had once existed, may be inferred from a passage in Saxo's History (v. p. 153), in which the following enactment is attributed to the mythical King Frothi the Peaceful: *Qui uero ex popularibus primipilum in acie anteiret ex seruo liber, ex agresti illustris (heþvarþer?) euaderet ; at si ingenuus foret satrapa crearetur.* It is probable therefore either that the evidence of the laws is incomplete or that the Danish social system

---

[1] Cf. Seebohm, *op. cit.* pp. 276 ff.

had undergone considerable simplification in the course of time.

On the other hand the Norwegian[1] laws disclose a somewhat elaborate social system. The amounts of the various wergelds unfortunately are not very clearly stated. In the old Gulathing Law, § 218, they are said to vary according to the *réttr*, a word which signifies both the privileges appertaining to each rank of society and the compensations payable for violation thereof. According to § 200 the compensations for breach of 'simple' *réttr* were as follows: freedman (*leysingr*) 6 ores (*aurar*), son of freedman 8 ores, *bóndi* 12 ores, *höldr* 3 marks (*i.e.* 24 ores), baron (*lendr maðr*[2]) and marshal (*stallari*) 6 marks, earl and bishop 12 marks. The *bóndi* and the *höldr* are both fully free men; but the latter is a man who has inherited land through a certain number of generations. In the regulations for the payment of wergelds, which are complicated and apparently by no means consistent, the *höldr* is always taken as the standard. In § 218 ff. the various payments which make up his wergeld are stated. For details it will be sufficient here to refer to Mr Seebohm's book (*Tribal Custom*), pp. 246 ff. Altogether they come to 242 ores. In § 243 ff. however we find a new statement of the wergeld, according to an entirely different scheme of distribution. The total in this case seems to be $247\frac{2}{5}$ ores. As to the relationship between the two

[1] I regret that I have not been able to take the evidence of the Swedish laws into account.

[2] The *lendr maðr* or 'baron' (cf. *Skaldskaparmál*, cap. 53) was a royal official (inferior to the earl) with territorial jurisdiction.

schemes we are not informed. But, since the difference in the totals is comparatively slight, we shall hardly go far wrong in concluding that the wergeld of the *höldr* amounted to about 240—250 ores.

Now in § 218 f. the value of the cow is said to be 2½ ores. The wergeld of the *höldr* will therefore amount to 96—100 cows. Hence Mr Seebohm has come to the conclusion that the *höldr* corresponds to the freeman of the continental laws. This conclusion seems to me hardly justified. The *bóndi* is also a fully free man, though his wergeld is apparently only half that of the *höldr*. Moreover it is to be observed that the valuation of the cow at 2½ ores—whatever the precise weight of the ore— must be comparatively modern. Certainly the cow was never worth anything like so much as this in England before the Norman Conquest. Consequently we have to ask which of the two valuations, the number of cows[1] or the weight of silver, represents the traditional amount of the wergeld. There can be little doubt that in very early times the cow was, as in England, worth no more than an ounce of silver. If the calculation in silver is old, the wergeld

---

[1] The appearance of the cow in statements of wergelds etc. is not necessarily a proof of their antiquity. We may compare a passage from the *Leges inter Brettos et Scotos* quoted by Mr See- bohm (*op. cit.* p. 308 f.), where wergelds are again stated both in ores and cows, the equation being 3 ores = 1 cow. In that case, as I have tried to show (cf. pp. 25, 104, above), some of the statements in ores are in accordance with ancient custom. The value of the cow however is that of the twelfth or thirteenth century.

of the *höldr* would in those days amount to 240—250 cows.

In the old Icelandic code (*Grágás*, VIII. § 114) we find only the wergelds of the ordinary 'man' and the freedman (*leysingr*). The former amounts probably to between 123 and 124 ores[1]. In the latter the chief items are half as much as the corresponding items in the former; but, since payments to distant relatives are wanting, the total comes to only 41 ores. No higher wergelds are mentioned in the laws. In narratives however referring to the tenth century and the early part of the eleventh century we find wergelds both of 'a hundred of silver' and of 'two hundreds of silver.' These expressions can hardly mean anything else than 120 ores and 240 ores respectively[2].

[1] Strictly the total is 120⅔ ores together with 5 *penningar* and 120 *thveiti*. Unfortunately it has not been determined how many *thveiti* went to the ore. 60 seems to be the most probable number.

[2] According to Dasent, *The Story of Burnt Njal*, vol. II. p. 404, Vigfússon's Dictionary, s.v. *hundrað*, and other authorities the 'hundred' in question was 120 ells of silver and equivalent to only 20 ores. If this is correct the wergelds of the tenth century must have differed very greatly from those of *Grágás*. Indeed it would be difficult to find a parallel for them in any Teutonic system. I confess that this view seems to me quite incredible. In *Nials Saga*, cap. 123, it is distinctly implied that six 'hundreds' was regarded as an enormous sum of money. According to Dasent's explanation it would amount to no more than 120 ores. Yet in a similar case (cap. 138) we find one of the defendants giving to a lawyer, in order to obtain his support, a gold ring which, according to Dasent himself (*ib.* p. 411), was worth 288 ores. We may further note that in the English Danelagh the term 'hundred' seems to mean 120 ores (cf. Aethelred III. 1, Edw. Conf. 27).

In exceptional cases we hear even of 'double' and 'triple' wergelds, by which, sometimes at all events, wergelds of 480 or 720 ores are meant. Thus in *Nials Saga*, cap. 123, it is stated that the amount to be paid for a magistrate (*goði*) named Höskuldr was "a triple wergeld, that is six hundreds of silver," but it is added that this was the greatest wergeld which had ever been paid in Iceland. At all events we may infer from such passages that a wergeld corresponding to that of the *höldr* was well known in that country and also that in the tenth century this wergeld already amounted to about 240 ores.

Moreover we have some evidence from a different source which leads us to infer that the silver amounts of the Norwegian wergelds were not raised in late times. The *réttr* of the king seems to have been reckoned at twice as much as that of the earl[1], *i.e.* eight times as much as that of the *höldr*. The king's wergeld therefore would presumably amount to about 1920 ores in the time of the laws[2]. Now in *Haralds Saga hins Hárfagra* (Heimskringla), cap. 32, we hear that King Harold exacted from the inhabitants of the Orkneys a wergeld of 60 marks of gold for his son Halfdan Háleggr. This took place about the end of the ninth or beginning of the tenth

[1] The king's *réttr* itself seems not to be given, but this is apparently the calculation used in other compensations due to him; cf. Seebohm, *op. cit.* p. 240 f.

[2] According to the *Saga Magnús Blinda* (Heimskr.) cap. 8, Bishop Reinaldr (of Stavanger) was required to ransom himself by a payment of 15 marks of gold. Reinaldr was of English birth, but it seems probable that this sum (*i.e.* 120 marks or 960 ores of silver) represents the Norwegian bishop's wergeld.

century. At a ratio 8:1 the sum in question would amount to 480 marks or 3840 ores of silver. If therefore that ratio already prevailed the sum in question must be regarded as a double (king's) wergeld. The circumstances under which Halfdan had been put to death were of such a character that an increased wergeld might reasonably be expected[1] But when all allowances are made it seems extremely unlikely that the proper wergeld at that time can have been less than it was in the twelfth century.

We may now briefly summarise the Scandinavian evidence. (1) A wergeld of about 15 marks or 120 ores (of silver) is known in Denmark, Norway and Iceland. In Norway it is the *bóndi*, in Denmark and Iceland the freeman, who is entitled to this wergeld. (2) The freedman has in all these countries a wergeld of half this amount or less. (3) A double wergeld of about 240 ores belongs in Norway to the *höldr*, in Iceland to certain freemen, apparently persons of superior social position. (4) Still higher wergelds belong in Norway to kings and officials, in Iceland to magistrates and other distinguished men.

These equations decidedly suggest that the *höldr* does not really correspond to the freeman of the continental laws. It will be well therefore now to examine the earliest records of Scandinavian wergelds, namely those passages in the English laws which refer to the Danelagh. In the Treaty of Alfred and Guthrum, cap. 2, the Englishman and the

---

[1] It is to be observed however that in the *Northleoda Lagu* (cf. p. 76) the king has a double wergeld (30,000 thr. as against 15,000 thr. for the aetheling and 8000 thr. for the earl).

Dane are valued alike at 8 half-marks of gold,
except the (English) ceorl and the (Danish) freedman (*liesing*), who are also valued alike at 200 sh.
The former sum, as we have seen (p. 50), appears to
correspond approximately to the West Saxon (thegn's)
wergeld of 1200 sh. The Danish freeman is therefore
put on a level with the English *twelfhynde* man.
If we turn to the *Northleoda Lagu* (cf. p. 76 f.) we
find mention of the *hold* (*i.e. höldr*). He is assigned
a wergeld of 4000 thrymsas, *i.e.* 2400 (West Saxon)
sh. or 12,000 pence, as against 2000 thrymsas for the
thegn and 8000 thrymsas for the earl[1]. Now in the
tenth century the ox was valued in England at
30 pence and the cow at 24 pence or less (cf. p. 2).
It appears then that the wergeld of the Danish
freeman amounted to 200 oxen or 240 cows and that
of the *hold* to 400 oxen or 480 cows. I do not
suggest that these figures truly represent the wergeld
of the Danish freeman and *hold* in their own
country. Doubtless they have been raised as a
result of conquest. But the *hold* would hardly have
obtained a wergeld twice as great as that of the
West Saxon noble unless he had been a man of some
importance; for it is to be remembered that Wessex had not been conquered by the Danes. This
inference moreover is confirmed by the fact that such
persons are occasionally mentioned in the Saxon

---

[1] It is worth while comparing the table given on p. 76 with the
statistics for *réttr* in Norway. In particular one may note that
the proportion between the thegn's wergeld (2000 thr.) and the
king's wergeld (30,000 thr.) is the same as that between the
wergeld of Alfr. and Guthr. 2 (4 gold marks) and the wergeld of
Halfdan Háleggr (60 gold marks).

Chronicle (*ann.* 905, 921, A). They were clearly regarded as leaders of the Danish forces—at least equal to the more important of the English king's thegns.

What I would suggest is that both the Danish wergelds have been doubled in England. We have seen that in the Gulathing Law the wergeld of the *höldr* amounts to 242—247 ores or 30—31 marks of silver. As the ratio of gold to silver at this time was only 8:1, the gold equivalent of this sum would be nearly four marks—the amount of the Danish freeman's wergeld in the Treaty of Alfred and Guthrum. It is the reckoning in bullion therefore which is traditional in the Gulathing Law; the reckoning in cattle has been modernised. The person with the wergeld of 100 oxen, corresponding to the freeman of the continental laws, was originally the *bóndi*. The *höldr* or *hold* had a double wergeld and must be regarded as a nobleman. Perhaps he is to be identified with the *illustris* of the passage from Saxo quoted above.

This discussion of the Scandinavian social system has produced one interesting analogy to English, or at least to West Saxon, custom. The essential difference between the *bóndi* or ordinary freeman and the *höldr* lies in the fact that the latter is in hereditary possession of land. But we have seen that in Wessex the difference between the *sixhynde* man and the *twelfhynde* man is that the former is 'landless' and the latter a landowner—or rather a member of a landowning family (cf. p. 96 f.). The two cases are probably not quite identical. But it is to be observed that even in Iceland the qualifications for the double wergeld seem to have differed considerably from those which prevailed in Norway. Now we have seen that in the ninth century the wergeld of the *höldr* like that of the *twelfhynde* man probably amounted to 200 oxen in his own country. At the same time the wergelds of the *sixhynde* man and the Scandinavian freeman would both amount to 100 oxen. These are analogies which certainly ought to be borne in mind, although the social position of the *sixhynde* man, standing as he does far above the ceorl, differs greatly from that of the Scandinavian freeman.

§ 4.   *The Ceorl's Wergeld.*

In the course of this chapter we have seen that among the Teutonic nations of the continent the amount of the freeman's wergeld apparently varied between 80 and 100 oxen. In those cases however where the lower figure occurs there seems to be some reason for suspecting that the amount has been reduced. We have also seen that in the ninth century the Scandinavian freeman likewise apparently had a wergeld of 100 oxen. Again, in all those nations which may be regarded on various grounds as more closely related to the invaders of Britain, namely the Frisians, 'Anglii and Werini,' Old Saxons and Scandinavians, we find a subordinate class, consisting of freedmen or *liti*, with wergelds considerably lower than that of the ordinary freeman[1].

[1] In Norway (possibly also elsewhere) there were gradations in

Lastly the same nations all possessed a class of hereditary nobles with higher wergelds. Among the Frisians and Scandinavians this higher wergeld was twice as great as that of the ordinary freeman; among the 'Anglii and Werini' the proportion was 3 : 1; while among the Old Saxons it was still higher.

All the characteristic features therefore of the Kentish social system recur in these kindred nations. We may conclude then with some confidence that these characteristics did not come into existence after the invasion of Britain. The closest resemblance to the Kentish system is clearly to be found in that of the 'Anglii and Werini.' Unfortunately however we have not in either case any information as to the origin of the nobility—the *eorlcund* class or *adalingi*. It may owe its existence to the hereditary possession of land, like the *höldr* class in Norway, or it may, in part at least, have originated in service to the king[1]. Indeed, if the theory suggested in the last Excursus (p. 376 f.) is correct, these two explanations are hardly incompatible; for

these lower wergelds. Mr Seebohm (*op. cit.* p. 484 f.) has pointed out that the three freedmen's wergelds of the Frostathing Law— apparently 40, 60 and 80 ores respectively—correspond to the three wergelds (40, 60 and 80 sh.) of the Kentish *læt*-class.

[1] It may perhaps be suggested in view of the *hold* of the Danelagh, that the *höldr* himself was originally an official. The corresponding English (poetic) word *hæleð* is used in much the same vague sense as *eorl*. Like the latter it sometimes occurs with a genitive. Thus in *Beow.* 1070 we find Hnaef (who elsewhere is called *þeoden*) described as *hæleð Healfdenes* (ms. -*a*), *i.e.* the *hold* of Halfdan (king of the Danes). It is to be remembered that even Norway had been governed by kings from early times, though the kingdoms were often of very limited area.

land held originally of the king or of his officials may in course of time have come to be possessed by hereditary right. In any case however it is clear that the origin of the nobility goes back to early times.

On the other hand the social system which prevailed in the rest of England, or at all events in Wessex, Mercia and Northumbria, stands quite isolated. For one of its features indeed, the distinction between the *twelfhynde* man or land-owning noble and the *sixhynde* man or landless noble, we find a certain analogy in the Norwegian distinction between the *höldr* and the *bóndi*. But the extraordinarily low wergeld of the ceorl or freeman (viz. 33 oxen) and the absence of any class corresponding to the freedmen or *liti*—these are features which find no parallel in any of the systems which we have discussed.

Mr Seebohm, in order to explain these difficulties, has put forward a theory that the English ceorl was not really a freeman: that his position in reality corresponded to that of the freedman or *litus* of the Kentish, Scandinavian and continental systems. From the evidence which we have discussed it is clear enough that the ceorl's value corresponded to that of the freedman. It seems likely that in regard to economic conditions he was in general no better off than the latter. In the absence of any evidence to the contrary, we may admit that he had probably little or no political power. But I cannot agree to Mr Seebohm's suggestion that the ceorl had an imperfect kindred. If that had been the case it is hardly conceivable that the laws should have failed altogether to convey any hint of the fact[1]. Indeed the laws seem to draw no distinction between the kindred of the ceorl and that of the *twelfhynde* man[2]. The passage in the *Northleoda Lagu,* which describes how the ceorl could become *gesiðcund* through the possession of land (cf. p. 81), has clearly no bearing on this question. The rise in social position there described is similar to that by which the Norwegian *bóndi* became a *höldr.* But the process by which the freedman (*leysingr*) passed into the *bóndi* was quite different; it was in no way connected with the possession of land. Unless the word *gesiðcund* has a different meaning in this passage from what it has elsewhere, the statement of the *Northleoda Lagu* must be understood to mean that a ceorlish family were rendered 'noble' by the possession of land for three consecutive generations.

Moreover there is another consideration which requires to be taken into account. If the vast majority of the English people were sprung from

---

[1] I cannot admit the derivation of *twelfhynde* etc. from the word *hynden,* proposed by Mr Seebohm. The argument put forward in *Tribal Custom,* p. 411 ff., seems to me erroneous. No doubt the total value of the oath which could be produced by the ceorl together with his relatives or associates was less than that of the oath which the *twelfhynde* man could produce under similar conditions. But surely the explanation of this is not that the ceorl had fewer co-swearers to draw upon but that the oath of each individual was of less value in the former case than in the latter (cf. p. 148 f.).

[2] In Aethelstan VI. 8 (cf. III. 6, IV. 3) provision is made for the possibility that a ceorlish family might become powerful enough to set the law at defiance.

freedmen, from whence did all these freedmen come[1]?
It has often been urged—and the truth of the contention can hardly be doubted—that the English
conquest of Britain must have been of an essentially
different character from the Frankish conquest of
Gaul. If after the conquest the bulk of the population, at least in the eastern part of the country, had
still belonged to the native stock, the native language
would surely have reasserted itself. The fact that it
died out, leaving only the slightest traces of itself in
the language of the invaders, seems to show that not
merely the nobility but the majority of the commons
also must have belonged to the invading nation.
On the other hand it is difficult to see how the
conquest could have had the effect of depressing the
condition of the poorer classes among the invaders
themselves[2]. Apparently it had no such effect in
Kent.

I think therefore that though Mr Seebohm has
correctly described the economic condition of the
ceorl[3]—more correctly, in my opinion, than any other
writer who has dealt with the subject—the explanation which he has furnished of the peculiarities of

[1] We have seen (p. 373, footnote) that in some districts the
slave-population was very large in early times. But I doubt
if such cases ought to be regarded as normal.

[2] Mr Seebohm (*op. cit.* p. 499 f.) seems to suggest some such
explanation as this; but one would like to have analogies for such
a phenomenon.

[3] Especially in regard to the condition of this class in the
seventh century, the earliest period for which records are available. It seems to me impossible to resist his conclusion that the
position of the ceorl was not less depressed at that time than in
any subsequent age.

that condition can hardly be maintained. It will be well then to try whether any other explanation is possible. Now, if we return for a moment to the Continental laws, we see that the Old Saxon system presents the greatest difference which is anywhere to be found between the wergeld of the noble and that of the freeman. It is very probable that this phenomenon is a result of the Saxon conquest[1]. Again we see that in England the wergelds of the Danish freeman and *hold* have apparently been doubled, and that this was a result of conquest there can hardly be any doubt. Is it not possible that the reduction of the English ceorl's wergeld may be due to a similar cause? In that case the *sixhynde* man with his wergeld of 100 oxen and the *twelfhynde* man with his wergeld of 200 oxen might represent respectively the freeman and the *hold* of the conquering nation.

It is true of course that the phenomena in England are not quite parallel to those in the cases noticed above. There we find the wergelds of the conquerors increased. In this case if the suggestion is to be admitted, the wergelds of the conquerors were probably unaffected, while the wergelds of the conquered were reduced. But, after all, any such arrangement must necessarily depend on the numbers of the conquerors and on the resources of the conquered country. The Danes who conquered

[1] Unless indeed the Old Saxon nobility really corresponded to the royal families of England. Unfortunately none of their genealogies are preserved. We do not know therefore whether they claimed divine ancestry.

the northern and eastern parts of England were an
army of fighting men from over the sea. Many of
them doubtless subsequently returned to their own
country. Indeed it is unlikely that the permanent
settlers ever constituted more than a comparatively
small minority of the population. If we were to
take the case of one nation conquering an immediately neighbouring nation of approximately
equal numbers, the conditions would obviously be
very different.

It may perhaps be urged that the use of the same
terms (*gesiðcund* and *eorlcund* or *eorlisc*) for the
higher classes of society both in Kent and in the
other kingdoms is an argument for believing that
these classes were of similar origin in both cases.
But, considering the character of the terms, this
argument can hardly be regarded as conclusive.
We have seen that *gesið* originally meant no more
than ' companion,' while the origin of *eorl* is altogether
obscure. If the conquerors and the conquered
differed from one another very slightly in language
and customs is it not possible that the fact that they
were originally of different nationalities might in
course of time be forgotten, and that the dominating
classes might come to be known by the ordinary
terms for nobility ?

But have we any record of such a conquest ?
The phenomena which require to be explained—the
absence of a freedman-class and the exceedingly low
value of the ceorl—are apparently common to the
three kingdoms of Wessex, Mercia and Northumbria,
perhaps to the whole of England except Kent.

Now it is true that Kent at one time held a short-lived supremacy over the other kingdoms of the South and the Midlands. But this supremacy was hardly of a character to bring about such far-reaching results; for even the native dynasties seem not to have been displaced. Moreover this explanation would not apply to Northumbria, for that kingdom lay beyond the limits of Aethelberht's dominions. But we have no tradition of any Kentish conquests before the time of Aethelberht. It is hardly possible therefore to avoid the conclusion that, if the theory of conquest is to be admitted at all, that conquest must have taken place before the invasion of Britain.

In Saxo's History, II. p. 51, we find a story which may very well have a certain bearing on this question. The story is concerned with the exploits of a Danish king named Helgo and is as follows: " He (Helgo) conquered in battle Hundingus the son of Syricus, king of Saxony, at the city of Stadium [1] and challenging him to a single combat overthrew him. For this reason he was called 'the slayer of Hundingus,' deriving a glorious surname from his victory. He took Jutland from the Saxons and gave it to his generals Hesce, Eyr and Ler to hold and administer. In Saxony he decreed that the freeman and the freedman should have an equal wergeld, wishing, as it seems, to make it perfectly clear that all the families of the Teutones were equally in

---

[1] It is not clear what town is meant, as place-names ending in *-stedt* are very common in Holstein and South Jutland. Holder suggests Hollingstedt, near Slesvig. Elsewhere in Saxo's History the name *Stadium* is applied to Stade.

bondage and that the whole nation had been degraded by the loss of their freedom to an equally dishonourable condition[1]. "

The context in which this passage occurs is hardly of such a character as to command unreserved confidence.   Indeed it is clear that Saxo has confused two distinct persons, the historical Danish king Helgi the son of Halfdan, who lived in the latter part of the fifth century, and the legendary hero Helgi Hundingsbani who is represented in the Older Edda as the son of Sigmundr (the son of Völsungr). From the passage itself it would seem that the conquest of 'Saxony' belongs to the latter of these persons.   The poems however merely say that Helgi conquered and slew a king named Hundingr.   They give no indication as to the locality of Hundingr's kingdom.

But is it altogether unreasonable to infer from this story that Saxo was aware of some tradition that Jutland, or some part of it, had once been in the possession of the Saxons, that the Saxons had been conquered by the Danes, and that, as a result of this event, the wergeld of the freeman in the conquered nation had been reduced to a level with that of the freedman ?

---

[1] *Hundingum Saxonie regis Syrici filium apud Stadium oppidum prelio uicit eundemque ex prouocacione adortus duello prostrauit.   ob quod Hundingi interemptor uocatus uictorie decus cognomine usurpauit.   Iutie Saxonibus erepte ius procuracionemque Hesce Eyr et Ler ducibus commisit.   apud Saxoniam ingenui ac liberti necem pari summa rependendam constituit perinde ac liquido constare uolens quod cunctas Teutonum familias equa seruitus teneret omniumque corrupta libertas parem condicionis ignominiam redoleret.*

Now it is to be remembered that Saxo constantly represents the Saxons as the southern neighbours of the Danes. Angel and the neighbouring districts he always regards as part of the kingdom of Denmark, and at least one English dynasty—that of Wihtlaeg (*Vigletus*), Wermund and Offa (*Uffo*)—figures in his list of Danish kings. In the same way he applies the term 'Saxon' to all tribes of Teutonic nationality beyond the Eider, though we have reason for believing that these districts (Holstein, Lauenburg, etc.) contained in early times tribes quite distinct from the Saxons. On the other hand he does not include any part of South Jutland (the province of Slesvig) in 'Saxony.' Moreover the frontier as depicted by him was by no means new. Even the earliest ecclesiastical writers, as far back as the eighth century[1], use language which implies that the west coast of Slesvig was then Danish. Yet we have seen (p. 387) that in the second century this country was the home of the Saxons. We must conclude therefore that the political geography of these districts had changed considerably during the intervening period.

The pirates who harried the coasts of the Roman provinces during the third and fourth centuries are always described as Saxons or Eruli. The name of the Angli never occurs in connection with these events. So far as our evidence goes the interests of this tribe appear to have lain entirely in the Baltic. In the first century of our era their chief sanctuary

---

[1] Alcuin, *Vita Willebrordi*, cap. 10, describes Heligoland (*Fositesland*) as lying *in confinio Fresonum et Danorum*.

seems to have been situated in one of the Baltic islands. The royal family of Wessex claimed to be descended from the eponymous ancestor of the Danish kings, whose residence according to both traditions was in Sjælland or Skåne. But before the invasion of Britain the Angli must obviously have obtained access to the North Sea, and it is likely enough that this access was gained by the conquest of the neighbouring tribes. What I would suggest is either that the Angli conquered the Saxons, *i.e.* those Saxons who remained in their old country, or that the Angli and Saxons in alliance conquered the tribes immediately to the south[1]. The evidence available is hardly sufficient to enable us to decide between these two hypotheses.

Perhaps it will not be out of place to suggest that the story told by Saxo of the reduction in the Saxon wergeld may originally have belonged to a different tradition. Helgo is not the only Danish king in his History who wins the kingdom of Saxony by single combat. The same incident is related (IV. p. 115 ff.) of Uffo, *i.e.* Offa, the most famous of the kings of Angel, in which case we certainly have to

---

[1] A third possibility, that the Angli together with the Saxons were conquered by the Danes or some other nation, need hardly be taken into account. The royal family of Mercia traced their descent from the dynasty which reigned in Angel during the fourth century. The royal family of Wessex claimed descent from princes who governed Slesvig at the same time. The Northumbrian (Bernician) royal family claimed to be of the same stock as that of Wessex. No such conquest therefore can have taken place after the third century at the latest. Beyond that point all that can be said is that neither the English nor the Danish traditions give any hint of such an event.

do with a historical event. It is true that English
tradition does not mention the Saxons in connection
with this story, though it records that Offa 'enlarged
his borders' and won permanently 'the greatest of
kingdoms.' His opponents are only described as
Myrgingas, which appears to be a dynastic rather
than a tribal name. But whether the conquered
nation were really Saxons or Swebi[1], it seems highly
probable, as the conflict is supposed to have taken
place at Rendsburg[2], that the kingdom which he
won included the basin of the Eider, together
perhaps with territories to the north as well as to
the south of that river. It will be observed moreover that the date of this occurrence—in all probability the latter half of the fourth century—suits
the requirements of our hypothesis extremely well.
By this time the Saxons had already succeeded in
establishing themselves in Western Germany; while
on the other hand a sufficiently long time is allowed
for the changes in the social system to have become
permanently fixed before the invasion of Britain.

[1] In *Widsith* (l. 44), we find the Swebi mentioned beside the
Angli, in such a way however that it cannot be determined with
certainty whether they are regarded as allies or enemies of the
latter.

[2] Cf. Langebek, *Scriptores Rerum Danicarum*, I. p. 152 and
note.

ADDENDA.

p. 4, note 2. The passage cited from Symeon of Durham is as follows: *anno DCCXLIX Elfwald rex Orientalium Anglorum defunctus est, regnumque Hunbeanna et Alberht sibi diuiserunt.* We should perhaps read *Hun, Beanna.*

p. 25, l. 1 f. Further evidence for the ore of 16 pence in the time of Aethelred II. is given by Aethelweard, II. 10, in his account of the compensation paid for Mul. He translates, wrongly of course, the *xxx. m̃.* of the Chronicle (*ann.* 694) by *solidos millia triginta per singulos constanti numero sexdecim nummis.*

p. 34. The dates for Aethelstan's accession and death should have been marked as doubtful. The last contribution to this difficult question is from Mr Anscombe, *Athenaeum,* 25 June, 1904. For the date of Cuthred's accession, cf. p. 271, note. Some of Aethelberht's coins may have been issued (in Kent, etc.) before 860.

p. 80, note 2. This regulation was in principle by no means new. In B. 201, dating from about 800, we find an agreement by which six hides provided a warrior. For similar regulations on the Continent cf. Meitzen, *Siedelung und Agrarwesen,* I. p. 72 f.

p. 87, note, ll. 1—9. From a comparison of Ine 23 and 32 (cf. *Northl. L.* 7) and from the fact that the expressions *terra—familiarum* and *terra—tributariorum* are synonymous I think it is a justifiable inference that the English *gafolgelda* also was a man who possessed (at least) one hide. It is generally agreed that the use of the word *hid* to denote a measure of land in itself points to a time when the hide was a normal holding. But it has hardly been sufficiently appreciated either that *gafolgelda* was the term applied to the person with this holding or that this holding was still apparently regarded as typical in the seventh century. It is quite possible that at this time the use of the word *hid* to denote a measure of land was comparatively recent. For the size of the early hide cf. p. 267, note.

p. 98, l. 18. Add reference to p. 379, note.

p. 100 f., note. Cf. p. 371, note. The suggestion (p. 101, note, l. 6 f.) that the *firma unius noctis*, etc. arose (exclusively or even mainly) out of these charges can hardly be correct. It consisted probably for the most part of payments derived from royal lands.

p. 102, ll. 12 ff. It is quite possible that 'five hides' may mean 'small village'; for in early times hidages seem to have been calculated very roughly (cf. p. 264 ff.). The term *landagende* in that case would mean that the person so described had a village of his own.

p. 130, l. 10. For the expression *to drihtinbeage* cf. the O. Norse *broeðrungsbaugr* etc.

p. 167, note. Cf. p. 347, note. That the earl like the king had men of high rank in his service may be seen (*e.g.*) from the poem on the battle of Maldon.

p. 168, ll. 4 f. But cf. p. 307.

p. 168, ll. 12 ff. Payment of the wergeld as ransom is familiar in cases of crime from the time of Ine onwards. A closer parallel to this case is afforded by the Norwegian example quoted on p. 396, note.

p. 169, ll. 10—12. Cf. Asser, cap. 106.

p. 171, note 1. Cf. p. 367 f.

p. 177, note 1. In spite of the hesitation expressed here the hypothesis that Huntingdonshire was under the jurisdiction of Byrhtnoth seems to me distinctly the most probable.

p. 182, note 1, ll. 6—8. The evidence of this charter has been taken into consideration in the notes.

p. 186, note 1. On Regnwald see Plummer, *Sax. Chron.*, II. pp. 130 f., 143.

p. 187, note 2. Account should have been taken of the possibility that changes may have taken place in the distribution of the eastern counties. Before Edgar's time the line of division between the two earldoms may have run from north to south rather than from east to west.

p. 190, l. 13. No Scandinavian names appear among the earls of Edward's charters.

p. 196, ll. 4 f. and note 1. This suggestion receives some confirmation from the fact that in B. 1296 Eadwine, earl of Sussex (cf. p. 176, note), is represented as exercising jurisdiction in Kent.

p. 200, note, l. 3. My reasons for taking *hundred* as 120 instead of 100 (in spite of the *an C* of Aethelred III. 7) are (i) that the equation 15 ores = 1 pound is known from Aethelred's time (cf. p. 24 f. and the additional note to p. 25, l. 1 above), whereas the equation $12\frac{1}{2}$ ores = 1 pound is, so far as I am aware, otherwise unknown ; and (ii) that the 'long hundred' is found elsewhere in the Danelagh (D. B. I. p. 336).

p. 202, ll. 5—7. Cheshire is mentioned in Chron. 980 C.

p. 205, ll. 11—13. It should have been mentioned that in Birch's text Wareham and Bridport do not appear, while the figures for the latter are confused with those for Christchurch —apparently through the omission of a line in the ms.

p. 213, note 2, l. 4. In later times Northampton seems to have been assessed at 25 hides (Round, *Feudal England*, p. 156). The suggestion put forward in this note rests of course on the assumption that the system of assessment (in the case of the boroughs) may have undergone considerable changes in the course of time. The purposes of assessment may also have changed to some extent.

p. 219, ll. 15 ff. This passage should read as follows : "if a man neglects to attend the *gemot* on three occasions he is to pay the fine due for disregard of the king's authority (*cynges oferhyrnesse*)...if he will not then do his duty or pay the fine, then the chief men," etc.

p. 220, note 1. Chester is assessed at only 50 hides in Domesday Book, but it seems probable that the assessment has been halved. The hundred of Chester contained apparently very few hides outside the borough (D.B. I. pp. 262 b, 266, 266 b). Shrewsbury was assessed at 100 hides (*ib.* p. 252).

p. 232, l. 28 f. Perhaps the expression *cyninges wicgerefa* ought to be translated : 'reeve of the king's *wic*.' In such cases the word *wic* may denote either 'residence' or 'quarter,' 'estate' (in a town).

p. 239, l. 14. For '*ealdermannes*' read '*ealdormonnes*.'

p. 240, l. 12. I am not inclined to attach much importance to the evidence derived from Malmesbury and Ingulf.

p. 243 f., note. Since this was printed the subject has been discussed by Prof. Vinogradoff in the *Eng. Hist. Review* (XIX. 282 ff.). With B. 1295 we may compare B. 780.

p. 247, note. It is interesting to compare the *Iud. Ciuit. Lund.* with the constitution of Malmesbury (cf. Gomme, *The Village Community*, p. 187 ff.), which is also connected by tradition (cf. B. 720) with Aethelstan. The question how far these burghal constitutions were derived from village organisations is one which I am not in a position to discuss. The case of Aston and Cote (cf. Gomme, *op. cit.*, p. 158 ff.), with its council of sixteen members, corresponding to the sixteen hides of the village, is of a form which surely must have come into existence in early times. Yet I doubt whether it is wise, in view of the silence of the laws, to credit such bodies with powers much exceeding those which we find them possessing in later times. My impression is that the boroughs were greatly influenced by those of the Danelagh, which must at first have been much more powerful organisations. Continental influence however is also to be taken into account.

p. 253, note. See the additional note to p. 280, l. 4 (below).

p. 260, l. 17 ; p. 262, l. 3. The use of the word *urbs* seems to imply that the town or village itself was fortified, though the question is one which can hardly be settled except by archaeological investigation. On the other hand it is generally supposed that in Wessex before the Danish invasions the word *burg* denoted only the fortified residence of the king or nobleman within the village, and such names as Tisbury and Shaftesbury are hardly evidence to the contrary.

p. 260, note 2. Cf. *H. E.* III. 19 : *Cnobheresburg id est urbs Cnobheri.* We may also compare the expression *urbs Cantuariorum* in charters.

p. 280, l. 4. Cf. p. 253, note. The explanation of the names 'Surrey' and 'Eastry' given by Mr T. Le Marchant Douse in the *Home Counties Magazine,* III. 198 ff., viz. that they originally meant 'South Rugii' and 'East Rugii,' seems to me quite incompatible with any of the forms in which these names occur in early texts. It is hardly necessary to point out that all the three examples which occur in texts of the eighth century, viz. *Sudergeona, H. E.* IV. 6 (MS. M), *Suðri[o]ena, ib.* (MS. C), *Eastrgena,* B. 254, would in that case have to be regarded as mistakes ; and the same remark applies to the form *Eosterge,* which occurs twice in an original charter (B. 332) of 811. Further, the only other forms which occur in original documents of this period, viz. *Eastorege, Eostorege, Easterege, Eostereye,* would be equally impossible, as there is no evidence for *-e-* in place of *-y-* before 850. It is true that *Suþrige* (in the Chronicle) and *Sudergeona* are plural forms, but they may be derivatives like *Eastrgena.*

p. 291, l. 9. I do not mean to imply by this that the number of English kingdoms in Britain was originally very large. I think it is likely that the first century after the invasion was a period of disintegration. But it does not necessarily follow that these new kingdoms were offshoots from Mercia. According to the Chronicle it would seem that the kingdom of the Hwicce had come into existence through a secession from Wessex. Indeed it is hardly probable that Mercia itself was one of the original kingdoms.

p. 295, l. 17. After "Northumbrians" add "and Danes."

p. 296, l. 27. Reference should have been given to Mr Plummer's note (*Sax. Chron.* II. p. 75), though I doubt whether his explanation is correct.

p. 301, ll. 3 ff. Eddius, cap. 17, speaks of *subreguli* beside the *praefecti* of Northumbria.

p. 301 (f.), note 2. In *Beowulf* the word *æðeling* seems to have a somewhat indefinite meaning. It is applied not only to members of the royal family, including kings, but also to king's thegns and princes' thegns whom we have no reason for believing to be of the blood royal. In the *Lex Angl. et Wer. adalingus* is the word for 'noble'; but this nation had almost certainly been under kingly government. It is further perhaps worth noting that in Alfr. 11 the oldest text uses the word *æðelborenran* of the *sixhynde* and *twelfhynde* classes.

p. 302, ll. 9 ff., and note 2. In St Olaf's Saga (Heimskr.), cap. 4, it is stated that, even as late as the beginning of the eleventh century, it was customary for young men of the royal family who led piratical expeditions to bear the kingly title (*konungsnafn*) though they governed no territories. This Scandinavian use, which I take to be due to confusion between *konungr* and *dróttinn*, seems to show an intermediate stage between what I have suggested as the original sense of the word and that which it has in Anglo-Saxon literature. The change in the character of kingship, in England at all events, was no doubt largely due to the introduction of the foreign rites of consecration and coronation. It is possible, as Mr E. H. Minns has pointed out to me, that the original meaning of the word may survive in Russ. *knjaz'* (O. Slav. *kŭnęzĭ*).

p. 304, ll. 5 ff. An interesting parallel to the position of Earl Aethelred is provided by the history of the earls of Lade who, with one short interval, held practically royal power in Norway for nearly forty years, yet never assumed the kingly title.

p. 372, ll. 13—15. By "the king's *feorm*" I mean of course the charge called by this name (*cyningfeorm*). The expression unfortunately is somewhat ambiguous, as the revenue derived by the king (or any other landowner) from his own lands was also called *feorm*. In Cnut II. 69 the reference is probably to the latter, but the meaning of the passage is obscure in several respects (cf. Maitland, *Domesday Book and Beyond*, p. 239, note). Here however I am speaking of the conditions of early times. For an interesting parallel to the king's *feorm* in Denmark, see Maitland, *op. cit.*, p. 238.

INDEX.